Disorganized Crime

DISORGANIZED CRIME

Jim Goodwin

VANTAGE PRESS
New York / Los Angeles / Chicago

FIRST EDITION

All rights reserved, including the right of
reproduction in whole or in part in any form.

Copyright © 1988 by Jim Goodwin

Published by Vantage Press, Inc.
516 West 34th Street, New York, New York 10001

Manufactured in the United States of America
ISBN: 0-533-06808-8

To the officers and men of Mobile Advisory Team (MAT) 48; and the villagers of Vo Xu, Houi Duc District, Bihn Tuy Province, Republic of South Vietnam

Contents

Preface

I believe the political and bureaucratic system that currently exists will soon collapse. The causes for this occurrence did not happen overnight and though most people know emotionally that the government is screwed up, they don't know to what degree. It was the result of nine years of auditing in three different federal agencies, the Departments of Army and Commerce and the Veterans Administration, that allowed me to see the extent of the catastrophe that is happening. In these nine years, I rose from an entry level of GS-7 to a supervisory GS-13. This exposure to several agencies, at several levels, and over a span of four administrations, provided a broad enough sample in which to base a prediction on what will happen in your lifetime; there is nothing you can do to prevent the collapse.

Disorganized Crime

Chapter 1

It's All Over

Prudence, indeed, will dictate that Governments long established should not be changed for light and transient causes; and accordingly all experience hath shown, that mankind are more disposed to suffer, while evils are sufferable, than to right themselves by abolishing the forms to which they are accustomed. But when a long train of abuses and usurpations, pursuing invariably the same Object evinces a design to reduce them under absolute Despotism, it is their right, it is their duty, to throw off such Government, and to provide new Guards for their future security

—The Declaration of Independence (July 4, 1776)

During the nine years (1973–1982) that I was a federal auditor, the federal bureaucracy squandered $4 trillion. This money was stolen from you in three ways: (1) by withholding money from your paycheck; (2) by stealing from businesses and business owners, who in turn charged you more for their products; and (3) printing worthless money to cover any possible bounced checks.

Now I'm not naive enough to believe that you would ever believe me that it's all over because of the theft of your money. It's been going on for your grandparents, parents, and your whole life. You've been conditioned that this theft is necessary, "Taxes are what we pay for civilized society," or "The only two sure things are death and taxes," et cetera. Anyway, if you didn't pay the money, someone from the IRS would come with a gun and interrupt your supper. What may get you to realize that it's over are two additional facts: (1) your money that was stolen was squandered in every instance that I'm aware of, no matter what political party was in office; and, (2) the national debt is so large that you have very little left to be stolen in order to continue Disorganized Crime.

1

Even if you do realize it is all over, it won't matter at all. You are absolutely powerless to do anything about the end. Are you actually thinking "I can vote?" This is going to be tougher than I imagined. What possible good is your one vote going to do at any level, much less a national election? We've had both political parties in office for over a hundred years. If you vote for a Democrat, your money will be stolen to support the social services program wing of Disorganized Crime. If you vote Republican, your money will be stolen to support the war program wing of Disorganized Crime. The sheer hopelessness of the situation has already convinced half of your fellow victims not to vote. During the last nine years, incumbents have usually won reelection.

Percentage of Representatives Seeking Reelection Who Win

1972	94%
1974	88%
1976	96%
1978	94%
1980	91%

That's called job security. What's your one vote going to do?

What's that I hear? "You won't pay taxes?" You aren't going to stop. First, the money is stolen from you before you even get your share. Second, it doesn't matter whether you pay or not. Disorganized Crime couldn't steal over $1 trillion just in the nine years I was a member. We just counterfeited enough currency to cover the shortfall. Most important, though, is the fact that you're not going to stop paying taxes because you're scared of having your supper go cold. Somebody might get upset with you. I mean you might actually miss TV.

However, all is not lost. A few brave souls reside among you. One example is Ray Garland, who stopped filing his taxes in 1976 because he considered it unfair of the government to require him to volunteer personal information. As a result, he has been charged with failing to file income taxes on annual incomes ranging from $16,000 to $33,000—a criminal misdemeanor.

This insurance salesman from Sycamore, Illinois, was found not guilty by a Chicago jury. After the verdict, Garland called the jurors "some of the bravest people there are in this country."

The fact that one taxpayer didn't get thrown away into the Gulag doesn't mean you wouldn't. In fact you wouldn't even think about not paying your fair share, because you are conditioned by Disorganized Crime to believe that your money is spent wisely. There are 120 agencies of government, spending over $165 million yearly on public relations. As reported in the May 30, 1983 *Washington Post*, the real cost may be far greater. The GAO has looked for a price tag without success. In 1975, the Associated Press computed that public relations and information services cost the government $1 billion. This did not include the money spent by the members of Congress for reelection propaganda.

What are some of the techniques that Disorganized Crime uses to make itself wasteful? According to an arcticle published by the Atlanta Chapter of the Association of Government Accountants (themselves members of Disorganized Crime), there were six major techniques utilized:

General

Hundreds of incompatible management systems using and producing incompatible data
Lack of information on cost and impact of program delivery in many cases
Computer technology for administrative services that is at least 10 years behind the private sector
No automated auditing, so prevention of waste, fraud, and abuse very difficult
Inadequate cash and debt management systems
Inadequate property and personnel management systems

Financial

A minimum of 325 separate agency financial/accounting systems that are:

Basically incompatible
Not online to OMB or Treasury or usually even within an agency
Only 60% approved by GAO
Separate from operational data, impeding results analysis
Without automated audit capabilities
Expensive to operate

Payroll

At least 350 different payroll systems that are:

Basically incompatible
Not online to Office of Personnel Management (OPM) or OMB
Lacking productivity or any other analysis capabilities
Without automated audit capabilities
Without consistent links to personnel systems
Expensive to operate

Personnel

The American Management Association recently reported that the ratio of personnel specilists in government is three times that in the private sector because of antiquated systems

Payment Centers

There are more than 2,300 administrative payment centers throughout the country, processing more than 700 million documents per year, where:

Documents processed per hour range from 2 to 18
Direct labor cost per payment in one department ranges from $3.30 to $29
Direct labor cost probably exceeds $600 million/year

Systems

The lack of comprehensive and integrated systems is a problem not only in managing the government but also in preventing waste, fraud and abuse. The information systems in many agencies are also far behind the state of the art or are incompatible across agency lines. The Federal Government cannot generally determine:

Property in the hands of contractors
Delinquency and aging of debt owed the government
Real time financial data—value of procurements, grants, obligations, commitments
Number of consultants in the government
Performance records of contractors and grantees (government-wide)
Total federal funds committed to individual states and localities
Effectiveness measures of programs and operations (as viewed by client groups, general population and Congress)

Now you're thinking, "Wait a second, isn't the current formal head of Disorganized Crime ending the size of the stealing?" That's not the case at all. Those were just his campaign visuals, which of course you believed. Let's examine three items that were to be either reduced or eliminated; the membership of Disorganized Crime, the Department of Energy, and the Department of Education. Worldwide, the government (as of December 1982) had 2,861,937 employees, including about 63,000 non-citizens employed overseas. That means the total membership of Disorganized Crime had increased by over 1,200 people during the year December 1981 to December 1982. The majority of the increase in membership is in the war arm of Disorganized Crime.

The Department of Energy has requested Congress to boost its fiscal 1984 budget request by over $21 million to fund 386 additional staff positions. Half of the new positions would go to the department's management and administrative division, with most of the other slots going to the regional offices.

Not only is the membership not going to be reduced, but the loot each member of Disorganized Crime receives is large. The President's Private Sector Survey on Cost Control (known as the Grace Commission) found that federal

4

employees are overpaid by $11 billion a year. This comes about because government wages are based on pay comparability studies performed by, you guessed, federal employees. Over 60,000 members of Disorganized Crime make over $50,000 a year. Those 60,000 salaries do not include the Postal Service, where the average salary of its 600,000 employees is over $22,000 a year, not counting benefits.

The real kicker is that though you understand all the preceding, I don't believe you know on what all your stolen money was squandered. That's what I will discuss in the next seven chapters. As you read, it's very important for you to emotionally and intellectually understand just one fact: you paid for all of it.

Chapter 2

Auditing Disorganized Crime

The people never give up their liberties but under some delusion.
—Edmund Burke (1784)

It took me years to understand the value system within Disorganized Crime. First, do away with your knee-jerk beliefs of right and wrong. The value system is based on visuals. What looks good? Will it float? Will I draw unfavorable attention to myself? Because of the need for visuals by Disorganized Crime, a limited system of internal review was developed after World War II. In 1978 these visuals were made into law by the Inspector General (IG) Act. Or in other words, there could now be a steady stream of propaganda to tell you that all your stolen money was spent in an organized and businesslike manner. By December 1982, the total cost savings reported by the various IG's exceeded $17 billion. This figure represents less than 2 percent of Disorganized Crime's budget for Fiscal Year 1982. In addition, the figure was incorrect because the Office of Management and Budget incorrectly added in $1 billion in error when compiling the cost savings figures from the various IG's reports.

The visuals value system dictates how auditors within Disorganized Crime will react. As I will describe in the following chapters, no matter at what level, what agency, what administration, what geographical location, or what function was being audited, visuals were the primary value system. Right or wrong, cost, waste, and abuse were not the primary drivers of our motives within Disorganized Crime. In the following chapters, there is one inescapable fact: you paid for everything I am about to relate to you. Whether you think it was good or bad, successful or not, you paid for all of it. The standards, training, salaries of the members of Disorganized Crime, the travel, the food and drugs, the golf courses, the buildings, the vendor's bills, and, the idle time, was all paid for by you.

There are several topics that need to be briefly brought to your attention before I go further. First, you paid for these topics and, second, each audit group I was a member of paid varying degrees of attention to them. These topics are standards, salaries, per diem, travel, and audit reports.

There are standards developed by the General Accounting Office branch of Disorganized Crime called the *Standards For Audit of Governmental Organizations* or among auditors the *Yellow Book*. Who paid for these standards? No, not Congress, try again. That's right, you paid for these standards. As a result of these standards, the auditing arm of Disorganized Crime can now present visuals to indicate that auditing will be done in a professional manner. However, bear in mind that whether the standards are used or not, you will pay for the audit effort, as well as what was being audited, the actual audit report, and the follow-up effort to the audit report. One of the most important standards was the standard of independence. It wouldn't do anyone any good if the auditors were in bed with who they were auditing. However, in practice, the lack of independence of auditors was all-pervasive.

A symptom of a lack of independence is apparent when the auditors are sent to look at minor issues, which wastes all their time (at your expense). For example, the GAO complained that Pentegon investigators are wasting their time checking unauthorized telephone calls and padded expense accounts, instead of focusing their attention on major cases of fraud. The report GAO/AFMD-83-33 stated that 62 percent of the military's fraud investigations involved sums less than $500, while only 4 percent involved loses over $5,000.

Training is given auditors for three reasons. The *Yellow Book* standards require it of audit organizations; to spend the money allocated from you for the purpose of training; and, to provide the visuals both within Disorganized Crime and to you, that your money is being spent in a businesslike manner and trained auditors are making sure that is taking place.

The salaries of auditors come every other week whether they are actually going through the motions of participating in an audit, doing personal business, or just "smoking and joking." These salaries are what make auditors go into auditing. Promotions in each group I was a member of were for the most part routine (annually) up through the GS-12 level. Salaries of auditors, effective as of October 3, 1982, follow:

Schedule of Government Salaries

Entry Level	GS-7	$16,559
	GS-9	$20,256
	GS-11	$24,508
	[GS-12	$29,374
Supervisory Levels	[GS-13	$34,930
	[GS-14	$41,277
	[GS-15	$48,553

Another form of income came to auditors when they were on the road conducting audits. This was called "per diem" and usually ranged from $50 to $75 daily. Per diem was affectionately know as "steak and lobster money," and it was difficult to envision how you could be living without per diem. We would get absolutely furious if it was suggested that we spend our own salary money and be reimbursed later. As a result, each group that I was a member of had travel advances, i.e., a free, no-interest loan of your money. (Just in case no one has said this to you before, thanks.) The amount of the loan varied from

$500 with the Department of Commerce (where I did very little traveling), $1,000 with Army Audit Agency, to $1,750 with the Veterans Administration. You paid the auditor's per diem after his submission of a travel voucher. In every group I was with, literally days were spent by the auditor, the next level supervisor, and his supervisor filling out and verifying the accuracy and authenticity of the travel voucher. You paid for this detailed review as well as the mathematical check of the voucher by the disbursing office located elsewhere. In addition, don't forget the payment you made to print the check (a green computer card), but I think (maybe?) you see my point.

Travel was a real motivator to the individual auditor. Happily married auditors hated to travel and after a couple of years would either divorce their mates, find another job (usually within Disorganized Crime), or complain to or "brownnose" their supervisors not to put them on the road. Other auditors (including myself) were more than happy to spend your per diem money and requested to be on the road as often as possible. For example, in 1979 I was doing the audit at VA Medical Center, Hampton, Virginia. I was provided a government car (paid for by who?) and was staying at the Sheraton Hotel on Virginia Beach. For various reasons I stayed there by myself (sending the rest of the auditors home for Christmas) from December 21, 1979 to January 8, 1980. By looking at your calendar, you will see I was paid nineteen days per diem (19 × $50 = $950); however, there were only eight workdays. Don't forget I also received my salary from you as well as the plane tickets. Not a bad vacation, if I do say so myself (the baked crab casserole was wonderful). One way for a supervisor to harass a subordinate to leave was to determine if the auditor wanted to travel or not and just do the opposite. It usually didn't take long for the subordinate to get the message (sent at your expense, of course).

Audit reports were the primary visuals produced by auditors. Audit reports were either internal or external. Internal audits dealt with other elements of Disorganized Crime. External audits dealt with others such as grantees, contractors, or local governments. Except for the production of these audit reports, there is no other document to show a reason for having auditors. Or in other words, you pay the auditors so that you can pay some more for them to print an audit report. The development of an internal audit report was the same in every audit group of which I was a member. The individual auditor would note something was not working correctly. The auditor would develop a condition, sometimes called a finding, a hit, a bodycount, a gottcha, or a burn. One audit supervisor would actually measure his performance as "burn rate." I'll let you decide if he was concerned how much it cost you for his high or low burn rate.

However, his visuals were good and that's what counted. After verbally discussing the various findings with the auditees, the draft report would be brought back to the office. It was then that the real audit would begin. The chain of audit supervisors would completely re-write the audit report. Usually this stage would last at least a year. The typing, writing, discussions of and re-discussions ("Why didn't you count the Mars Bars instead of the Snickers?") of the report would be paid for by you. After the report was finally approved (sometimes the auditors who actually conducted the audit would recognize the subject of the report), the final report was available to the public. If the draft audit report was not finalized, it was not open to the public (and was said to have been "thrown away," "filed 13," or "filed in the circular file"). But whether the report was finalized or thrown away, you paid for the effort to produce it.

I will present to you the three audit groups as I experienced them. This gives a certain logical chain of events; however, it gives the most recent events last. I decided to go back to the beginning of my exposure to Disorganized Crime because it was all the same story.

Chapter 3

Army Audit Agency

He has erected a multitude of new offices, and sent hither swarms of officers to harass our people, and eat out their substance. He has kept among us, in times of peace, standing armies; . . .
—Declaration of Independence (July 4, 1776)

After leaving the Army, I went back to school and received an accounting degree. I wanted to go back to the Orient. A friend of mine was working with a group that would send me overseas after being with them two years. I interviewed and two weeks after graduation was going to the Pentagon to work with U.S. Army Audit Agency in September 1973. My first day was spent being photographed and receiving my assigned audits. I was instructed to show up the next day at my first audit assignment at Fort Ritchie (Hagerstown), Maryland. Before I left the Pentagon, I received a travel advance of a thousand dollars. Not bad for the first day, one day a poor student—the next day King Midas. I was hooked on your per diem money and couldn't get out of your wallet for the next nine years.

The next day I met the rest of the audit team and introduced myself to a beleaguered auditor-in-charge. He was over halfway completed with the audit and was winding down the audit effort. All he needed was a low grade (the lowest to be exact), with literally only one day in the agency. He asked me if I knew anything about the Army. Duly impressed, he assigned me to audit the Facility Engineers, and off I went to fight the good fight. No audit guide, no training, no idea about findings but ready to do my duty. I stayed there five weeks and predictably enough came up with nothing. Now besides the five weeks salary ($1,100), plus the per diem ($875), and the mileage ($150), this cost you over $2,000 for nothing and I didn't produce any paper (which would have cost you more money if I had produced something).

Now just in case you are worried I'm only going to brag about my derring-do, let me describe the rest of the audit effort. The audit was conducted from approximately July through November 1973; however, the twelve-page audit report itself was issued a year later, on January 30, 1974. The audit team was composed of seven auditors; however, there were only two findings (body count). It's important to remind you (I know that you have forgotten) that you paid for the problems we found and just not our haphazard efforts to create visuals to show that your money was wisely managed by Disorganized Crime.

11

The first of the two findings concerned the power plant operations at the Alternate National Military Command Center. Army Audit recommended to purchase electrical power from the local electric company, Potomac Edison. The Army arm of Disorganized Crime had been supplying their own electricity by means of five 1000-kilowatt generators. Literally, you had paid for them to have their own power company. The auditors had found that the utilities cost to you would be reduced by $177,000 plus the conservation of over 1.3 million gallons of diesel fuel. Though the audit stated that the Commander, Fort Ritchie, had agreed to the recommendation, he had actually only stated that he would submit a plan to the Joint Chiefs of Staff for approval to operate the system in accordance with USAAA's recommendation. Through a Freedom of Information request, I found that all correspondence relating to actions taken by either USAAA or the Department of the Army had been discarded.

In addition to the five generators already at Fort Ritchie, the Army was installing a sixth generator. You (and the auditors) would think that the Army would have agreed to stop the installation of this sixth generator, especially in light of the fact that you were about to pay for commercial electrical power. The savings were over $200,000 of your stolen dollars. The Deputy Chief of Staff for Military Operations (no fooling, that was his title) disagreed because "It is anticipated that the power requirements will increase. . . . The expected future power requirement will require all six generators—three on line, one up-to-speed as backup, one as standby and one down for maintenance." Army audit replied, "It appears from the comments provided by Command that four generators could supply the total power requirements during an emergency." And there the disagreement, whether or not to save your stolen $200,000 (so it could be spent on some other boondoggle) by not installing the sixth generator, stood in the final audit report. Through a Freedom of Information request, I found that all correspondence relating to this matter had also been discarded.

The second finding found excess repair parts to support the communications equipment. Though the stockage list contained about 9,000 line items valued at $100,000, over $26,000 of these items were excess. You had paid for too many items. To make matters worse, the auditors found in a review of 131 of 250 requisitions that were on back order, 32 should have been canceled because enough stock was on hand. There were also 42 requisitions where the amount ordered could have been reduced. In other words the auditor doing this review had a "burn rate" of 74 out of 131, not bad.

Why was your money squandered on excess parts on hand and more being ordered? Because a member of Disorganized Crime (government employee) had not kept accurate stock record cards. For example, the stock records showed zero balances for 18 line items that were on requisition; however, our inventory revealed that sufficient stocks were on hand. Though the Commander, Fort Ritchie, agreed with the motherhood-and-apple-pie recommendation, he stated, "A physical inventory is currently under way at which time the stock record cards will be brought into agreement with quantity of items on hand."

Because I was green, I just couldn't believe that someone would actually state it took over 80 days to inventory 9,000 line items and that his staff didn't update the stock record cards then, but had to go back and count them again. That's right. Not only did you pay for one slow inventory, but they had to go back and have you pay for a second inventory. But look at this from a visuals viewpoint. Not only is he going to correct the situation, but he's going to invest a lot of effort to make sure it gets done. And that ended my first audit with USAAA. My first exposure at being a member of Disorganized Crime. Of the seven members, six are still members of Disorganized Crime.

My second audit was of the Commissary Operations at the Walter Reed Army Medical Center in Washington, D.C. I know this is hard for you to believe, but the War arm of Disorganized Crime runs their own private chain of grocery stores. This started in the days of the Old West because the process of feeding troops was difficult without neighborhood 7–11's. I found it hard to believe there was a shortage of grocery stores in the nation's capital; however, you were paying for four commissaries in the nation's capital, of which Walter Reed was only one. The six-member team was at Walter Reed from November 1973 to January 1974. The problems were so obvious I even found four of the twelve that made up the final report dated 27 March 1974 (only a couple of months to produce fifty-five pages). The audit report stated that Walter Reed Commissary was a real disaster.

> *During calendar year 1973, the resale commissary sustained excessive unidentified losses. The losses were concealed and passed on to the patrons in the form of higher prices through the mill rule system of pricing and by selling meat at prices substantially in excess of costs.*

The twelve problems that you paid both to have and to be reported on were all caused by the War arm of Disorganized Crime wanting a chain of grovery stores. It reminds me of the USSR where party members have their own special grocery stores to avoid waiting in long lines. The irony about Disorganized Crime is their chain of grocery stores are so bad, their members pay more for the privilege (?) of shopping for groceries than they would if they went to a commercial grocery store. The audit report had the following twelve findings.

1. Continued use of a 1-mill rule in determining selling prices during the last 6 months of calendar year 1973 kept losses from commissary grocery store operations within acceptable tolerances. By not reverting to a 3-mill rule and thus reducing prices when the accountable inventory disclosed a reduced loss at the end of June, the commissary was able to reduce future losses or recoup prior losses from customers in the form of higher grocery prices. Although the commissary remained on a 1-mill rule, the net loss on grocery sales of $7,726,057 was $29,912 for the first nine months of 1973.

In theory, commissaries should not incur a gain or loss in their conduct of day-to-day operations of selling subsistence items. In practice, however, gains and losses do occur and the variable mill rule pricing system is designed to adjust selling prices to compensate for these variances. Significant losses are recouped by increasing prices, and gains are reduced by decreasing prices. Tolerance ranges and mill rules are:

Gain (Percent of Sales)	Mill Rule
1.50 and higher	5
.75 to 1.49	4
.00 to .74	3

Loss (Percent of Sales)	Mill Rule
.00 to .74	3
.75 to 1.49	2
1.50 and higher	1

At 31 December 1973, the commissary was operating on a 1-mill rule as it had during the calendar year 1973.

Or, in other words, the commissary was charging the highest prices it could and still was losing money. Also, the $29,912 loss did not include a one-time write-off of the cumulative loss account balance on 31 March 1973 of $31,680. This write-off was authorized by Department of Army in order to start fresh (so to speak).

2. Controls over meat market operations were not adequate to ensure that all meat products were properly accounted for. The commisary reported a loss of $16,520 for October and November 1973 meat market operations, although cutting tests showed that prices were more than would be needed to recover costs. In addition, fat content tests showed excessive quantities of fat in ground meat which would further add to profits. Consistent over-pricing of processed meat items results in overcharging patrons and could conceal losses. These losses on meat market operations could result from any one or a combination of the following: (i) inadequate receiving proce-dures, (ii) errors on the part of cashiers to identify meat market sales properly, and (iii) pilferage or theft. Therefore, it is important that prompt action be taken to determine the causes for losses in meat market operations.

Based on the results of the cutting tests and the prices established for the beef available for sale to the customers during October and November 1973, the meat market should have realized a profit of $20,596 on the sale of beef cuts. However, the commissary reported a loss of $16,520 for October and November meat market operations, or a 2.09 percent loss of total sales. In an attempt to identify the possible causes for this loss, we expanded our review to include the following areas.

Most of the fat content test results showed excessive quantities of fat in the ground meat, which would further add to the profit per pound of beef. For example, the fat content of ground chuck should not exceed 15 percent. However, the actual fat content ranged from 14 to 25 percent and exceeded the allowable 15 percent on 10 of 13 ground chuck tests.

Based on cutting tests, the 388,040 pounds of beef carcass, reported as received during October and November 1973, should have generated 271,640 pounds of salable beef and 116,400 pounds of fat and bone. However, an additional 19,650 pounds of fat and bone were generated. From this we concluded that actual cutting practices in the meat market were not nearly as efficient as beef carcass cutting tests.

The apprarent policy and procedure followed by the meat market was to overcharge patrons, to preclude reporting losses in excess of authorized tolerances on the quarterly accountability report instead of identifying causes for losses.

In another part of our review, we found that procedures were not adequate to assure that all beef paid for was actually received. The commissary's veterinarian was assigned responsibility for receiving the meat, weighing it, examining it for quality, and recording the weight of each carcass. In order to expedite the process of receiving beef carcasses, the veterinarian noted the amount each carcass was overweight or short-weight according to the tags placed on the carcasses. After all the beef was weighed, the veterinarian simply netted the overages and underages to determine how much the total shipment was over or under. But he did not always tally up the total beef received to ensure that all of the carcasses on the vendor's invoice were actually received. As a result, the commissary did not have adequate assurance that all beef paid for was received.

We informed the Commissary Officer of the above receiving practices,and he took immediate action to implement improved controls for the receiving of beef. As a result of these procedures, the veterinarian detected 406 pounds of carcass beef shortweighted on the next two shipments after the controls were instituted.

A more complete analysis of meat market operations would have been possible if mandatory trial balances had been taken twice a month and maintained. This trial balance would compare sales with the cost of sales and identify gains and losses on a current basis.

3. Internal controls and physical security measures did not provide the necessary safeguards over commissary merchandise valued at about $500,000. Adequate receiving procedures were not always followed, and physical security needed strengthening. During 1973, the commissary sustained unidentified losses which were concealed and passed on to patrons in the form of higher meat and grocer prices. Good preventive measures are necessary to minimize the possibilities of losses from theft or pilferage.

The commissary stocks many items of merchandise that are particularly vulnerable to theft and pilferage. This merchandise bears no commissary markings to distinguish it from similar products sold in civilian stores.

4. Controls over cash receipts needed strengthening to provide greater assurance that all cash receipts are accounted for properly and deposited intact. Our review showed that:

Breaks in sequence of cash register lock and unlock numbers and transaction numbers were not reviewed to identify and explain missing numbers.

Large amounts of cash were unnecessarily retained in the commissary store both during and after working hours.

Cashier's credit slips were not controlled to insure proper usage or to identify those cashiers in need of additional training.

Before, during and after any business day, more than one individual had access to commissary funds.

Responsibilities for handling and accounting for cash were not adequately separated.

Coupons were not controlled and properly accounted for.

Basic accounting controls over cash sales were not adequate.

Cash receipts are susceptible to theft, diversion, or other misappropriation either before or after they have been recorded. However, once the receipt of cash has been recorded, successful embezzlement becomes more difficult.

The internal control features on the commissary's cash registers were not fully used. These controls were designed to preclude misappropriation of receipts and to insure that the cash registers were not being tampered with. The 22 cash registers in the commissary had 2 basic internal control features as follows:

An internally stored tape records the amount and sequential number of each transaction. Misplaced or destroyed records of transactions can be identified by determining if there are missing numbers in the sequence. We found that reviews were not made to determine whether transaction numbers were missing from the cash register tapes. We reviewed the closing numbers for selected registers on one day and the starting numbers on the next day and found that numbers were missing. Management personnel had not taken any action to determine why the numbers were missing.

Another counter shows the number of times the cash register has been cleared and reset. Cash registers not used were not cleared at the close of business or before the start of business the next day as required by regulations. Records to account for each time the register was cleared were not maintained. Also, breaks in sequence were noted in the register lock and unlock numbers appearing on the Summary of Daily Fund Receipts (DA Form 3292) during the months of September and October 1973. The primary controls over cash receipts reported on DA Form 3292 are the cash register lock and unlock numbers. Whenever there is a break in sequence of numbers, the Commissary Officer is required to include a statement of reason for the break. Personnel clearing the registers did not document the lock and unlock numbers on the itemized clearing slips, and records were not maintained to show these numbers. As a result, the lock and unlock numbers on DA Form 3292 disclosed breaks in lock and unlock numbers sequence daily for each register. We noted in many instances that the opening number was less than the previous day's closing number. This discrepancy should never occur unless the machine is broken. Examples are:

Register #	Date & Closing #	Date & Opening #	Difference
4	18 Sept. 0554	19 Sept. 0556	2
2A	20 Sept. 0580	21 Sept. 0576	− 4
3A	19 Sept. 0425	20 Sept. 0429	4
10A	2 Oct. 0576	3 Oct. 0559	− 17

The breaks in sequence of the lock and unlock numbers, coupled with the missing customer transaction numbers, provide the opportunity for misappropriation of funds.

The commissary did not document and reconcile each day's sales activity in accordance with procedures prescribed by regulation. The cash register clearing tapes form the basic accounting record for all cash sales in the commissary store. Register tapes and the Cashier's Daily Report (DA Form 3291) are used to support all entries documented on DA Form 3292. Also, the DA Form 3292 is a summary for Report of Deposits (DD Form 707) which supports the Certificate of Deposit. We compared the total value of checks reported on these four forms for 2 through 6 October 1973. In no instance did the value of checks for this period agree on all four documents. However, on 4 and 5 October, two documents did show identical dollar totals for checks. An illustration of this review follows:

Dollar Amount of Checks as Reported on Accounting Records

Date October 1973	Cash Register Tapes	DA Form 3291	DA Form 3292	Certificate of Deposit
2	$33,957.34	$34,413.80	$22,928.05	$34,212.57
3	42,822.57	(i)	42,239.09	43,651.71
4	53,049.38	52,551.60	53,715.31	53,715.31
5	36,516.00	37,589.54	37,576.02	37,576.02
6	39,999.11	37,703.15	(i)	40,226.98

(i) Not documented.

5. Periodic reconciliations were not made between the Commissary Officer's records and records maintained by the Finance and Accounting Office (FAO). Overall differences ranging up to $196,230 had accumulated between the inventory balances on the two records. A reconciliation identifying detailed or individual differences between the two records would permit necessary accounting adjustments, provide greater assurance that records represented the actual status of the account, and ensure that accurate financial data was supported to higher command.

A comparison of the commissary and FAO inventory records disclosed the following differences:

Date	Iventory Balance on Commissary Records	Inventory Balance on FAO Records	Difference
30 June 73	$614,394	$579,700	$ 34,694
31 July 73	619,300	753,850	134,550
31 Aug 73	668,605	864,835	196,230
30 Sep 73	645,008	823,037	178,029

Similarly, cumulative sales data as shown by FAO did not agree with the data reported by the commissary. A comparison of cumulative sales, reported by the two activities for the same periods, is shown below:

Period	Cumulative Sales Reported by FAO (i)	Cumulative Sales Reported by Commissary (ii)	Difference
3rd Quarter FY73	$15,608,723	$11,272,016	$4,336,707
4th Quarter FY73	15,452,344	15,499,227	46,883
1st Quarter FY74	4,248,821	4,237,211	11,610

(i) Data obtained from FAO consolidated final trial balance.

(ii) Computed from reports submitted to the U.S. Army Food Service Center, Fort Lee, Virginia.

Periodic reconciliations between the two records were not made, and installation personnel were not aware that differences between the two records existed.

6. The prices on about 734 or 33 percent of the grocery items in the store were incorrect. Of these 734 items, 346 were overpriced and 388 were underpriced. In addition, most cashiers were not charging correct prices for produce items. Although the individual grocery and produce price variances were small, the sales volume of about $10 million annually could generate large differences causing significant over- or under-charges to customers and unnecessary gains or losses. These pricing errors were not disclosed by the monthly price verifications by disinterested officers because their reviews were not adequate to determine the extent of pricing errors.

Selling prices are established at the commissary store based on the cost of each item. The selling prices are shown on a master price list which is to be the source of all store prices. A verification of commissary store sales prices to the master price list is required to be accomplished during each month. This verification is to be performed by a disinterested person and must include at least 20 percent of the grocery, meat, and produce items. When this verification shows a 5 percent or greater pricing error rate, a complete review of commissary pricing procedures is required.

On a monthly basis, the commissary obtained a statement from a disinterested officer that selling prices in the store were verified to the master pricelist. These independent statements indicated that 20 percent of the sales items in the store were reviewed and that pricing errors did not exceed 5 percent of the items verified. Because documentation was not adequate to support these independent statements, we performed a review of selling prices. This review showed that grocery and produce prices were not correct and that the master pricelist was not current.

Using statistical sampling techniques, we compared prices for resale items on the pricelist to prices marked on items on the shelves of the commissary store. Based on the sample results, we estimate that 644 of the 2,220 grocery items were incorrectly priced on the master pricelist. The selling prices for 734 grocery items were not correct. Of these 734 items, 346 were overpriced and 388 were underpriced. Listed below are examples of price discrepancies that existed for extended periods.

Item	Effective Date of Price Change	Correct Price	Pricelist on 2 Nov 1973	Elapsed Days
Soup, Chicken Noodle	19 Aug 73	$0.28	$0.25	75
Kidney Beans	19 Oct 73	0.18	0.14	14
Flour, Gold Medal	24 Oct 73	0.39	0.33	9

A meaningful verification of the accuracy of selling prices could not be accomplished without a current pricelist. Unless there is prompt notification of price changes, prices of items on the store shelf cannot be changed within the prescribed 2-day timeframe.

Produce items were not always sold at the correct price because cashiers were not properly preparing their pricelist which was used to identify produce prices. Our review of 20 cashiers lists disclosed incorrect prices on 13 lists. Our review also showed that the pricelists were not consistent in the number of items appearing on the lists. Cashier pricelists should be prepared centrally and kept up to date. Without complete and accurate pricelists, cashiers could charge commissary patrons incorrect prices or delay customer processing.

Accurate pricing of merchandise is necessary to maintain control over commissary operations and to provide products at the best possible price. Financial control, ultimately represented by gains and losses, forms the basis of measuring the effectiveness of commissary operations. Although incorrect pricing is not the only cause for gains or losses, with $10 million in annual sales it constitutes an important factor and could conceal practices that actually cause losses.

    7. The commissary did not maintain required inventory consumption records. As a result, management reorder decisions were based primarily on personal judgment and about 30 percent of the items carried on the current stockage list were not on hand. In addition, excessive quantities of other items were on hand and the number of items stocked for some product groups exceeded the number recommended by regulation.

Commissary consumption records (DA Forms 3293 and 1297) provided data on each line item as to quantities on hand, on order, and consumed, replenishment leadtime, turnover rate, and other information needed to manage stocks effectively.

The commissary had not maintained required consumption records for its resale items since September 1972. Prior to that time, the commissary maintained consumption records manually for both resale and troop issue consumption. The manual records were abandoned when conversion was made to an automatic data processing system. The commissary experienced operational difficulties with the automatic data processing equipment and a large amount of machine downtime. Consequently, receipt and issue information needed for determining requisitioning objectives was not promptly recorded. Attempts to maintain the records manually were not successful due in part to personnel shortages. For more than a year, therefore, the commissary has not maintained the data needed to determine the correct stockage requirements. As a result, the commissary did not stock enough of some items and stocked too much of others.

This lack of consumption data was probably a major factor in the overstockage of many items. At the commissary, as a result, the quantity ordered was based on the judgment of the individual preparing the order. In addition, orders were not always placed in a timely manner. Using statistical sampling techniques, we estimated that about 30 percent of the items stocked by the commissary had zero balances. The following schedule shows the status of this condition as of 2 November 1973:

Items out-of-stock but on order	525
Items out-of-stock and reportedly unavailable	300
Items out-of-stock and not on order	48
	873

We also found that the items on hand for about 200 line items exceeded the authorized stockage levels. Another problem was that the number of line items stocked for resale exceeded the number recommended by the regulation for certain items. The number of line items recommended for stockage is designed to provide a choice of selection for patrons and at the same time restrict the total number of items stocked. To insure adequate inventory turnover, reduce fund and shelf space requirements, and prevent accumulation of slow moving items, the commissary should not stock items in excess of the maximum number. Product groups should be reviewed to insure that the number of items stocked is consistent with the number recommended and that sales of each item justify continued stockage.

8. Closer supervision was needed to make sure that the basic records that controlled outstanding commissary bills were maintained in the manner prescribed by regulation. Commissary bills remained unpaid for extended periods, and discounts amounting to $4,402 for 5-month period were not realized. In addition, overpayments of over $400 to vendors were not detected because finance and accounting records were not reconciled with commissary records.

Closer supervision was needed to assure that basic accounting records were maintained as required by regulation. FAO did not have a complete record of all outstanding commissary obligations to vendors. One former employee had caused this problem by not recording many of the outstanding amounts due to vendors. This condition should have been detected by reconciling FAO records with the commissary records. The needed reconciliations, however, were not accomplished. This need for improved control over outstanding amounts due to vendors also contributed to the following problems.

Vendors were not paid in a timely manner. FAO paid vendors only after receiving a bill for merchandise delivered and matching this bill to the commissary receiving report. Our review of 170 accounts payable files showed that 23 had complete documentation available to authorize payment. However, these vendors had not been paid, and only about 60 percent of all vendors were paid within 30 days.

The delays in paying the vendors also resulted in the loss of discounts which were available in return for prompt payments. An analysis of bills received from vendors from 1 July through 7 December 1973 showed that the $7,410 in cash discounts which were offered by vendors in return for prompt payment only $3,008 were realized. The loss was passed on to the commissary patrons in the form of higher prices. The commissary provided FAO with documentation indicating the goods received and the amount to which the vendor was entitled. FAO then matched this documentation to the bill submitted by the vendor and paid the vendor. The commissary was not comparing receiving reports documentation with the amounts actually paid by FAO. As a result, the commissary did not reduce prices and adjust its inventory records downward when price changes or voluntary vendor discounts resulted in the vendor charging less than authorized by the commissary. During the most recent 5-month period, there were 119 such price changes with a total reduced cost of $8,210. In another eight instances, the amount paid exceeded by $418 the amount authorized by the commissary. The overpayment resulted because FAO did not take note of the shortage in the amount received as indicated by the documentation provided by the commissary.

9. The commissary was not provided with a complete and current list of individuals who had redeemed bad checks. As a result, some individuals were permitted to pass several bad checks. In addition, checks were accepted with incomplete or invalid information and accountability controls over unredeemed bad checks were not adequate.

Remember, all these bad checks are received from members of Disorganized Crime.

At the commissary, dishonored checks were averaging about $1,500 per month. Because of the volume of uncollected checks, we expanded our review to evaluate the adequacy of and compliance with established procedures. Several problems were noted:

The bad-check list was not promptly distributed to the commissary. For example, the check-cashing privilege of one individual was revoked 22 August,

21

1973. The local check-cashing revocation listing with this information, however, was not distributed until 12 October 1973. As a result, the individual was able to cash six more bad checks totaling $337 after revocation of check-cashing privileges. Distribution of the local listing or supplements to the listing could have prevented this occurrence.

Our observations of the check approval process showed the following problems:

As of mid-December 1973, the commissary was using a January 1973 Walter Reed bad-check list and an August 1973 Military District of Washington bad-check list.

Both bad-check lists were not always screened prior to approving checks.

Checks were returned because they were not endorsed or because they were postdated.

The system used to record checks returned by the bank because of insufficient funds did not provide reasonable assurance that all checks were recorded for subsequent collection attempts. The bank provided a memorandum with the balance of returned checks. These checks were then listed by the commissary cashier section for collection action. Our review of this list showed that the individual amounts listed did not equal the bank memorandum totals:

Date During 1973	Amount Per Bank	Amount Per Cashiers' Control Records	Difference
3 July	$589.59	$546.18	$43.41
2 August	577.11	452.61	124.50
4 September	455.86	162.28	293.58

10. The automatic data processing system in use at the Walter Reed Army Medical Center Commissary did not provide the timely financial and quantitative data needed for effective management. The commissary had not fully implemented the DA-adapted 0488 system for automating commissary record keeping due, in part, to the downtime and personnel shortages. The downtime could have been reduced had the maintenance contractor reacted within specified timeframes. In order to provide the needed management data, a concerted effort should be made to either promptly implement the system as intended or abandon it and return to manual records.

(The first of my nine years auditing computer systems that did not work. Every computer system I ever audited had problems with it.)

In 1971, DA adopted a standard system for automating the maintenance of the commissary records.

Currently, the commissary leases one set, paying about $712 a month for rental and maintenance. A second set which would increase rental and maintenance to approximately $1,400 per month is expected in February and March 1974. There were eight applications to the computer, however, the commissary

22

was granted an exception to implementing three of these applications.

The implementation of the 0488 system began in 1971. DA directed that commissaries submit monthly reports identifying problem areas that could impede meeting target dates. The commissary replied that there were no problems to report other than that the one configuration was not adequate to implement all applications.

In May 1973, U.S. Army Computer Systems Command Support Group submitted a one-time request to all commissaries for information. One specific item of data requested was the status of the number of applications implemented. The commissary reported that of the five applications to be implemented, four had been implemented. However, as of December 1973, implementation of the four applications reported as complete were not completed.

The Walter Reed Army Medical Center Commissary was not alone in experiencing problems with the mechanization. A U.S. Army Audit Agency Report (5074–1, dated 25 July 1973) indicated that other commissaries were having similar problems.

Another limiting factor was maintenance of the equipment. The maintenance contract states that the contractor should grant a credit to the Government if the contractor, upon notification of malfunction of equipment, does not arrive within four hours to repair equipment, except for causes beyond the control of the contractor. However, a credit is not granted if any portion of the applications is operational and productive. The contract also states that the contractor is required to specify in writing the frequency and duration of preventive maintenance required for the equipment and should coordinate with the Government as to the time convenient for the contractor to perform the preventive maintenance. The contractor is paid a flat fee for performing preventive maintenance.

A malfunction assistance log should be prepared for each system malfunction. This log provides for documentation of the time and dates the contractor representative was notified and arrived.

Our discussion with responsible personnel and review of documents relating to automatic data processing equipment disclosed the following:

Preventive maintenance was not performed. The repairman came only when notified of equipment malfunction.
After notification of machine malfunction, repairmen took long than specified before arriving to repair equipment. In one instance, Fort Lee, the support center, had to call the contractor to speed up the repair process.
Malfunction logs were not always prepared.

Because of the frequent breakdown of equipment, we feel that the contracting officer representative should request that the contractor provide the Government with a required preventive maintenance schedule and perform maintenance as required. Maximum production depends on all functions of the equipment being operative. We feel that the contract should be rewritten to grant the Government a credit if any portion of the equipment is inoperative.

A final limiting factor was the staffing assigned to implement this automated system. The commissary had only one person working in the automated data processing section.

In view of the continuing outlay of about $720 a month for equipment rental and maintenance, a prompt decision should be made either to make a determined and systematic effort to fully implement the system, and thereby realize maximum return from the outlay, or to abandon the system and avoid the recurring cost. If it is decided to go with the system, assistance should be sought from DA to make the system work.

The Army's Health Services Command response was to acquire more equipment. The most expensive and least effective use of your money. But think of the visuals all this new equipment would make.

11. Full economic and ecological benefits were not realized from the disposal of cardboard. Army installations in the Washington metropolitan area were profitably recycling cardboard; however, Walter Reed Army Medical Center was paying about $40,000 annually to have cardboard compacted, hauled away, and burned. In addition, the contractor was paid at least $126 per week for a service which was not provided. The use of incinerators for cardboard disposal disrupts the natural environment, prevents recycling of valuable timber products, and increases disposal costs.

The commissary store cardboard was separated from spoilage waste and compressed with a compactor. When filled, the compactor was transported to an incinerator in the suburbs, where the cardboard was burned. The disposal cost of cardboard in 1973 was about $40,000 for the commissary store alone. The contractor was paid for 5 to 7 tons of cardboard transported and burned each trip at $126.40 per trip. Alternative disposal practices would provide significant economic and ecological benefits. For example, another commissary in the Washington metropolitan area had purchased its compactor equipment and is receiving $20 per ton for the waste cardboard at a local salvage yard. We realize that certain costs are incurred in obtaining this $20 per ton return but an overall profit results.

The commissary store operated and stocked shelves only 5 days a week. The refuse collection and disposal contract, however, provided for cardboard pickups 6 days per week at $126.40 per day. Observation of the compactor unit on two Saturdays and discussion with commissary receiving personnel disclosed that there were no pickups on Saturday. However, the truck driver was getting the warehouseman to sign two service tickets when he made the Monday pickup. This practice would not have been necessary because the contracting officers representative was not comparing tickets for service actually received with the amount billed by the contractor. Instead, the receiving report was certified for the amount billed by the contractor. Because this procedure did not provide reasonable assurance that all service paid for was actually received, there is a possibility that other refuse pickups were not actually made.

12. The food service program at Walter Reed Medical Center was not adequately controlled to preclude unauthorized persons from receiving meals without charge. Meal cards were issued to persons not authorized free use of Army dining facilities. Also, the headcounters stationed in the dining facilities to check admissions either did not require meal cards and identification to be presented or did not check them adequately. In the absence of these needed internal controls, unauthorized persons were eating in the dining facilities.

Rigid controls are necessary to preclude misuse of these services. Although controls specified in the regulations were present in name, the controls were not fully implemented nor strictly followed.

Meal cards are numbered and issued to unit commanders from the Food Service Division. The numbering machine did not function properly and sometimes printed the same number on more than one card. It was found that fifty-eight meals cards with duplicate numbers and two meal cards without numbers were issued to the unit. In addition, some of the duplicate meal cards were issued to individuals. Duplicate meal card numbers provide the opportunity for misuse.

Our review of meal card procedures at eight units disclosed that meal cards were not adequately controlled. When meal cards were issued, personnel did not always sign the register. When new meal cards were issued, the register was not revised to show what disposition was made of the old cards. Personnel had not signed for 440 meal cards, and 10 individuals had signed for more than 1 meal card. In addition, at three of the units, meal cards were not issued in numerical sequence. The issuing agents could not account for 50 meal cards that were issued to them.

From a review of the meal card registers it was not possible to determine whether the 3,485 meal cards listed as outstanding were currently valid. For example, one unit's register showed that four persons had meal cards authorizing them free subsistence in the dining hall. Financial records, however, showed that in lieu of free subsistence, they were receiving separate rations of about $51 per month. Additionally, personnel were not required to turn in meal cards when departing from the unit.

What is interesting about Disorganized Crime is that it is noncorrecting. As a result, you not only pay for the screw-up, the first reporting of the screw-up, but the continuance of the previously reported screw-up and the second reporting of the continuance of the screw-up. The second audit of the Walter Reed Commissary was performed during the seven-month period of September 1976 to April 1977. They reported basically the same problems as USAAA had previously reported three years earlier. Though the problems remained the same, the cost to you of course increased (did you think that your paying for an audit was going to save you money?).

Whereas the commissary lost only $29,912 of your money for the first nine months of 1973 (say $3,300 monthly), the loss had exploded to about $590,000 for the eighteen months ended 26 September 1976 (say $33,000 monthly)—a tenfold increase—not bad. Though I wasn't on this second audit, it should be very instructive to you to show all the good it did to spend your money sending me on the 1973 audit. The second audit disclosed that ineffective controls over merchandise and cash as well as inadequate management reviews were the major causes for the commissary losses. These operational weaknesses were due largely to a lack of strict supervision over commissary operations. Many of the internal-control deficiencies noted during our audit had been identified in prior audits, inspections, and reviews, but were never corrected.

Most of the losses incurred by the WRAMC Commissary for the eighteen month period ended 26 September 1976 were attributable to the commissary's grocery operation. Of the $590,000 in losses, about $551,000 occurred prior to 1 July 1976, the date on which Troop Support Agency assumed management responsibility for the WRAMC Commissary. For five consecutive quarters prior to 1 July 1976, the commissary exceeded its authorized loss tolerance for the grocery operations. As a result, a Report of Survey was conducted following each of these quarters by a disinterested officer appointed by command. In addition, other reviews and inspections were conducted by the WRAMC Internal Review and the local US Army Criminal Investigation Division during this same time frame. Our audit disclosed that many of the internal control weaknesses identified in these reviews still existed.

The losses incurred by the commissary were not attributable to any one cause or event. Weaknesses in merchandise and cash controls, physical security, and merchandise pricing contributed to the losses. In addition, deficiencies in preparing accounting records may have contributed to management's inability to detect the specific causes for the losses. These control weaknesses did not develop recently,and many had been identified by previous independent reviews. Allowing the same deficiencies to continue showed that the commissary did not have the strong managerial attention it required. Management personnel needed to ensure that corrective action on deficiencies was thorough and of a continuing nature.

The commissary operation had shown improvement since July 1976 as evidenced by its Statement of Gains and Losses for the accountability period ended 26 September 1976. The net loss from all operations for this period was about $39,000. While this is still a significant loss, it was the first time in six accountability periods that the commissary was within its *authorized loss tolerance*.

Controls over tobacco products were not adequate to safeguard merchandise on hand or to detect inventory shortages. Sales accountability tests were not performed, and thus, large inventory shortages went undetected. We performed sales accountability tests for two different periods and found cash receipts were about $37,000 less than what the dollar sales should have been.

a. The Walter Reed Army Medical Center (WRAMC) Commissary's average monthly tobacco sales were about $108,000. Cigarette sales accounted for about 97 percent of the tobacco sales. Cigarettes are a highly marketable item and are therefore more susceptible to misappropriation. Thus, tight controls must be followed to ensure that they are properly safeguarded.

b. Quarterly accountability inventories were required for the commissary's grocery, meat, and produce operations. Tobacco products were not accounted for separately, but instead were included as a grocery item. However, the tobacco sales were rung up using a separate cash-register key, which provided the sales data needed for making a sales-accountability test. The purpose of making such tests is to disclose differences between the actual dollar sales and the sales that should have resulted based on the beginning inventory plus purchases less ending inventory. Sales less than the dollar value of the inventory consumed indicates potential losses or diversions of merchandise, which should be investigated.

c. Commissaries are required to prepare a Statement of Gains and Losses Report (DA Form 4170) each quarter to reflect their results of operation. For the six quarters ended 26 September 1976, the WRAMC Commissary reported cumulative net losses of about $590,000.

Inventory Shortage—1 March to 30 June 1976. Our sales accountability analysis of tobacco transactions during the period 1 March to 30 June 1976 showed unexplained inventory losses of $32,714. Computation of the losses follows:

Inventory Value 1 March 1976	$ 49,116
Purchases 1 March through 30 June 1976	441,765
Total Available for Sale	$490,881
Inventory Value 30 June 1976	25,843
Computed Consumption	$465,038
Recorded Sales 1 March through 30 June 1976	432,234
Unidentified Losses	$ 32,714

The Statement of Gains and Losses Report for this period showed losses of $137,448 in the grocery operation. Based on the above accountability computation, $32,714, or 24 percent, was due to losses in tobacco inventory.

Inventory Shortage—26 September to 22 November 1976. In September 1976, the commissary attempted to increase its control over tobacco products by securing them within a fully enclosed wire cage located in the warehouse. To determine the effectiveness of this control, we performed a second accountability analysis for the period 26 September to 22 November 1976. This analysis, provided below, showed unexplained inventory losses of $4,287:

Inventory Value 26 September 1976	$ 45,333
Purchases 26 September through 22 November 1976	257,985
Total Available for Sale	$303,318
Inventory Value 22 November 1976	84,306
Computed Consumption	$219,012
Recorded Sales 26 September through 22 November 1976	214,725
Unidentified Losses	$ 4,287

Although the tobacco product losses were much lower than those shown in our previous analysis, the losses were still significant, and thus additional controls seem warranted.

Inventory Accountability. Although dollar sales figures were available, sales accountability tests were not made to detect inventory losses. However, under the current system, even if such tests had been made, it would have been very difficult to determine the actual cause of the losses. Our accountability analyses showed that significant tobacco losses had occurred, but we were unable to fix the responsibility for these losses or even to determine whether the losses occurred in the warehouse or the sales store. To have complete control over tobacco products requires that a system be established whereby accountability can be fixed to specific commissary personnel from the time tobacco products enter the commissary warehouse until they are sold.

The lack of adequate management reviews and effective internal controls prevented the detection of losses in the commissary meat market. For the accountability period 1 July to 26 September 1976, the commissary meat market operation should have realized a gain of at least $21,300 instead of the net gain of $4,781.

Generally, resale prices should be established to recover the cost of items without incurring a gain or loss. Resale pricing policy varies depending on whether the item is unprocessed or processed. Unprocessed items, i.e., items sold in the form originally received, are specifically identifiable units. They are sold for the invoice cost per unit, with application of the current mill rule, and should result in no gain or loss from the transaction to the commissary. Prices for processed items, however, are based on cost and other influencing factors, such as patron demand, standardized cutting procedures and yield of salable cuts, balanced movement of processed cuts, and cumulative gains or losses carried forward from the preceding accounting period. Because of the variability of these factors, the commissary officer can adjust prices to preclude gain or loss to the government from overall operation of the meat market.

Quarterly accountability inventories were conducted at the commissary to determine the results (gains or losses) of the meat, produce, and grocery operations. For the period ended 30 June 1976, the WRAMC Commissary reported a cumulative gain of $2,180 in the meat market, and for the period ended 26 September 1976, a cumulative gain of $6,961. So, for the accountable period 1 July to 26 September 1976, the commissary had a reported net gain of $4,781.

Unrealized Gains. Periodic cutting tests are required to ensure that prices are established correctly for processed meat and that operating gains and losses do not exceed acceptable levels. Our review showed gains of as much as $30 on cutting tests for each side of beef, and an average gain of $14.85 for all carcass beef cutting tests for the accountability period ended 30 June 1976. Yet, the meat market operation showed a net operating loss of $2,143 for the same period. This was determined by subtracting the cumulative gain for the previous accountability period from the cumulative reported gain for the period ended 30 June 1976 ($4,323 − $2,180 = $2,143).

Because of the results of this limited view, we decided to perform an analysis of the meat market operation for the most current accountability period, 1 July to 26 September 1976. This analysis showed that the meat market operation should have realized a minimum gain of at least $21,300 instead of the reported net gain of $4,781. The gain of $21,300 was determined by using the results of the commissary's cutting tests, which established the selling price and the percentage yield of salable retail cuts from carcass beef. This data, applied to the number of pounds of carcass beef processed during our test period, provided what the retail gain in carcass beef sales should have been. Meat market personnel told us that cutting tests were performed when significant price changes occurred. During our test period, we used the results of seven cutting tests. We determined the dates of all carcass beef purchases so we could apply the results of each cutting test against the appropriate proportion of poundage applicable to that cutting test period. Also, our review of the documentation supporting these tests, as well as personal observation of cutting tests during the audit, showed that these tests were accurately performed. In order to determine the reasonableness of the cutting test yields, we established the projected amount to be received from the sale of fat and bones for the quarter 1 July to 26 September 1976. We concluded that the cutting test projections for fat and bones were within 2 1/4 percent of the actual amount received. We selected fat and bones for this analysis because these items (i) represent about 30 percent of carcass beef weight, and (ii) are sold in such a manner that the receipts from their sale can be specifically identified, whereas sales of all other carcass beef items are not distinguishable from other meat sales.

In our opinion, our computed gain of $21,300 for the meat market operation was a conservative figure. This computation was based on what the expected gain should have been just from the sale of carcass beef cuts alone. We estimated that carcass beef sales account for about 50 percent of total meat sales. The

29

remaining 50 percent comes from the sale of the other processed meat items (e.g., lamb carcass, veal, pork loins, and loins of beef) and the unprocessed or prepackaged items. Cutting tests during this period for these other processed meat items showed that sales of these items should have produced at least nominal gains. We were told that all unprocessed or prepackaged meat items were sold at their purchase price, thus producing no gains or loss. In addition, our computed gain from carcass beef sales was based solely on purchases made during the test period, and did not include carcass beef already on hand at the beginning of the period. Meat inventory at 1 July 1976 was valued at about $45,000, and the ending meat inventory at 26 September 1976 was about $14,000. We assumed that the difference, $31,000, was sold at the purchase price. It seems reasonable to assume that at least a nominal gain would have occurred from the sale of this $31,000 of meat items since the cutting for the period ending 30 June 1976 indicated gains.

Segregation of Duties and Responsibilities. An effective system of internal controls must include "checks and balances," which require adequate segregation of duties and responsibilities. However, these "checks and balances" were not present in the meat market operation. Meat market personnel were responsible for all phases of the meak market operation to include (i) procuring, receiving, and processing meat items, (ii) establishing sales prices on carcass meat items, (iii) merchandising meat items, and (iv) performing accountability functions (e.g., taking inventories and preparing trial balances). Our audit showed that independent reviews or analyses of the meat market operation were not made. Supervisory personnel tended to assume that if the quarterly reported gain or loss for the meat market was within the allowable tolerance, then the meat market was operating efficiently. This was especially true where gains were reported. Lack of independent reviews of the meat market operation provides the opportunity for meat shortages or management inefficiency to go undetected. We believe that an analysis similar to the one we performed should be done on a regular basis by supervisory personnel who are not directly involved in the meat market operation.

Controls over cashier operations were inadequate. Control features on cash registers were not effectively utilized; responsibilities for handling and accounting for cash were not segregated; and tests to measure cashier accuracy were not performed as required. These control weaknesses may have contributed to the commissary's reported operating losses for the six quarters ended 26 September 1976.

The commissary has annual sales of about $17 million. The large amount of cash receipts and the large number of commissary employees who handle cash make it imperative that the commissary follows strict internal controls to account for cash proceeds. The commissary's cash registers have built-in mechanical control features that can be used to verify cash sales. In addition, AR 31-200 specifies the control procedures necessary for monitoring cash from receipt to deposit.

Sequential Transaction Numbers. Each cash register has two paper tapes on which transactions are printed as they are rung up. One tape is given to the customer, and the other tape remains inside the cash register for audit purposes. Sequential numbers are printed beside each transaction. The person responsible for preparing the Summary of Daily Fund Receipts (DA Form 3292) did not compare the ending transaction number on cash register detail tapes for one day to the beginning transaction number the next day to determine that all sales transactions were accounted for. Also, commissary personnel could not locate the cash register detail tapes for the month of April 1976. Therefore, we could not compare the daily beginning and ending transaction number or validate the amount of sales for that month. Without detail audit tapes and close monitoring of the tapes by management, there is no assurance that all sales and cash receipts are accounted for.

Lock-Unlock Numbers. Cash registers are equipped with a lock/unlock number meter, which counts the number of times the cash register is cleared. Clearing procedures require each cash register in operation to be cleared twice. Each clearing produces a tape. The first tape shows the total dollar sales rung up by merchandise category, which the second tape should show all zeros. The second clearing is done to ensure that the register is cleared. Prior to 4 May 1976, the commissary did not retain the second tape. In addition, when the sequence of lock/unlock numbers registered more than two clearings per cash register, the unexplained breaks were not investigated. Retention of both clearing tapes and investigation of unexplained clearings are necessary to be assured that cash is turned in for all sales rung up on the cash register.

Cumulative Sales Readings. Commissary cash registers are equipped with two sales meters, which accumulate the dollar value of sales that is rung up. One of these meters is automatically reset to zero each time the cash register is cleared; the other meter is not resettable. By taking the difference between the beginning and ending cumulative sales, it can be determined if all sales rung up are reported. Prior to 4 May 1976, clearing procedures did not include taking a reading of the cumulative sales meter totals. After 4 May 1976, cumulative sales readings were taken and recorded; however, the readings were not used to verify reported sales.

No Sales. One of the cash register meters records the number of times that the cash drawer is opened when "no sale" rings are recorded on the cash register. When the cash drawer is opened with a "no sale" ring, there is a possibility that sales are not being recorded and cash tendered is being diverted. Beginning on 4 May 1976, the number of "no sale" rings were recorded on the cashier's Summary of Daily Fund Receipts report. We reviewed the number of "no sale" rings recorded for all registers for a one-week period beginning 4 May 1976. Of the 10,299 transactions recorded, 795 or 7.7 percent were "no sale" rings. However, there was no indication that management had investigated what appeared to be an excessive number of "no sale" rings. Since "no sale" rings provide cashiers an opportunity to misappropriate funds, more stringent controls are necessary to minimize the number of such transactions.

Cash Register Readings. Cashiers were routinely provided with cash register readings prior to documenting their cash receipts and turning them in to the head cashier. At the end of each day, cashiers should count and record their receipts and turn in this amount without knowing amounts recorded on the cash register. Providing cashiers with readings defeats the purpose of having personnel other than cashiers take readings and clear cash registers and may encourage the misappropriation of funds.

Segregation of Duties. Internal accounting controls over handling and accounting for cash were inadequate because these functions were not always segregated. According to AR 31-200, the person receiving and handling funds should not prepare the Summary of Daily Fund Receipts report and the Report of Deposit (DD Form 707). However, we found the person responsible for preparing these reports served as a cashier frequently.

Tests of Cashier Accuracy. Neither monthly shopping tests nor surprise cash counts were being conducted as required by AR 31-200 and AR 37-103. Tests of cashier accuracy should be made periodically to provide management assurance that receipts are not being misappropriated and to act as a psychological deterrent to employee theft. Between 19 May and 1 November 1976, commissary personnel performed only one check of cashier accuracy. The one test pointed out the need for more frequent spot checks. It revealed that a customer had passed a cashier's check-out area with merchandise totaling $326, but the cashier had rung up only $111 on the cash register. This incident was reported to the military police and is now being reviewed by the Federal Bureau of Investigation.

The lack of adequate controls over merchandise coupons made it possible for coupons to be substituted for cash. This practice could be detected only by observation or surprise cash counts. Therefore, it was not possible to determine the total amount of merchandise coupons that may have been substituted for cash.

Merchandise coupons, generally found in newspapers and magazines, are discounts allowed by manufacturers to introduce new items or to stimulate sales. Commissary patrons may use these coupons as partial payment toward the purchase of the specific merchandise designated on the coupons. Upon receipt, cashiers are to record the value of the coupons on their cash registers. As cashiers go off duty, they are to record the total value of coupons received on a Cashier's Daily Report and give both the coupons and the report to the head cashier. For the seven months ended 31 October 1976, the commissary had received credit for merchandise coupons valued at $41,749 by forwarding them to Northeast Field Office, US Army Troop Support Agency.

Surprise Cash Count. The condition discussed in this finding was first detected during a surprise cash count we performed on 20 September 1976, when the commissary was not open for business. At the time of our count, the commissary had all coupons on hand that had been accepted as payment for commissary merchandise for the period 1–20 September (thirteen operating days). The coupons were separated by date of transaction and by cash register. We reviewed these coupons on a selective basis and found the following:

Of the total number of coupons on hand, 997 were Johnson and Johnson coupons valued at $135.70. For one day, 18 September, the cashier for one of the 19 cash registers in operation had turned in 73 of the Johnson and Johnson coupons worth $12.85. For that day, this cashier was the only one of the 19 that received Johnson and Johnson coupons. Since coupons could be and were redeemed at any one of the 19 cash registers, it seemed highly unlikely that all Johnson and Johnson coupons would be redeemed at only one cash register position. For the entire 13-day period the same cash register, normally operated by the same cashier, accounted for about one-half (408 of the 997) of the turn-ins for these coupons. Also, 172 of the 408 coupons, worth $29.50, were expired coupons.

Two different cashiers redeemed $9.50 and $8.00 each on "O Cedar Broom or Mop" coupons, an item which, according to the commissary officer, was not carried in the commissary.

As part of our coupon review, we also compared the dollar amount of coupons rung up on selected cash registers to the dollar amount of coupons turned in for the same cash registers. We found in all instances that the amount of coupons rung up on the cash registers was equal to the amount of coupons turned in. We performed a second cash count during business hours to see if we could determine if coupons were being substituted for cash.

Follow-up Cash Count. On 11 November 1976, we performed a second cash count during the store's normal hours of operation. With the assistance of the commissary officer, we closed six cash register positions and took a reading of each cash register. Then, with each of the six cashiers present, we counted the cash receipts and coupons and compared these totals to the cash register readings. The table below shows that one of the six cashiers had a cash balance due overage of $14.90 and a coupon shortage of $14.93.

Type of Receipt	Cash Register Reading	Physical Count	Difference Over (Short)
Coupons	$ 25.58	$ 10.65	$(14.93)
Checks	1,627.29	1,627.29	-0-
Balance Due	1,075.66	1,090.56	14.90
Total	$2,728.53	$2,728.50	$(.03)

Upon completion of our cash count, the cashiers were allowed to return to their cash registers until the close of business.

At the end of the day's operations, we performed a second cash reconciliation for the cashier who had the cash overage and coupon shortage. As shown below, for some reason there was no longer a cash overage or coupon shortage.

Type of Receipt	Cash Register Reading	Physical Count	Difference Over (Short)
Coupons	$ 28.99	$ 28.99	$-0-
Checks	2,279.77	2,279.77	-0-
Balance Due	1,312.92	1,312.92	-0-
Total	$3,621.68	$3,621.68	$-0-

Based on this review, it appeared that cash sales were rung up on the coupon tendered key, thus causing a coupon shortage and cash overage. At the close of business, coupons representing the difference between the coupons tendered reading and actual coupons submitted by customers could have been substituted for corresponding cash overages. Cashiers were provided coupons readings before turning in their receipts. Thus, the opportunity to substitute coupons for corresponding cash overages was much greater.

Merchandise Coupons. Commissary patrons could obtain merchandise coupons from newspapers and magazines or through vendor distribution. Our review of coupons redeemed at the commissary showed that one of the major sources of coupons is magazines—two in particular, *Lady Com* and *Family*. Both magazines are distributed commercially to the commissary on a no-charge basis. Bulk shipments of these magazines are sent to the commissary monthly for distribution to commissary patrons as they enter the store. The coupons contained in these two magazines can be redeemed only at commissaries.

Once the magazines are received at the commissary warehouse, the procedures for distributing them to the commissary patrons differ for each magazine. The commercial firm that distributes the *Lady Com* magazine employs an individual who is responsible for handing out the magazines to the commissary patrons. When the *Lady Com* magazine arrives at the commissary, commissary personnel are to contact this individual to come to the store and make the distribution. However, the commercial firm responsible for distributing *Family* magazine does not provide anyone to hand out the magazines to the commissary patrons. Instead, commissary personnel are tasked to make the distribution.

Our audit showed that large quantities of both magazines were received at the commissary warehouse but were never distributed to the commissary patrons and could not be accounted for. For example, a shipment of 1,800 *Lady Com* magazines, containing coupons valued at about $8,600, was receipted for by the commissary on 1 October 1976. Once received, the magazines were left unsecured in the commissary warehouse. The person responsible for distributing the magazines was never notified by the commissary that the shipment had been received. We brought this matter to the attention of the commissary officer, who tried to locate the shipment of magazines but was unsuccessful. We also found that *Family* magazines were not being properly controlled or distributed. The commissary received monthly shipments of about 1,500 of these magazines. However, the commissary maintained no records of these shipments. We were told by commissary personnel that most of these magazines were disposed of rather than distributed to the commissary customers. According to the commissary officer, this was done because he did not have the personnel available to make the distribution.

The 15 June 1976 Criminal Investigation Division Report of the WRAMC Commissary also pointed out a lack of control over merchandise coupons. This is especially significant since our audit indicated that coupons may have been substituted for cash.

Accounting procedures and reviews were not adequately administered to ensure that the results of operation were accurately presented. Posting errors of about $42,500 to the accounting records caused the commissary's Statement of Gains and Losses for the period ended 26 September 1976 to be unreliable. Thus, commissary management was not provided with the data necessary to accurately measure operational efficiency.

Commissary merchandise is accounted for in a relatively simple manner. In each accounting period, all merchandise receipts and price increases are added to the beginning inventory while sales, destroyed merchandise, and price reductions are deducted. The net figure is the recorded or book inventory. A physical inventory is taken quarterly, and the value is compared to book inventory to determine gains or losses. Gains or losses exceeding allowable tolerances must be investigated. AR 31–200 prescribes the methods and procedures to be used in accounting for, and conducting inventories of, subsistence supplies at commissaries.

The basic commissary accounting record is DA Form 3295, Voucher Register and General Control (Control). The Control record is used to record the dollar value of book inventory showing increases, decreases, and balances on hand. Vouchers are the documents from which data are entered into the Control record. Correct posting of vouchers is essential to the eventual determination of results of operations. Erroneous postings can distort recorded gains or losses.

Posting Errors. We reviewed entries posted to the Control record prior to, during, and subsequent to the accountability period ended 26 September 1976. Our review disclosed errors totaling about $42,500, which had a significant effect on the reported gains and losses for that period:

The 31 August entry for deliveries in August under a Consolidated Agreement was understated by $13,825.

Good received in this period, totaling about $17,100, were erroneously posted as being received in the subsequent accountability period. A potential cause for part of these errors was that some of the goods were received in several shipments as called for in Blanket Purchase Agreements. Some goods were received prior to 26 September and some after 26 September. Only one payment was made in such agreements and that being at the end of each month. So accounting personnel posted the entire amount of shipments received during the month on 30 September and therefore understated the 26 September book inventory.

Three vouchers totaling about $11,580 for meat purchases were erroneously posted to the grocery account. In our opinion, the erroneous posting could have been easily detected by commissary personnel if a quick and simple comparison had been made. Meat market personnel prepared bimonthly a trial balance to measure the cumulative gain or loss for the meat market operation. The cumulative gain at 26 September 1976, as measured by the meat market's trial balance, was $5,129, or $13,412 less than that recorded in the Control record. Most of this difference was evident as early as 31 July 1976. The trial balance prepared in the meat market is an estimate, and therefore the gain or loss determined from it is not expected to be exactly the same as that shown in the Control record. However, the two

35

figures should be relatively close. Comparisons between the trial balance and the Control record should be made on a regular basis, and if significant differences exist, immediate action taken to determine the cause for the differences.

Actual versus Reported Gains and Losses. The effect of the posting errors we disclosed is presented in the following schedule:

Grocery and Meat Market Operations
For the Period 1 July — 26 September 1976

| | Actual Gain or (Loss) | | Authorized Tolerance | |
	Grocery	Meat	Grocery	Meat
Amount Reported	$(27,466)	$18,540	$49,502	$8,536
After Audit	(46,813)	6,960	49,502	8,536

The major impact of these posting errors was that the loss in the grocery operation was understated by about $19,000, while the meat market gain was overstated by about $11,500. Even though the actual loss in the grocery operation was still within the allowable tolerance, the significance of the loss warrants an intensive review by commissary management.

Accounting records were not always given the management attention they deserve. However, management decision-making was based, to a large extent, on what those records indicated. Unless accounting records are accurate, command and commissary management may be misled with respect to the efficiency of the overall commissary operation. This situation could result in some elements of the total operation being needlessly overmanaged and other areas requiring management's attention being seriously undermanaged.

Management personnel did not make adequate reviews of the selling prices of commissary merchandise. Independent price verification by disinterested persons were not conducted during the period 1 July to 31 October 1976. These conditions resulted in commissary patrons being charged incorrect prices and may have contributed to operational losses.

The selling prices of items sold in the WRAMC Commissary are supposed to be based on the prices quoted on purchase orders or on invoices submitted by vendors in accordance with Blanket Purchase Agreements. Commissary personnel are required to prepare a master pricelist each quarter and have it updated by supplemental pricelists to reflect inertia price changes. Accurate pricing of retail merchandise is necessary for the commissary to recover its annual acquisition costs of about $17 million and to preclude substantial gains or losses from overall operations.

A master pricelist is generated quarterly by the WRAMC Management Information Systems Office and provided to the commissary's accounting department. When price changes occur, the accounting department processes three copies of the changes. They retain one copy and forward the other two copies

36

to the day and night shift personnel who stock the commissary shelves. The copy retained by the accounting department is supposed to be used to update the master pricelist by preparing a punched card for each change and forwarding the cards to the automatic data processing section for a computer run. The copies given to the day and night shift personnel should be used to verify and update the prices on the new merchandise being stocked.

Price Changes. We selected sixty-nine items from the master pricelist for review and found that the most current prices were not shown for 7 percent of the items. In some instances, more then eighteen days elapsed from the time price changes were received until the master pricelist was updated. Some examples of this condition are shown below.

Date of USAAA Review	Date of Receiving Report	Item	New Price Per Purchase Order	Price Per Master List
29 Oct 76	11 Oct 76	Soup, Italian Style	$0.48	$0.45
29 Oct 76	14 Sep 76	Soap, Liquid Palmolive	0.75	0.60
29 Oct 76	10 Oct 76	Spice, MSG	2.20	2.45
29 Oct 76	10 Oct 76	Asparagus	0.50	0.54

Pricing Verification. Army regulations required that a disinterested person appointed by the installation commander selectively verify two hundred of the commissary's marked prices to the current master pricelist within three days of the beginning of each accounting period. If the verification discloses an error rate of 4 percent or greater, the commander is required to direct that an internal review be made of the commissary's pricing procedures.

We selected the twelve-month period ended 31 October 1976 as a basis to review the results of disinterested officers' price verifications. We found that price verifications were not made subsequent to 1 July 1976. There seemed to be some confusion as to who was responsible for making price verifications since operational control of the commissary was transferred from the Commander, WRAMC to the Commander, US Army Troop Support Agency on 1 July 1976. The verifications that were made were performed up to nine working days after the beginning of the accounting period. Unless price verifications are made at the beginning of each accounting period and excessive error rates are promptly investigated, pricing errors could go undetected and could result in operational losses.

After the Walter Reed Commissary audit, I was assigned to my first Army-wide audit. Army-wide audits involve numerous auditors and numerous audit sites. There is one audit site called the Audit Control Point, which is responsible for issuing guidance to the other audit sites and usually writes the audit report. Though you pay through the nose for these large-scale audits, they are the most productive in terms of detecting large amounts of your wasted money. This system-wide audit was of the Army's leased communications. I worked on this job for the first six months of 1974. The audit report was published on 27 September 1974.

The U.S. Army Communications Command (USACC) is a major field command of the Department of the Army. Its major missions are to engineer, install, operate, and maintain the Army's nontactical communications and other communications as directed. In addition, it functions as the Army leasing agency for all leased communications requirements.

The missions are accomplished in the Continental United States (CONUS) by USACC-CONUS, a major subordinate command of Headquarters, USACC. At 30 April 1974, the combined military and civilian strength of the Communications Command, including foreign nationals, was about 30,000. About 8,700 were assigned to USACC-CONUS. At 30 April 1974, the FY 1974 funding program for leased communications in CONUS included about $80.3 million in Operation and Maintenance, Army funds.

USACC estimated that a cost avoidance, or dollar savings, in the amount of $10 million would be realized from the reorganization by July 1977. As part of a continuing U.S. Army Audit Agency program for assessing the CONUS Army reorganization, we separately evaluated the basis for the projected $10 million cost avoidance or savings. We issued a Reorganization Advisory Letter to USACC on 6 May 1974, stating that the basis for the projected savings was not documented, and therefore, an evaluation of its reasonableness could not be made. Included in this report, however, are recommendations for corrective action, which, when implemented, will result in savings that can be reported as realized from the reorganization. Our recommendations concerning Commercial Long Distance Services will result in hard dollar savings for USACC. Also our recommendations concerning Lease-Purchase Analyses, relating to equipment and facilities that were acquired at installations, could similarly result in hard dollar savings. Other recommendations affecting short haul communications may also result in additional reportable savings.

Prior to the Army's CONUS reorganization of 1 July 1973, USACC was responsible for all long-haul communications and short-haul communications in support of the U.S. Army Air Defense Command, Military Traffic Management Command, U.S. Army Intelligence Command, and four Health Service Command Installations. In addition, USACC was responsible for communications in support of designated DOD organizations, such as the Defense Civil Preparedness Agency. Effective with the reorganization, USACC assumed the responsibility for short-haul communications support for TRADOC, FORSCOM, and AMC installations. In addition to this mission, USACC was also given the responsibility for the Army's Communications Economy and Discipline Program, Military Affiliate Radio System, outside plant television cable systems, Army Civilian Career Program for Communications, and the Army's air traffic control systems.

A major change in command authority and responsibility resulted from the reorganization. To accomplish this organizationally, the Commander, USACC-CONUS, was appointed executive agent for the overall control of CONUS communications, and intermediate commands responsible to USACC-CONUS were established at TRADOC, FORSCOM, and AMC Headquarters. The commanders of these three intermediate commands also function as the major commands' communications-electronics (C-E) officers, thereby performing in a dual-hat capacity. Eighty C-E activities at installations became USACC agencies or detachments. (A detachment has seventy-five or fewer personnel.) The agencies or detachments are under the command and technical control of the newly established intermediate commands; however, they are under the operational control of the local installation commander. The commander or chief of the agency or detachment also functions in a dual-hat capacity as the installation's C-E officer.

With the establishment of three additional intermediate commands at the major Army command level and eighty agencies and detachments at the installation level, an effective organizational structure was developed for the management of nontactical communications in CONUS. The new organizational concept provides an excellent vehicle for centralized control of communications management and can result in substantial dollar savings and increased effectiveness. However, the CONUS reorganization plan did not assign the U.S. Army Communications Command (USACC) total responsibility and necessary authority and did not transfer all Army nontactical communications management to USACC. In addition, USACC did not establish methods to measure the effectiveness of communications management. In any major reorganization, new ground has to be broken, new problems fielded, and effective management techniques devised to meet the new mode of operation. Establishing the new communications organization in itself required a herculean effort. The problems facing USACC are substantial. The auditors pointed out some of the problems still faced in the area of leased communications and suggested management improvements.

To achieve further savings, there was a need to assign USACC the responsibility and authority to enforce communications economy and discipline at all levels. There was also a need to identify agencies that retained responsibility for managing their own nontactical communications and to transfer these responsibilities to USACC. Meaningful performance indicators were needed to measure the effectiveness of USACC's operations. The programs for annual review and rejustification of voice communications facilities and for equipment lease-purchase analyses required clarification and additional command emphasis. Intensified management of a telephone traffic recorder program could help hold down costs and eliminate delays in implementation. With respect to the telephone system, costs could be reduced by using the most economical systems for making long-distance calls and limiting the number of official Class A telephone lines in accordance with established criteria. In the area of fund management, responsibilities had to be defined and guidance needed to be issued to USACC's newly established agencies and detachments.

As a result of the Army's 1973 reorganization, the U.S. Army Communications Command (USACC) was given the responsibility for programming, budgeting, funding, accounting, and reporting for base communications. An elaborate system of some eighty allottees was established to control the funds. However, DA staff agencies, major Army commands, and their subordinate activities, together with USACC, share the responsibility for ensuring the proper and efficient use of base communications. Since these organizations do not pay for the base communications they use, they have no incentive to make, and have not made, proper and efficient use of the communications. Without the responsibility for and authority to enforce communications economy and discipline, USACC has no means to ensure that its funds are used effectively, and many of the economies and benefits that could have resulted from the 1973 reorganization will not be realized.

The Department of Army stated that an objective of the CONUS reorganization was to streamline management and reduce overhead. The letter also stated that guidance for detailed planning by all commands should consider full management at the installation level and exception management at the higher levels.

In conjunction with the 1973 CONUS reorganization, the Army Chief of Staff directed that responsibility for certain functions be transferred from the DA Assistant Chief of Staff for Communications-Electronics (ACSC-E) to USACC on 1 May 1973. These included responsibility for the operational aspects of the Communications Economy and Discipline Program and becoming the proponent of AR 105-10, Communications Economy and Discipline. With the reorganization, USACC was also given the responsibility for programming, budgeting, funding, accounting, and reporting for the base communications activities in CONUS. Inherent with fund control is the authority and responsibility to exercise control over the base communications to ensure their effective and efficient use.

Need for Assignment of Responsibility and Authority. Although the Army Chief of Staff directed that responsibility for the operational aspects of the Communications Economy and Discipline Program be transferred to USACC, USACC's responsibility and authority to require the efficient and proper use of communications at all command levels was not set forth in the reorganization plan or in subsequent guidance from DA. Without the assignment of such responsibility and authority, USACC has provided telecommunications services requested and given advice on communications economy and discipline but contends it has no direct authority to require that efficient and proper use is made of the services provided. In this regard, USACC provided the following comments on its interpretation of responsibility and authority for communications economy and discipline.

The activity (either DA staff agency or Major Army Command (MACOM)) receiving telecommunications support from a USACC agency or detachment has no inherent command responsibility to ensure efficient and proper use of telecommunications service. The Communications-Electronics (C-E) staff officer at such an activity likewise has a staff responsibility to ensure efficient and proper use of telecommunications service. The C-E staff officer as Commander of the USACC agency or detachment has technical control responsibilities to discharge in ensuring efficient and proper use of telecommunications services. Responsibility for management of the Army communications system is shared by USACC and other MACOM's receiving communications support.

40

This command shares responsibility for compliance with DA policy concerning the use of communications with heads of DA staff agencies and commanders of MACOM's. The degree to which responsibility is shared as well as the level of responsibility varies among DA staff agencies, major Army commands, and installations. The general assignment of the shared responsibility is made by the revised regulation (AR 105–10); however, specific responsibilities of this command and other MACOM's receiving communications support from this command must be determined on a case-by-case basis.

Difussion of Responsibility and Authority. Without specifically assigning USACC the responsibilities for the operational aspects of communications economy and discipline and the necessary authority with which to carry out those responsibilities, a meaningful Communications Economy and Discipline Program cannot be established. In becoming the proponent of AR 105–10, Communications Economy and Discipline, USACC took action and prepared a revised AR, which was issued on 13 May 1974. Because USACC was not assigned the responsibilities for the operational aspects of communications economy and discipline, the revised AR left these responsibilities diffused throughout various Army command levels and activities.

As users, DA staff agencies and MACOM's and their subordinate activities are responsible for the efficient and proper use of telecommunications. However, USACC and its subordinate commands should be responsible for ensuring that efficient and proper use of telecommunications is made. Specific direction from DA and major changes to the revised AR 105–10 will be necessary to assign these responsibilities to USACC. The revised AR still assigns responsibilities for the Communications Economy and Discipline Program to heads of DA staff agencies and commanders of MACOM's rather than to USACC and its subordinate commands, agencies, and detachments. Paragraphs 4c(1) through 4c(11) of AR 105–10 show the following responsibilities as assigned to heads of DA staff agencies and commanders of MACOM's rather than to USACC.

Ensure efficient and proper use of telecommunications service at all levels.

Ensure that newly assigned personnel are informed of available communications services and systems and the regulations governing their use.

Establish telecommunications service monitoring (surveillance) responsibility within each activity to maintain proper standards of economy, discipline, and efficiency.

Emphasize that written messages will be released and delivered to telecommunications centers promptly so that workload may be distributed as evenly as possible throughout the business day.

Ensure that emergency plans prescribe actions to be automatically executed when emergencies arise to preclude increasing message traffic.

Ensure that staff members, drafters, and releasers of messages are instructed in the meaning and importance of MINIMIZE.

Ensure that access to and use of long distance telephone capabilities are restricted to that which is essential for mission accomplishment.

Ensure that procedures for the economical and disciplined use of communications systems for transmitting data formatted traffic are established, promulgated, and periodically reviewed.

Communications Economy and Discipline. Many of the economies that could have resulted from an effective communications economy and discipline program will not be realized. Since USACC has not been assigned the authority to require that efficient and proper use of telecommunications services is made, but contends it has only supervisory and advisory responsibility for communications economy and discipline, action has not been taken to ensure communications economy and discipline at the user level. To have an effective economy and discipline program, USACC's subordinate activities must require that the users whom they service make efficient and proper use of the telecommunications that are provided to them. Since USACC's subordinate activities did not require efficient and proper use of telecommunications by users, the control necessary for effective communications economy and discipline has not been established.

Our review at the installation level disclosed that, in the absence of such control, effective communications economy and discipline were not being practiced and the least costly methods of communication were not being used. Some of the problems noted, which will continue to exist until USACC is assigned the necessary authority and responsibility, are discussed in the following paragraphs.

Economical Use of Telephone Communications. USACC agencies and detachments were not informing users of available communications services and the regulations governing their use. For example, at Fort Lewis, users were making toll calls to areas that were already serviced by tie-lines. The cost of the unnecessary toll calls was estimated at about $27,000 annually. At Sacramento Army Depot, during a one-month period, 82 percent of toll calls made in Northern California were made to areas where tie-lines were available.

Transmission of Data. USACC agencies and detachments did not ensure that only essential material was transmitted over the automatic digital network (AUTODIN). In most cases, they depended upon reviews made by installation economy and discipline boards established in accordance with AR 105–10. In some cases, reviews were made by USACC agencies and detachments but were limited to identifying problems in the preparation and processing of messages. The reviews did not consider the contents of messages to determine if they should have been sent by other means. For example, AR 105–31 provides that routine messages that qualify for electrical transmission will normally be sent by mail when released on Friday afternoons or on afternoons preceding national holidays so that AUTODIN traffic can be kept to a minimum. At Fort Benning, 822 messages were transmitted through AUTODIN on Fridays during the period 1 September to 31 December 1973. Of this quantity, 539 messages, or 66 percent, were classified routine and should have been considered for dispatch by mail. Similar situations were noted at other installations.

Purchasing Essential Telephone Services. USACC agencies and detachments did not take the necessary actions to ensure that only essential telephone services were purchased to satisfy customer requirements. Semiannual reviews of toll calls, wide area telephone service (WATS), and foreign exchange (FX) costs, as required by AR 105–23, would have disclosed unnecessary services and uneconomical configurations of lines. For example, at Fort Huachuca, annual savings of about $37,000 could be realized by reconfiguring WATS and FX lines. At Fort Benning, addition of WATS lines in lieu of making toll calls could result in an annual savings of about $29,000.

Operational Control of Facsimile Services. USACC agencies and detachments had not obtained operational control of facsimile devices at DA staff agencies, MACOM's, or CONUS installations. Although DA policy and written procedures regarding facsimile devices were established in August 1972, USACC and its subordinate command levels did not enforce them. As a result, the actual quantity of devices remained unknown. This prevented USACC from realizing cost savings through bulk leasing and purchasing methods. Also, the USACC agencies and detachments did not have control of automatic voice network telephone traffic resulting from use of the devices. Our review showed that USACC activities did not control most of the devices at six of the eight installations included in our audit.

Now, in spite of the fact that USAAA proved their point, DA disagreed with the auditors.

The Department of the Army stated U.S. Army Communications Command's (USACC) responsibility to ensure that efficient and proper use of telecommunication is made by DA staff agencies, major commands, and their subordinate activities is contained in AR 105–10, Communications Economy and Discipline, dated 13 May 1974. Paragraph 4b of the subject regulation assigns to USACC the responsibility for supervision and monitoring the operational aspects of the program. Paragraphs 4c (2) through (12) define those operational aspects of the program for which heads of DA staff agencies and major commanders have responsibility, to include among other things, the commander's responsiveness to queries from Headquarters, USACC, regarding the use of telecommunications facilities and assets. Further, paragraph 4c (1) directs that both the Inspector General and Headquarters, USACC, through annual inspection and staff visits include communications economy and discipline a matter of inquiry.

In addition to the regulation, USACC is in a dual-hat role and has a direct command line to the installation communications-electronics officer in most cases. Through this channel, information and statistical data can be made available to provide background data in the preparation of the semiannual summary due Headquarters, DA. USACC, in its semiannual summary evaluation report, should surface the problem arising beyond its control.

Major commanders are coordinate elements of the Department of the Army. Directives and matters of command direction are issued to major commanders by the Chief of Staff, United States Army. Being co-equal in the chain of command, and as command channel structure is vertical, it is neither practical nor desirable to authorize, or give, directive authority to one major commander

43

over another major commander. In addition, AR 105–10 has given sufficient authority to USACC to accomplish its responsibilities so far as they pertain to the communications economy and discipline program.

As a result, from a practical standpoint, it appeared that the 1973 CONUS reorganization, as it related to base communications, served little purpose except to provide information and statistical data that would not have required a major reorganization to obtain. The control of base communications has remained under each and every using command and activity throughout CONUS and communications economy and discipline have not been enforced. The requirement for commanders to be responsive to queries from Headquarters, USACC, in itself, will not ensure effective use of base communications. An effective communications economy and discipline program cannot be established until a single command element is given both the program responsibility and the execution authority.

In any sound organization, responsibility and authority must remain together. Assigned responsibility cannot be effectively discharged without the authority to require necessary action. Inspector General annual inspections and Headquarters, USACC, staff visits do not take the place of normal day-to-day controls and procedures required for effective communications economy and discipline. Instead, such visits are another means for management to periodically ensure that established procedures are followed and controls are effective.

It was not the auditor's intent that USACC should have directive authority over another major commander but rather the USACC should have the directive authority to enforce the proper and efficient use of the leased communications systems for which it pays. Since DA staff agencies, major commands, and their subordinate activities have not responsibility for programming and funding of base communications, they have not incentive to make proper and efficient use of the communications. As long as the responsibility and authority remain separate, it is doubtful that the 1973 CONUS reorganization will serve its purpose. In fact, many of the current problems, which existed prior to the 1973 reorganization, will continue to exist.

As long as USACC has the responsibility for programming, budgeting, funding, accounting, and reporting for base communications activities, it should be given directive authority or some other means to enforce the proper and efficient use of the leased communications that are purchased with its funds. If a means is not provided for USACC to effectively control base communications, then individual users should be required to pay for their own leased communications so that there is at least some incentive for communications economy and discipline.

Under the Army's 1973 CONUS reorganization, the U.S. Army Communications Command (USACC) assumed the responsibility for the management and control of most Army nontactical communications in CONUS. However, some DA staff support agencies and major commands were allowed to retain responsibility for management of their own nontactical communications. We believed this fragmentation was not in the best interest of management efficiency. USACC provides communications support to these activities on a reimbursable basis but

44

has no responsibility for managing or funding the communications. Accordingly, (i) the regulatory procedures and controls applicable to most nontactical communications are not applicable to these activities, (ii) the same technical communications guidance and support provided to others is not available, and (iii) communications costs are not kept at a minimum.

Unsupported Activities. The Army's 1973 CONUS reorganization plan did not assign USACC the responsibility to provide nontactical communications support to certain DA agencies and major commands within CONUS, such as the U.S. Army Recruiting Command, the U.S. Army Security Agency, the U.S. Army Club Management Agency, the Army National Guard, the Corps of Engineers, and some medical service activities. These activities still receive direct funding for all or part of their leased communications costs and reimburse USACC for the communications support provided. The total annual reimbursement to USACC by these and other DA activities is not known but is believed to be significant. For example, the communications costs for the U.S. Army Recruiting Command for FY 1974 were estimated at $5.9 million, based on actual costs for the eight months ended 28 February 1974.

Communications Support. The same support and technical assistance provided to installation commanders under the communications control of USACC were not always being provided to other DA activities supported on a reimbursable basis. USACC agencies and detachments did not (i) review the telephone bills of tenant and satellited activities to determine whether toll costs could be reduced through the lease and use of toll-free telephone circuits, (ii) verify the telephone bills for these activities to ascertain whether the bills were accurate and all toll calls were official, and (iii) obtain from satellited activities the information needed for annual rejustifications of leased communications facilities. Also, some DA staff agencies and major commands did not coordinate their new communications requirements with USACC prior to submitting telecommunications requests through command channels. By placing the responsibility for management and control of all Army nontactical communications under USACC, management of leased communications facilities could be improved and communications costs reduced, as illustrated in the following paragraphs.

Reduction of Telephone Toll Calls. Since USACC was not required to make periodic reviews of the monthly telephone bills of DA activities to which communications support was provided on a reimbursable basis, these activities did not always use the least costly type of telephone service available. We found that the cost of the long distance calls could be reduced for these activities by the lease and use of toll-free lines, such as wide area telephone service (WATS).

The toll costs for the Third Recruiting District of the U.S. Army Recruiting Command are expected to exceed $900,000 for FY 1974. Our analysis of monthly telephone bills for selected activities of the District showed that the costs of toll calls significantly exceeded the lease prices of comparable WATS coverage. For example, about $6,500 annually could be saved by leasing an incoming intrastate WATS line costing about $500 a month in lieu of $1,040 in monthly toll calls made by twenty-three recruiting stations reporting to the Recruiting Main Station at Raleigh, North Carolina. Leased WATS lines were not always used when they were available. About $4,000 annually was being spent for toll calls to Fort McPherson, Georgia, by activities of the Third Recruiting District although there was an incoming WATS line that could have been used. Periodic reviews by USACC would detect many instances in which significant savings would result from the installation and maximum use of leased toll-free telephone circuits.

Verification of Telephone Bills. Monthly telephone bills for many DA activities where communications were not under the control of USACC were not being verified to ensure that the bills were accurate and that all toll calls were made for official business. The telephone company mailed the telephone bills for 297 recruiting activities directly to the Third Recruiting District, which, in turn, forwarded the bills to the Fort McPherson Finance and Accounting Office for payment. The telephone bills were not reviewed or verified by individual recruiting activities or the District nor were they sent to the USACC Agency at Fort McPherson for verification or analysis.

Telephone bills for the Madigan Army Medical Center at Fort Lewis, Washington, were paid by, but not verified by, the USACC Agency at Fort Lewis. The USACC Agency verified the telephone bills of other Fort Lewis activities; however, because the Medical Center was a tenant activity and reimbursed USACC for the communications costs, the USACC Agency had no responsibility for the Center's telephone bills. Further, the Medical Center's internal review staff had noted that (i) no verification was made of toll calls estimated at $21,000 annually, (ii) about 40 percent of the toll calls were not documented on a Report of Authorized Official Toll Telephone Calls (DA Form 360) as required by AR 105–23, and (iii) many of the toll calls were unofficial.

Rejustification of Leased Facilities. Certain satellited activities did not respond to USACC's requests for rejustification of existing leased communications facilities because USACC did not have management responsibility for and operational control over the communications facilities used by those activities. California Army National Guard elements satellited on Fort Ord would not provide the USACC Agency at Ford Ord with requested rejustifications because the requests were not made through the National Guard Bureau. As a result, the USACC Agency did not determine whether the leased facilities used by those National Guard elements were justified. Assigning USACC the responsibility for managing the communications of satellited activities would provide for proper rejustification of those communications facilities.

Establishment of Requirements. Some activities determined their own communication needs and prepared requests for communications services without obtaining technical assistance from USACC. Without proper reviews and analysis of communication needs and alternative methods of accomplishing the needs, the most economical method may not be selected. For example, the U.S. Army Management Agency (USACMA), which was formed to exercise technical direction and supervision over the Army club system worldwide, developed a management information system to monitor the operations of individual clubs on a daily basis. The key to the system was to install a facsimile device (telecopier) in the office of each installation club manager and at each regional headquarters to

46

enable direct transmission of operational data. This system was estimated to cost about $132,000 per year for all CONUS installations.

Approval for the system was obtained from DA Assistant Chief of Staff for Communications-Electronics without first coordinating with USACC. Had USACMA requested technical assistance from USACC, a less costly alternate proposal could likely have been developed. Arrangements could have been made to use other telecopiers already located on installations or those used by the Army-Air Force Exchange System. Also, installation club managers within close proximity to a USACMA regional office may have been able to mail required data rather than use facsimile devices. The leasing of facsimile devices for the system was discontinued 1 April 1974 due to withdrawal of appropriated funds from USACMA. However, the example illustrates the need for USACC technical control and assistance on all requests for communications services to ensure proper evaluation of all alternatives.

USACC is the Army's prime communications manager and has developed a high degree of expertise in communications matters. Providing USACC with the full responsibility for management of all Army nontactical communications would promote efficiency and eliminate fragmentation of communications functions. As noted above, economies could have been achieved if USACC had been exercising full management resonsibility over the communications function of DA agencies and activities where its role is now restricted. This has been recognized by the Commander, U.S. Army Recruiting Command, who, during our audit, requested DA to require USACC to provide technical assistance on a communications survey of the Recruiting Command. USACC-CONUS has been tasked by USACC to provide this assistance. The Commander, U.S. Army Recruiting Command, also requested directly to USACC that he be provided the same communications support being provided other major Army commanders. Pending any assumption of communications responsibility for additional DA activities, USACC agencies and detachments should be tasked to provide whatever expert advice and assistance they can render to the DA activities not now under USACC's cognizance.

Meaningful performance indicators had not been developed to measure the effectiveness of leased communications operations. Service objectives or standards were not consistently defined and applied in measuring the effectiveness of telephone service. One goal of the Army's 1973 CONUS reorganization was to improve communications support to installations, and at the same time reduce communications costs by the elimination of unneeded leased communication facilities and services. The extent to which this goal is achieved, as well as the effectiveness of communications support to all other Army elements, cannot be fully evaluated without the application of service standards to measure performance.

The Supplemental Guidance for Implementation-CONUS Reorganization-1973 tasked the U.S. Army Communications Command (USACC) during May 1973 with developing and submitting criteria to measure the effectiveness of reorganization actions as they relate to improved communications support and resource management. The Comptroller, USACC, was assigned the responsibility to develop the indicators of communications improvements and savings. In the area of telephone service, USACC stated that traffic studies would be made to disclose excess telephone circuits and equipment, and that improved customer satisfaction and cost savings would be the measure of success of the program. These objectives were more in the nature of goals, rather than acutal criteria against which USACC could evaluate the effectiveness with which leased communications are managed. Dollar savings in themselves are not adequate to measure improvements arising from the reorganization. Improvements in communication services provided all USACC customers should also be measurable. One type of measurement, telephone service objectives, is discussed in the following paragraphs.

Telephone Service Objectives. Telephone service objectives are predetermined standards or goals set to determine the quality or grade of service provided users of telephone systems. These objectives cover (i) the allowable proportion of attempted calls that may be delayed because a circuit is not available, (ii) speed of dial connections, (iii) speed of operator answer, and (iv) speed of call connections. Service objectives are the starting point from which circuit and equipment requirements are developed. As more stringent grades of service objectives are established, more facilities and increased costs result. All telephone service objectives must be clearly defined so that increased effectiveness of telephone services, can be measured.

Established Service Objectives. Relatively few service objectives have been officially established to measure the quality of telephone service. The Joint Chief of Staff (JCS), in Memorandum of Policy Number 151, established a service objective of P.05* for incoming calls on the automatic voice network (AUTO-VON) and stated that service objectives for outgoing AUTOVON calls should be determined by each activity based on mission requirements. Communications Command Regulation 105–14, 17 July 1972, specifies that the USACC Deputy Chief of Staff for Plans, Operations, and Automation has the responsibility for establishing telephone service objectives and performance grades of service. Communications Command Pamphlet 105–7, 17 July 1972, contains some service objectives pertaining to telephone equipment but does not require their use.

Undefined Service Objectives. Unofficial service objectives are currently in use which either differ between installations or are not consistent with JCS policy. For example, USACC-CONUS applied an unofficial service objective of P.03 to outgoing local telephone lines. On the other hand, the USACC Agency at Fort Huachuca used P.01 based on an acceptable industry standard and the USACC Detachment at Sacramento Army Depot used P.05 because it provided acceptable telephone service. For outgoing AUTOVON calls, USACC-CONUS chose a service objective of P.10 in analyzing requirements for AUTOVON circuits at various installations. For telephone equipment (line connectors), USACC-CONUS used a service objective that differed from the objective set forth in Communications Command Pamphlet 105–7.

*Represents the probablilty of not completing a call expressed as a decimal fraction. A service objective of P.05 denotes that 5 calls out of 100 will probably not be completed because circuits will be busy. Similarly, P.10 denotes that 10 out of 100 will probably not be completed.

In view of these inconsistencies, USACC should determine which service objectives would be the most appropriate for each type of telephone circuit or equipment and establish them as the official service objectives for management purposes. When a particular objective is not appropriate for all installations, USACC should coordinate with each major Army command to arrive at one that would be appropriate for its installations. Although we basically confined our analyses to telephone service, we noted that, in the area of data traffic management, similar indicators of performance effectiveness were apparently unavailable or not used. By development and application of appropriate standards of service, USACC will be in a better position to ascertain whether improved customer satisfaction at reduced cost is being achieved as envisioned under the reorganization.

The annual review and rejustification program for leased communications facilities and services at CONUS installations could be accomplished more effectively and with less effort. The initial cyclic review and rejustification of voice communications, for which the U.S. Army Communications Command (USACC) assumed responsibility on 1 July 1973, identified few unneeded facilities or services and provided no assurance that all pertinent facilities and services were included. Facilities or services required to meet operational requirements and leased for a satellited activity were not required to be rejustified in the review by that user's major command. Further, the review duplicated other annual requirements for reviewing traffic data or verifying the need for facilities/services when renewing leases.

USACC was required by AR 105–22 to establish procedures and manage a program for the annual review and revalidation of leased communications services. For CONUS communications, this responsibility has been delegated to USACC-CONUS. The provisions of the AR apply to automatic voice network (AUTOVON), automatic digital network (AUTODIN), and other nontactical voice and data facilities and services which are centrally leased. These communications are commonly referred to as long haul. Short-haul communications, on the other hand, are those leased services contracted for by local installation purchasing and contracting officers for tenant USACC agencies and detachments. At present, there are about 16,000 leased communications facilities and services that require annual review and rejustification of which 6,000 are short-haul voice and 700 are short-haul data facilities and services.

The primary criteria for justifying retention of leased communications facilities and services are operational necessity and usage. The review and rejustification process is programmed on a time-phased basis so that USACC agencies and detachments do not have an excessive number of communications facilities and services to review at any one time. Reviews are scheduled quarterly as follows: AUTOVON—first quarter; long- and short-haul voice—second quarter; AUTODIN—third quarter; and long- and short-haul data—fourth quarter. Rejustification of short-haul communications is obtained from USACC agencies and detachments designated to provide Communications-Electronics support to Army elements within their respective geographical areas and then submitted to USACC-CONUS after review by intermediate commands.

Initial Review of Leased Communications Services. The initial cyclic review and rejustification of leased communications, for which USACC assumed responsibility on 1 July 1973, resulted in a large volume of administrative document processing but little identification of unessential or uneconomical services. Rejustifications for long- and short-haul voice communications were solicited during the second quarter of FY 1974. Our review at 31 March 1974 showed that of 1,500 responses received by USACC-CONUS, 1,000 had been reviewed and 31 had been reported as disconnected or no longer required. Only 18 of these actions, with a total monthly lease cost of $1,296, occurred during the rejustification process. The other 13 had been disconnected prior to the rejustification.

In addition, the mission statements and usage data shown on the rejustification sheets were either lacking detail or were too general to enable USACC-CONUS or subordinate agencies and detachments to evaluate the need for retention of the services. A random review of 106 of the 1,000 rejustification sheets showed that 42 responses contained no information on usage, while another 56 contained only estimated usage or general statements such as "light" or "varies." Only 8 of the 106 had adequate rejustifications. Also, the mission statements were too general to enable evaluation as to whether the service was justified on the basis of operational necessity for 36 of the selected rejustifications. Revision of existing procedures could make the rejustification program more effective.

Rejustification Procedures. There was no assurance that all leased communications facilities and services were rejustified in the initial review because not all customers supported by USACC agencies and detachments were contacted. In addition, the solicitation to rejustify services already reviewed under other analyses resulted in unnecessary duplicate paperwork processing by USACC agencies and detachments.

Supported Activities. The USACC agencies and detachments process communications requirements for many satellited off-post activities as well as on-post tenants and installation activities. Many of the services obtained for tenant and satellited activities are justified solely on the basis of operational necessity, not on actual usage. The USACC agencies and detachments frequently do not have the knowledge of the mission or operational requirements of the activities for which they provide support; therefore, they are unable to evaluate the need for retention of the communications justified solely on the basis of operational necessity.

Instructions for completing the rejustification process did not always adequately define how the USACC activity should obtain the rejustification from satellited activities. As a result, some USACC activities did not contact all users. One USACC intermediate command, USACC-U.S. Army Training and Doctrine Command (TRADOC), instructed its subordinate USACC agencies and detachments to make direct contact with the user wherever possible and forward the rejustifications to the user's major command for review if the user was not a TRADOC subordinate command. However, USACC-CONUS and USACC-U.S. Army Forces Command did not instruct direct contact with the users and their major commands.

For example, the USACC Agency at Fort Lewis was responsible for rejustifying 380 leased short-haul voice services. About 50 percent of those leased services were for off-post customers located throughout a five-state area. Individual users were not contacted because of a lack of specific instructions to do so. Further, agency personnel stated that they did not have the necessary personnel resources to contact all users within the time allowed. This resulted in wasted effort by the USACC personnel at Fort Lewis and did not ensure that all services provided to supported activities were identified.

Existing procedures should be revised, and detailed instructions provided to all USACC-CONUS intermediate commands, agencies, and detachments requiring direct contact with the user. Procedures should further require that the rejustification be forwarded to the user's major command for review and validation when communications are justified as an operational necessity.

Duplicate Rejustification of Service Retained Based Upon Usage. The rejustification of leased communications services whose usage data is required to be periodically analyzed resulted in unnecessary duplicate effort at USACC activities. For example, the USACC activities were required to submit a rejustification for each wide area telephone service (WATS) and foreign exchange (FX) line procured locally even though AR 105–23 already required a semiannual review of the cost effectiveness of toll calls, WATS, and FX. The traffic management practices of USACC-CONUS further prescribed procedures for cyclic analysis of usage data for other services such as AUTOVON circuits, dial central office facilities, and trunks. USACC-CONUS was performing traffic studies for AUTOVON circuit configurations using traffic data obtained from American Telephone and Telegraph Company and, therefore, did not solicit customers to rejustify the circuit configurations. Customers were solicited only to rejustify AUTOVON special features justified as operationally necessary. Like AUTO-VON, other leased communications services for which usage is analyzed on a cyclic basis should be rejustified in accordance with existing requirements for analysis of usage statistics.

Duplicate Processing. The annual rejustification of leased short-haul facilities and services duplicates the requirement in AR 105–23 to determine the necessity for continuation of the service when renewing leases. Leases are issued for a definite period of time, normally not to exceed a fiscal year. The lease can be reissued at the beginning of each fiscal year if continuation of the service is necessary. While the actual contracting is performed by the installation purchasing and contracting office, the requirements for the services are processed by the USACC agency or detachment. The annual review and rejustification of the leased short-haul voice and data services are also solicited from the USACC agency or detachment. Duplicate determinations of the need to continue the service could be eliminated by coordinating the annual renewal of leases with the rejustification for short-haul voice and data facilities and services.

The U.S. Army Communications Command (USACC) has requested funds for FY's 1976 and 1977 to purchase 67 computers for communications use, 58 of which are currently being leased. However, the amount requested was incorrect and the urgency for immediate funding not defined. At the time of our review, at least $1.1 million in lease payments could have been saved by procuring the computers at an earlier, more cost-effective time instead of continuing to lease them. Guidance for preparing and monitoring lease versus purchase analyses needed to be disseminated to ensure that the analyses are performed as required.

The basic criteria for economic analyses and similar management evaluations are prescribed in AR 105–22 and AR 37–13. An economic analysis is a management tool used to select the most economical alternative to satisfy a specific operational requirement. An integral part of an economic analysis of leased equipment is the determination whether it would be more economical to lease or purchase the equipment. The Comptroller, USACC, is responsible for providing staff assistance and guidance concerning performance of economic analyses to USACC subordinate activities. The lease-purchase analysis can also be used to support fund requirements for a project. As a result of the CONUS Army reorganization on 1 July 1973, USACC also assumed the responsibility to ensure that equipment leases of subordinate USACC agencies and detachments would be evaluated to determine if it would be more cost effective to purchase rather than lease equipment.

Purchase of Computers. As of 31 May 1974, USACC was leasing 58 UNIVAC DCT 9000 computers and had programmed 9 more for installation by the end of FY 75 for a total of 67. The 58 computers were leased from UNIVAC under two separate contracts; 23 under a bulk lease contract by the Defence Communications Agency (DCA) and 35 under the provisions of the standard General Services Administration (GSA) contract. Although USACC managed the computers, lease-purchase analyses either had not been made or were inadequate. At the request of DA, USACC performed a lease-purchase analysis of 14 of the computers during September 1973 and reported that the cost effective alternative was immediate procurement. This analysis showed that the optimum time to purchase had already passed on all 14 computers.

During March 1974, USACC requested funds to purchase the aforementioned 67 computers during FY's 1976 and 1977. The total amount of funds requested was based on a current average price under the GSA contract for the 14 computers included in the lease-purchase analysis. The fund estimate did not consider the additional lease credits that would accrue subsequent to the time of the analysis. Also, the contract provisions allowing purchase differed for those computers leased under the DCA contract. Because these two factors were not reflected in the fund submission, errors totaling about $2 million were made and the request for funds was understated by a net amount of about $70,000.

In the interim, the 58 computers currently installed were to continue to be leased. We advised command in a letter dated 31 May 1974 that, unless the computers were procured at the most cost-effective time, more than $1.1 million would be unnecessarily expended during the period 1 July 1974 to 30 June 1976 by continuing to lease the 58 computers. Our computation was based upon the number of months subsequent to 1 July 1974 that each computer would be leased with no lease credit accruing towards purchase price.

Lease-Purchase Analyses. Lease-purchase analyses were not effectively monitored or controlled and were made more than once for some equipment and not at all for other equipment.

Monitorship of Analyses. During May 1974, USACC-CONUS was making a lease-purchase analysis of leased computer communication terminals within CONUS. The analysis included the same 14 computers that had already been analyzed by Headquarters, USACC, in September 1973. Neither command was aware of the other's analysis. Effective monitorship of lease-purchase analyses could have avoided this duplication of effort. Although a policy had been established by Headquarters, USACC, to require a lease-purchase analysis of equipment leased for more than one year, an analysis was not performed for all equipment. During our audits at the Fort Huachuca and Fort Lewis USACC Agencies, we found that neither agency had made a lease-purchase analysis of leased copier equipment used in their communications centers within prescribed time frames. Fort Huachuca had performed a lease-purchase analysis of its copier prior to the 1 July 1973 reorganization, but the analysis had been done incorrectly. In both cases, purchase would have been more economical than continued leasing. More effective monitorship is needed to ensure that the requirements for lease-purchase analyses are applied to all pertinent equipment.

Control of Analyses. Telecommunications requirements for new communications equipment or services frequently did not include a management evaluation showing alternative ways to provide the service or facility, such as lease versus purchase. Although AR 105–22 requires such an evaluation, internal procedures did not require that telecommunications requirements involving leased equipment be reviewed by the USACC Systems and Economic Analysis Division prior to approval to ensure that an evaluation was made. We reviewed five telecommunications requirements for replacement of automatic digital network terminal equipment with UNIVACDCT 9000's and none included a lease-purchase analysis. The lease-purchase analysis should be performed as early as possible so that funds may be programmed if procurement is the most feasible alternative.

A $1.5 million telephone traffic recorder program was not provided intensified management. Rather, the program was fragmented into routine communications-electronics projects, which were afforded a lesser degree of management. As a result, Headquarters, U.S. Army Communications Command (USACC), was not directly involved in decisions that have increased the cost of the program or in resolving problems that have delayed its full implementation. Further, the program did not provide for training of individuals in telephone traffic analysis or for standard methods for analyzing automatic voice network (AUTOVON) traffic data.

In 1972, a telephone traffic recorder program was initiated to provide for the development, implementation, and management of a centralized telephone traffic collection and analysis system. All government-owned telephone exchanges were to participate in the program. The program was estimated to cost about $1.5 million and would involve (i) procuring traffic recorders and installation material, (ii) design engineering for each telephone exchange, and (iii) training of individuals who would operate and maintain the equipment. The capability for collecting traffic data on all AUTOVON, city, foreign exchange, point-to-point, and intra-office exchange lines would result from this program. Traffic data would be transmitted to USACC-CONUS for subsequent analysis by telephone traffic engineers. Recommendations for adding or deleting services could then be made by the engineers and sent to each agency or detachment for action.

The U.S. Army Communication-Electronics Engineering Installation Agency (USACEEIA), a major subordinate command of USACC, was tasked to prepare standardization guidance for the design work and installation of traffic recorder equipment. USACEEIA's subordinate activity, USACEEIA-CONUS was directed to provide detailed drawings for installation of the equipment at each dial central office.

Program Status. As of 1 June 1974, purchase of the traffic recorders had been completed. Procurement of additional equipment costing about $50,000 was in process, and another procurement action for equipment costing about $80,000 was planned. There were 91 separate design engineering packages of which 14 were completed, 46 were in process, and 31 were being held in abeyance. Training of key personnel who would oversee the operation and maintenance of the equipment had also been completed. Training literature had been published for individuals who would use and maintain the traffic recorders in the field. Actual on-site training was scheduled to begin as soon as the first telephone exchange was fitted with the equipment.

Program Control. The traffic recorder program had been fragmented into separate telecommunication requirement projects that were not afforded the intensified management at the Headquarters, USACC, which might normally be expected for a project of this size and impact. Instead, it only received routine management. Because the program was fragmented, Headquarters, USACC, did not become directly involved in certain decisions, which have increased program costs and delayed implementation.

Increased Costs. In September 1973, USACEEIA-CONUS decided to use a wiring technique different from the one originally planned (fixed panels in lieu of patch panels). Headquarters, USACC, did not become directly involved in the decision, even though it required fifty additional items of equipment (scanners) and increased program costs by about $50,000.

In April 1974, USACC-CONUS decided to change installation mode from portable to fixed for thirty-one telephone exchanges. Basically, this change requires recorders to be permanently installed at those telephone exchanges. Implementation requires additional equipment costing about $80,000, which was not included in the original program. Again, Headquarters, USACC, was not directly involved in the decision.

Delays Experienced. In March 1973, USACEEIA submitted to USACC standardization guidance for design engineering and installation of the traffic recorder equipment. The guidance was to be used by USACEEIA-CONUS engineers in their design plans. We were informed by USACEEIA-CONUS that the design engineers had never received the guidance. Because intensified management procedures were lacking, it could not be ensured that each functional group involved in the program received all necessary information.

54

Another delay occurred on routine supply requests for installation material processed through the Lexington-Blue Grass Army Depot. On 23 November 1973 and 4 January 1974, the material required to install the traffic recorders was ordered. The material was to be received by 1 April 1974 and installation was scheduled to start in June 1974. However, on 26 February 1974, the depot advised Headquarters, USACC, that permission for sole source procurement was required. The matter was referred to USACC-CONUS since the individual projects were not being managed by Headquarters, USACC. Subsequently, the depot requested action on the matter from USACC-CONUS on 25 March and again on 22 April and 2 May with no response. As of 31 May 1974, the situation had still not been resolved. At least a three-month slippage in installation of the traffic recorders is expected since the essential material will not be available. This slippage will cause other delays in the training phase because training cannot start until installation is completed. Had Headquarters, USACC, been continually aware of the program's status, the supply problems could have been resolved so as not to delay overall implementation of the program.

Traffic Analysis Training. The recorder program does not include training for new personnel entering the traffic analysis field. Presently, personnel at USACC-CONUS provide the necessary expertise to analyze traffic data collected from each telephone exchange and make recommendations on the most economical and efficient service available. To avoid losing this expertise through resignation or retirement of the present staff, a formal program is needed to train new personnel in traffic analysis procedures. The training program should emphasize standard methods for analyzing and configuring routine automatic voice network (AUTOVON) lines in CONUS where the bulk of the traffic data will originate. Routine AUTOVON lines are those justified on the basis of traffic volume, rather than operational need. Although a standard method is described in Communications Command Pamphlet 105–7, it is not the primary one used by the traffic engineers at USACC-CONUS. USACC needs to settle on a standard method and ensure its application throughout the command.

Installation of commercial telephone services were not reviewed semiannually as required to determine the most economical system for making long-distance calls. Guidance had not been prepared and provided for conducting these reviews. If the reviews were performed and used to establish the most economical combination of toll calls, wide area telephone service (WATS), and foreign exchange (FX) lines, substantial savings could be realized. Some reviews of commercial long-distance services had been made by U.S. Army Communications Command (USACC) and subordinate commands at selected installations, but they were not accomplished by the most economical method and did not make use of information readily available from local telephone companies.

WATS and FX lines are leased commercial telephone services used to provide long-distance communications to those areas not covered by the automatic voice network (AUTOVON). WATS permits toll-free calls within a specified geographical area referred to as a band. Band 0 covers the state of the subscriber. Band 1 covers an interstate area close to the subscriber, and each additional band allows telephone access to an expanded interstate area. Rates can be selected for full-time or measured-time service, and the rates increase with each additional WATS band. An FX line is a leased line that permits unlimited calls from one telephone exchange to another for a flat monthly rate. When none of the above telephone services are available, commercial toll calls are authorized to meet official requirements.

About $10.6 million is spent annually for toll calls, WATS, and FX telephone services at those installations in CONUS where communications are managed by USACC. AR 105–23 requires that the cost of toll calls, WATS, and FX lines be reviewed at each installation not less than semiannually to determine the most economical method of providing necessary long-distance telephone communications. Prior to the Army's 1973 CONUS reorganization, installation commanders were responsible for the review. Since that date, USACC agencies and detachments at each installation have been charged with this responsibility.

Semiannual Reviews. Audit at eight USACC agencies and detachments disclosed that the semiannual reviews required by AR 105–23 were not being made primarily because detailed guidance had not been prepared by Headquarters, USACC, and provided to the agencies and detachments.

Problems Noted. We analyzed toll call, WATS, and FX costs at the eight installations to determine if the most economical long-distance telephone service was being used.

Similar situations were noted at the other four installations. Overall, our review showed that annual toll call, WATS, and FX costs of about $855,000 could have been reduced by a potential $154,000, or 18 percent, if the semiannual reviews had been performed and acted upon. If the results of our reviews are representative at all installations in CONUS, the potential exists for reducing the Army's annual $10.6 million expenditure for toll calls, WATS, and FX by about $1.9 million.

At Fort Huachuca, annual costs of toll calls placed to areas covered by WATS and FX were about $9,000. A five-day traffic study disclosed that most of the existing 23 WATS and FX lines were not in alignment with the geographical areas to which most telephone traffic was directed and were used less than 30 percent of the time during the normal business day. By reconfiguring WATS and FX lines to facilitate WATS and FX in lieu of toll calls, leased telephone services culd be reduced and a potential $37,000 could be saved annually.

At Fort Lewis, commercial toll calls were placed at additional expense to areas already served by FX. The unnecessary use of the toll call telephone service resulted in additional communication costs of about $27,000.

At Sacramento Army Depot, toll calls and FX telephone services were used for long distance communications to those areas not covered by AUTOVON. If toll calls and FX were replaced by WATS, an annual savings of $27,000 could be realized.

At Fort Benning, there were no WATS lines. An analysis of toll calls for one month showed that about $29,000 could be saved annually by using WATS instead of toll calls.

Actions Taken. USACC-CONUS and some of the USACC intermediate commands had recognized the need for analyzing toll call, WATS, and FX costs to determine potential economies. For example, USACC-CONUS performed analyses of these costs at seven U.S. Army Training and Doctrine Command (TRADOC), U.S. Army Forces Command (FORSCOM), and U.S. Army Material Command (AMC) installations during FY 1974. USACC-AMC awarded a contract to a commercial firm to perform a study at one AMC installation and was considering a contract for performance of a toll-WATS-FX analysis at all AMC installations. USACC-TRADOC was testing a toll-WATS-FX analysis program at Fort Monroe. No action had been taken by USACC-FORSCOM.

The actions taken by USACC-CONUS and the intermediate USACC commands were not consistent and did not provide for standard application throughout CONUS. Administrative costs to develop a program for review of toll-WATS-FX costs were increased because each command was developing its own procedures. Further, the programs developed by USACC-CONUS and the intermediate commands were primarily one-time reviews and did not meet the criteria of AR 105–23, which required that semiannual reviews be performed. Also, the program developed were not the most economical approach for making the reviews either because of contract costs or personnel and travel costs. If detailed guidance were provided to USACC agencies and detachments, the semiannual reviews could be performed with little or no additional costs.

Actions Needed. To accomplish the prescribed semiannual reviews, all outgoing long-distance telephone calls, including toll calls, WATs, and FX, should be analyzed to determine the most economical service possible. Outgoing toll calls should be identified with the WATS band areas called and then the costs of WATS bands should be compared with the toll costs. When a sufficient number of toll calls fall within one or more WATS band areas, consideration should be given to leasing one WATS line to cover two or more WATS areas. If a high concentration of toll calls are made to one city, a comparison should be made to determine whether it would be more economical to lease an FX line instead of making toll calls. Where WATS or FX lines are already being leased, usage data by WATS band or FX line should be reviewed to determine if the most economical configuration of lines is being used. In addition, an analysis should be performed to ensure that toll calls are not being placed to areas covered by other leased communications services.

All of the data needed for the review and analysis of toll call, WATS, and FX can be collected manually or readily obtained from local telephone companies in the form of computer printouts. The computer printouts show, among other things, (i) number of calls and total number of minutes of chargeable time for each WATS band, (ii) a cost comparison of calls if they were placed on toll circuit and if they were made on WATS or FX circuits, (iii) percent of usage for each WATS or FX line, and (iv) a listing of all toll calls that could have been made over WATS or FX lines. We found that USACC agencies and detachments were generally not aware that such information was available.

The number of official Class A telephone lines, including those with access to the automatic voice network (AUTOVON), exceeded limitations established for CONUS installations. Reductions in both types of lines could generate substantial economies. The number of Class A telephone lines at each CONUS installation is required to be limited to 40 percent of the total number of official telephone lines being used. Based on the total number of official telephone lines in use, a reduction of some 33,000 Class A telepohone lines is required in major CONUS commands to meet the 40 percent limitation. Limitations could continue to be exceeded because there was no reporting system for determining the number of official telephone lines with access to AUTOVON.

Joint Chiefs of Staff (JCS) Memorandum of Policy Number 151 states that direct AUTOVON access will be restricted to 40 percent of the total number of official mainlines of a military service. Official mainlines have been defined by DOD as circuits between a switchboard and telephone instruments designated either as Class A (official) or Class C (official restricted) telephones. Class A phones are those used to transact official business over commercial off-post or AUTOVON lines, while Class C phones are used to transact official business only within an installation or activity. To meet the JCS limitation on AUTOVON access within DA, USACC-CONUS issued Supplement 1 to AR 105–10 limiting the number of Class A lines to 40 percent of the total number of official lines at each CONUS installation. A similar limitation, to be applied at the major Army command level, is contained in the pending revision to AR 105–23.

Class A Telephone Lines. Within CONUS, Class A telephone lines at most installations exceeded the limitation of 40 percent of the total number of official telephone lines. As of 31 December 1973, the annual Fixed Telephone Communications Facilities report prepared by USACC indicated that CONUS installations had a total of 85,549 (54.7 percent) Class C telephone lines. Of the 141 installations and activities having Class A lines, only 31 were at or below the 40 percent limitation in total. For Class A lines, USACC had 67.9 percent, U.S. Army Material Command had 55.2 percent, U.S. Army Forces Command had 56.3 percent, and U.S. Army Training and Doctrine Command had 47.7 percent. A reduction of about 33,000 Class A lines would be required for the four commands to meet the 40 percent limitation, assuming that the total number of Class C lines did not increase.

A comparison of the number of official lines reported for December 1973 and for December 1972 showed that the number of Class A lines within CONUS had increased by 2,148; the ratio of the number of Class A to the total number of official lines increased from 52.5 to 54.7 percent. Action should be taken to reverse this trend. Any reduction in Class A lines would result in a substantial reduction in equipment or circuit costs, as well as reducing the number of individuals who have access to AUTOVON or to commercial numbers.

Access to AUTOVON. At the time of our review, the Army did not have a system for determining the total number of official telephone lines that had access to AUTOVON. Prior to 1 July 1973, AR 105–10 required that this information be provided as part of a quarterly report on the Communications Economy and Discipline Program. DA Circular 105–28, 24 August 1973, which summarized the reports for the third quarter of FY 1973, showed that overall within the Army the number of official telephone lines having access to AUTO-

58

VON was 39.3 percent of the total number of official telephone lines or just under the JCS imposed limitation of 40 percent. The requirement for this quarterly report was rescinded by DA effective the first quarter of FY 1974. Therefore, the Army no longer accumulates information to show whether they are still meeting the restrictions imposed by JCS Memorandum of Policy Number 151.

Effective with the publication of the new AR 105–23, this information will be required annually on the Telephone Equipment Data Report. However, this AR is still in draft form and may not be issued for some time. Since the latest information on the percentage of official lines with AUTOVON access is about a year old and issuance of revised AR 105–23, which would enable reduction of the number of Class A lines to 40 percent of total official lines, would probably not occur until calendar year 1975, action should be taken as soon as possible to obtain current data on the total number of Class A and Class C lines and the number of Class A lines that have access to AUTOVON. If the data obtained indicates that the JCS limitation has been exceeded, then a determination should be made as to where lines can be reduced without a serious effect on mission accomplishment.

Funds were being obligated by U.S. Army Communications Command (USACC) activities at installation level without sufficient attention to fund availability. Available accounting records and reports were not used to establish fund control. The Financial Management Report, designed to identify financial problems, was not sufficiently detailed to serve its purpose and projected fund requirements shown on the report were not adjusted when actual experience proved the projections to be inaccurate. Additionally, review and analyses of financial data were not made by USACC activities and responsible personnel were not trained in financial management. Because of these conditions, funding targets imposed by USACC-CONUS were exceeded and the potential for an overobligation of funds was created.

Control of Funds. In conjunction with the 1973 CONUS reorganization, USACC was required to establish procedures for the administrative control of funds and provide financial management to the USACC agencies and detachments. Memoranda of understanding were established between USACC and (i) the U.S. Army Training and Doctrine Command, (ii) the U.S. Army Forces Command, and (iii) the U.S. Army Materiel Command, which provided that installation FAO's would provide USACC agencies and detachments with accounting support. However, this guidance did not specifically define the responsibilities of both the USACC agencies and detachments and their servicing FAO's for the administrative control of funds.

Certification of Funds. Three activities at an installation had authority to obligate USACC funds. Personnel offices prepared the payroll for the civilian personnel working at the USACC agencies and detachments and cited USACC funds for payment, purchasing and contracting offices cited USACC funds for contractual services, and USACC agencies and detachments prepared obligation documents for the lease of telephone lines and the purchase of supplies. However, certifications of fund availability were not being accomplished prior to incurring obligations. Key personnel in the comptroller directorate at USACC-CONUS and management personnel of several installation FAO's and USACC agencies and detachments differed in their opinions as to who was responsible for certifying fund availability. Funding targets could be exceeded or funds could be overobligated when obligations are incurred without predetermination of fund availability.

Funding Targets. During the second and third quarters of FY 1974, eleven USACC agencies and detachments exceeded funding targets without obtaining prior approval from USACC-CONUS. In seven of eleven instances, no action had been taken by the agencies and detachments to identify additional funding requirements. In four instances, the Financial Management Reports submitted to USACC-CONUS indicated that a potential funding problem existed; however, the reports had either been received too late to take corrective action or USACC-CONUS had not given sufficient attention to the indications of problem areas. There was no record at USACC-CONUS to show that any of the eleven activities had previously reported that funding targets would be exceeded without additional funds.

Availability of Accounting Reports. Various accounting reports were available from servicing FAO's to assist USACC agencies and detachments in performing financial management analyses. Reports were prepared on a daily, weekly, or monthly basis and contained status of fund data concerning obligations and reimbursements. In addition, exception listings were available to identify elements of expense, major programs, and allotments that had exceeded established targets or available funds.

USACC agencies and detachments had not received guidance on what reports were available and how they could be used as an aid to financial management analyses. For example, only a weekly detailed cost report was received by the USACC Agency, Fort Eustis. In January 1974, a management team from USACC-CONUS visited the Agency and pointed out the availability of other reports such as the aforementioned exception listings. At the time of our visit to Fort Eustis in May 1974, exception listings were still not being provided to the Agency. Definitive procedures need to be established to ensure that such reports are made available to all USACC agencies and detachments.

Financial Management Analyses. The Transition Plan for USACC-CONUS Management of Army CONUS Communications, dated 15 May 1973, and a subsequent letter from USACC-CONUS, dated 15 June 1973, contained guidance for financial administration for use by USACC agencies and detachments. A requirement was established for preparation of a monthly Financial Management Report that could be used to inform higher command of existing or potential financial problems. However, we found that the report provisions contained several shortcomings, which restricted the report's use as an effective financial analysis tool.

Financial Management Report. Without additional features, the Financial Management Report could not be relied upon to identify potential funding shortages and differences between budget estimates and actual obligations and reimbursements. The report showed actual cumulative obligations and reimbursements earned through the reporting month and projected cumulative obligations and reimbursements for the remaining months of the fiscal year. The report did not show a comparison of (i) direct obligations with allotments received, (ii) reimbursements earned with reimbursement orders received, and (iii) actual obligations incurred with previous estimates. Without these features, potential financial problems could be overlooked and needed corrective action might not be taken.

We reviewed the Financial Management Reports for the eleven USACC agencies and detachments that exceeded funding targets during the second or third quarters of FY 1974. Examples of problems that should have been identified on the Financial Management Reports are described below.

Actual cumulative personnel and communications costs at Fort Eustis consistently exceeded programmed budget costs during the 5-month period ended 31 March 1974. At 31 March 1974, actual personnel costs exceeded budgeted costs by about $21,000. In addition, reimbursements earned were about $81,600 less than had been projected through March 1974.

At Fort McPherson and at Fort Buchanan, actual personnel costs exceeded budgeted estimates by about $11,000 and $13,000, respectively, as of 31 March 1974.

Since none of the above discrepancies had been identified, funding targets were exceeded by USACC activities at the installation level.

Budget Projections. Subordinate agencies and detachments were required to show, on the Financial Management Report, cumulative expenditures and reimbursements through the reporting month, and updated budget estimates for the remaining months of the fiscal year. This data was used for comparison to the total annual budget requirements. Our review showed that USACC agencies and detachments did not adjust their budget projections in line with actual expenditure and earnings data. As a result, direct funding requirements were misstated and USACC-CONUS was not apprised of the need for additional funds to cover operating costs. As an example, in December 1973, total direct obligations of the USACC Agency, Fort Eustis, exceeded budgeted estimates because personnel costs increased and some reimbursable earnings did not materialize. However, action was not taken for several months to adjust the programmed requirements to show this trend and that additional direct funds would be needed to finance operations for the remainder of the year. Similar situations were noted at ten other agencies and detachments.

Accounting Surveillance. In April 1973, Headquarters, USACC, initiated an accounting surveillance program intended for use by subordinate elements of USACC for monitoring accounting records. However, since the accompanying instructions to USACC-CONUS did not specify that the program was to be implemented at the agency and detachment level, actions taken at USACC-CONUS were only directed toward establishing a surveillance program for the Finance and Accounting Division, Fort Ritchie. Accounting surveillance procedures were to include, as a minimum, specific actions to be performed to (i) identify accounting reports to be reviewed, (ii) determine the methods to be used

61

to verify the accuracy of accounting data, and (iii) verify all accounting transactions.

Accounting data must be accurate so that management can be apprised of the status of the funds available. Our review showed that accounting data was frequently inaccurate. For example, in December 1973, USACC-CONUS erroneously showed an overobligation of about $28,100 on its records because the installation FAO had not made an adjusting entry of more than $50,000, to deobligate funds based on actual billings for July 1973. Had the $50,000 not been available, USACC-CONUS would have been overobligated.

Our review of records at Fort Eustis disclosed several accounting errors, such as (i) credits of $18,050 due from the telephone company were not recorded, (ii) $6,000 of delivery orders for another Fort Eustis activity were charged to the USACC Agency's funds, (iii) receipts of $20,100 in reimbursable orders were not recorded, and (iv) about $12,600 for commercial telephone bills incurred during the nine-month period ended 31 March 1974 had been paid but not recorded. In the latter instance, the necessary correction was made in March 1974. However, by the time the error was detected, it was too late for the USACC Agency to evaluate the fund situation and acquire additional funds from USACC-CONUS.

Financial Management Training. Beginning 1 July 1973, USACC agencies and detachments assumed responsibility for the administrative control of base communication funds. Various management personnel of the USACC agencies and detachments informed us that they did not have the necessary background to perform financial management analyses and that such analyses would have to be performed by either installation comptroller personnel or by USACC-CONUS. On the other hand, comptroller personnel from USACC-CONUS stated that the analyses should be performed by the agencies and detachments since only those activities have the pertinent records and can identify a potential funding problem in time to avoid exceeding funding targets or overobligating funds. Despite this condition, USACC-CONUS had not informed subordinate agencies and detachments of their responsibility to make financial analyses. As a general rule, we found that USACC activities did not have personnel sufficiently oriented in financial management to (i) ensure that imposed funding limitations were not exceeded, (ii) perform financial management analyses, and (iii) perform accounting surveillance. Consequently, the need exists for a formal training program to educate key USACC agency and detachment personnel in their new responsibilities.

My last two weeks in the United States was when I received my first formal training.

In my being sent to Okinawa, you were kind enough to pay for my new MGB to be sent over. I received free room (BOQ) and a cost-of-living differential.

Chapter 4

Army Audit Agency—Overseas

It is true, as the GAO report points out, that Israel's debt service to the United States is growing, and Israel shares the conclusion of the report that the debt service might become too burdensome in the years to come. Therefore, we repeat that more of the future military assistance should be in the form of grants and not loans.

—Dan Halpern, Minister of Economic Affairs
at the Israeli Embassy (July 14, 1983)

Before I go into specific audits that were performed overseas, let me give you a few overall facts to keep in mind. Why is there a large membership of Disorganized Crime overseas? The United States spends more than twice as much of our Gross National Product on defense than our NATO allies do, and seven times as much as Japan. Several of these nations have a higher per-capita wealth than we do. These countries combined have twice the Gross National Product of the Soviet Union (our largest friend during the First and Second World Wars). These countries are perfectly able to defend themselves. However, they can save their money while Disorganized Crime is spending yours defending them. Why won't the U.S. withdraw its subsidies (not its membership, just its subsidies) from NATO? One reason is that the War arm of Disorganized Crime is quite content with the arrangement. The Pentagon has a strong stake in expanding its budget by preserving its European presence. The maintenance of a large garrison in Europe offers openings for thousands of U.S. career officers. We are currently spending a third of the Pentagon's budget on our forces stationed in Europe. But it's not just in Europe; Disorganized Crime is worldwide. For example, on June 1, 1983, the U.S. and the Philippines signed a five-year renewal of their bases agreement, increasing by $400 million the current American payment of $500 million being provided during the five years of the current pact that expires next year. Think of it, $900 million so we can send members of Disorganized Crime to the Philippines!

My first audit in Okinawa was conducted from July through November 1974. During my time overseas, I found that Disorganized Crime is an international conglomerate. You are paying for all of it. It was an audit of the Facilities Engineering Program at the U.S. Army Garrison, Okinawa. At 31 October 1974, the Facilities Engineer had an assigned strength of 18 military and 1,503 civilian personnel, including local national employees. The FY 1975 annual funding program for Facilities Engineer support totaled $22.5 million. The recorded value of real property was about $245 million. You recall my first assignment with Army Audit was the Facilities Engineer at Fort Ritchie, Maryland.

The Directorate for Facilities Engineering (DFAE) had not implemented an effective work management system. Maintenance and repair work was not coordinated and accomplished in order of priority because annual work plans were not prepared on time and did not identify and specify all work requirements. The Work Coordinating Division did not schedule and control all work effectively. Performance standards were not always used to estimate man-hour requirements, and completed work was not adequately analyzed. As a result, optimum utilization of the work force had not been achieved and causes of inefficiencies were not identified and corrected.

Facilities Engineers are required by Army regulations to establish a work management system for planning, estimating, and scheduling work. The primary objectives of a work management program are to provide a standard efficient method of work control, increase productivity of the work force by applying industrial engineering techniques, and attain the maximum practical return from resources expended. The system contemplates using a Work Coordinating Office to ensure that these objectives are met. Work is normally authorized and controlled by the following types of work orders:

Standing Operation Orders (SOO). For operations and services for which specific work and manpower requirements are relatively constant and predictable. The work should be planned and scheduled for periods not to exceed a year.
Individual Job Orders (IJO). For maintenance, repair, and minor construction requirements that exceed 16 man-hours or cost more than $200. Estimated man-hours and other required resources are predetermined for each job. IJO's are subdivided into major and minor. A major job order exceeds 80 man-hours, whereas the man-hours required for a minor job order fall between 16 and 80.
Maintenance Service Orders (MSO). For maintenance jobs that do not exceed 16 man-hours or that cost less than $200.

Planning. Advance planning was not used to coordinate the maintenance and repair work effort. An annual work plan should be developed and submitted to the installation commander for approval in advance of each fiscal year. Work plans are needed so that all work requirements can be analyzed and priorities can be assigned commensurate with mission requirements.

Annual work plans for FY's 1974 and 1975 were not prepared on time and did not identify total work requirements. The FY 1974 work plan was not submitted to the installation commander until October 1973, while the FY 1975 plan was not submitted until August 1974. In addition, the workload shown in the plan was not specific nor realistic. Total workload requirements were not considered. The unit work plans, which are part of the annual plan, did not show

64

any work that needed to be deferred although workload requirements exceeded available resources. Work to be accomplished was based upon the available labor force and was shown in general terms such as total man-years to be expended on Standing Operation Orders, Individual Job Orders, and Maintenance Orders.

Unit work plans should detail all work requirements for each shop. Then, based upon available resources, the total workload should be divided into two categories—work to be done in the coming year and work that must be deferred. Unless detailed work plans are prepared properly, work might not be accomplished in the proper priority. For example, in June and July 1974, DFAE received two jobs requesting construction of dugouts and bleachers at three baseball fields. The projects were started immediately. The carpenter shop used more than 1,200 man-hours completing these job orders. Because this project was given a high priority, the mission requirements to repair leaky roofs on family housing quarters was deferred. Some of the requests to repair the roofs had been outstanding since March 1974. Had command been aware of the total workload and the specific requirements, the construction of dugouts and bleachers might have received a lower priority.

Work Controls and Scheduling. Shop personnel acted almost autonomously in deciding on the jobs and the pace of work to be performed. To effectively and efficiently utilize available resources, as much of the labor force as possible should work on jobs that are included in the master schedule. The master schedule should be prepared and controlled by the Work Coordinating Division and should include all work except MSO's (Maintenance Service Orders) and minor IJO's (Individual Job Orders) for work required to be done by only one shop. The Work Coordinating Division, however, only maintained a master schedule for minor construction jobs exceeding $1,000, major repair jobs exceeding $5,000, and special command interest jobs. By maintaining a complete master schedule, the Work Coordinating Division would be able to exercise better control over jobs, which would in turn increase efficiency and reduce the length of time a job remains outstanding.

MSO's were scheduled by the individual shops. However, the Work Coordinating Division did not monitor the completion of MSO's. Our review of all MSO's outstanding in the carpenter, electrical (interior), and plumbing shops as of 8 September 1974 showed that 76.7 percent exceeded the standard time limits. Details of our review follow:

Work Priority	Standard for Completion (Number of Days)	Number Of MSO's	Number of MSO's Outstanding (By Periods of Time in Days)				
			0–1	2–5	6–15	16–35	31–60	Over 60
1	0–1	25	4	8	5	2	3	3
2	2–5	401	45	55	118	37	94	52
3	6–15	167	6	9	19	24	57	52

Our review of MSO's completed during August 1974 also showed that priorities were not always followed. For example, a Priority 1 MSO received by the carpenter shop on 31 May 1974 and a Priority 2 was received on 25 June

65

1974. The Priority 2 was completed on 3 September 1974, whereas the Priority 1 was still outstanding as of 8 September 1974. Monitoring of jobs scheduled by the shops would enable the Work Coordinating Division to determine causes for delays in completing work and reasons for not following priorities.

Performance Standards. The use of acceptable performance standards is essential for providing a sound basis for evaluating work performance. However, estimates of man-hour requirements for jobs were not always made. When estimates were made, they were not always based on work performance standards established by DA. In those instances where DA standards were not used to prepare estimates, DFAE personnel used their own estimates, which were based on judgment rather than valid job engineering techniques.

SOO (Standing Operation Orders) Man-Hour Estimates. During FY 1974, DFAE performed work on 48 SOO's. We reviewed the estimates for 15, which involved 153 individual shop work orders. Of the 153 work orders, estimates were prepared for only 88, or 56 percent. The actual man-hours charged for the remaining 65 shop requests totaled 23,150 hours and represented about $107,500 in labor costs.

IJO Man-Hour Estimates. DFAE completed about 3,000 IJO's during FY 1974. To evaluate the adequacy of man-hour estimates, we randomly selected 167 IJO's for review. The results of our review showed that estimates were not needed for 35 job orders because the jobs were for emergencies or for issues of material only; man-hour estimates, although required, were not made for 4; and estimates were maded for the remaining 128. The 128 IJO's comprised a total of 196 shop work orders. Man-hour estimates for the shop work orders were determined as follows: 112 were based on the estimator's experience, 41 on Army standards, and 43 on a combination of Army standards and estimator's experience. Unless DA standards are consistently used or any deviation from them supported, management has no scientific means to measure the effectiveness and efficiency of the work force.

Evaluation of Work Performance. The Work Coordinating Division did not evaluate and analyze completed work to determine if time estimates and standards were realistic or to determine causes for significant variances between the time estimates and actual work performance. Consequently, the reasons for consistently low production were not known. Evaluations are required and involve periodic inspections, work sampling, and analysis of work performed. Evaluation should be made to determine the effectiveness and quality of work and to ensure that idle time is not charged directly to work authorizations.

Standing Operation Orders. The Work Coordinating Division had no documentation indicating that an evaluation to determine reasons for variances between estimated and actual man-hours for SOO's had ever been made. Our review of 15 of the 48 SOO's in FY 1974 showed that over $220,000 in labor, material, and equipment costs were charged by shops that did not have an authorization to work on these SOO's. We also compared man-hour estimates for those shops authorized to perform work on these 15 SOO's with the actual time charged and found that 93 percent of the estimates differed with the man-hours charged by more than 10 percent. For example, estimates were exceeded by 5,848 man-hours (170 percent) in the refrigerator shop on SOO number 340002. Conversely, estimates exceeded actual by 325 man-hours (551 percent) in the petroleum, oils, and lubricants shop on SOO number 3400004. If actual and estimated man-hours had been analyzed, management would have been aware that shops made unauthorized charges to SOO's and that actual man-hours varied significantly from estimates.

Individual Job Orders. Significant variances between estimated and actual man-hours on IJO's were not evaluated to determine causes for the variances. We reviewed the estimated and actual man-hours recorded for 128 IJO's completed in FY 1974. The review showed that 95 were completed within 10 percent of the estimated man-hours, 13 required from 12 to 88 percent less time, and 20 required from 11 to 180 percent more time. Shop supervisors were required to state the reasons for variations of plus or minus 10 percent on the back of the IJO. However, this requirement was not enforced.

Maintenance Service Orders. In March 1974, the Work Coordinating Division compared actual performance to the DA standards for all MSO's completed during the period 23 January to 28 February 1974. The comparison disclosed significant variances for all tasks completed, but no action was taken to determine the causes. Examples of the variances are shown below:

	Average Man-Hours of Craft Time	
	Actual	Standard
Repair or replace switch	9.2	0.59
Replace fuse	11.6	0.37
Replace glass window	9.7	0.81
Replace screen window or door	10.5	0.81
Paint repaired window	1.2	1.58

Our review of MSO's completed in June 1974 disclosed that performance had not improved. This analysis and our observation of MSO teams also showed that much of the inefficiency was due to sending more workers to do a job than could possibly be used productively. As an example, we observed a four-man MSO team spend six man-hours repairing an electric clock cord. On another occasion, three workers who were sent to replace a faulty wall switch spent six man-hours performing the job. While this was better than the average noted above, it is still far in excess of the DA standards.

Command was aware of some of the problems in the work management program, and, at command's request, we agreed to emphasize the review of work management during our audit. Continued command interest is needed in the work management area to ensure that maximum productivity is obtained from available resources.

The Directorate for Facilities Engineering (DFAE) did not compare actual work performance with established standards or use prescribed work sampling techniques to evaluate the performance of preventive maintenance (PM) teams. During FY 1974, the number of PM inspections made was less than 50 percent of the number that should have been achieved, based on established standards. Had performance of the PM teams been evalutated, causes of inefficient performance could have been identified and corrected. We found that:

Team leaders did not usually perform work and employees who had finished assigned tasks consistently waited for all team members to finish their individual tasks before proceeding to the next work site.

Some employees quit work prior to quitting time.

Occupants of Government quarters were not always given advance notification of planned PM team visits.

PM is the systematic inspection, care, and serrrvicing of buildings, structures, ground facilities, utility plants, and systems and equipment for the purpose of detecting and correcting beginning failures and accomplishing minor maintenance. As of 30 June 1974, the PM section of DFAE consisted of sixty-three local nationals assigned to 20 teams. Because of the physical location of buildings requiring PM, the teams were divided into two sections, the northern sector with 13 teams and the southern sector with 7 teams. Additionally, DFAE operated a supply section and self-help centers in each sector.

Use of Work Standards. In order to determine the efficiency of work performance and to identify areas where improvements are needed, DA Pamphlet 420–6 provides for an analysis and evaluation of completed work. The actual time expended on PM should be compared to standards shown in DA Pamphlet 420–5. DFAE, however, had not analyzed the efficiency of PM by comparing actual performance with work standards or by making work sampling studies. Without analyses of completed work, the PM teams can perform at a slower pace and management would be unaware of the poor performance. Based on DA standards, the size of the PM staff, and the size and type of buildings supported, the PM teams should have been able to perform PM on all buildings 5.6 times per year. However, only about 2.6 visits were made during FY 1974. During our observations of the PM teams, we noted that team members frequently spent more than the standard amount of time to perform minor maintenance tasks. For example, we saw one worker spend thirty minutes changing a faucet washer. According to DA standards, this job should have taken twelve minutes.

Work Performance. During our audit, we made frequent observations of work performance to identify nonproductive effort of the PM teams. Based on the results of our observations, we estimated that productivity could be increased significantly by reducing unnecessary delays, ensuring that employees work until quitting time, and giving advance notice of PM visits.

Unnecessary Delays. Delays occurred because PM team leaders did not perform craft work to assist the teams in performing the required maintenance. In addition, team members were not assigned to the next building to perform PM after they had completed their tasks at the current work site. Although PM team leaders were required to perform craft work, this was seldom done. Team leaders were responsible for performing certain administrative tasks, such as inspecting buildings to determine what maintenance work needed to be done and preparing PM record cards. After the administrative tasks were completed, team leaders spent the rest of their time observing other members' work. Team members also were not always productively employed. PM teams normally consisted of three or four members. Sometimes one or more of the members would complete their tasks before the remaining team members. When this situation occurred, team members who had completed their work waited until the remaining employees finished before starting work on another building. Productivity could be increased by having employees who have finished their tasks proceed to and start work on the next building.

Quitting Early. PM teams assigned to the southern sector quit work and left about 20 minutes early each day. The working hours of the PM were from 0730 to 1615. To minimize transportation delays, however, the drivers of PM trucks were paid for an additional 30 minutes of work each day. This allowed the drivers 15 minutes to pick up the trucks at the motor pool so that teams could depart from the PM section at 0730 hours and also allowed 15 minutes to leave the trucks at the motor pool at the end of the day so the teams did not have to return prior to 1615 hours. The average time the teams returned was 1555 hours, or 20 minutes early.

Advance Notification. PM teams in the southern sector did not provide advance notification to family housing occupants of the date and approximate time of the team's visit. As a result, many occupants were not home when teams arrived to perform PM. The DFAE had designed a form to show the scheduled time and date of the PM team visit, and the form was to be left with the occupant the day before the team's scheduled visit. Occupants were to indicate on the form the type of PM work they considered necessary. During our three days of observations of PM teams assigned to family housing in the southern sector, we noted eighteen instances where the occupants were not at home. We believe that most of the occupants would have been home if they had been notified in advance of the PM team's scheduled visit, thereby increasing productivity.

We believed that many of the problem areas discussed above could have been detected and corrected if DFAE had used work sampling techniques and analyzed work performance. On 29 August 1974, we discussed the results of our review of the PM teams with command personnel, and action was promptly initiated to implement our recommendations.

The automated management information system in use did not provide adequate data for effective management of the work force. The work management reports produced were either rarely used or could not be used at all. Deficiencies existed in the system because objectives were not clearly defined before the computer programs were written. In addition, Directorate for Facilities Engineering (DFAE) personnel did not follow up and coordinate corrective actions with data processing personnel to ensure that programming errors were eliminated.

The primary objectives of the Army Management Information System program are to design, develop, install, and maintain systems that efficiently and economically satisfy the information requirements of managers at all levels.

Before these objectives can be met, the type of information needed for management decisions must be defined and the system must be continually monitored to ensure that the data produced meets the stated objectives. DFAE, with the assistance of the Directorate for Data Systems, developed an automated management information system to control funds and evaluate work performance. About $25,000 a year was expended for computer time to produce the various management information reports. The information contained in reports for financial management purposes was reliable, but the reports for work management did not provide management with meaningful information. Because of the various problems that have existed since the inception of the current data processing system, we believe that the objectives should be redefined and programs revised where necessary.

Problems Within the System. The objectives of the automated system for work management were not adequately defined nor monitored. The present automated system became operational in July 1972. However, the reports for work management purposes have never been satisfactory. A study was not made to define the information needed for management purposes and to determine how a data-processing system could provide this data. Also, objectives were not clearly defined before the computer programs were developed. If the study had been made and objectives clearly defined and understood, some of the errors in computer programs might not have been made. The Work Coordination Register, for example, could not be effectively used to monitor actual performance. The size of the fields on the register for recording the number of man-hours and the amount of funds expended on a job were five or six digits, respectively. But the program was written so that the most significant digit was omitted when the number of man-hours expended and amount of costs incurred exceeded the size of the field. As a result, fourteen Standing Operation Orders completed in FY 1974 were understated by two million man-hours and $5 million.

Once the automated management information system was implemented, DFAE did not adequately coordinate corrective actions with data-processing personnel to ensure that program deficiencies were eliminated. Periodically, DFAE held meetings to identify improvements needed in the data processing system. A representative of the Directorate for Data Systems also attended the meetings. Although errors in various reports were noted and discussed during the meetings, the errors continued to occur. In May 1973 for example, DFAE personnel noted that the Individual Job Order—Maintenance Service Order Effectiveness Report provided meaningless data. This report was to provide an analysis of major and minor Individual Job Orders and Maintenance Service Orders to show the effectiveness of the work force by comparing actual man-hours expended to the number of man-hours that should have been expended. The report did not provide the desired results. Rather than showing the effectiveness of each category of job order, the report combined major and minor job orders and only showed an average effectiveness of both. The analysis of the effectiveness of Maintenance Service Orders also could not be used. Due to a programming error, a zero was printed in every column devoted to analysis of service orders. The same deficiency was noted again at a meeting in February 1974 but still

70

remained uncorrected at the time of our audit. Followup action should have been taken to ensure that the deficiencies caused by programming errors were corrected.

Timeliness of Data. In addition to costs and accuracy of information, timeliness should also be considered. The primary objectives of work management is to ensure maximum utilization of the labor force. The most important method of evaluating efficiency is to compare man-hours expended against estimated man-hours and determine the reasons for significant variances. This information is needed as soon as work is completed so corrective actions can be initiated. In most instances, data currently being produced was not timely and could not be effectively used. As a result, DFAE maintained manual records, which, to some extent, duplicated the information generated by the automated system. Unless the data-processing system can be fully responsive, the need for maintaining manual records will continue to exist. Response time may become more of a problem in the future. In March 1975, all data-processing support is scheduled to be transferred from Okinawa to Camp Zama, Japan. Because of the distance involved, however, the information contained in reports for work management may still not be responsive to management's needs.

Supplies were not managed effectively. About $1.7 million of expendable supplies on hand at 20 August 1974 were excess of requirements. Several conditions led to the accumulation of excesses.

Stockage levels were not reviewed for accuracy at least every ninety days. Accomplishment of these reviews was impracticable because of the excessive number of line items stocked.

Some stockage levels were erroneously established and supplies requisitioned on the basis of recommendations by shop personnel without consideration of prior demand experience or current job requirements.

Open requisitions for supplies no longer needed were not canceled.

The list of standby items stocked for emergencies had not been properly reviewed and updated since 1970.

In addition to the generation of excesses, replenishment actions were not always initiated when reorder points were reached. Also, the value of the inventory was inaccurate because current prices were not always used.

Procedures provide for establishing a Requisition Objective (RO) for any item having at least three demands during the most recent ninety-day control period. Generally, items with less than three demands in ninety days are not authorized for stockage. Reorder points (ROP) should be established for each item having an RO to assure that replenishment actions are initiated promptly. RO's and ROP's are required to be reviewed and revised before submitting a requisition or at least every ninety days. Stocks on hand that are excess to authorized levels should be reported for redistribution or disposal. Certain items of supply essential to life, to the health and welfare of installation personnel, and to the continued uninterrupted mission of the installation may be stocked for emergencies. Items stocked only for emergencies should be reviewed at least semiannually. The inventory should be valued at either standard prices published

71

in DA or Federal Supply Catalogs for items requisitioned from government supply sources or at prices established by the Directorate for Facilities Engineering (DFAE) for locally procured items.

Excess Stocks. As of 20 August 1974, about $1.7 million, or 77 percent, of the $2.2 million worth of expendable supplies on hand were excess to authorized stockage levels. The inventory consisted of about 24,000 line items* of which about 9,100 line items worth $750,000 had been on hand for at least two years without any quantities having been issued. In December 1973, DFAE identified items valued at about $1.5 million that did not qualify for stockage. However, during the period 1 December through 31 August 1974, DFAE only turned in approximately $175,000 worth of expendable supplies to the supply system for redistribution or disposal. Many of the items that were turned in were repair parts for equipment that was no longer in use. DFAE received credits of about $33,000 for the items turned in. As is discussed in the ensuing paragraph, the excessive number of line items and quantities on hand contributed to ineffective stock control procedures.

Review of Requisitioning Objectives and Reorder Points. RO's and ROP's were not being reviewed and revised every ninety days. The large number of line items stocked made timely review a virtual impossibility. The RO and ROP for only about 5 percent of the line items stocked were reviewed during the three-month period ended 20 August 1974. All of the reviews were made at the time the items were requisitioned. We found that many of the RO's were incorrect. As an example, a fuse had an RO of 25 each; however, the item did not qualify for stockage because only one issue had been made within the last twenty-three months. That meant that each reorder of 25 resulted in a fifty-year supply! DFAE had not computed the RO for this item since 19 November 1968. Conversely, the RO shown for an incandescent lamp was zero, but it should have been 5. The last time that stock control personnel reviewed this RO was 13 December 1973.

Requisitioning of Excess Supplies. In many instances, excess supplies were requisitioned because shop personnel, rather than stock control personnel, determined the quantities of items to be requisitioned and stocked without adequate consideration of past demand experience or current job requirements. On 1 December 1973, for example, shop personnel recommended that ten V-belts be stocked. Based on the recommendation, stock control personnel established a stockage level of ten and requisitioned ten V-belts. However, only three belts were issued during the 22-month period ended 31 August 1974. In another instance, one float valve assembly was needed to repair an icemaker. However, at the request of shop personnel, five assemblies were requisitioned on 6 June 1974. This item did not qualify for stockage because only five had been issued during the past five years. To preclude accumulating excess supplies, stock control personnel should requisition supplies only on the basis of RO's that are

---

*The facilities engineering activity in Mainland Japan stocked only about 3,200 line items. The repair and maintenance responsibility for Mainland Japan in terms of building space was equal to about 80 percent of the facilities supported by the facilities engineer in Okinawa.

support by demands. When the need arises for non-demand supported items, shop personnel should be required to request only the quantities needed for current job requirements.

Requisitions for Closed Work Orders. The Stock Control Branch was not notified when work orders for which supplies had been ordered were canceled or completed. Sometimes work orders awaiting supplies can be completed by using substitute items or fabricating parts. The Scheduling Branch was aware of the status of jobs and notified the Storage Branch when jobs awaiting supplies were closed. However, the Stock Control Branch was not notified. Consequently, requisitions for items no longer needed were not canceled. To minimize receipt of unneeded supplies, the Stock Control Branch should be notified when work orders are closed so that all applicable open requisitions can be canceled.

Standby Items. Standby items are minimum quantities of supplies that must be available for emergencies. These items need not be demand supported. The type and quantity of items stocked must be justified and approved by the facilities engineer. The stockage list of standby items was last approved on 15 April 1970. The list originally contained 849 line items valued at about $121,000. Since April 1970, items have been added and deleted without any documented justification. Shop supervisors could not readily determine if the type of items or the quantities stocked were still needed without a detailed examination of the standby list and analysis of current mission requirements. However, some items did not require detailed examination. For example, the supervisor for the electrical shop readily recognized two items for support of missile sites that should have been deleted. DFAE lost the mission to support missile sites in 1972. To avoid accumulation of unneeded stock and to ensure that items needed for emergencies are available, the list of standy items should be reviewed and updated semiannually.

Replenishment Requisitions. Replenishment requisitions were not always processed when reorder points were reached. We reviewed ninety line items and found that the on-hand balance for 18 percent of the items had reached the ROP; however, requisitions had not been initiated. Storage personnel estimated that they could review each line item only once every two weeks because of the large number of line items stocked. Review time can be reduced by disposing of excess stocks and by identifying the quantity of stock for each line item representing the ROP. For example, the ROP quantity for small items could be identified by placing it in a bag or taping it together. When the bag or tape is broken, replenishment action should be initiated.

Excess stocks have been a continuing problem for DFAE. Although DFAE disposed of some excess stocks, our audit showed that the value of stocks on hand in excess of authorized levels increased by about $700,000 since 1971. In addition, the number of line items stocked remained about the same even though DFAE lost the mission of supporting several island-wide functions in May 1972. By reducing the number of line items stocked, DFAE should be able to manage supplies more efficiently, increase the efficiency of storage operations, and utilize warehouse storage capacity more effectively. If excess stocks are disposed of, stock control clerks would be able to review RO's and ROP's every ninety days, and the number of man-hours needed to take physical inventories should be reduced significantly. About ten thousand man-hours were expended taking the physical inventory in November 1973. In addition, stocks that are deteriorating outdoors could be stored in warehouses. Quality control inspectors from the Directorate for Industrial Operations condemned about $10,000 worth of metal products stored outside. Some of the items should have been stored inside.

Storage practices needed improvement to (i) protect supplies from deterioration, (ii) ensure supplies on hand were available for issue, (iii) avoid loss of time searching for supplies, and (iv) maintain control over supplies and prevent unauthorized issues. Our review showed that:

Metal products valued at about $10,000 that were stored outside had become unserviceable.

About $3,100 worth of supplies reserved for work orders should have been returned to stock or disposed of.

The locator file was inaccurate; some locations were not marked with location codes, and items stored in open areas were not always properly identified. Corrections that should have been made during the last locator survey were not made. Consequently, additional time was needed to search for supplies and some supplies could not be found.

Supplies were issued to individuals who did not have signature cards on file.

As of 20 August 1974, the Directorate for Facilities Engineering (DFAE) maintained ten warehouses and four outdoor supply yards to store about $2.6 million of supplies. Good storage practices require that only supplies that resist deterioration may be stored in open areas. All other supplies should be stored in warehouses. Once items have been placed to storage, a locator system must be maintained to control supplies and to facilitate processing of receipts and issues. Policies and procedures for storing and locating facilities engineering supplies are contained in AR 420–32.

Deteriorated Stocks. Many items stocked by DFAE were stored outside. Some items were subject to deterioration by the elements and should not have been in outside storage. To determine the extent of the deterioration, we requested quality control inspectors from the Directorate for Industrial Operations to inspect metal products stored outside. The inspectors recommend that supplies valued at about $10,000 be disposed of. Because some pipeline valves, which were not condemned by the inspectors, were rusty, we requested that personnel of the petroleum, oils, and lubricants shop determine the condition of these valves. They stated that many of the valves would require reconditioning before they could be used. Technical Manual 30–460 recommends that the valves be stored indoors and the openings be covered to protect the flanges and internal parts. The majority of the valve openings were not covered, and some were positioned so that the unsealed openings faced upwards. Supplies stored outside in Okinawa are subject to faster than normal deterioration because of constant high humidity. Therefore, as many items as possible should be stored indoors. Additional warehouse storage space could be made available after disposition of excess stocks.

Reserved Supplies. When supplies needed for work orders are not on hand, the needed supplies are requisitioned. Items on hand that are also needed for the same work order are reserved, tagged, and placed in holding areas. Reserved supplies are referred to as "frozen items." When all required supplies are received, they, along with the "frozen items," are issued to the shops. On 9 October 1974, storage personnel estimated that between 1,500 and 2,000 line items were reserved for work orders. We randomly selected 66 line items reserved for 43 work orders to determine if the items should remain "frozen." We found 42 line items valued at about $1,800 that were for work orders that had been canceled or completed. A control assembly, for example, was "frozen" for a work order that had been completed in 1970. Many other items were "frozen" for work orders that had been closed in 1972 and 1973. The individual in charge of the holding areas stated that the tag identifying the work order for which the item is "frozen" is marked with an "X" when notification is received that a work order has been completed or canceled. However, the items were not always returned to normal storage locations. We also found four line items valued at about $1,300 that were stored in the holding area without tags. Storage personnel were unable to determine if these items should have been "frozen." Items that remain in the supply holding area are not available for issue for use on other work orders.

Locator System. Using statistical sampling techniques, we evaluated the accuracy of the 26,167 locator cards for expendable items. We found an error rate of 24 percent. Primarily, there were two types of errors. Locations shown on locator cards were incorrect for 4,448, or 17 percent, of the locations and another 1,832 cards, or 7 percent, were maintained for items no longer stocked. An inaccurate locator system could cause delays in processing receipts and issues as well as a loss of control of supplies.

Incorrect Locations. About 785 locator cards at Warehouse 360 were incorrect because the location codes shown had not been changed when a five-digit locator system was established in July 1973. Serious problems in finding supplies had not occurred because storage personnel were familiar with the warehouse. Delays, however, were encountered at Warehouse 358 where about 2,878 locator cards were inaccurate. In this instance, not all of the locator cards for line items transferred to the warehouse in May 1974 had been updated by 31 August 1974 and warehouse personnel had difficulty finding items. For example, it took 1 hour and 45 minutes to find thirteen line items.

Although the locator cards were inaccurate, we were eventually able to find most of the items. However, storage personnel could not find the items for 3 percent of the locator cards in our sample.

Inactive Locations. About 7 percent of the locator cards were for inactive line items. An item is considered to be inactive when the stock on hand is exhausted and restockage of the item is no longer required. When this occurs, the locator card for the inactive line item should be removed from the master file so that the storage location can be made available for another item.

Locator Surveys. To ensure that recorded locations are accurate, locator surveys should be performed concurrently with annual inventories. Discrepancies found should be corrected immediately. DFAE had not prepared specific instructions for performing and completing annual locator surveys. A locator survey, performed concurrently with the last inventory in November 1973, was not completely effective. The inaccurate locator cards in Warehouse 360 should have been detected and corrected during the survey. On 7 August 1974, we also found that not all storage locations, specifically Yard A and Warehouse 354, were marked with the five-digit code established in July 1973. At these two areas, storage personnel had to go from one location to another searching for items. Storage personnel began marking storage locations with the five-digit code the day after our visit.

Identification of Supplies. According to AR 420–32, bulky items should be identified by stenciling the proper nomenclature, including the stock or part number, in a conspicuous place on the item with permanent weatherproof paint. Large items should be tagged. DFAE procedures required that items in open storage areas be identified with small wooden tags. However, wooden tags were not always attached to the items, particularly at Yard A and C. Furthermore, the information on some of the tags had become illegible due to the weather. For example, we attempted to locate and inventory several types of large air conditioners and other cooling equipment. Not all of the items were tagged, and the markings on the containers were no longer visible. Storage personnel had to open several creates to identify the contents.

Issue Procedures. Supplies were issued to individuals who did not have signature cards on file. We reviewed twenty-four issue documents prepared on 16 September 1974 and found that signature cards were not available for four of the eight individuals who signed for the supplies. Storage personnel stated that the signature cards were being updated by DFAE activities, and the signatures of the four individuals would appear on the updated cards. Although supplies are issued from six issue points, signature cards were on file at only two of the points. Copies of current signature cards are needed at all issue points to ensure that only authorized persons pick up supplies.

Contract administration procedures needed improvement to ensure that contracts are modified when the scope of work is changed, payments are made only for work actually performed, and issues of government-furnished supplies are controlled. Our review disclosed that:

An inspector increased the scope of work on one contract without coordinating with the contracting officer to have the contract modified. Also, there was no assurance at the time that additional funds were available to cover the increased costs.

A painting contractor was overpaid about $6,700 because the amount of work actually performed was not verified.

The custodial services contractor did not acknowledge receipt of about $55,000 worth of government-furnished supplies. In addition, about $11,000 of government-furnished supplies were issued in excess of the amounts specified in the contract.

Some facilities engineering support, such as painting and custodial services, was provided under commercial contracts. When engineering services were provided by a contractor, the Directorate for Facilities Engineering (DFAE), as the contracting officer's representative, was responsible for (i) administering contractor performance to ensure compliance with contract provisions, (ii) verifying the amount of work performed, and (iii) ensuring that government-furnished supplies were utilized properly and in reasonable quantities.

Contract Modification. An inspector changed the scope of a painting contract without coordinating with the contracting officer, determining if additional funds were available, or requesting a contract modification. Contract number DAJB09–C0088 was awarded to paint 301 family housing units. Under the provisions of the contract, the units were to be painted using government-furnished paint. One coat of paint was to be applied to 250 family housing units and two coats to the remaining 51 units. As of 13 September 1974, the contract inspector's worksheet showed that the contractor had completed 47 family housing units that were scheduled for one coat of paint. Of the 47 units, only 28 had been accepted for payment to the contractor. However, we found that the quantities of paint used varied by as much as twelve gallons per unit. Responsible personnel stated that to adequately cover the surface, two coats of paint were applied to some quarters although the contract provided for only one coat. A local national inspector directed the contractor to apply the second coat. However, the change had not been coordinated with either the requesting activity or the procurement activity, and the contract was not modified to include the additional work. According to the inspector's worksheet, two coats of paint had been applied to 16 units that had been contracted for only one coat. Based on the rates in the contract, the cost of applying the second coat of paint amounted to $2,000. After we brought this condition to the attention of responsible personnel, action was initiated to ensure the availability of funds and appropriate modification of the contract.

Verification of Work Performed. The amount of work actually performed was not always verified. Our review of contract DAJB09–C0110 showed that the contractor received payments of $6,651 for work that was not performed. The contract, which was completed in March 1974, was for interior painting of various types of family quarters. Payments were to be based on the number of square feet certified as having been painted. To determine the size of the painted surface and to certify payment, DFAE inspectors were required to measure each type of quarters. However, some measurements were not accurate. Our comparison of the measurements taken for contract DAJB09–73–C0110 with measurements subsequently taken in July 1974 for another contract, which included the same type of quarters, disclosed that the number of square feet to be painted in each type C and type D-2 quarters was overstated on the earlier contract by 1,770 and 1,632 square feet, respectively. At our request, contract inspectors measured type C quarters on 17 September 1974. This measurement was in line with the one taken in July. DFAE personnel also agreed that the measurement of D-2 type quarters taken in July were also more reliable. Thus, the contractor was paid for painting a larger area than was actually painted. Based on the contract price, the difference amounted to $59 for each type C quarters and $54 for each type D-2 quarters. Excessive payments totaled $2,655 for the 45 type C quarters painted and $3,996 for the 74 type D-2 quarters painted. To preclude overpayments to contractors, the amount of work actually performed should be verified.

Control of Government-Furnished Supplies. Controls over government-furnished supplies for the custodial services contract were not adequate. Under the provision of the contract, the government provided the contractor with supplies, such as soap, paper towels, and toilet tissue. During FY 1974, DFAE issued supplies valued at about $55,200 to the contractor. DFAE rarely enforced the requirement for the contractor to acknowledge receipt by signing a copy of the issue document. Signed issue documents only accounted for supplies valued at $285. Government-furnished supplies cannot be properly controlled unless the contractor acknowledges receipt by signing each issue document.

We also found that the quantity of toilet tissue issued to the contractor exceeded the quantity specified in the contract. According to the contract, the government was required to furnish the contractor about 15,000 rolls of toilet tissue a month. During FY 1974, DFAE issued an average of 21,000 rolls a month to the contractor. The value of the excess quantities issued amounted to $10,800.

Personnel costs could be reduced by approximately $90,000 a year by transferring the functions of the Taiwan Sub-Post Engineer to the U.S. Navy's Officer-In-Charge of Construction (OICC) in Taiwan. We also believe that the transfer would provide for more efficient and economical procurement and contract administration support because the U.S. Army does not have a procurement office in Taiwan. Our review of the Taiwan Sub-Post showed that contracts were not administered properly. Contractors were directed to perform work that was outside the scope of the contract. Payments to contractors were authorized for work that had not been performed. In other instances, contractors were erroneously paid at trouble-call rates although the work was performed during normal duty hours.

The Taiwan Sub-Post was established in December 1968 primarily to provide facilities engineering support to the U.S. Army Communications Command (USACC) in Taiwan. Before 1968, facilities engineering support was provided by the U.S. Navy's OICC. In Taiwan, OICC has the mission of providing construction, maintenance, and repair support to all Naval activities and to activities of other military departments on an Inter-Service Support Agreement basis. All of the support currently provided by the Taiwan Sub-Post Engineer was performed under four maintenance and repair contracts. Two of the contracts were for maintenance and repair of facilities, which included custodial services and air conditioning repair services. The other two contracts were for generator maintenance. At the time of our audit, the staffing for the sub-post engineer consisted of one enlisted man, three Department of the Army civilians, and eleven Taiwanese nationals. Combined salaries totaled about $104,000, while the value of the contracts administered totaled about $195,000.

Transfer of Taiwan Sub-Post Functions. Personnel costs could be reduced by about $90,000 a year by transferring the functions of the Taiwan Sub-Post Engineer to the Navy's OICC in Taiwan. Responsible Navy personnel told us that only four additional local national spaces would be needed by their organization to absorb the increased workload. Thus, the overall current staffing requirements would be reduced by eleven spaces resulting in savings in personnel costs of about $90,000 per year. Moreover, we found that the rates generally paid for services performed under contracts administered by the Navy's OICC were lower than the rates paid for similar services under contracts administered by the sub-post engineer. Examples of differences in unit prices are:

| | | Unit Price | |
| | | Sub-Post | |
Type of Service	Unit	Engineer	OICC
Interior Painting	Sq. Ft.	$ 0.06	$ 0.03
Replace Incandescent Bulbs	Each	$ 0.80	$ 0.66
Replace Wire Type Fuse	Each	$ 0.30	$ 0.08
Cutting Grass*	Acre	$38.00	$ 7.90

*The auditors recognized that the cost of cutting grass depends on the frequency and the terrain of the area to be cut. However, we believed that $38 per acre, which is more than four times the price paid by OICC, might be excessive.

In addition to the reduction in personnel costs that would be realized from transferring the facilities engineering function to OICC, we believe that OICC could provide better procurement and contract administration support. Effective 30 June 1974, the Taiwan Field Office of the Directorate for Procurement, U.S. Army Garrison, Okinawa (PROV), was closed. The sub-post engineer now receives all procurement support from Okinawa. In December 1974, all procurement functions on Okinawa are scheduled to be transferred to the U.S. Air Force. After the transfer, procurement support for U.S. Army activities in Taiwan will continue to be provided from Okinawa. Under this situation, responsiveness to the needs of USACC would be decreased, especially for emergency procurement, because the contracting officer would not be present in Taiwan to process procurement actions. Day-to-day problems of contract administration that also require the attention of the contracting officer would not be resolved promptly. Furthermore, the cost of numerous trips to Taiwan by the contracting officer will significantly increase the cost of providing procurement support from Okinawa. We believe that the problems regarding contract administration, which are discussed below, occurred mainly because of the lack of procurement support and technical supervision in Taiwan.

Contract Administration. The maintenance and repair contracts were not properly administered by the sub-post engineer. Indefinite quantity items, such as changing light bulbs and cutting grass, were ordered as required. As ordering officer, the sub-post engineer was responsible for administering delivery orders placed for indefinite items, establishing controls necessary to ensure that all contract terms were complied with, and that services were performed before payment was authorized. The sub-post engineer did not have the authority to direct the contractor to perform work outside the scope of the contract or to modify contracts. However, our review of work orders completed during July and August 1974 showed that (i) contractors were directed to perform work outside the scope of the contract, (ii) payments to contractors were authorized for work that was not performed, and (iii) contractors were erroneously paid trouble-call rates for work performed during normal duty hours.

Work Performed Outside the Scope of Contracts. When work must be performed that is outside the scope of current contracts, coordination with the contracting officer is necessary to either modify an existing contract or to initiate new procurement. We noted several instances where contractors were directed to perform work that was outside the scope of the contracts. As an example, a carpet was installed in a dining facility at a cost of $1,920 under one of the maintenance and repair contracts. This work was outside the scope of the contract. On another occasion, security lights were installed by another maintenance and repair contractor at a cost of $3,008. An analysis of the work performed revealed that most of the work was not included in the contract provisions.

The award of generator overhaul work to one of the maintenance and repair contractors, rather than to one of the generator repair contractors, also illustrates the problems that can be encountered if procurement office support and technical supervision are not readily available. In July 1974, a 60-kilowatt backup generator was overhauled at a cost of $616, and the job was given to a contractor for maintenance and repair facilities. Since that contractor did not have the capability of performing this type of work, he sublet the job to one of the generator repair contractors.

Payments for Work Performed. Payment to the contractor should be authorized only after an inspection has been made to ensure that the work has actually been performed. We found that contractors had been paid for work that had not been done. To illustrate, the ceiling of a dining facility, which measured about 1,200 square feet, was painted. According to the provisions of the contract, only one coat of paint was to be applied at a rate of 6 cents a square foot. The contractor, however, was paid for painting 2,400 square feet at 12 cents a square foot. Sub-post engineer personnel stated that the rate per square foot was doubled because two coats of paint were applied. However, no one could explain why both the rate and the size of the area painted were doubled. In another instance, we noted that the maintenance and repair contractor was paid for cutting about 30,000 square feet of grass around the USACC headquarters building and the motor pool. The grass was cut twice a month at a cost of $53.20 a month. However, we were only able to find two areas of grass, totaling about 700 square feet. The remaining areas around the headquarters building and the motor pool were concrete.

Trouble-Call Rates. During normal duty hours, contractors for the maintenance and repair of facilities were required to keep qualified individuals on duty at selected locations to provide trouble service maintenance, inspections, and general maintenance. If trouble service maintenance, such as replacing a fuse, was required during off-duty hours, the contractor would provide the service but at a higher rate because someone would have to be sent to the site to perform the work. On twelve different occasions during July and August 1974, the contractor was paid for performing services at the higher trouble-call rate during normal duty hours.

80

My second audit was of the Army's fixed communications system. This was the "sister" to the previously discussed Leased Communications audit. My attempt to obtain a copy of this audit was unsuccessful. In response to my Freedom of Information Request, I was informed that all copies of this audit were destroyed. As a result, I'll ask you to believe me when I say there were lots of problems and move onto my next audit.

My third audit overseas was of the Army Medical Matériel Agency. During the audit, your foray into Vietnam ended. This report was published on May 8, 1975.

The major missions of the U.S. Army Medical Matériel Agency, Pacific (USAMMAPAC), are to provide depot level supply support, optical fabrication, and equipment maintenance support to authorized customers in the Western Pacific. These customers include designated U.S. Forces, Free World Military Assistance Forces, and activities supported by the U.S. Agency for International Development (USAID) and Military Assistance Programs (MAP).

USAMMAPPAC was the principal source of medical supplies in the Pacific and received vast amounts of retrograde medical matériel during the Vietnam era. With the reduction of U.S. military involvement in the Western Pacific and the increasing trend toward filling customer requisitions by direct delivery from CONUS depots, the extent of supply support provided by USAMMAPAC has declined considerably and is expected to continue to decline. Stock fund sales of medical matériel, which totaled $46.5 million in FY 1973, declined to $33.7 million in FY 1974 and amounted to $11.1 million during the first seven months of FY 1975. Moreover, the number of customer requisitions filled by direct deliveries from CONUS is increasing. Nearly 60 percent of the sales made thus far during FY 1975 were for direct deliveries of matériel from CONUS supply sources to USAMMAPAC customers.

In view of the declining supply mission, USAMMAPAC has, in addition to reporting excess matériel for redistribution, taken various management actions to accelerate the drawdown of its medical supplies, which includes a number of items with limited shelf life. USAMMAPAC's largest mission customer was the Army of the Republic of Vietnam (ARVN), which accounted for nearly 50 percent of its sales in FY 1974. Although it lost the mission of directly supporting ARVN in July 1974, USAMMAPAC has been furnishing the U.S. Army Medical Matériel Agency (USAMMA) in CONUS with periodic listings of long supply assets available in Okinawa. ARVN requisitions submitted directly to USAMMA were screened against the listing, and referral orders for matériel valued at $850,000 were forwarded to Okinawa for fill during the seven months ended 31 January 1975. Also, USAMMAPAC, anticipating losing the mission to support USAID and other MAP customers after 1 July 1975, initiated action in December 1974 to delete the stockage of a thirty-day safety level established to support these customers, thus making additional assets available for redistribution. In addition, USAMMAPAC has been furnishing the Pacific Command Utilization and Redistribution Agency (PURA) visibility of some permissive overstockage assets, that are authorized for retention and are not normally reported for redistribution, as a further means to maximize the utilization of medical matériel.

81

Our audit showed that USAMMAPAC had taken actions to improve the management of its medical supplies. There were opportunities, however, for additional improvements in the areas of redistribution of medical assets, management of optical stocks, allocation of maintenance costs to job orders, and inventory adjustment procedures. The recommendations on the conditions summarized below were addressed to the Commander, U.S. Army Medical Department Activity, Japan.

As of 31 January 1975, USAMMAPAC was authorized 384 personnel consisting of 143 military, 23 U.S. civilians, and 218 local national employees; 227 were assigned. During fiscal year 1975, $1.4 million of operations and maintenance, Army funds, and $14.8 million in stock funds money was made available to USAMMAPAC.

The U.S. Army Matériel Agency, Pacific (USAMMAPAC) can achieve greater utilization of matériel by making more of its medical assets available for redistribution. Potency-dated and narcotic items retained as permissive overstockage (POS) were not reported to the Pacific Command Utilization and Redistribution Agency (PURA) because the computer program was not revised to provide the means of reporting these previously exempt assets. Some assets that no longer met the criteria for stockage also were not reported to PURA. Consequently, at least thirty-one requisitions for matériel valued at $10,800 that were submitted by medical activities to PURA during a 24-day period were passed to supply sources in CONUS although USAMMAPAC had sufficient assets to fill the requisitions. In addition, potency-dated and deteriorative items held in pre-positioned war reserve (PPWR) accounts, which have little likelihood of being rotated because of the lack of peacetime operating requirements, should be made available for redistribution promptly instead of waiting until their remaining shelf life is nine months or less.

USAMMAPAC was the recipient of vast amounts of retrograde medical matériel during the phasedown of U.S. operations in Vietnam. Because of declining customer demands, many medical assets at USAMMAPAC are now in a long-supply position. Long supply refers to a situation wherein the quantity of an item on hand exceeds its requisitioning objective.* The long-supply quantity authorized for retention is known as POS. USAMMAPAC was authorized a thirty-six-month POS. The long supply quantity on hand over and above the requisitioning objective and POS is excess stock.

PURA is a Pacific Command (PACOM) agency that maintains a record of excess matériel reported by supply activities in PACOM and monitors the program of intra- and inter-service utilization and redistribution of these reported excesses. Supply activities submit their routine requisitions through PURA. PURA matches the requisitions with reported excesses and directs redistribution when possible. Excess matériel reported by USAMMAPAC included narcotic items and those potency-dated items with more than twelve months remaining shelf life.

In addition to the reporting of excess medical matériel, a special computer program was developed in September 1972 to ensure greater use of medical

*The maximum quantity of an item authorized to be on hand and on order to sustain current operations.

assets held in POS at USAMMAPAC by providing visibility of these assets to PURA. Following the monthly computer restratification of USAMMAPAC assets, all items with POS assets, except potency-dated and narcotic items, are reported to PURA. Requisitions submitted through PURA by selected Army, Navy, Air Force, and Marine Corps medical activities (non-mission customers) are screened against PURA's POS file before the requisitions are sent to supply sources in CONUS. If the item is available, the requisition is referred to USAMMAPAC and processed as a normal funded requisition. Requisitions submitted by mission customers of USAMMAPAC are excluded from this screening because their requisitions pass through USAMMAPAC on the way to PURA.

Reporting of Matériel. POS quantities of potency-dated and narcotic items and items that no longer qualified for stockage were not reported to PURA for redistribution. Consequently, some requisitions received at PURA for these items were passed to supply sources in CONUS although the assets were available at USAMMAPAC.

Potency-dated and Narcotic Items. Medical items retained for POS that were reported to PURA in November 1974 excluded potency-dated and narcotic items. We were told that these items were exempt from reporting and that the computer program for reporting POS assets to PURA was designed to exclude these items. However, our review of CINPACINST 4600.10, dated 30 October 1974, showed that the procedures for reporting POS assets had been revised and that USAMMAPAC was required to report narcotic items and those potency-dated items with more than twelve months remaining shelf life. The computer program had not been changed to incorporate the revised reporting procedures.

Our review of requisitions passed by PURA to supply sources in CONUS during the period 14 November to 7 December 1974 showed that at least sixteen requisitions for potency-dated items and two requisitions for narcotic items could have been satisfied by USAMMAPAC. The eighteen requisitions were for matériel worth about $10,000. For example, PURA received a requisition in early December 1974 from the medical depot in Korea for 4,800 bottles of penicillin powder. The requisition was passed to CONUS because the requested item was not PURA's POS file. USAMMAPAC had about 752,000 bottles of this item in POS in early December 1974. All of these bottles had a remaining shelf life of thirty-six months.

The ideal solution for the reporting of potency-dated and narcotic items to PURA is to revise the computer program. However, past experience has shown that changes to computer programs take time and we were told that the Computer Systems Command in Hawaii, which has the responsibility for making program changes, is working on the implementation of SAILS, a high-priority requirement. To expedite the redistribution of these assets, PURA and medical activities should be made aware of the availability of these items. We were told by computer personnel at PURA and the Directorate for Data Systems, U.S. Army Garrison, Okinawa, that it may be possible to manually report potency-dated and narcotic items to PURA. USAMMAPAC should pursue this area further and determine how this can be accomplished. If it is determined that reporting by manual means is not feasible, USAMMAPAC should broadcast the availability of these items to medical activities by electrical messages or correspondence. USAMMAPAC has a procedure to manually review and identify potency-dated items when they reach nine and three months of remaining shelf life and offer these items to authorized customers at reduced prices. Potency-dated items with POS assets that have more than twelve months remaining shelf life could also be identified during this manual review. As previously mentioned, USAMMAPAC had about 752,000 bottles of penicillin powder with a remaining shelf life of thirty-six months. Under existing procedures, medical activities may not become aware that this item was available at USAMMAPAC until its remaining shelf life reached nine months.

Nonstockage List Items. USAMMAPAC assigned stockage list code (SLC) A to items that were previously on the authorized stockage list but no longer qualified for stockage due to insufficient demands. This code was intended to be used to retain the assets until they could qualify for stockage again, or until they could be disposed of through attrition rather than reporting them to PURA. Our review of requisitions passed by PURA to supply sources in CONUS between 14 November and 7 December 1974 showed that at least thirteen requisitions for matériel valued at $800 could have been satisfied by USAMMAPAC had these SLC A items been reported to PURA. Although USAMMAPAC personnel had been deleting the SLC A from a number of items, there were 734 SLC A items with on-hand assets valued at $573,000 as of 28 December 1974. We were told that an item was generally retained if at least one demand was recorded during a twelve-month period; otherwise, the SLC A would be removed. Our review of 20 SLC A items, however, showed that seven items had no demands for at least twelve months. SLC A items should be reviewed more closely so that unneeded assets can be reported for redistribution.

Rotation of Stocks. PPWR stocks stored at USAMMAPAC included potency-dated and deteriorative items for which USAMMAPAC had insufficient peacetime operating requirements to establish stockage levels. USAMMAPAC therefore is experiencing difficulty in rotating these stocks before they become unusable. Recognizing the problem of nonrotatable stocks, the U.S. Army, Pacific, established a procedure in February 1973 to delete shelf-life type assets from PPWR accounts at USAMMAPAC. Under this procedure, USAMMAPAC and the U.S. Army Medical Matériel Agency (USAMMA) in CONUS jointly manage the levels and assets on hand of shelf-life items stocked for PPWR items. As the potency-dated and deteriorative items on hand at USAMMAPAC are reduced through attrition, they are not replenished. USAMMAPAC's level is subsequently adjusted to equal the quantity on hand and the authorized level at USAMMA is increased.

USAMMAPAC has a procedure to broadcast the availability of potency-dated and deteriorative items nearing their shelf-life expiration dates. When items reach nine and three months of remaining shelf life, they are offered by message to medical activities in PACOM at 50 percent and 90 percent reductions in prices, respectively. However, responses have been minimal. For example, of the sixty-one line items valued at $47,000 that were offered at reduced prices in October 1974, requests were received for only fifteen line items valued at $640. The requests were all for items with nine months of remaining shelf life.

We selected for review forty-one potency-dated items that were in the PPWR accounts and did not have peacetime operating levels. We found that medical activities (non-mission customers of USAMMAPAC) had submitted eleven requisitions to PURA for nine of the forty-one line items during the period 15 October through 9 December 1974. These requisitions were all forwarded to supply sources in CONUS. Since our review indicated that medical activities in PACOM needed some of these assets, we believe that better use of USAMMAPAC assets could be achieved if potency-dated and deteriorative items in the PPWR accounts that do not have a rotatable base were offered to customers now rather than waiting until they have nine months of remaining shelf life. Past experiences has shown that, even at reduced prices, customers seldom requisition assets that have short remaining life.

Plastic lenses, valued at approximately $100,000, were on hand at the depot supply activity and Property Management Division of U.S. Army Medical Matériel Agency, Pacific (USAMMAPAC), although the majority of the stocks did not qualify for stockage. Excessive quantities of spectacle components, including unusable items, also were on hand at the optical laboratory. In addition, our review of 681 line items at the Property Management Division showed that stock record cards had not been established for 287 line items and the quantities on hand for 168 line items did not agree with the recorded balances.

USAMMAPAC's Optical Division operates an optical laboratory to fabricate and repair spectacles for authorized customers. The laboratory maintains bench stocks of spectacle components and repair parts. The bench stocks are replenished from the operating stocks managed by the Property Management Division, which in turn receives its replenishment stocks from the depot supply activity of USAMMAPAC. Our review showed that management of optical stocks needed improvement at all three levels of supply.

Stockage of Supplies. The Property Management Division and the depot supply activity had a total of about $100,000 of plastic lenses on hand. Most of these lenses did not qualify for stockage. The optical laboratory also had more bench stocks than were needed.

Plastic Lenses. About 25,000 pairs of plastic lenses were stocked at the Property Management Division and an additional 12,000 pairs of similar lenses were on hand at the depot supply activity as of 26 December 1974. These plastic lenses were valued at about $100,000. Stockage levels had not been established for these lenses at either level of supply and requirements were not sufficient to justify retention of the majority of the lenses. Correspondence showed that a decision was made in May 1973 to buy about $60,000 of plastic lenses that were on hand at the depot supply activity in order to utilize consumer funds remaining at year end. We were told that the original acquisition of the plastic lenses by the depot supply activity and the purchase of plastic lenses with year-end consumer funds were made in anticipation of increased prescriptions for plastic lenses. However, the anticipated requirements did not materialize.

The conditions under which plastic or glass lenses will be used to fill prescriptions for spectacles are specified in AR 40–3. Plastic lenses can only be used to fill certain prescriptions and they are subject to faster deterioration than glass lenses while in storage. During the three-month period ended 31 December 1974, the optical laboratory completed about 9,600 prescriptions. About 50 prescriptions, or less than 1 percent, were for plastic lenses. Optical laboratory personnel estimated that they would continue to use about 50 pairs of plastic lenses each quarter. Because of the low rate of usage, the optical laboratory did not stock plastic lenses as part of its bench stocks. These lenses were requested from the Property Management Division on an as-needed basis. Compared to the estimated annual requirement of 200 pairs of plastic lenses, the 37,000 pairs on hand at the Property Management Division and the depot supply activity were clearly excessive.

In view of the large quantity of plastic lenses on hand, the low rate of consumption, and the susceptibility of these lenses to deterioration, prompt action is needed to determine stockage requirements for plastic lenses and report unneeded quantities for redistribution. Consumption data should be reconstructed to the extent possible and used together with estimated future requirements to establish stockage levels. By maintaining accurate consumption data in the future, stockage levels can be purified over a period of time.

Bench Stocks. The optical laboratory's bench stocks consisted of about 1,900 line items of spectacle components and repair parts valued at $18,000. Our review of selected items showed that some of the spectacle components either could not be used or were not needed and excessive quantities of other components were stocked. The bench stocks included 132 line items of pink-tinted glass lenses valued at $2,700. The optical laboratory discontinued using these lenses about a year ago after notification from higher headquarters that their use was suspended. We found a box containing 56 line items of various lenses valued at about $430. After inspecting the items, optical laboratory personnel stated that quantities on hand of 20 or more showed that 12 line items had stocks on hand that exceeded the prescribed fifteen-day stockage level; 7 line items had seventy or more days of supply on hand.

Accounting for Supplies. The Property Management Division maintained about 2,000 stock record cards for optical stocks as of 6 December 1974. Together with operating personnel, we took a physical inventory of 681 items of spectacle components valued at about $67,000. We found that stock record cards had not been established for 287 line items of plastic lenses, with stocks on hand valued at about $32,000. Our inventory counts did not agree with the recorded balances for an additional 168 line items. The quantities on hand were greater than the recorded balances for 53 line items and less than the recorded balances for 115 line items. Operating personnel could not explain why accountability had not been established for the 287 line items of plastic lenses, which were received in July 1973, nor why these items were excluded from the inventories of optical stocks that were taken in March 1974 and August 1974.

Accountability and control of optical stocks can be improved by establishing a program similar to the Project Condition/Count 5 used at the depot supply activity. This project provides for conducting physical counts of all recorded locations for each selected item; verifying the count, location, and condition code to the accountable record; and researching discrepancies to determine the causes. Such a program will identify areas of supply management that need improvement.

The accuracy of accountable records for depot stocks could be improved by strengthening inventory adjustment procedures. Adjustments to the accountable records were not always correct, and some were not supported by required physical inventory counts. Prompt action was not always taken to research discrepancies between recorded and on-hand balances, thereby delaying clearing of discrepant items from the suspense account beyond the prescribed time period. Because recorded balances were inaccurate, some requisitions were submitted to the supply source in CONUS although sufficient assets were on hand to fill these requisitions. In addition, statistics on causes of inventory discrepancies were not being accumulated and analyzed to identify supply problem trends and to facilitate corrective action.

AR 740–26 prescribes procedures for conducting physical inventories and researching discrepancies between recorded and on-hand balances. The U.S. Army Medical Matériel Agency, Pacific (USAMMAPAC), inventoried its depot stocks by the single-count method. Under this method, the first count is compared to the accountable records and is subject to post-count validation if the recorded balance and inventory count do not agree. Discrepant items with extended monetary values of $200 or more are referred to as major discrepancies; minor discrepancies are those that are less than $200. Although AR 740–26 authorizes the use of sampling to research discrepant items, USAMMAPAC's policy was to increase its research efforts by performing causative research* of all major discrepancies with extended monetary values over $100. However, this policy was not always followed.

Research of Discrepant Items. During a six-month period ended 31 December 1974, USAMMAPAC reported inventory gains of $624,000 and inventory losses of $494,000 in its Report of Inventory Control Effectiveness. Our review showed that adjustments made to the accountable records were not always correct nor supported by validated physical inventory counts, and some discrepant items in a suspense account were not always researched promptly and cleared within the prescribed thirty-day time period.

Our review of thirty major inventory adjustments showed that ten adjustments were posted to the accountable records on the basis of single-inventory counts. The inventory count cards, whether they were first count or recount cards, were all maintained in file trays at the Inventory Performance Branch. Although we were told that post-count validations were performed when recorded balances differed from quantities on hand, the recount cards for these ten items could not be located. Together with operating personnel, we took a physical inventory of the ten items to determine the propriety of the adjustments made to the accountable records. We found that the quantities on hand exceeded the recorded balances for three items, with the variances ranging from quantities of 107 to 336. Because the recorded balances were understated, seven requisitions

*Causative research is an investigation of variances consisting of a complete review of all transactions occurring since the last inventory.

were subsequently submitted to supply sources in CONUS for the three items.

As an example, the recorded balance of 27 gas cylinders, valued at $1,485, was ajusted to a zero balance because the inventory count card showed that there were no gas cylinders on hand. We counted 107 gas cylinders at the location shown on the count card, and our review showed that there had been no gas cylinders received since the last inventory. Because the accountable records showed that none were on hand, 18 cylinders were requisitioned from the supply source in CONUS. One of the cylinders was needed to fill a high-priority requisition. After we informed operating personnel that on-hand quantities for these three line items exceeded the recorded quantities, we were told that action would be taken to fill the priority requisition, cancel the open requisitions, and correct the recorded balances.

We also inventoried 25 potency-dated items and found that the quantities on hand for 14 items differed from the recorded balances. We requested that the Inventory Performance Branch research six discrepancies for matériel valued at over $200 each. Their research showed that at least two discrepancies resulted from past erroneous inventory counts. They were not able to locate recount cards to show that post-count validations were performed for these two items.

In addition, some discrepant items held in a suspense account pending research to verify the quantity on hand and, when applicable, to adjust the accountable records, were not being researched and cleared from the account within the thirty-day period specified by AR 740–26. Our review showed that research efforts had not been initiated for seven items that had been in the suspense account for thirty-five days as of 16 January 1975. During the period the seven items were in the suspense account, USAMMAPAC received seven customer requisitions, including three high-priority requisitions, for three items and submitted two depot replenishment requisitions to the supply source in CONUS for one of the items. Discrepant items should be researched promptly because past research efforts have resulted in the discovery of assets that previously could not be located.

Tabulation and Analysis of Causes. Cause codes were assigned to each inventory discrepancy that was researched. However, statistics were not being accumulated and analyzed to identify and correct problem areas. Our review showed that cause code statistics were previously compiled, but for some unexplained reason, this practice was discontinued at the end of calendar year 1973. As stated in AR 740–26, an analysis of causes of inventory discrepancies is vital in order to:

Provide the item manager with indications of the failures in the control systems and where improvements can be made,
Reduce similar variances in the future,
Ensure that the proper adjustment was made, and
Evaluate, for corrective actions, trends or system problems.

My next audit was of the Sagamihara Commissary at Honshu, Japan. The report was published November 7, 1975.

The Sagamihara Commissary, consisting of a main store and two annexes, is an operating activity under the jurisdiction of the Commander, U.S. Army Garrison, Honshu, who is directly responsible to the Commander, U.S. Army, Japan. The mission of the commissary is to order, receive, store, issue, and sell subsistence items to authorized individuals and activities. Sales to patrons amounted to about $3.5 million during FY 1975. In addition, $900,000 of issues to troop dining facilities and sales to authorized activities were made during the same period.

One military and seventy-three U.S. civilian and local national employees were assigned to the commissary at 31 August 1975.

Operations and Maintenance, Army, funds made available to the commissary during FY 1975 totaled about $776,000. The commissary's inventory of subsistence items at 30 June 1975 was valued at about $1.1 million.

Personnel costs at the Sagamihara Commissary can be reduced by changing annex operating hours and terminating some cashiers at the main store. Also, further personnel reductions are possible by refining the stockage of subsistence items.

Operating Costs. The Sagamihara Commissary, which operates a main store and two annexes, reported operating costs of about $776,000 during FY 1975, and about 90 percent of this amount represented personnel costs. In this respect, it is significant to note that in recent years annual pay increases for local national employees have substantially increased payroll costs. In 1972, 1973, and 1974, pay increases were 10.68, 15.39, and 29.64 percent, respectively. An increase of about 15 percent is expected in 1975.

Annex Operating Hours. The Sagamihara Commissary operates a main store and two annexes, which are located about three and eight miles from the main store, respectively. Monthly sales averaged about $230,000 at the main store, $47,000 at the Zama Annex, and $15,000 at the Sagami Annex. The two annexes operated six days (48 hours) a week. However, the main store was open for business only five days (40 hours) a week. We believed that it would not be necessary for the annexes to remain open for business longer than the main store. Reducing annex operating hours from 48 to 40 hours a week would eliminate an estimated $7,000 of overtime annually that is currently being paid to five employees.

Reductions in personnel costs could also be achieved by reducing the number of days of operation at each annex, possibly to three days a week, and staggering the days so that fewer employees could operate both annexes. Although this action would inconvenience employees who must work at two locations and could cause some other problems, we believe that management should pursue this area further as reductions of about $40,000 in personnel costs annually could be realized.

We were informed that the two annexes are needed because hazardous traffic conditions in Japan make it difficult for customers to get to the main store, and that the annexes are conveniently situated for personnel living in the surrounding areas. On the other hand, personnel living in Yokohama, which is located about twenty miles from the main store, and at Atsugi, about five miles from the main store, commute by automobile to the main store to do their shopping. Conversely, personnel billeted in the Camp Zama area frequently patronize the Navy commissary in Yokohama. Also, a number of personnel billeted in the Zama and Sagami areas, where the annexes are located, patronize the main store frequently. Therefore, morale and welfare versus cost considerations will be the deciding factors in determining the need for operating the annexes on their present schedule.

Cashier Positions. Nine cashiers were employed at the main store to operate a maximum of seven checkout counters as of 30 June 1975. One cashier checked customers' identification cards and approved checks for payment of purchases. Another was used as a relief cashier. We observed the main store's operation about once every hour during part of June and most of July 1975. On Saturdays and paydays, which were the busiest days, four to six checkout counters were generally in use, and about 75 percent of that time, only one to three customers were waiting to go through the checkout counters. On the other days of business, two to four checkout counters were generally in use, and only one or two customers were waiting in line about one-half of the time. The busy hours on most days were in the late afternoon. At other times, because of minimum workload, cashiers were often assisting floor workers in restocking shelves. On the basis of our observations, we believe that the number of checkout counters in use can be reduced and the services of some cashiers terminated without having an adverse impact on the main store's operation. Having a maximum of five checkout counters could result in the termination of at least two to three cashier positions at an annual savings of about $6,500 per cashier. Further reductions in the number of checkout counters in use and cashiers on board could be made, but it is probable that there would be a longer waiting line of customers. However, the waiting time probably would not exceed that of other nearby commissaries. At the Fort Buckner and Kadena Air Base commissaries in Okinawa, Japan, on paydays and on some Saturdays customers must wait in line to get into the stores. Further, there is a line of six to twelve customers, with waiting periods of about thirty minutes to go through a checkout counter.

Stockage Items. The Sagamihara Commissary stocked about 4,600 line items, including 900 perishable items, as of 30 June 1975. Nine percent of the line items reviewed did not meet the stockage-retention criteria. Moreover, compared with the number of line items stocked by other commissaries, the Sagamihara Commissary is probably stocking more brands of each item. The Fort Buckner Commissary in Okinawa, Japan, stocked about 3,300 line items and the Navy commissaries at Yokohama, Hokosuka, and Atsugi each stocked about 2,900 line items. A substantial reduction in the number of line items being stocked would reduce the amount of funds being tied up in inventories. Also, there would be a reduction in the workload of the commissary, which would result in a related personnel savings.

Commissary consumption records contained errors in both recorded balances and issue data; requirements objectives were not revised when warranted, and some items did not qualify for retention; and quantities of items force-issued or sold at reduced prices were not excluded from requirements computations. Also, items were displayed on store shelves in larger quantities than necessary, and some items were not displayed.

The Commissary Consumption Record is the basic record used to manage commissary stocks. This record is adjusted by the results of monthly physical inventories, and shows the balance on hand, receipts, dues-in, and consumption of an item. Its stockage position should be compared with the requisitioning objective (RO)* to determine whether stock replenishment is necessary. As of 30 June 1975, the commissary stocked about 3,700 nonperishable line items and about 900 perishable line items valued at about $1.1 million.

Monthly Inventories. Consumption records could not be used effectively to manage commissary stocks because monthly inventory counts of stocks on hand often were not accurate. Erroneous inventory counts also caused consumption data to be inaccurate. A review of fifty consumption records cards showed that thirty-one contained one or more errors in recorded balances during the twelve-month period ended 15 May 1975. These errors were obvious because the ending inventory quantities were greater than the sum of the beginning inventory quantities and any quantities received during the month. Some examples follow:

| | | | | Unit Price |
Examples	Beginning Inventory	Receipts	Ending Inventory	Month of Inventory
Rug Cleaner	84	0	252	Mar 75
Rice-A-Roni	192	0	336	Apr 75
Fish, Flounder	0	96	228	Apr 75

Erroneous inventory counts caused both recorded balances and consumption data to be in error and resulted in the ordering of either excessive or insufficient quantities of replenishment stocks.

The problems with the inventory could have been lessened considerably had a stock locator system been established at the two warehouses used for storing commissary stocks. Our review showed that inventory personnel would not always position the inventory count cards with the applicable items, prior to the taking of the monthly inventories, because of difficulty in locating the items. In these instances, the count cards were annotated to show that no stocks were on hand. However, we were told by inventory managers that their review of consumption records cards frequently showed that stocks were on hand for these zero-balance count cards and that the items were located after warehouse personnel had been directed to make a search of the warehouse.

We also found that requests for commissary items were being denied although stocks were on hand. For example, on 21 and 23 July 1975, requests for issues were forwarded from the commissary store annexes to the warehouse activity. Of about 180 items requested, 40 were annotated as being not on hand by warehouse personnel because the items could not be located. We selected 25 of

*The RO, computed on the basis on consumption data, represents the greatest quantity of subsistence items authorized to be on hand and on order at any one time.

these items, searched the warehouse on 24 July 1975, and found stocks for 8 of the items. We were also told that difficulties were experienced in specifically identifying items for inventory because the descriptions shown on the inventory count cards were too brief and, in other cases, there were no stock numbers on the containers of some items. A stock locator system could greatly facilitate locating and identifying items in the warehouses. Technical Manual 743–200 contains instructions for establishing and maintaining such a system.

As an additional control over physical inventory procedures, inventory managers should watch for indications of erratic consumption and require that recounts be made to verify the reported inventory counts. A significant increase or decrease in consumption, when compared to the prior month's consumption, indicates that an erroneous inventory count may have been made of the item. To illustrate, the consumption of Rice-A-Roni in March 1975 was recorded as 312 on the basis of an inventory count of 192. The prior month's consumption of this item was only 48. The monthly inventory taken of this item in April 1975 showed that the consumption and inventory amounts recorded in March 1975 were both in error.

Requirements Review. RO's were not reviewed monthly and revised as necessary, although required by established procedures. We were told that because of the effort devoted to the phase-in of the Direct Commissary Subsistence Support System and a locally developed automated commissary system, manual reviews and revisions of RO's by the inventory managers were limited mainly to fast-moving items. Also, the RO was normally revised only when the newly computed requirement differed from the existing RO by more than 10 percent. We reviewed the consumption record cards of 25 perishable and nonperishable items that had frequent consumption activity and computed the RO's as of 15 May 1975. The commissary's established RO for perishable items was two and a half months of supply; and for nonperishable items, five and a half months of supply. For 15 of the 25 items reviewed, RO's recorded on consumption records at 15 May 1975 exceeded actual requirements by more than 10 percent. The difference ranged between 19 and 82 percent. The recorded RO's of eight items had not been updated since March 1973. Consequently, quantities in excess of requirements had been requisitioned, as shown by the following examples.

Item	On Hand and On Order	Auditor's Computed RO	Excess Quanity	Months Of Supply
Rug Cleaner	384	204	180	4.8
Fruit Cocktail	1,848	1,298	550	2.3
Seasoning, Bon Appetit	576	50	526	58.0

Cancellation action could not be initiated for the excess quantities on order since they either had been received or were in transit at the time we completed our review. To avoid unnecessary procurement of commissary stocks, RO's should be reviewed at prescribed intervals and revised when warranted.

Included in the estimated 3,700 nonperishable line items stocked by the commissary were items that did not meet the stockage retention criteria prescribed in AR 31–200. Our review of 400 line items showed that 36 items, or 9 percent, did not qualify for retention. Also, items that no longer qualified for retention were sometimes identified by the commissary officer during his spot checks of the consumption records rather than by the inventory managers who should have been performing recurring reviews for this purpose.

Abnormal Consumption. Slow-moving items and items subject to spoilage not consumed within a short time were usually force-issued to supported activities, or sold at reduced prices. These types of transactions totaled about $7,700 between January and May 1975. Although identified on commissary documents, these transactions were not identified separately from normal sales transactions on the consumption records. Since RO's were computed on the basis of consumption data, the inclusion of abnormal consumption quantities in the RO computations causes them to be overstated and could result in unnecessary procurement.

Store Shelves. We were told that about 7 days of supply should normally be stocked on the commissary store shelves. The shelf stocks should be kept to a limited quantity because of space considerations and because these stocks are not considered when determining the commissary's monthly replenishment requirements. Our review of 21 items showed that 18 were stocked on the shelves in quantities excess to normal requirements. The excesses ranged between 12 and 212 days of supply; seven items had more than 50 days of supply on the shelves. Because replenishment quantities were based on stocks on hand only in the warehouse, placing more quantities than needed on the shelves resulted in unnecessary replenishments. For example, seven cases of grape perserves, about 60 days of supply, were stocked on the shelves as of 11 June 1975. Because the commissary's established requirement for this item was about 16 cases and 11 cases were on hand in the warehouse, 5 additional cases were requisitioned. In addition, we traced about 150 items in the commissary's warehouse to the shelves in the store. Ten items were not displayed on the shelves and therefore were not available for purchase by commissary patrons.

Selling prices of processed meat items were adjusted only once a month although biweekly trial balances of meat market operations and meat cutting tests during the month indicated the need for more frequent changes. As a result, accumulated monetary gains exceeded allowable limits. In addition, unidentifiable gains and losses disclosed by the trial balance were not investigated to determine and correct the underlying causes.

Policies and procedures for processing, pricing, and accounting for meat products sold in commissary meat markets are set forth in AR 31–200. The basic policy is that sales prices of meat products will be set at prices that result in recovering their costs. Prepackaged meat items should be priced on the basis of costs. However, salable meat cut from carcasses should be priced based on pricing charts or cutting tests that take fat and bone waste into consideration. The meat should be priced so that the sales proceeds will equal the cost of the carcass. The regulation authorizes commissaries a gain or loss tolerance of 1 percent of the total sales of the meat market for the period between the quarterly accountability inventories. When this tolerance factor is exceeded, management is required to make a review to determine the reasons, and take appropriate corrective action. To further control sales prices of meat and minimize gains or losses, accountability studies (trial balance) should be prepared at least twice a month to determine the extent of cumulative gains or losses for possible adjustment of current selling prices.

Price Adjustments. Trial balances were prepared every two weeks to determine the results of meat market operations and the extent of gains and losses. The trial balances prepared during the six-month period ended 16 July 1975 showed that cumulative gains frequently exceeded the prescribed tolerance limit and cumulative gains as much as 7 percent had been reported. These gains or losses, when they occur, should be passed on to commissary patrons either by decreasing selling prices when gains are realized, or increasing prices when losses occur. Although the biweekly trial balances showed that the cumulative gains frequently exceeded the allowable limit, the commissary's practice was to adjust selling prices only once a month. However, the adjustments were not sufficient, as illustrated by the trial balance, which reported gains of 2.6 percent and 1.6 percent for the quarters ending in March and June 1975, respectively. Since the trial balances were prepared every two weeks and showed the extent of gains or losses, management should adjust selling prices promptly rather than waiting until month end.

In addition to the reported gains or losses, commissary personnel relied on cutting tests of carcasses to determine selling prices of processed meat items. Four shipments of carcasses, each averaging about 16,000 pounds, were generally received each month. Although cutting tests were made of carcasses from each individual shipment, selling prices were adjusted only monthly on the basis of the results of the cutting tests obtained from the last shipment. The results of cutting tests made of other shipments of carcasses were not considered for price adjustments. Depending on the weight, grade, and extent of waste, the amount of salable meat obtained from a carcass varies. Our review showed that the amount of salable meat obtained from a carcass varied by as much as 9 percent from that obtained from a carcass received earlier the same month.

Since selling prices were established based on the cutting test results of one shipment, differences in the amount of salable meat obtained from carcasses in other shipments were partly responsible for the excessive gains reported on the trial balances. For example, the trial balance prepared for the period between 22 May and 25 June 1975 showed a gain of $5,300 from the meat market operation. Our analysis showed that, on the basis of cutting tests, the gain of $5,300 was attributable partly to differences in the amount of salable meat obtained from carcasses. Therefore, prices should not be established only on the basis of the cutting tests of carcasses from one shipment on a once-a-month basis. Instead, results of the cutting tests obtained from each shipment and the reported gains or losses on the biweekly trial balances should be analyzed together to determine when and to what extent price adjustments are necessary. Reestablishing prices more often also tends to minimize large month-to-month fluctuations in selling prices. The use of more cutting tests to determine price adjustments should also reduce the amount of unidentifiable gains or losses reported on trial balances.

Only three operational reports were prepared of the two annexes' operations during a one-year period, although the reports were required monthly to determine the extent of gains or losses. In addition, stockage at the two annexes included items that were not required for daily customer needs, and one annex experienced high rates of deterioration of produce.

The commissary operates two annexes, with monthly sales averaging $47,000 at the Zama Annex and $15,000 at the Sagami Annex. AR 31–200 requires the commissary to maintain a record of receipts, sales, and inventories pertaining to annex operations. This data should be summarized monthly by preparing a trial balance to determine the dollar value of transactions and the extent of unidentifiable gains or losses. Because operational data at both annexes is accounted for as part of the overall commissary store operation, weaknesses that may exist at the annexes can be hidden unless closely monitored by means of monthly trial balances.

Trial Balance. Grocery markets in overseas commissary stores are authorized a loss allowance of 1 percent of the grocery market sales, the meat market is authorized a net gain or loss tolerance of 1 percent, and the produce market is authorized a net gain or loss tolerance of 1.5 percent. Only three trial balances of annex operations were prepared during the twelve-month period ended 11 June 1975, although they were required monthly. When prepared, the trial balances showed that both annexes had realized operational gains and losses that exceeded the allowable limits permitted for commissary sales departments by AR 31–200. For example, the trial balance prepared as of 11 June 1975 for the Sagami Annex showed losses of $1,092, or 1.6 percent of grocery market sales; losses of $138, or 1.9 percent of meat market sales; and losses of $306, or 14.3 percent of produce market sales. Although the three trial balances showed that both gains and losses were incurred by the two annexes, reviews had not been initiated by management to determine the underlying causes so that remedial action could be taken.

Stockage Items. The trial balances of annex operations were not prepared monthly because an inventory of the stocks on hand, which was required as part of the data needed for the trial balances, was not always taken. We were told that the inventory could require as much as a full working day at each annex. Both annexes stocked about 1,300 line items of meat, produce, and grocery items. Items such as metal and furniture polish, window cleaners, and many other household and kitchen items, were also stocked. We believe that the annexes should stock primarily essential items, such as milk, eggs, and bread, and some meat and vegetable items that are required daily by most patrons.

Produce Items. An average of 20 percent of all produce items received at the Sagami Annex was subsequently returned to the main store during the six-month period ended 30 June 1975. On several occasions, we observed lettuce and cabbage on displays at the annex that did not appear to be in a salable condition. Moreover, the chief of the produce market at the main store stated that most of the items returned were not salable and were usually condemned by veterinary personnel. To minimize losses of produce items, quantities stocked at this annex should be reduced and potentially unsalable items returned promptly to the main store before they reach advanced stages of deterioration.

Chapter 5

Department of Commerce

A government that robs Peter to pay Paul can depend on the support of Paul.
—George Bernard Shaw (1900)

I was employed by the Office of Audit, Department of Commerce in Atlanta, Georgia, for two years 1977–1978. Though I was generally located in Dixie, the same funny story was told throughout the land. My work was spent on four different areas: 1) Economic Development Administration (EDA) audits, 2) Office of Minority Business Enterprise (OMBE) audits, 3) internal audits; and, 4) personal business.

The EDA is a large organization within the Department of Commerce. It provides grants of your money to local governments, businessmen, and associations to promote economic growth (at least that's the visuals). In reality it's a way for Disorganized Crime to spread around your money so that it can steal some more of your money. Sort of like Robin Hood in reverse. The EDA audits that I will discuss were just two of thousands of EDA grants worth billions of dollars issued between 1976–1978 under a special program called the Local Public Works (LPW) program. The two grantees were Hobson City, Alabama, and Mound Bayou, Mississippi.

Hobson City, Alabama (with a population below a thousand people), received an EDA grant of $757,900 and started spending this treasure on April 25, 1977. The money was to provide financial assistance for the construction of a municipal complex. Needless to say, it was the most money the Mayor (the local Baptist preacher) had ever received. Because of several newspaper articles about the lack of progress made on this project, an interim audit effort was performed and an audit report was issued on September 13, 1977. What is interesting is that no final audit was performed on this Hobson City grant for the next five years.

Of the $126,347 spent by August 29, 1977, over $41,000 (32 percent) was either questioned or qualified by the auditors. For example, fee of over $4,700 for project coordination were questioned. The City Planner was paid $4.81 an hour from project funds from April 25 to June 3, 1977. He resigned from his position with Hobson City on June 1, 1977. That same date Hobson City entered into a $24,000 agreement with his "consulting firm" to provide coordination services over a fifteen-month period at $20 an hour! The Mayor told us he wanted someone he could rely on to stay on top of the project; that the former City Planner was the logical choice as he had been involved with the project from the beginning. Amounts billed to the project were based on the number of hours worked; however, the Project Coordinator did not keep time records and the invoices were his estimates of work performed. We also found out that $144,000 had been withdrawn from the bank, even though the project books reported that only $126,000 had been spent. To summarize the situation:

Hobson City, Alabama, Status of Funds

Total authorized costs per grant budget	$757,900
Project Costs (per Hobson City)	$126,347
Less: Questioned & Qualified Costs	41,397
Project Costs net of Questioned & Qualified Costs	84,950
Less: Cash Drawdowns on Letter of Credit	144,000
Project Balance at August 29, 1977	($ 59,050)

Not bad, over $59,000 in the hole, and the project was only four months old. Just one final note: the newspapers were correct, no construction had taken place; however, the land where the new municipal center was to be located had been cleared of bottles and litter. Within the next few years, the Mayor was indicted on several counts of CETA (a Department of Labor program) fraud.

A final audit was at least prepared for Mound Bayou, Mississippi. Like Hobson City, Alabama, Mound Bayou has a population that could fit into a chartered 747. And as you read on, that's just what might have happened to the $4,834,900 that EDA granted on December 23, 1976. I left the Department of Commerce before the final audit report was issued in June 1983, seven years after the grant was awarded. The grant was to provide financial assistance for the construction of a municipal complex, maintenance area, street improvements, and a water tank.

Of the $4,835,014 spent by August 5, 1982, over $3,987,152 (82 percent) was either questioned or unresolved by the auditors. For example, $3,431,703 of construction and project improvement costs were unresolved because:

1. No "as-built" drawings for the street improvements work performed were furnished. Those drawings could have provided detailed descriptive and graphic information on the type, location, and extent of individual work elements performed, and would constitute the bsaic documentation addressing the other audit reasons that these costs went unresolved.

2. The engineering firm reduced the "total contract work completed" amount on the contractor's final payment request by $152,809, from $3,284,953 to $3,132,144, which would have been within the total contracted amount of $3,145,139. The contractor disputed the reduction and has taken legal action against the City of Mound Bayou for nonpayment for work performed. Although engineering firms provided the basics for its computations of the various work elements performed, the grantee could not furnish conclusive documentation to

verify either the A/E firm's or the contractor's computations of allowable contract charges.

3. For some work elements, the work performed by the contractor departed considerably from that scheduled according to the contract awarded, as evidenced by our following schedule taken from the engineering firm's cost computations:

Element	Scheduled	Performed	Difference
Allowance for Obstructions	$ 75,000	$ 101,543	$ 26,543
Inlets, Structures, and Manholes	159,071	184,706	25,635
Concrete Streets	852,029	784,299	(67,730)
Sidewalks	113,620	51,482	(62,138)
Concrete Ditch	39,200	2,075	(37,125)
Concrete Curbs and Gutters	39,249	21,560	(17,689)
Concreted Overlay	127,540	-0-	(127,540)
Piping	446,973	435,203	(11,770)
Pumping Stations	275,740	273,000	(2,740)
Other Elements	215,265	226,971	(11,706)
Total Original Contract	$2,343,687	$2,080,839	$ (262,848)
Change Order No. 2	677,707	516,416	(161,291)
Change Order No. 3	(8,727)	79,945	88,672
Additive Alternative	-0-	322,472	322,472
Other Change Orders	132,472	132,472	-0-
Total Amended Contract	$3,145,139	$3,132,144	$ (12,995)

We found no evidence in the grantee's files to document the reasons for these differences.

4. The grantee used a substantial bid underrun and the basic contract underrun detailed above to finance additional work not specifically approved by EDA. In the grantee's grant application package to EDA, the engineering firm estimated the total construction costs of the street improvements portion of the project to be $3,480,930 plus an additive alternate of $208,758, yielding total contracted costs for street improvements of $2,676,688. The grantee used the resulting difference of $804,297, plus the basic contract underrun of $262,848 computed above, a total of $1,067,145, to finance the additional work identified below and performed on the contract. A major factor influencing the $804,297 bid underrun was that the scheduled values of the paving work element in the contract awarded to the contractor were only $156,115 and $852,029, respectively, or $228,481 less than the engineering firm's estimated paving costs of $1,236,625. This difference apparently primarily resulted from an overstatement of the width of streets within Mound Bayou, which are narrower than the thirty-two feet indicated.

99

Change Order No. 1	$ 59,894
Change Order No. 2	516,416
Change Order No. 3	79,945
Additive Alternate	322,472
Change Order No. 4	72,578
Total Additional Work	$1,051,305

We found that the grantee's files (1) contained only a copy of the engineering firm's bid recap summary but not copies of bid specifications released to interested contractors nor of subsequent bids received; (2) contained only a copy of Change Order Number 1, which was not signed by either a grantee or EDA representative; and (3) did not indicate that any of the change orders or the additional additive alternates were submitted to EDA for approval of the expanded scope of work to be performed. We noted from the engineering firm's description of the additional work that $226,170 from Change Order Number 2 and the entire $322,472 from the additive alternate related to work performed in the eastern portion of Mound Bayou, an area that EDA had specifically excluded from the project by approving the grantee's LPW grant application for work to be done in the western portion of the city, and disapproving the LPW application for work to be done in the eastern portion. We further noted from the engineering firm's description that the $59,894 from Change Order Number 1 was not itemized by the locations of the work performed, the $79,945 from Change Order Number 3 appeared to be related to maintenance and repair work, specifically unallowable under the LPW program, and the remaining $322,824 related to additional work performed for which we are uncertain from its description if EDA would have included it within its approved project scope.

5. Based on our physical verification of work performed, we could not determine if all street improvements work contracted to the contractor was performed as approved by EDA or as charged by the contractor, according to the engineering firm's computation of acceptable charges, as detailed below.

a. EDA approved the construction of two concrete-lined storm water pumping stations, estimated to cost $60,000 each, to be located off Maginnis Street near the Delta Health Center and off West Main Street near Jerome Street. The grantee paid the contractor $273,000 for the two stations, and paid another contractor $36,300 on a separate contract for related work; however, the West Main Street station was not constructed at the designated site and we were unable to determine its alternate locations. Since the station was designated as a major component of the storm water drainage system, we are uncertain if the drainage piping leading to that station was laid as approved by EDA and charged by the contractor.

b. EDA approved the construction of a 4,400 linear-foot concrete storm water drainage channel, estimated to cost $209,220, between South Street and the stream named Mound Bayou. The channel was to pass under Maginnis Street through a double-barrel box culvert, estimated to cost $27,152. The portion of the channel between South Street and Maginnis Street was not constructed, which negated the need for the culvert; we did not locate the point at which the channel enters the stream of Mound Bayou; and only a minor portion of the channel was concreted. The grantee paid the contractor only $2,075 for channel construction; however, since the channel was designed as a major component of the storm water drainage system, we are again uncertain if the drainage piping leading to the channel was laid as approved by EDA and charged by the contractor.

c. The contract with the contractor included a concrete overlay on Maginnis Street to cost $127,540, or about 10 percent of the total estimated paving costs of $1,236,625 approved by EDA. This construction was not performed or charged; however, the grantee did pay the contractor $15,889 on Change Order Number 3 for work charged to Maginnis Street.

d. We were unable to verify the extent of street paving performed nor of the construction of sidewalks, curbing, and guttering, total contract charges of $857,341, because a portion of the total work of that type done within Mound Bayou was funded through earlier grants from the U.S. Department of Housing and Urban Development (HUD). The grantee was unable to furnish information; e.g., "as-built" drawings, identifying the exact scopes by individual streets of street improvements accomplished under either the LPW project or the earlier HUD projects. In other words, Disorganized Crime may have paid for the same work twice.

e. We noted apparent problems in the quality of street paving in that the concrete in some locations was breaking up or retaining storm water for extended periods, and that our measurements in various of those locations revealed that the concrete ranged from 1 1/2 to 4 inches deep instead of the required 6 inches. Although we are uncertain what paving was done under which of the grants referenced in d. above, we did note that these problems typically occurred along Davis Street, Lampton Street, and other locations not originally designed to be included within the LPW project.

g. The grantee paid the contractor a total of $236,853 for the paving of nine streets that apparently do not exist within Mount Bayou; however, we verified the existence of paving on seventeen streets that was not charged. We do not know if these discrepancies resulted from improper contract charges, confusion on street names, or paving laid before the LPW project.

In spite of the fact that there are specific EDA projects with problems, the total EDA/LPW program cost in the billions, no overall internal audits were performed on the program. Perhaps some visuals are better left unfound.

The Office of Minority Business Enterprise is another major unit within the Department of Commerce that also doled out your money to groups in order to steal more of your money. The visuals for OMBE were different than EDA. EDA was to pass out your money as grants, while OMBE was to pass out your money as contracts.

We performed an audit of costs claimed on Contract Number 5–36582 with Southern Rural Action, Inc. (SRA), Atlanta, Georgia. On June 30, 1975, the

U.S. Department of Commerce, in furtherance of the Office of Minority Business Enterprise (OMBE) program, entered into Contract Number 5–36582 with SRA. SRA was to perform the scope of work for an Experiment and Demonstration Program to meet certain specific needs of minority businesses engaged in the manufacturing of products for the commercial market in the Southeast region. The contract provided for reimbursement of costs incurred in an estimated amount not to exceed $193,036. The period of contract performance was from June 30, 1975, to June 30, 1976.

We performed a final audit of costs incurred under this contract in order to determine whether (i) financial operations were properly conducted and in compliance with contract provisions and OMBE instructions, and (ii) the costs incurred from July 1, 1975, to June 30, 1976, were allowable. As reported in our previous audit report number SE-179–303–76–065, dated August 27, 1976, we (1) found that the accounting system and internal controls in effect during the contract period were inadequate to safeguard the assets, check the accuracy and reliability of accounting data, promote operating efficiency and encourage adherence to prescribed management policies and OMBE requirements, (2) believed that SRA had not complied with five of the contract terms and provisions, and (3) questioned costs of $160,000 primarily because of (i) noncompliance with contract terms, (ii) inadequate documentation, and (iii) no basis for the amount charged.

In addition, on February 9, 1977, we issued supplemental report number SE-194–303–77–015. This report stated that we attempted to determine the amount of accrued salaries paid and to analyze the interfund accounts. Our review disclosed that about $7,100 had been paid, but we were unable to determine if the payments were for accrued salaries or salaries earned subsequent to the contract period. The books and records for the contract had not changed since our final audit, and the books and records of SRA were not available. Because of this, we were unable to analyze the interfund accounts.

SRA located documentation, reconstructed some records, and submitted an informal claim for costs incurred of $163,460. Consequently, we performed an audit of these claimed costs to ascertain whether they were allowable under Contract Number 5–36582.

SRA's claim was predicted upon revised earnings statements, affidavits for salary payments from employees, travel vouchers, invoices, bills, and canceled checks from various bank accounts. The official books of original entry for the contract showed no changes since the time of our previous audit. The conditions relative to time and attendance and labor distribution records remained the same. These items were not considered in preparation of the claim.

The books available for our review were:

	Books and Periods Covered			
Program/Bank	General Ledger	General Journal	Cash Receipts	Cash Disbursements
CETA—Fulton National	12–31–75	12–31–75	2–7–75 to 12–31–75	9–1–75 to 1–26–76
SRA—Trust Company	7–31–75 to 6–30–76	—	7–14–75 to 6–30–76	7–1–75 to 4–19–76
OMBE—Citizens & Trust	7–31–75 to 6–30–76	9–30–75 to 6–30–76	7–3–75 to 4–30–76	7–28–75 to 4–28–76
SRA—Citizens & Trust	7–31–75 to 6–30–76	—	7–7–75 to 6–2–76	1–2–75 to 6–30–76

Other records available consisted of time cards, sign in/sign out sheets, check stubs, bank statements, and canceled checks.

The results of our audit are summarized below and detailed later:

Costs Claimed	$163,460 (1)
Add: Net Adjustments to Claim	698 (2)
Less: Costs Questioned	154,342 (3)
Costs Accepted	$ 9,816

(1) Costs claimed are the contractor's representations, based upon revised earnings statements, affidavits from employees, travel vouchers, invoices, statements or bills, and canceled checks.

(2) Various adjustments were required to reconcile the costs claimed with the supporting details.

(3) Costs questioned consisted primarily of personnel, fringe benefits, and printing and publication costs.

Southern Rural Action, Inc.
Summary of Costs Claimed and Audit Recommendations
June 30, 1975, to June 30, 1976

Description	Budget	Costs Claimed (1)	Adjusted Costs Claimed (2)	Audit Recommendations Costs Accepted	Costs Questioned	Reference Notes
Personnel	$141,475	$114,164	$114,164	$ —	$114,164	3
Fringe Benefits	17,521	9,865	9,865	—	9,865	4
Consultants and Contract Services	3,000	500	500	—	500	5
Local Travel	1,200	3,807	2,213	—	2,213	6
Out-of-Town Travel	14,600	included in local	included in local	—	—	
Facility Costs	3,600	3,318	3,318	517	2,801	7
Other Direct Costs	11,640					
Consumable Supplies		2,245	2,245	—	2,245	8
Postage		642	623	—	623	9
Printing and Publications		11,435	10,081	—	10,081	10
Telephone		6,821	11,182	3,138	8,044	11
Utilities		5,006	4,429	2,174	2,255	12
Workshops and Conferences		5,657	5,538	3,987	1,551	13
Total	$193,036	$163,460	$164,158	$9,816	$154,343	

Reference Notes:
1. The amounts shown as costs claimed for the contract period are the contractor's representations, based upon reconstructed earnings statements, affidavits from employees on the amount of salary paid, travel vouchers, invoices, statements, or bills and canceled checks.
2. Adjustments were made as needed to reconcile the costs claimed with the supporting details.
3. In total, personnel costs claimed were $22,229 less than the amount recorded in the general ledger and reported as cost incurred in our prior audit report. Because of the variances in the salary amounts claimed, recorded, reconstructed and indicated in our review, it was not possible for us to express an opinion on the amount of personnel costs allowable. The variances noted on the personnel cost and the salary payments for one employee are illustrated in the following paragraphs.

104

Employee A was approved for employment, effective August 1, 1975, at an annual salary rate of $12,000. According to the budget, 100 percent of the salary was chargeable to the contract. The maximum salary chargeable to the contract for Employee A was about $11,000.

In February 1977, Employee A signed an affidavit that he worked under the contract for the period August 1, 1975, to June 30, 1976. The affidavit is annotated with the amount of salary, $12,000, and states that all back salaries under the contract have been paid in full.

Informal records of SRA dated July 22, 1975, and August 5, 1975, showed that Employee A was owed net salary payments totalling about $1,957 and $1,722, respectively. These records were not available for the entire contract period, and they did not show the amount of gross salary.

The original earnings statement for Employee A showed a gross salary of $9,254. During the final audit of costs incurred, we reviewed records that showed that the gross salary for Employee A for the contract period was $12,688. This amount included accrued salary of $2,884.

After the audit report was issued, SRA personnel reviewed checks issued, identified certain checks as salary payments, and calculated a gross salary for a period. The net amount of each check and the calculated gross amounts were posted to an earnings statement. Generally, the canceled checks were filed with the earnings statements.

The reconstructed earnings statement for Employee A showed a gross salary of $12,409. We attempted to reconcile the total on the reconstructed earnings statement to the amount shown in the audit report. Primarily because of the mix of net and gross amounts, we were unable to do so.

Since the contract period corresponded with four quarters of payroll tax returns, we attempted to verify the personnel cost claimed by reviewing payroll tax returns and Forms W-2. The Forms 941 for the calendar year 1976 showed $8,755. The Form W-2 for calendar year 1976 showed $9,255. We could not determine which amount was correct and, acordingly, could not determine if the salary for Employee A during the contract period of $9,605, according to the Forms 941, was correct.

We reviewed records which indicated that checks totalling $7,672 were made payable to Employee A during the period August 1, 1975, to June 30, 1976. Checks totalling $8,718 were made payable to Employee A during the period of July 1, 1975, to June 30, 1976. These checks represent payments for all purposes. Because of the conditions of the records, we are not assured that our review identified all of the checks payable to Employee A.

4. All fringe-benefit costs of $9,865 are questioned because they are associated with the salary costs questioned in note 3. The fringe-benefit costs claimed are comprised of $5,136 for FICA, $1,542 for unemployment compensation, $473 for workmen's compensation, and $2,714 for health insurance. In several cases there were errors in the base or in the period used in the computations. In addition, it was not possible to determine all of the actual amounts paid. An overall percentage rate should not be applied, if the salary

costs are resolved; items of cost should be calculated on an individual basis.

5. *Consultant and Contract Services*—We have questioned $500 in consultant and contract services cost. There was no documentation to support the cost other than canceled checks. In addition, one payment of $200 was made three months after the contract expired. We could not determine the nature of the service provided or if any approvals were required. We were advised that the services were accounting and related to the audit.

6. *Travel cost*—We have questioned $2,213 of travel cost. These travel costs are related to contractor employees whose salary costs are questioned. If the related salary costs were accepted, $765 of travel cost would be accepted. The remaining $1,448 of travel cost would be questioned because there were either no travel vouchers, no supporting documentation for the travel, or no approval for travel outside the geographic scope of the contract. Two checks were payable to an employee who was not funded under the contract.

7. *Facility cost*—We have questioned $2,801 in facility cost. The amount $2,658 of cost questioned is for payments that were labeled equipment and furniture by the contractor. There were no invoices to support $2,585 of these payments. We could not determine if the remaining $73 was allowable to the contract. In addition, the negotiation memorandum for the contract indicates that all furniture and equipment would be provided by the contractor at no cost to the government.

The contractor has claimed space cost based on the square footage of space utilized by employees funded under the contract. However, the contractor excluded the square footage in certain common areas from his calculations. We recalculated the percentage of space allocable (47 percent) to the contract and, accordingly, have questioned $143 of the space cost claimed.

8. *Consumable Supplies*—We have questioned $2,245 of consumable supplies because we could not determine that the supplies were allocable to the contract.

9. *Postage*—We have questioned $623 of postage cost because we could not determine that the costs were allocable to the contract. In addition, $237 of this cost was represented by checks payable to individuals or organizations, and we could not determine the purpose of these payments.

10. *Printing and Publications*—We have questioned $10,081 of printing and publication costs because we could not determine the method the contractor used to arrive at the cost. There was insufficient documentation to support the charges and some costs appear to be estimates rather than actual cost. For example, the contractor claimed printing cost of $945 for a report on a meeting of minority manufacturers. Invoices for paper totaled $512. The remaining cost was an estimate of labor costs.

11. *Telephone*—We have questioned $8,044 of telephone cost because of missing invoices and a difference in the method of determining the amount allocable to the contract. Based upon the number of telephones, the contractor claimed that 61 percent of the total telephone costs were allocable to the contract. We accepted 61 percent of the telephone base costs for which there were

106

telephone bills plus all long-distance calls which the contractor indicated were for the OMBE program.

12. *Utilities*—The contractor claimed utility costs by applying the percentage used for space costs (refer to Note 7 of this exhibit) to the bills for utilities. One adjustment was required to reconcile the base costs to the supporting details. We questioned $2,757 of $7,382, adjusted base costs, because (i) bills were missing, (ii) the period to which the payment applied was not determinable, or (iii) a payment was for a period prior to the contract. We accepted 47 percent of the $4,625 and questioned $2,255.

13. *Workshops and Conferences*—We have questioned $1,551 of cost for workshops and conferences because there was no documentation, such as invoices, to support the payments.

What is of interest concerning the SRA audit was what happened to its leader, Reverend Ralph Blackwell. Remember only 22 percent ($42,852 out of $193,036 awarded) of his (SRA's) costs were accepted on his OMBE contract. After Jimmy Carter was elected president, the Reverend was put in charge of the total OMBE program!

The overall OMBE program was given a Vulnerability Assessment by the Department of Commerce Inspector General in September 1982. Nothing had changed over the five years since I had audited OMBE contracts. The Vulnerability Assessment is structured around what we view as the four basic management processes in MBDA. These are (I) Planning and Direction; (II) Award and Implementation; (III) Monitoring and Administration; and (IV) Evaluation and Assessment. Highlights of our findings follow.

PLANNING AND DIRECTION

**A.   Failure to Effectively Communicate or
Implement MBDA Policies and Objectives**

MBDA programs and activities have had major problems because stated Agency policies and objectives have not been effectively communicated or implemented. Frequently, when this occurred, MBDA has had no assurances that its funds were spent in accordance with its overall mission and current objectives.

This lack of communication and policy enforcement has been widespread and its adverse consequences can be illustrated by MBDA's:

1. Failure to ensure that its funded organizations complied with revised program policy.
2. Failure to effectively implement the policy on monitoring recipient performance.
3. Failure to implement the competitive awards policy on a timely and uniform basis.

B. **Questionable Year-End Spending**
Large Year-End Carryovers

MBDA's program funds are "no-year" appropriations and, as such, any year-end surpluses can be carried forward, reprogrammed, and used in subsequent fiscal years. This authority, however, has resulted in two troubling situations at opposite extremes. First, we have found a noticeable increase in the number of questionable projects hastily awarded at the end of the fiscal year. We attribute this problem, in part, to poor planning by MBDA officials and an attempt to literally get rid of the money. Obviously, projects awarded under such circumstances are more vulnerable to fraud, waste, and abuse. Conversely, MBDA has carried-over proportionately large sums of monies that it has not spent during the periods for which the funds were originally appropriated. This has been a continuing problem and, according to early projections, this fiscal year's carryover into fiscal year 1983 may reach alarming proportions in excess of $25 million dollars. We again attribute this situation to poor planning and see it as an embarrassment to the Department and a disservice to the minority business community.

C. **Ineffectiveness of Travel**

During the past few years, MBDA, like most agencies, has been called upon to reduce its travel expenditures. In complying with these travel reductions, however, MBDA, in our opinion, has not planned and directed its available travel funds in the areas that would offer the greatest return on its primary investments—i.e., monitoring its funded projects. In this respect, we have found that although approximately $1.8 million has been spent on travel during the last three fiscal years, many project officers have failed to travel to some of MBDA's largest and most significant projects to oversee and monitor recipient operations and accomplishments— purportedly because of a lack of travel funds. This situation has occurred while other MBDA personnel have attended conferences, meetings, and pursued travel of a seemingly less crucial nature.

D. **Lack of Corrective Action on**
Reported Deficiencies and Weaknesses

Some programs, projects, and activities needlessly remain vulnerable to waste and abuse because MBDA officials have failed to implement management recommendations made by the MBDA staff, OIG, and GAO, or take prompt corrective actions on known weaknesses and deficiencies. Examples of this include: (1) the lack of action on recommendations involving the recovery of significant amounts of money due MBDA by contractors and grantees; (2) MBDA's slowness in deobligating unliquidated obligations, and (3) the failure of MBDA to correct major shortcomings in its grant award and administrative procedures and practices.

108

AWARD AND IMPLEMENTATION

A. Problem Program Recipients

The ultimate success of MBDA depends largely upon the effectiveness of its grantees and contractors. Services to minority businesses have suffered because "problem" contractors and grantees repeatedly have been refunded although their prior performance records were less than satisfactory. Compounding this situation is the fact that MBDA has frequently ignored problems identified in the high percentage of OIG investigative actions required on MBDA-funded organizations and in serious audit findings about these organizations.

In addition, MBDA has yet to adequately address the OIG management report on *patterns* of significant and recurring deficiencies with recipients, which: (1) indicated major weaknesses in project award practices, (2) revealed major flaws to project oversight, and (3) jeopardized the financial integrity and programmatic accomplishments of MBDA programs.

B. Wasteful Project Modifications and Extensions

The frequent use of modifications and extensions in project agreements has been wasteful and raises questions about MBDA's ability to effectively administer its programs. Modifications and extensions have been used excessively to overcome planning and administration deficiencies. In addition, many of the extensions and modifications granted have often permitted recipients to merely deplete unspent monies remaining at the end of the original performances period since they were granted with few, if any, additional work or program requirements.

C. Sole Source Awards

There is a widespread perception that many of the projects awarded are politically motivated or awarded to close or former associates of some MBDA officials, In this regard, it must be noted that until recently, the majority of projects were awarded sole source, which made it easier to target who received awards. MBDA personnel have acknowledged that justifications for many sole source awards were sometimes very shallow, unsupported, or not even prepared. To the extent that projects are awarded for reasons other than the best qualified at a fair price, government funds may be wasted and there exists a distinct likelihood of abuse and favoritism.

D. Questionable Awards from Salaries and Expense Funds

In a review of selected projects from Salaries and Expenses (S&E) funds, we found that some were questionable as to the propriety of being funded with S&E funds. In discussing this and related matters with various MBDA personnel, we believe that there is still a great deal of confusion

109

as to what projects can be funded with S&E funds. In addition, we have observed that there are inadequate internal controls and safeguards over potential disbursements for projects awarded from S&E funds.

E.   Project Award Violations

Work has frequently been allowed to commence on many projects prior to finalizing the official project agreements. This practice violates prudent grant management procedures and has caused numerous complications. In a review of the 87 grants awarded from October 1, 1980 through August 26, 1981, we found that 77 (89 percent) were actually awarded *after work had already started*. The time from work-start to actual award in these instances ranged from one day to as much as ten months before the official award.

F.   Vague Project Work Requirements

Some funded projects contain such vague and ambiguous scopes of work that it is difficult to determine what they are actually expected to accomplish. This made is extremely difficult to objectively measure and assess programmatic accomplishments and other results reported for such projects. Our greatest concern, in this regard, centers around those non-General Business Service (GBS) projects that are awarded to stimulate, interact, encourage, and perform other non-quantifiable tasks, which are very difficult to verify.

G.   Improper Use of Sub-Projects

We have uncovered improper as well as questionable cases where funded projects have been used as a vehicle to "pass through" monies to individuals and organizations for purposes totally unrelated to the purpose of the primary project. This is an area of concern to us and one that we view as highly vulnerable to fraud, waste, and abuse.

MONITORING AND ADMINISTRATION

A.   Ineffective Project Monitoring

The lack of routine and effective project monitoring by project officers represents one of the most significant weaknesses and, therefore, vulnerable areas confronting MBDA. In addition, the vulnerability of projects to waste, abuse, and other problems appears to increase when certain project officers are involved. In this respect, we have found a correlation between some projects plagued with abuses, waste, and other problems (programmatic and financial/compliance) and with certain individual project officers assigned to oversee these projects.

110

B. Incomplete Project Files/Record Keeping

Our review of numerous official project files revealed that they are often incomplete, and in general disarray. We have found that many project files lack adequate documentation necessary to relate the historical progression, financial status, programmatic progress, and/or current status of many projects. The condition of the project files has long been a problem at MBDA and continued through the period of our assessment.

C. Excess Advances—A Costly and Wasteful Practice

MBDA-funded organizations frequently have been permitted to draw-down and improperly retain monies in excess of their incurred costs or reasonable projected costs. This problem is still evident and will continue unless MBDA project personnel work closely and actively with the Office of Financial Assistance (OFA) to ensure that recipients only receive monies commensurate with need and performance.

D. Ineffective Oversight of Subcontracting Activities Under Funded Projects

We have found instances where recipients have engaged in improper subcontracting practices. Such practices for example, have included:

Improper sole-source awards;
Possible conflict-of-interest situations; and
Lack of demonstrated need or benefit.

In some of these cases, project officers failed to stop such practices even though they were aware of them. In projects where improper subcontracting activities occur, the government usually does not receive the best products or services for the funds expended. In such instances, it is also unlikely that all applicable rules and regulations are followed.

E. Inappropriate Project Performance Cerfitications

The practice of some project officers to certify that project performance is adequate to allow advance payments to recipients, without an adequate basis, has contributed to substantial waste and other problems. The practice has continued because some project officers habitually certify the adequacy of recipient's performance when, in fact, they know that the performance is questionable, or had little, if any, knowledge of the actual project performance.

F. Inaccurate Business Assistance Reporting

There is strong evidence to show that many of the Business Assistance Reports (BARs) and the replacement Business Development Reports

(BDRs) submitted by some MBDA recipients have been inaccurate. Given the purpose, significance, and use made of the BAR/BDR data, we are concerned that programmatic accomplishments and other reported information may have been significantly misrepresented. Further, we have reason to believe that some of these inaccuracies may have been deliberate and, therefore, fraudulent.

G. **Improper Solicitation of Contributions and Fees from Clients**

Although MBDA has traditionally funded its General Business Service (GBS) organizations to allow them to provide "free" management and technical assistance to qualified individuals and organizations, we are aware of a number of situations where some have solicited fees or contributions in conjunction with this assistance. Such solicitations have been accomplished through a variety of means and were a violation of the terms and conditions of MBDA agreements. In addition, there is always the possibility that involved individuals personally profit from such situations. As MBDA's newest GBS concept and resultant organizations (Business Development Centers) commence operations with the special user fee requirements, there are increased possibilities for problems with improper solicitation of contributions and fees from clients.

H. **Inability to Account for Government-Owned Property in Possession of Recipients**

MBDA has failed to implement and operate an adequate system to properly account for and control government-owned property in the possession of contractos/grantees. This, despite the fact that millions of dollars worth of federal property has been furnished to or purchased by recipients. Because the proper controls have not existed, we believe that substantial funds have been wasted on unnecessary purchases. It is also very probable, as selected cases indicate, that a few recipients have abused or fraudulently diverted property for personal gain.

EVALUATION AND ASSESSMENT

A. **Lack of Training and Expertise of Personnel**

Some MBDA programs, activities, and projects experience an increased susceptibility to problems and failures because some MBDA personnel do not possess the expertise necessary to ensure that they are capable of meeting the day-to-day challenges associated with their positions. Our concerns in this regard are based on personal interviews and other findings, which clearly demonstrate, for example, the lack of *basic* and *essential* knowledge that many "project officers" have for addressing crucial contract/ grant matters. Likewise, other MBDA personnel—some admittedly—do not possess the technical capabilities necessary to effectively oversee specific projects assigned to them. Compounding this situation are our findings that MBDA personnel often have not been provided the training necessary to reduce vulnerabilities and better ensure success of certain MBDA programs and projects.

B. Wasteful Demonstration, Experimentation and Other Special Initiatives Projects

Significant amounts of funds have been wasted on demonstration, experimentation, and other special initiative-type projects. Demonstration and experimentation projects are essentially those special, pilot, or innovative projects that are intended to exploit ideas and areas potentially beneficial to minority business development. We have found that, despite the significant sums spent on such projects, the Demonstration and Experimentation (Projects) Program, as such, has generally been a failure. We attribute this failure to the fact that many of these projects (1) were ill-conceived, (2) awarded under highly questionable circumstances, (3) received inadequate monitoring, and (4) were poorly coordinated and evaluated.

C. MBDA PROFILE System—Is It Needed?

MBDA's PROFILE System represents a potentially wasteful expenditurb. The PROFILE System, formerly the National Minoroty Data Bank, is a specifically designed computerized directory of minority-owned business, listed by size, industry, and capacity. PROFILE, however, closely parallels and, may in fact, duplicate much of the Small Business Administration's PASS System. At the time of our assessment, there was little available data to support the merits of continuing with the PROFILE System in its present form.

D. Questionable Research and Information Projects

MBDA's Office of Research and Information (R&I) funded nineteen projects from FY 1978 through FY 1981 at a cost of $2.4 million. Many of these projects are highly questionable with regard to need, purpose, and value to MBDA program objectives. MBDA officials have even acknowledged that seven of these projects totaling $413,011 had produced little

My internal audit within the Department of Commerce was of the National Climatic Center during August and September 1976. The audit report was published January 4, 1977. The National Climatic Center in Asheville, North Carolina, is the largest of six major facilities administered by NOAA's Environmental Data Service. NCC is responsible for the receipt, archival, and dissemination of weather and climatic data. Meteorological observations made by NOAA's major line components are received and processed at NCC. These data are entered on magnetic tape, computer edited for quality control, and formatted for publication.

NCC's publications serve the needs of broad user audiences. For example, the Climatic Atlas of the United States presents widely used climatological data in graphic forms and tabulations. The monthly Climatic Data National Summary Lists pressure, temperature, and wind data for a large sampling of stations. Local Climatological Data publications also are issued monthly for about 300 cities. In July 1976, there were about 18,000 paid subscribers for NCC publications. In fiscal year 1976, NCC expected to respond to an estimated 60,000 requests for data from planners, designers, engineers, lawyers, academic groups, other government agencies, and from the general public. These requests are serviced, in major part, by sending a copy of an existing NCC publication or a microfilm of an original manuscript, as appropriate. However, there are some requests that require special analysis or interpretive comment by NCC's professional staff.

For fiscal year 1976, NCC had an authorized funding level of about $6 million and had about $2 million from reimbursable activities. As of August 1976, NCC employed 318 full-time permanent personnel.

NCC's management processes did not provide information necessary to evaluate actual operating results achieved for printing activities nor has NCC established a means for periodically assessing and determining the extent to which operating objectives and milestones were being achieved. This condition exists, in our opinion, because annual plans for printing operatins were not developed to show (1) designated priorities and estimated costs for printing various NCC publications, and (2) estimates of productivity that could be expected from efficient use of available printing resources. The availability of an annual plan and criteria for comparing, measuring, and assessing actual results of printing operations would provide EDS officials with information needed to assure that (1) priority work was being completed in a timely manner, (2) efficient use was being made of available equipment and other resources, (3) printing requirements for various NCC divisions were being effectively coordinated, and (4) the best mix of in-house and contract printing was being achieved.

NOAA is authorized by the Joint Committee on Printing to operate a printing facility at Asheville, North Carolina. Printing is defined as the reproduction of materials for publication and includes the process of composition, preparation of illustrations, film making, plate making, presswork, and binding. While the Department defines publishing as the issuance of printed materials for distribution to the public, the Department's "Handbook of Publishing and Printing" points out that economical and effective publishing requires planning and coordination that begin early in the preparation of a manuscript, or the prototype of a series.

Most of NCC's publications are printed in-house for reasons of cost and quality, except for color printing, which is done by or through the Government Printing Office. NCC has made limited use of commercial contractors to fulfill its printing requirements.

NCC does not prepare an annual printing and publishing plan to show (1) expected printing requirements for various publications and estimated costs, (2) designated priorities for printing publications, (3) estimates of productivity to be expected from the efficient use of printing resources, and (4) comparative printing costs for determining the most economical and best mix of in-house and commercial printing to be achieved. However, NCC does prepare an annual Program Report to show actual results of printing operations for the period and a variety of other internal reports that show actual results of operations, such as the volume of printing by publication and number of paid and free publications distributed. At present, however, the information shown in internal reports on actual results of operations serves as a historical record of printing and publishing activities performed by NCC.

Printed schedules are prepared to show the expected day of the month on which publications are to arrive in the print shop and the expected date the printed material is to be available for publishing. However, the latest NCC printing schedule that was available for our review was prepared in 1969.

This schedule listed nine publications for printing by NCC on a regular basis and one for printing on an intermittent basic. NCC's printing schedule, which was revised and updated during our audit, listed five publications for printing by NCC on a regular basis and four for printing on an intermittent basis. For example, two publications printed on an intermittent basis are the quarterly publication, *High Altitude Meteorological Data,* for October-December 1974, which was printed in August 1976 while the monthly publication, *Northern Hemisphere Historical Weather Maps,* for May 1969 was scheduled for printing in September 1976.

We noted that NCC does not plan for or monitor the use made of certain photo, microfilm, and printing equipment. However, NCC provided us with its estimates of the use made of forty-one items of equipment during fiscal year 1976. For sixteen items of equipment in the photo laboratory, one item was used 57 percent of the available time, one 50 percent, one 26 percent, and the remaining thirteen items were used less than 20 percent. For eleven items of microfilm equipment, four items were used 100 percent of the available time, one item 67 percent, three items 43 percent, and the remaining three items less than 20 percent. For fourteen items of equipment in the print shop, four items were used over 80 percent of the available time, four items 60 to 80 percent, two items 38 to 42 percent, three items less than 20 percent, and one item was not used during the period.

In our opinion, without an annual printing and publishing plan, NCC lacks a management tool that could serve as a means for (1) allocating available resources and assigning operating priorities to accomplish designated printing activities, (2) measuring "how well" NCC is operating in terms of actual results achieved versus expected accomplishments, (3) ascertaining that efficient and economical use is being derived from resources used to carry out printing and publishing activities, and (4) determining that the best options of in-house and commercial printing are being identified for accomplishment during the ensuing fiscal year.

NCC pricing policies were not being uniformly applied and, in certain respects, did not provide for full cost recovery. Also, NCC did not obtain certain required approvals before publishing and distributing printed material. Moreover, initial free distribution of NCC publications appeared high—about 67 percent—and may not be in full accord with Department policy, which is to hold such distribution to a minimum. These conditions existed because the management controls and related responsibilities for implementing, reviewing and monitoring the application of these policies were fragmented and uncoordinated at the NCC level. Effective, cohesive management controls over implementation of pricing and free distribution policies are necessary to reasonably assure that Department and NOAA requirements are being uniformly and consistently applied and that all possible revenues are being realized from services and printed materials provided by NCC.

The Department's general policy and related requirements for imposing fees and charges for supplies and services rendered are set forth in DAO 203–5. It is the Department's policy to make reasonable and equitable charges for services rendered consistent with program and legislative requirements and to recover the full cost of rendering such services, unless one or more of the exceptions set forth in DAO 203–5 are applicable. A determination of full cost includes all direct costs associated with rendering the service and a proportionate share of indirect costs for such elements as (1) supporting service costs, (2) Office of the Secretary expense, (3) depreciation on government-owned equipment, and (4) building space and maintenance costs.

NCC determines the unit price to be printed on a publication by applying a predetermined fixed-cost-per-page to the number of pages in the publication and adding a unit cost for postage. Cognizant NCC officials advised that fixed-cost-per-page was based on NCC's printing and distribution costs. However, NCC did not have current cost analyses available to show the type of costs and amounts used to arrive at the fixed-cost-per-page or to show that such costs were based on NCC's actual printing and distribution costs. In addition, NCC officials advised that proportionate share of costs associated with computer programming and processing and manual editing were not considered in determining unit prices for NCC publications. In these circumstances, there is less assurance that NCC's price determinations include all direct costs and a proportionate share of indirect costs, as required by DAO 203–5.

NCC maintains an inventory of publications for responding to inquiries or requests for climatic data and information. The cost of providing this service would include the cost of publishing, storage space, and personnel required to maintain the inventory and fill customer orders. However, we were advised that these publications were sold to the general public at the price printed on the publication and to other agencies for the cost to retrieve the publication from stock. In the latter instance, the price of the publication was not recovered and in neither instance were storage costs considered.

NCC has issued guidelines, which include a user charge list that contains prices for frequently requested NCC services, such as copies of original documents and film. Included in the guidelines are a user charge-price list and internal estimating guides for use by Branch and Section Chiefs for pricing products and services rendered; however, NCC has not periodically monitored the use made of these guidelines to ensure uniform application throughout NCC.

We noted that NCC submitted user charges to the NOAA Finance Division for review and approval but did not submit for approval the fees for NCC publications. NCC provides free data services up to (a) $25 for each instance involving federal, state, and local governments and certain non-profit organizations and (b) $49 for foreign governments and United Nations related organizations. However, information available did not indicate that NCC had obtained the appropriate administrative exception to the Department's and NOAA's policy of full cost recovery. In this regard, NOAA Directive 34–39 states that Directors of Primary Organization Elements or their designee will make no commitment to waive any element of cost without prior approval of the Associate Administrator, NOAA.

The Department's *Handbook of Publishing and Printing* (DAO 201–32) states that it is the policy of the Department to hold free distribution of priced and unpriced publications to a minimum. This DAO points out that care should be exercised to assure that distribution of free publications should not exceed reasonable requirements for the publications in relation to the purposes they are intended to serve.

NOAA Directive 25–03 sets forth the basis for free distribution of priced publications and designates the type of recipients who were entitled to receive free copies of NOAA publications. Generally, these exceptions are in accord with the Department's policy guidelines set forth in DAO 203–5. NOAA Directive 25–03 assigns to the Environmental Scientific Information Center (ESIC) the responsibility for assuring compliance with Department and NOAA distribution policies and are subject to approval by ESIC, acting as the NOAA liaison with the Department's Office of Publications.

Close control to limit free distribution of priced publications to selected recipients was not evident in certain respects. Information available at NCC showed that about 67 percent of NCC's initial distribution of publications—about 700,000 copies annually—were sent to recipients free of charge. As of July 1976, NCC had a total of 53,727 subscribers to its various priced publications of which 35,515—or 66 percent—were sent free publications. To illustrate, in August 1976, NCC printed about 275 copies of the quarterly publication, *High Altitude Mereorological Data,* for October-December 1974. Of this total, 11 copies were sent to paid subscribers and 166 were distributed without charge. The quarterly subscription price for this publication of about 600 pages was $11.20. Accordingly, quarterly revenue from sales of this publication would be $123 while priced publications valued at $1,859 were sent to recipients included on NCC's free distribution list.

We also noted that certain recipients were being sent more than one free copy of priced publications and that certain foreign recipients were being sent free copies of publications without approval by ESIC, as required by NOAA or NCC directives. While mailing lists were generally circularized, information available did not indicate that the mailing list for free distribution of certain priced publications to cooperative observers had been circularized annually, as required.

In our opinion, there is a need for NCC to improve and strengthen internal management controls over the free distribution of priced publications. In this regard, NCC should more closely review and control its free distribution lists for priced publications with a view toward reducing to a minimum the number of recipients who are sent free copies of priced publications. By this means, NCC may be able to increase, to some extent, revenues from sales of priced publications to interested recipients.

Internal financial management and operational controls exercised by NCC over billings, collections, and inventory were inadequate and ineffective. Due to weaknesses in existing internal controls over recording and reporting of transactions, the balance of outstanding accounts receivable could not be accurately determined, receipts on-hand could not be reconciled to cash receipts journals, customers with delinquent accounts continued to receive services from NCC, and inventories of shelf-stocks were in excess of limits prescribed by NOAA. Effective internal management controls over billings, collections, and inventories are necessary to reasonably assure the safeguard of assets, integrity of employees, efficiency of operations, and adherence to prescribed managerial policies and procedures.

Billings

Department Organization Order 25–5B provides that the Assistant Administrator for Administration, NOAA, shall provide administrative management and support services for all NOAA components, except as otherwise directed to do so. Cognizant NOAA officials advised that they were not aware of an exception to authorize NCC to perform a billing function. However, NCC has been performing the billing function for an extended period of time and apparently without a specific delegation of authority from NOAA Headquarters.

NCC Directive 34–02 sets forth procedures for billing and collecting from non-federal customers for providing services costing less than $5,000 and for certain publications. Division/Branch Chiefs are responsible for invoicing the services provided while NCC's Fiscal Section is responsible for maintaining accounts receivable and collecting all debts dovered by NCC invoices. No individual had been designated specific responsibility for monitoring accounts receivable. To bill for services of less than $5, NCC uses an unnumbered invoice. Numbered invoices are used to bill for services of $5 to $9.99. These invoices are filed numerically. Neither the numbered or unnumbered invoices show the customer's name.

NOAA's policy is to request an advance of funds for services unless the customer is (1) prohibited from doing so by statute, (2) is determined to be reliable in paying bills, or (3) receives a waiver from NOAA Headquarters. In this regard, NOAA waived the requirement for EDS to obtain advances for services under $5,000, with the proviso that costs incurred are recovered promptly. For bad debts, NCC Directive 34–02 specifies that when a customer's account becomes ninety days old, it is to be added to the "Bad Debt List" and that these customers are not to be provided additional services until the amount owed is resolved. For collecting debts, NCC follows a practice of sending one follow-up

118

request after thirty days if payment is not received for invoices over $10 and does not send a follow-up request for invoices under $10.

Since customer names were not on all invoices and since numbered invoices were filed numerically, some payments received could not be identified with specific billings. Accordingly, the correct balance of outstanding accounts receivables could not be readily determined. However, available information indicated that, as of August 1976, NCC had an estimated $77,000 in outstanding accounts receivable of which about $21,000 was outstanding ninety days or more. This includes about $3,000 in overdue amounts that were not included on NCC's bad debt lists. In addition, there were three customers who made advance payments and who had negative balances totaling $930 that were over nintey days old. These amounts were not included on the bad debt list.

To improve management controls over billings, bad debts, and advance payments, we believe that NCC should (1) designate a central billing unit, (2) control accounts receivable by customer name, (3) use and account for all prenumbered invoices, (4) fix responsibility for monitoring accounts receivable and for handling customer's checks returned by the bank, and (5) consider requiring customers with delinquent accounts to make advance payments before providing additional services. In addition, NCC should indicate the frequency and the level at which no further follow-up action will be taken to collect delinquent accounts and should require that write-offs of uncollectable accounts be approved by the NCC Director, or his designee.

Collections

Collections received by mail are opened in the mailroom and picked up by NCC's Fiscal Section where total receipts are verified and recorded. However, each day's receipts are not deposited intact but are held in various statuses until NCC determines that the requested service or information is available. On September 1, 1976, NCC had over $12,000 on-hand. In these circumstances, daily cash receipts could not be compared to deposits made. In addition, stamps received as payment for services are held by NCC's cashier for sale to NCC personnel. This cash, along with other cash received, is used by the cashier to make refunds up to $5 and to purchase money orders for refunds of $5 to $25. Refunds of $25 or more are made by the NOAA Finance Division. Moreover, NCC accepts signed blank checks on which NCC enters the cost of services requested by the customer.

Our reconciliation of receipts shown in NCC's Cash Receipts Journal to deposits made and receipts on-hand showed a cash overage of about $24,000. Of this amount, $15,000 represented the deposit of checks that were not processed through the cash register nor recorded as receipts in the Cash Receipts Journal. The remaining cash overage of about $9,000 could not be identified but was probably due to a variety of processing errors and ineffective internal control procedures over cash receipts and deposits.

In our opinion, the internal control procedures exercised by NCC over receipts and deposits were inadequate and weak, did not effectively protect the government's interests nor safeguard the integrity of NCC's accountable employees. To strengthen internal control procedures, NCC should (1) prepare a list of all receipts at the time mail is opened in the mail room; (2) deposit receipts intact daily; (3) verify deposits to lists of daily receipts; (4) return blank checks to customers; (5) make periodic independent reconciliations of the Cash Receipts Journal; and (6) assign specific functional responsibility to individuals to ensure adequate segregation of duties.

Inventories

The Department's *Handbook of Publishing and Printing* requires operating units to dispose of excess or obsolete publications under an effective system of inventory control. NOAA's Directives Manual (NDM) 62–38 provides for disposal of shelf-stock after two years. According to NDG 37–11, a tickler file is required to assure that shelf-stock items will be used before shelf-life expires. In this regard, a stock locator system would provide information for ready location of publications and serve as a perpetual inventory record. This record could be used for taking periodic physical inventories and for identifying for disposal any excess or obsolete publications.

Although NCC has placed on microfiche about 2,650 square feet of publications over two years old, no publications have been disposed of, pending approval of quality assurance procedures. Also, NCC has 1,370 square feet of stored publications over two years old that have not been put on film and 1,360 square feet of empty shelves. We did note that for the period August 1975 through April 1976, NCC disposed of about 700 square feet of stock, including older publications and the bulk of data received from closed State climatological offices.

Our test check of publications on hand at NCC showed that shelf-life of publications was exceeding NOAA requirements. For publications printed during April, May, and June 1972, shelf-stock copies ranged from zero for one publication to 120 copies of another monthly issue. Some multiple copies were on hand for periods in the early 1940s. For publications printed in fiscal year 1973, there were 20 to 220 shelf-stock copies on hand for a particular month. These situations can be attributed to the absence of an effective inventory system for disposing of excess or obsolete publications and from the lack of a periodic inventory of publications.

Although NCC does not currently have a stock locator system to facilitate locating publications needed to fill customer orders and to serve as a perpetual inventory record, cognizant NCC officials advised that a rotary file for this purpose was placed on order in May 1976. The implementation of a stock locator system should improve NCC inventory systems for shelf-stock publications and provide a basis for discharging accountability functions for priced publications from production through appropriate disposition.

Commercial Printing

NCC has made limited use of commercial contractors to fulfill its printing requirements. Generally, comparative cost analyses made by NCC have shown that it was more economical to do the work in-house. However, these analyses were not made in accord with OMB Circular A-76. In addition, NCC's printing contracts did not (1) provide for a COTR to monitor, inspect, and approve contractors' production processes at critical stages so that technical inadequacies could be identified and corrected during the early stages of printing work; and (2) include provisions for terminating contracts for convenience of the government and for default, as provided by existing regulations. Compliance with existing requirements is necessary to reasonably assure that the most economical and best mix of in-house and contract printing is being achieved and that government's interest is being adequately protected.

We recommend to the Director, EDS, that he require NCC managers to (1) prepare future comparative cost analyses in accord with the principles contained in OMB Circular A-76; (2) designate, in future contracts, a COTR to monitor contract performance; and (3) incorporate into future contracts appropriate clauses for termination for the convenience of the government and for default. The Director, EDS, stated that he would require NCC managers to take the actions necessary to implement our recommendations regarding future comparative cost analyses and contract provisions.

Responding to Inquiries

NCC follows a practice of assigning professional staff members to initially respond to telephone inquiries for weather and climatic data. Our random selection of such inquiries indicated that about 90 percent were acted upon by technicians. Most inquiries appeared to be normal routine requests for publications or for weather and climatic data (not requiring interpretive comment, analysis, or consultation), which were readily available from NCC files and which could have been furnished by trained technicians or clerical personnel. This situation appears to have evolved over periods of time during which the telephone numbers of professional staff members were listed in NCC pamphlets and letters. This practice results in less than efficient use of available professional staff time and increase the cost of providing this service to the public.

We recommended to the Director, EDS, that he have NCC managers determine the feasibility of having all future telephone inquiries for weather and climatic data initially screened by trained technicians or clerical personnel. To accomplish this, technicians should be provided with a general guideline for determining the type of inquiries that require substantive, interpretive comment or analysis for referral to and response by the professional staff. The Director, EDS, advised that NCC managers would be instructed to review the present practice of assigning professional staff members to initially screen telephone inquiries to determine whether a general guide can be developed for use by technicians or clerical personnel to perform this function and to refer appropriate inquiries to the professional staff for response.

Internal Reports

Some NCC computerized internal financial and administrative reports duplicated, in certain major respects, information provided by, or available from,
established NOAA reporting systems. Computerized reports are generated in
response to internal requests for data, apparently without determining whether
the requestors' needs can be satisfied from existing NOAA reporting systems.
In these circumstances, NCC may be foregoing certain economies that could be
achieved by making greater and more efficient use of information available from
existing NOAA reporting systems.

We recommended that the Director, EDS, require NCC managers to identify
and review existing requirements for all NCC computer-prepared reports with a
view toward eliminating or reducing the number of internal reports to that needed
for efficient office management. This should include a determination as to whether
as to whether NCC's information requirements can be met by or through established NOAA reporting systems. The Director, EDS, advised that a review was
in process to identify NCC requirements for internal reports and to determine if
such requirements can be satisfied from existing reporting systems. The results
of this review will be used to eliminate redundancies in reports and to reduce
the number of internal reports, as appropriate.

Customer Complaint File

Customer complaint files maintained by NCC did not contain sufficient
documentation to show the actions taken to resolve the complaint. For 17 of 25
complaints we reviewed, there was insufficient information in the files to show
that the complaints were appropriately resolved. Most complaints concerned
non-receipt of requested subscriptions or publications, and in certain instances,
indicated that canceled checks were in the possesesion of the complainant. Subsequent follow-up on these matters indicated that the checks were properly
processed and deposited to NCC accounts. Without complete files, weaknesses
in internal operating processes could continue undetected and uncorrected for
extended periods of time and could perpetuate certain undesirable practices, such
as those relating to accountability for cash receipts.

We recommended to the Director, EDS, that he require the Director, NCC,
to provide for: (1) maintaining a control log to show the nature of the actions
taken on specific complaints, (2) making a periodic review of the complaint file
for completeness and for detecting weaknesses in internal operating processes,
and (3) having the Director (or his designee) sign all responses to complaints.
The implementation of these internal management controls is needed to safeguard
the integrity of accountable employees. The Director, EDS, advised that appropriate implementing actions would be taken by the Director, NCC.

User Survey

At the time of our review, NCC had sent questionnaires to a limited number
of NCC data users and held a workshop for selected members in the scientific

community. These inquiries were made to determine the value and usefulness of NCC services to data users and to define user requirements and recommend ways for meeting user needs. In our opinion, the initial actions taken by NCC are a move in the right direction. However, NCC should expand such efforts to obtain feedback from a broader spectrum of data users. Such feedback would provide NCC with type of basic information needed for determining (1) whether current publications are meeting the needs of various classes of data users, and (2) the extent to which NCC is meeting program responsibilities. The Director, EDS, advised that he intended to broaden the coverage of NCC users through additional surveys of user needs.

To wrap up my two years of experiences at the Department of Commerce. I need to describe what I did more than anything else. I spent most of my time (at your expense) doing nothing. Specifically I would either talk on the telephone, look for another job, prepare tax returns for my friends and acquaintances, or simply call in sick. What's important for you to know is, I wasn't alone—not by a long shot.

Chapter 6

Veterans Administration Hospitals

There are several major flaws in the analogy between consumer demand for goods provided in the market, and the political pressures for government services. Consumers purchase the amount of goods they desire. The level of government spending, however, is always greater than the level the voters would choose if programs and their budgets were put to a direct vote. Government programs bestow concentrated benefits on organized groups (the Merchant Marine, Chryslyer Corporation, the dairy cartel, etc.) that find it profitable to invest millions in political contributions and lobbying fees, since this will "produce" millions more in subsidies. On the other hand, the cost to the individual taxpayer of even finding out how much he or she pays in taxes, or on which purchases or sources of income the taxes fall, or how this might be stopped, may be as great a burden as the taxes themselves.

—Libertarian Party News (January 1983)

There are 174 VA Hospitals. These hospitals contain 82,000 beds, which are occupied by Surgical, Medical, Intensive Care, Alcoholic, and Psychiatric patients. You pay 234,000 members of Disorganized Crime to operate these 82,000 beds, of which 16,000 beds (20 percent) are without patients. The first thing I learned at the VA is the "squeaking wheel gets greased." A veteran, if persistent, will get anything he desires from the VA. This is due to the strength of the veteran lobby groups, such as the American Legion, Veterans of Foreign Wars, Disabled American Veterans, just to name a few. These groups demand and get lots of your money for the Veterans Administration. In return the VA provides these groups with offices, furniture, access to veterans, and most importantly, access to the VA membership of Disorganized Crime. It's not important that these veterans haven't won a war in the last thirty years, they are still going to get benefits (or at least they think they are receiving benefits). The veterans of the last war, which we officially won, forgot to tell their children and grandchildren, because hundreds of thousands of them are still stationed in Germany and Japan. Perhaps someday our economic competitors will forgive the World War II veterans and release these hostages.

My first audit of a VA Hospital was as a team member at Oklahoma City,

Oklahoma. The audit team was there in September and October 1978. The audit report was published one year later in September 1979.

The medical center had a total of 433 operating beds consisting of 169 medical, 157 surgical, and 107 psychiatric. As of September 30, 1978, there were 1,066 full time employees and 286 part-time employees and trainees. The annual budget for fiscal year 1979 is $34.4 million, and the center had nonexpendable equipment costing over $8.9 million. There were 59 recommendations in the report. The Director concurred in 53, did not concur in four, and provided qualified concurrences in two recommendations.

Improvement was needed in resource planning and equipment utilization. The Five-Year Facility Plan had inadequate justification for some proposals for construction, equipment purchase, and building renovation. The planned $229,000 purchase of electron microscopy equipment for Laboratory Service, $4 million planned research construction, and the $350,000 renovation of the Drug Treatment Unit should have been eliminated. These three projects totaled over $4.5 million of your money.

Workload figures for laboratory did not justify purchase of an electron microscope. This service was available through a sharing agreement with the University of Oklahoma.

There were four laboratory rooms not currently in use in research at the time of the audit, and a Central Office site visit identified a number of laboratory rooms that were not assigned. There was no detailed plan or justification available for the auditors to review.

The patient demand for an inpatient Drug Treatment Unit had fallen to a level that did not justify the continued operation of the unit. The inpatient Drug Treatment Unit occupied Building 3, which had 8,431 square feet of space. A $350,000 project was planned for fiscal year 1980 to renovate portions of this building, to correct fire and safety deficiencies since patients were housed in the building. This project would not have been necessary if patients were no longer in the building.

Physician and patient scheduling needed improvement. A study made by facility personnel during May and June 1977 on staff utilization and timeliness showed that physicians were not properly scheduled. Based on our observations during the audit, the condition still existed a year later.

On Wednesday, October 18, 1978, we visited two of the clinical areas comprised of eight clinics. We found the patient waiting room with fifty patients scheduled to be seen, beginning at 10 A.M., but there were no doctors available in any of seventeen examination rooms as of 11:30 A.M. A nurse on duty in one of the clinics stated that many times the doctors do not come to the clinic until after 1:00 P.M. It was also noted that additional patients were scheduled to be seen in the afternoon.

Patients are scheduled for blocks of time, although VA manual requirements provided that patients would be scheduled at specific time intervals based on determination of time required for each patient to complete the visit at one clinic. Physician coverage for the clinics was also scheduled by blocks of time set aside for clinical coverage, but there was no assignment of specific responsibility to ensure that the clinical coverage was provided.

We also noted that each group of clinics maintained its own patient schedule and made changes, cancellations, and adjustments as it desired many times without the knowledge of the Associate Chief of Staff for Ambulatory Care. Additionally, the schedule did not always show the physicians responsible for coverage.

A special purpose visit's recommendations had not been complied with. The report of the VA Central Office Special Purpose visit in April 1978 stated there was a "perceived" linen shortage at this facility and that linen handling within the facility was very loose and did not promote security or sanitation and aggravated the apparent linen shortage. Linen purchases in fiscal year 1978 were over $46,000. The report recommended:

a. Conduct a complete inventory of hospital linens to determine the current par value of all items and use this information to guide action that ensures the routine availability of linens.

b. Perform a complete review of linen handling within the facility and implement corrective measures in cooperation with the using services.

The service chief reported to VA Central Office, by letter of August 4, 1978, that only a linen inventory comparison with the par level required to support the facility workload could determine that there was a linen shortage. A linen inventory had not been performed as of October 25, 1978. Most VA Hospitals had problems with linen losses (your losses).

The hospital canteen vending machine contract began May 1, 1974, and paid the Canteen Service 14.3 percent of gross sales. The contract provided for a hostess, clean-up in the vending machine area, and for inspection of the vending machines and contractor's plant for sanitation and housekeeping reasons.

The contract provided for a hostess six and a half hours per weekday and two hours per day on weekends. The hostess was to: (1) ensure that vending machines were at the proper temperature and are well stocked with merchandise; (2) keep the vending machines and nearby table and chairs clean; (3) assist customers in the selection of products vended; (4) keep condiment stand well stocked and clean; (5) remove litter and clean occasional spillage from the floor; (6) maintain the vendor's storage area in a neat and clean condition. In addition, the hostess and clean-up service were to be provided from 6:00 P.M. to 9:00 P.M., seven days a week.

Our spot checks of hostess and clean-up service showed the following:

1978	Observations
October 8 (Sunday)	Hostess not present from 12:15 P.M. to 1:30 P.M.
October 9 (Monday)	No clean-up from 6:00 P.M. to 9:00 P.M. by vendor.

The Chief, Building Management Service, told us his staff routinely cleaned the vending-machine area between 8:30 A.M. to 10:00 A.M. daily. By obtaining the services for hostess and clean-up service specified in the contract, Building Management Service would have more time in other areas.

Limited merchandise was available for sale. The contract calls for specific items that were to be offered, such as salads, casseroles, and ice cream, in the vending machines. Salads, casseroles, and ice cream were not offered to the customers because the installed vending machines were unable to dispense these products. The lack of choice of items that can be purchased was placing an undue hardship on patients who cannot leave the medical center.

We found that electron microscopy equipment was not needed. The Facility Five-Year Plan showed that electron microscopy equipment, valued at about $229,000, was planned for the pathology section during fiscal year 1980. The electron microscopy procedures were being performed by the University of Oklahoma, Department of Pathology, under a fee-basis agreement with the VA Medical Center, Oklahoma City. Review of pathology's electron microscopy workload showed that during fiscal years 1977 and 1978, only twenty-seven electron microscopic procedures were performed by the University of Oklahoma, at a cost of $4,590 ($170 each). Because the electron microscopy procedures were obtained at a reasonable rate when needed, and since the current workload would not result in the efficient use of the equipment, it was not economically justified to purchase electron microscopy equipment. The Hospital Director did not concur and stated,

> There are approximately 50 biopsies done per month, a high percentage of which should receive electron microscopy. All kidney, muscle, GI and the majority of liver biopsies should have electron microscopy for the sake of good patient care. We feel that only 5 percent of the biopsies go to electron microscopy and expect the demand to increase because of aging population which should receive this testing. The availability of electron microscopy will require additional staff, a pathologist and a technician. The presence of the equipment itself will attract a pathologist.

The nonconcurrence of a member of Disorganized Crime to a recommendation to save your money was common, though usually unfounded, as was this nonconcurrence. Electron microscopy testing, as previously noted, was already available to the VA Medical Center through a sharing agreement with the University of Oklahoma, Department of Pathology, and therefore, necessary services could have been provided in the past if needed. However, based on fifty biopsies per month, only 2 percent of the biopsies received electron microscopy testing during the period October 1, 1976, to September 30, 1978. Another electron microscope (paid for by you) was also available within the VA's medical district. To economically justify the purchase of the electron microscopy equipment, the medical center would have had to perform at least eleven microscopy tests per month for ten years. Based on the tests provided during fiscal years 1977 and 1978, the eleven tests per month would equate to approximately 1,000 percent increase in workload. Also, there was no assurance that the presence of electron microscopy equipment would attract a pathologist (whose salary you would have paid) to operate the new electron microscope.

Excess laboratory equipment costing about $20,000 had not been reported to Supply Service. The length of time the equipment had been stored could not be determined because utilization records were not being maintained by Laboratory Service personnel. The members of Disorganized Crime in charge of the Consolidated Memorandum Receipt told us some of the equipment had been in storage for as long as four years.

During the consolidation of the patient library with the medical library, the patient library was reduced by over 3,700 books. The Chief, Library Service, could account for 588 books, and told us these books were given to Supply Service for disposal. The Chief, Supply Service, said the books were destroyed, but did not have any documentation showing the disposition of the books. There was no further record on the remaining 3,112 books and we never found them.

Veterans are paid to go to VA hospitals. This ensures as high a usage of hospitals as possible (at your expense, of course) and is called beneficiary travel. Our review of thirty-three beneficiary travel claims (twenty by individuals, twelve by groups, one multiple payment) showed 30 percent of the expenditures were made for claims with some type of discrepancy. We estimate that $203,000 of the $4,010,250 budgeted for beneficiary travel during fiscal year 1979 could possibly have been saved if additional controls were implemented.

Our review of travel vouchers of twenty outpatients paid beneficiary travel during a two-day period (March 1 and September 29, 1978) showed that 25 percent of the veterans were not seen by health care personnel.

Our review of the scheduling logs maintained in the clinics and the travel office found no record of scheduled visits for some patients. We reviewed medical records to determine what medical services were provided to patients receiving beneficiary travel. No record of scheduled appointments or indications of the reasons the visits were necessary were found for five of the twenty patients reviewed. They would show up in Oklahoma City simply to collect your money.

A review was made of twelve medical records from four groups of outpatients from the same town, who visited the medical center on the same day. Five of the patients came to the hospital without a scheduled appointment, but were seen by health care personnel. Round-trip travel claims were paid to all twelve people. There were no special circumstances documented in the records of those without appointments, as required by VA Regulations, which state that payment without advance approval is authorized only in those cases where the VA determines that there was a need for prompt medical care, or circumstances prevented a request for prior authorization, or due to VA delay or error prior authorization for travel was not given, or there was a justifiable lack of knowledge on the part of a third party acting for the veteran, or based on a finding by the administrator or his designee that failure to secure prior authorization was justified. These decisions may be made by telephone or telegraph but are subject to confirmation in writing by the authorizing employee. Our review did not identify written documentation for the five patientrs in our sample who were paid beneficiary travel.

Further, thirty-six persons are authorized to certify beneficiary travel vouchers. Thus, it would be possible for a patient to receive multiple payments for a single visit by requesting a voucher from different persons in the system when more than one clinic is scheduled. This was noted during our observations of personnel processing travel vouchers. We noted that two patients with more than one clinic scheduled had their vouchers processed, and only one clinic was marked off the scheduling log. This could allow the patients to collect beneficiary travel twice for the same visit.

Of the 280 vouchers processed in a two-day period, 3 vouchers were approved by a staff person not authorized to approve beneficiary travel. Medical center officials and the Federal Bureau of Investigation had found some patients had abused the beneficiary travel system by providing out-of-town addresses when in fact they live in Oklahoma City.

An electrical grinder in Prosthetics Service, purchased in 1972 for $255 for use by the Orthotics Laboratory, had never been used because the present laboratory did not have a 220 single-phase electrical outlet. At the time of our audit (1978), there was no work order with Engineering Service to install the proper electrical outlet so that the machine could be used.

The next problem area is the first (but by no means last) indication that the auditors "were in bed with" management (and why not, both are paid by the same person). The patient demand for an inpatient Drug Treatment Unit had fallen to a level that did not justify the continued operation of the unit, which had an annual expenditure of $240,000 for staff salaries. The 25-bed inpatient Drug Treatment Unit had an average occupancy rate of only 48 percent for fiscal year 1978 and an average daily census of 12 inpatients. There was no waiting list of veterans to enter the program. During fiscal year 1978, there were 257 admissions, but only 5 treatments were completed. Of the 261 discharge from the inpatient Drug Treatment Unit in fiscal year 1978, 29 percent were not medically discharged but just walked away from the program.

VA Circular 10–77–103 stated that the occupancy rate and the monthly turnover rate for this type of unit should be 85 percent. In fiscal year 1978, the turnover rate was 181.3 percent, which indicated that many of the patients left the program with continuing drug problems. The occupancy rate ranged from a high of 72 percent in October 1977 to a low of only 40 percent in April 1978. This circular also stated that, if a special medical service is inefficient and poorly utilized, the overall requirements of patient care may be better served by closing the unit and obtaining the specialized services from another VA or non-VA hospital.

Since fiscal year 1975, there has been a significant workload reduction in the inpatient program as shown below:

| | Fiscal Year | | | |
	1975	1976	1977	1978
Inpatient admissions	344	369	298	257

130

The Medical Center Director stated in an October 11, 1978 letter to the ADCMD for Operations, in VA Central Office:

In November 1977, we experienced a critical and potentially dangerous incident in our Drug Dependence Treatment Center. As a result, one staff member was removed; the Unit Director sought transfer out of the state; the head nurse requested reassignment; and the psychiatrist resigned. We could not deliver quality care under these circumstances. On December 2, 1977, the then Director of our Hospital phoned the Deputy Director, Mental Health and Behavioral Sciences Service in VACO, and informed him fully of our situation and of the necessity to phase down and restructure the program.

Other alternative drug treatment programs were available if the medical center's inpatient Drug Treatment Unit was closed. At the time of our audit, all eleven inpatients were residents of Oklahoma and therefore eligible for treatment by the State of Oklahoma, which had both an inpatient and outpatient drug treatment program. The state program would have been able to accommodate these veterans if the medical center's program were closed. If a nonresident needed inpatient treatment, he could have been transferred to nearby VA Medical Centers that have programs, such as Dallas, Little Rock, and Topeka.

The inpatient Drug Treatment Unit occupied Building 3, which had 8,431 square feet of space. Because of space shortage, the VA Medical Center, Oklahoma City, rented space in the nearby Rogers Building. The Fiscal and Supply Services are accommodated in 6,986 square feet on the third floor, costing $36,000 annually. Personnel Service occupies 6,131 square feet on the fifth floor, costing $37,200 annually. If the inpatient Drug Treatment Unit had been closed, some of the administrative services occupying this leased space could have been moved to Building 3, thereby reducing rental costs. These leases could have been terminated by the VA with a sixty-day notice.

A project, estimated to cost $350,000, was planned for fiscal year 1980 to correct fire and safety deficiencies because patients stay in the building. A project estimated by Engineering Service to cost $65,000 would have been needed to correct the fire and safety deficiencies to meet requirements so that the building could have been used for administrative purposes. If the inpatient Drug Treatment Unit were closed, the much smaller project would be all that was necessary.

The Director did not concur with the recommendation that the inpatient Drug Treatment Unit be closed. The Director stated:

The program has been operating with a reduced census because of a potentially dangerous incident in November 1977. This incident resulted in the loss of a psychiatrist, head nurse, the unit director and a counselor. We are implementing changes in the program which should restore its effectiveness, and propose that the program be reevaluated in two years before a decision is made concerning its continuation.

In other words, the Director wanted to spend over $37,000 (construction cost plus two years' salaries) of your money for a two-year period, in order to speculate if the unit could have been made effective. What's interesting is the reply from the Deputy Chief Medical Director, who agreed with the hospital Director. No further mention was made of dropping this underutilized drug treatment unit by the auditors.

Construction for research services was also unjustified. Planned research construction should have been removed from the Five-Year Facility Plan. The Five-Year Facility Plan (1980–1984) showed planning phase funds of $80,000 to be spent in 1982 for a research building addition. The design and construction phase was shown for fiscal year 1984 at a cost of over $4 million. There was no detailed plan or justification available for our review. However, the Associate Chief of Staff for Research believed that justification could have been developed to spend your money. He told us that his office had not participated in preparation of the Five-Year Facility Plan.

Central Office site visit identified a number of laboratory rooms that were not assigned. During our tour of the research facility, we found four laboratory rooms that were not currently in use, although they had been assigned to projects. Elimination of the research construction would save the expenditure of $4,080,000.

As we found later at the VA hospital in New Orleans, the veteran's consent to be a guinea pig in experimental research was not always obtained. Our review of eleven medical records for patients participating in research showed five records (45 percent) had no consent forms and that six (55 percent) had consent forms, but four were not complete. This problem was also noted in a study conducted by Medical Information on March 28, 1978. The study indicated that fourteen patients during the first quarter of fiscal year 1978 had no consent forms in their medical record. Medical Center Memorandum 151–1, dated April 20, 1978, requires the investigator to file the original consent document in the patient's medical record at the time the patient is entered on the research study. Lack of consent forms provides for potential liability or legal action by the patient or his family against the Veterans Administration and the investigator. These liabilities, of course, would be paid for by you.

Emergency cardiopulmonary resuscitation (CPR) carts were improperly stocked. Also, periodic inspections were not made to ensure that the carts contain the proper equipment and that the drugs had not exceeded their expiration dates. Our inventory of one sealed cart in the physical therapy area showed that an endrotracheal guide with stop adapter was missing. We also found that the Pronestyl and Glucagon drugs had expired on September 1, 1978, and October 1, 1978, respectively. Information received from Nursing Service showed that equipment had been missing from the carts on four separate occasions during the past twelve months.

The Supply Processing and Distribution Section (SPD) was responsible for 133 items in each of the emergency carts. We noted the SPD's logbook showed the carts were not inspected for expired items. Our inventory of nine additional carts showed that *all* contained expired items. In addition, Pharmacy Service, which was responsible for the twenty-four pharmaceuticals in the carts, inspected the carts for outdated drugs but the inspections were inadequate. For example, the cart inventoried on October 25, 1978, contained a drug that had expired on September 1, 1978. However, the drug had not been removed when pharmacy personnel inspected the cart on September 14, 1978.

As a result, the quality of patient care was threatened by improperly stocked carts. In addition to potential health hazards, Disorganized Crime was not concerned with the litigation from injured parties, if outdated drugs were administered.

Stockage of inventory needed to be improved. This is similar to what you previously read in the chapters on Army Audit Agency and the Department of Commerce. At the end of fiscal year 1978, Supply Service was responsible for an inventory exceeding $395,000. The inventory quantity exceeds 304,000 separate items for the 1,162 line items stocked. To control this inventory and the necessary procurements, the medical center used the computerized LOG I system.

We conducted a statistical sample to determine whether the stockage level was appropriate. The stockage was appropriate for only 475 lines (41 percent) and was over or short for 684 line items.

	Number of Lines	
	Sample	Total
Lines with appropriate stockage	59	475
Lines with overages	20	162
Lines with shortages	65	522
Lines without computed safety level reorder point nor economic order quantity	1	3
Total line items	145	1,162

The overage value of the 20 line items overstocked was over $6,400. If this trend held for all 162 lines overstocked, the overage value for the entire inventory would exceed $46,000. Stock overages were partially caused by requests by user services for purchases of items in order to use end-of-the-year funds received from VA Central Office. Our review of the first and last 100 purchases for the month of September 1978 showed that purchases were made for four line items that were overstocked. The value of the overstockage was over $4,000.

The degree of shortage of line items was shown by the fact that 128 lines were below their safety levels. We sampled 522 line items with shortages to determine if they were being reordered promptly and in the most economical

133

quantities. We found that line items with shortages are not being reordered promptly, nor are the orders in the most economical quantity.

| | Amount | |
	Sample	Total
Lines with due-in September 29, 1978	38	302
Lines without due-in September 29, 1978	27	220
Total lines with shortages	65	522

Of the 302 lines with due-ins, 128 lines had due-ins of the economic order quantity. Of the 220 lines with no due-ins, 163 lines continued to have no due-ins as of October 12, 1978. Seventy-three of the 163 line items did not have due-ins because Supply's Purchasing Section took longer than fourteen days to initiate a purchase order after it was notified by the Personal Property Section that the line item needed an order.

At the conclusion of my first audit within the VA, I had found that (as with the Departments of Army and Commerce) spending your money on visuals was the name of the game. What amazed me, though, was the willingness of the VA arm of Disorganized Crime to take an undefendable position in writing against saving your money. I was later to learn the audit team at Oklahoma City was lucky; at least the report was published.

I was the Auditor-in-Charge of the Kerrville, Texas, VA Hospital. Myself and my two fellow members of Disorganized Crime were there for three weeks in February 1979. The report was published September 24, 1979. There were over 150 employees and over 340 beds. Several findings in Engineering Service indicated that improved control and direction were needed by top management to insure efficiency and economy in Engineering Service operations.

A properly functioning fire alarm system is an absolute necessity to the safety of patients, employees, and property; the prolonged period of unsatisfactory alarm system functioning culminating in disconnection of the system from the fire station represents a situation that requires immediate management attention.

The lack of an effective preventive maintenance program had resulted in the premature replacement of some equipment and unnecessary repair of other equipment. The lack of required preventive maintenance had been brought to management's attention on several occasions since May 1976 by reports from the Engineering Officer and Building Management Service. Appropriate management attention to the preventive maintenance program was necessary to prevent recurring equipment failure and unnecessary expenditures for repair and replacement.

Quarters occupancy should be of primary concern to management to insure appropriate coverage of medical activities. However, we found that only the Director and Assistant Director lived on the station and that no documentation exists to justify why other essential employees did not live on station. Calculations of quarters' rental rates also showed a need for increased management concern.

Underutilized resources in biomedical maintenance and unsatisfactory contract maintenance in this area reflected another area for improved control and direction by top management to insure efficient and economical use of resources.

The five-year plan for the medical center needed improvement. There were two areas where problems were noted:

a. Proposed projects for Dental, Engineering, and Laboratory Services, with a total proposed cost of over $2.2 million, were either not needed or the planned costs were overstated.
b. A proposed 120-bed Nursing Home Care Unit (NHCU) is planned for fiscal year 1981. Officials from Health Care Facilities Service, Office of Construction, VACO, stated that the earliest the NHCU would be operational is the end of fiscal year 1983. In addition, the proposed NHCU must be approved by Congress before funds can be allocated for its construction. This delay of a minimum of two years has a major effect on current plans. The alcohol treatment unit had been proposed, based on the construction and completion of a proposed $7.8 million 120-bed NHCU, in fiscal year 1983. Space was available to accomplish this goal without waiting four years for the NHCU to be completed.

Management should have been able to plan more efficient and economical use of resources by documenting need and accurately computing the costs required to obtain the medical center's goals.

We also found that the $125,000 renovation of the laundry building should have been delayed until a Consolidation Feasibility Study (CFS) was conducted. The five-year facility plan for fiscal year 1981 through 1985 included $125,000 in 1981 for renovation of the laundry building. This renovation should have been delayed if a decision on consolidation with VAMC San Antonio had not been made before that time.

In October 1977 the District Executive Council initiated a feasibility study for consolidation of the two laundries. The study was completed in February 1978 and recommended against consolidation. However, the problem was deferred until the Veterans Administration Central Office (VACO) made a CFS. VACO's scheduled visit was postponed several times in 1978 and is now tentatively scheduled for July 1979. Should the visit again be postponed, it was recommended that building renovations not be initiated prior to a decision on consolidation. A decision in favor of consolidation would result in wasted funds if renovations were done prematurely. Renovations had been delayed from fiscal year 1980 to 1981 because of consolidation uncertainties.

Although the District Executive Council CFS was generally not in favor of consolidation, we noted that Kerrville's laundry handled all of San Antonio's 110-bed workload for six months during installation of San Antonio's laundry in 1974. Also, during the replacement of Kerrville's washer-extractors, VAMC San Antonio did Kerrville's washing for a two-week period. We felt that this led credence to the possibility of consolidation as well as the fact that laundry equipment utilization at Kerrville had been below 60 percent.

We found in Dental Service that the renovation plans needed revision. The medical center five-year plan (fiscal year 1981–1985) lists Dental Service renovation costs of $354,000, which were unnecessary, to correct space deficiencies. The medical center had identified space deficiencies in the service that could have been corrected at less than the proposed amount. The Chief, Dental Service, told us these problems could have been resolved with the acquisition of a storage room that was used by Pharmacy Service for conversion to a waiting area. The cost for this project and correction of the other following deficiencies is approximately $33,000, according to the Chief, Engineering Services.

Likewise, the boiler plant replacement was not justified. Problems with the medical center's boiler plant did not warrant its replacement as a minor construction project in fiscal year 1983. This $1.5 million project was included in the five-year facility plan for fiscal year 1981 through 1985.

These boilers were installed in 1958. There was no VA established replacement date for boilers, but thirty years was considered a useful lifetime in the VA system. Twenty-five-year replacement would have been out of line without a history of repair problems that indicates the necessity for replacement. Boiler inspection reports prepared semiannually and dating back to 1969 documented no problems with the station's boilers.

A special-purpose visit by VACO on September 21, 1978, to review and evaluate boiler safety, operation and maintenance procedures, and to identify problems and recommend improvements in operating procedures resulted in a recommendation to submit an interim project for fiscal year 1979 to replace burner, instrumentation, and flame safeguard equipment. The station concurred in that recommendation in December 1978. This major renovation should preclude the need for boiler plant replacement as planned in fiscal year 1983. An age of twenty-five years is not sufficient justification for replacement.

The fire alarm system was sending many false alarms to the Kerrville Fire Department. As a result, the alarm system had been disconnected from the fire department. Since January 12, 1979, the procedure in case of fire was for the switchboard operator to phone the fire department. Upon our arrival the Director had asked us to review this problem.

There had been two projects since 1975 to install a fire alarm system at the medical center. The first project, Contract Number V591C-88–74, was awarded June 27, 1974, for over $185,000. The medical center obtained the manufacturer's certificate December 29, 1975. The manufacturer certified that:

> The system has been properly installed, adjusted, and tested to insure that the system meets all the requirements of the plans and specifications.

The second fire alarm project, Contract Number V101C-183, was a portion of the installation of a $2.2 million air-conditioning system with a requirement for another fire alarm system. Contract Number V101C-183 called for seven items that we were not able to locate or verify:

Item

(1) "A certificate by the manufacturer of the fire alarm system equipment that the systems have been properly installed, adjusted and tested."
Audit Results
    Could not locate the manufacturer's certificate.

(2) "Furnish the services of a competent, factory-trained engineer or technician for two 4-hour periods for instructing maintenance personnel on the dates requested by the Resident Engineer."
Audit Results
    Could not verify that training had been requested by Resident Engineer nor received.

(3) "New components for additions to fire alarm system shall be made by the same firm which made the firm alarm equipment in the new system which is being or has been installed at the VA station or shall be approved equal and shall be compatible with and compatibly connected to the systems so the systems together with the new components operate satisfactorily in every respect, including coding characteristics. It shall be this contractor's full responsibility to supply full compatible components and/or modify the existing or newly installed fire alarm system in such manner that the operational requirements are fully attained and met."
Audit Results
    A letter dated September 19, 1975, from the contractor for Contract Number V101C-183 to the Resident Engineer, stating:

    This is to clarify that our approval of the subject submittal data does not indicate compatibility of this equipment with the equipment already installed under Contract No. V591C-88–74. Last May I attempted to obtain internal wiring diagrams for the system being installed under Contract No. V591C-88–74, and was informed by (name deleted) that such diagrams are not available. Because of this, our firm has no way of determining compatibility between the equipment of the two contracts.

    The contractor for Contract Number V591C-88–74, on August 17, 1976, wrote:

    This letter is to notify you that our warranty on the above referenced contract is hereby considered null and void for the following reasons:

1. Alterations and modifications to existing console by others.

2. Air Conditioning contractor in relocating existing smoke detectors to

new locations is not wiring to the same terminals as were existing, this puts the code transmitter in trouble alarm.

3. None of the new equipment being tied into existing equipment by the Air Conditioning contractor has been coordinated with our supplier as for compatibility with the existing system.

4. Characteristics of the equipment and the resistance of the circuits throughout the system shall be such that the systems will operate satisfactorily in every respect.

5. Adjust the sensitivity of each of the detectors as recommended by manufacturer of the detectors and mount them as required to insure satisfactory detection of the products of comubstion at the locations where they are being installed without causing nuisance actuations of the detectors.

6. When the systems have been completed and prior to the final inspection, furnish testing equipment and perform tests in the presence of the Resident Engineer to indicate that all of the equipment is operating properly.

Audit Results (Items 4–6 above)

The amount of testing of the fire alarm system by the contractor before acceptance of the system by the VA was limited.

a. The Resident Engineer, on May 4, 1977, stated the fire alarm system was only 85 percent complete.
b. The contractor stated on April 22, 1977, that the system was only tested two of the three scheduled days for testing.
c. The subcontractor could not check out all of the fire alarm system because the existing fire alarm system was not working on May 11, 1977.
d. The Resident Engineer, on June 3, 1977, stated:

"Bldg. #11 is now ready for completion of your contract requirements.

"Station personnel are still working on the circuitry for Bldgs. #1 and #2 and hope to have this area ready soon."

There was no documentation that any further testing was performed after May 11, 1977.

7. At the final inspection, demonstrate that the systems function properly in every respect in the presence of a VA representative.

Audit Results (Item 7)

The fire alarm system installation was a portion of the larger air-conditioning project. The final inspection conducted from June 14–17, 1977, resulted in twenty-five pages of deficiencies. Relating to the fire alarm system, deficiencies noted with the fire alarm system included relocating smoke detectors and missing smoke detectors.

The Post Final Inspection, on September 12–14, 1977, resulted in another seven pages of deficiencies; however, only one item mentioned the fire alarm system.

The Chief, Engineering Service, contacted the manufacturer in an attempt to correct this problem. The manufacturer sent a letter to the Chief on January 30, 1979, concerning the false alarms. The manufacturer stated:

Please be assured we will assist you in any way possible to resolve this problem as quickly as possible.

You will note that accumulation of dust or other foreign matter in the chamber area can cause the units to become more sensitive . . . it is imperative that when an adustment is made, that the pulse rate be maintained between the specified limits. Adjustments beyond the upper ranges will result in the unit's inability to respond to products of combustion.

The manufacturer's comments indicated that proper maintenance was necessary. Without the necessary maintenance training that should have been received, per the contract, there was no assurance the smoke detector units will function correctly. The fire alarm system was extremely important to the safety and protection of patients, employees, and property at the medical center and should have been corrected immediately. Only Disorganized Crime would have spent so much of your money for nonworking fire alarms for a hospital.

The medical center had not conducted an effective preventive maintenance (PM) program in several areas. This had resulted in some unnecessary repair costs and contributed toward early equipment replacement.

A review of preventive maintenance logs showed no documentation of completed PM during fiscal year 1978 for air conditioning and other machines. Documentation of PM for plumabing and steamfitting was not evident in over half of the months. This PM represented monthly, quarterly, semiannual, and annual schedules for a considerable amount of station equipment.

As early as May 10, 1976, the Engineering Officer reported in his Report of Systematic Review:

Required preventive maintenance within the Mechanical Shop has not been performed during the year of FY 76.

139

A year later he reported to the Administrative Executive Board in April 15, 1977, that:

The Machine Shop's work load is too great to permit any time for Preventive Maintenance Inspections.

Laundry equipment scheduled for PM was reviewed for PM documentation through July 1977, the oldest available records. There was no recorded documentation from July 1977 through June 1978. Administrative reports dating back to January 1977 indicated the Building Management Chief's concern over the inactive PM in the laundry service. For example:

MANAGEMENT REPORT, JANUARY 31, 1977
There is no preventive maintenance being performed on the laundry equipment at the present time. It is done via work orders. I have been informed by *(name deleted),* Asst. Engineering Officer, that they do have a program on paper but no manpower to accomplish it. I feel this is one of the reasons that we have so many breakdowns on the laundry equipment.

BUILDING MANAGEMENT BI-WEEKLY REPORT, JUNE 21, 1977
During the past two weeks, we have had one motor repaired on one of our washer-extractors. Upon questioning Engineering, they indicated that they did not have time to accomplish PM Maintenance.

On January 27, 1977, the Assistant Director reported to the Director that:

Engineering Service should be doing preventive maintenance on laundry equipment which is not being done. They should be checking the belts and bearings especially.

A review of work orders, related to repairs of laundry equipment for 1978, showed only one of twenty-six work orders in which preventive maintenance had been conducted on the machinery at the time of repair.

PM on laundry equipment was now provided by contract services at a cost of $150 per month, since December 1978. In other words, you paid for PM twice but it was too late.

The medical center had a request approved, based on excessive repair costs to date, to replace the laundry's folding machine at a cost of $29,000. The present equipment was purchased for $6,339 and had been scheduled for replacement in January 1982.

We also found the quarters' rental rates were too low. Besides the Director's single dwelling quarters, there were four detached duplexes, one of which was to be converted to administrative uses. Quarters' appraisals were required every three years unless five-year appraisals had been approved. Appraisals were also required when quarters were reconditioned, altered, or improved.

The last quarters' appraisal was by HUD in January 1976. The appraisal resulted in raising monthly rental for the Director's quarters, for example, from $156.46 to $210 in 1976. The significance of timely three-year appraisals was important. With Consumer Price Index (CPI) adjustments, the current rate was $230.83. The station estimated a net loss of $2,766 for quarters for the first half of fiscal year 1979, although a net profit of $382 was estimated by the station through the end of fiscal year 1979.

By November 1977 a central heating and air conditioning (A/C) project had been completed in all quarters. This improvement should have initiated a reappraisal of quarters, which Engineering Service failed to accomplish. The improvement would have increased rental rates.

Management had failed to insure timely appraisal of quarters. When advised in January 1979 that the three-year appraisal was due in January, the Director, on January 11, 1979, issued a request to VACO to change to five-year appraisals. The history of CPI adjustments did not suggest that approval of five-year appraisals could reasonably be expected by VACO. On February 2, 1979, VACO requested the required three-year appraisal, deferring a decision on five-year appraisal until the required appraisal was evaluated.

Also the quarters' utility rates were not properly determined. Our review of available records disclosed several problem areas. Adequate controls were not in effect to insure that utility rates were accurately computed. Station personnel were also not totally familiar with manual requirements, and station records were not readily auditable.

VA policy requires that quarters' utility rates must be adjusted whenever local domestic rates are changed. In no case should recomputation be delayed more than thirty days following the local adjustment. It had been the station's policy to adjust rates annually at the time of CPI adjustments in February each year.

This station used measured utility rates. For each type of utility, an estimate of the quantity used in an average month should have been made, based upon estimated hours of usage (life-style, occupancy) and using services in the quarters (lighting, TV, etc.). The medical center's utility rates did not accurately reflect these factors. For example, when the Assistant Director increased occupancy from three to four on April 9, 1978, utility rates were increased 42 cents per pay period, reflecting only a water charge increase. Currently, the Chief, Rehabilitation Medicine Service, with two quarters occupants, and the Chief, Laboratory Service, with four quarters occupants, are charged the same rates for electricity ($44.17 per month) and gas ($19.95 per month). Although the measured system was supposed to be in use, annual CPI adjustments were made in February 1977. Measured utilities are not subject to CPI adjustments.

Biomedical Maintenance Engineering Resources had not been effectively utilized. Planning involved in establishment of the biomedical maintenance engineering technician (BMET) shop had resulted in underutilization of space and equipment. Only one technician operated BMET facilities available to support a staff of four employees.

During 1976 a BMET was established at the medical center. Its mission included responsibility for maintenance, modernization, and operating safety of all medical equipment. It also was responsible for operational safety of all patient areas' electrical systems. It should have provided advice and expertise to medical personnel concerning operation and safety of all medical equipment. The present one-man shop could not accomplish this requirement.

Some of the preventive maintenance, which could be accomplished by a properly staffed BMET shop, was done by contract. It was common for PM-contracted services by the VA Supply Depot to be canceled. The present BMET said that the Supply Depot contracted services had not been highly efficient because the workload was high and was often rescheduled or canceled. Some medical equipment breakdowns and repair costs were a result of the current preventive maintenance program. Preventive maintenance contracts through this shop with the private sector and VA Supply Depot exceeded $27,000 annually. Another example of your paying twice for the same service.

The medical center five-year plan (fiscal years 1981–1985) lists laboratory renovation costs of $350,000. However, the Chief, Laboratory Service, had identified space deficiencies as potential JCAH deficiencies that could have been corrected at less cost than the proposed amount. The space deficiencies were computed prior to the receipt of more compact laboratory equipment that required less space to operate. While some relocation of certain laboratory rooms will be required, it was obviously unnecessary to spend the proposed amount of $350,000 to effect the changes.

The collection of claims due to ineligible hospitalization was not always prompt and aggressive. As of December 5, 1978, the accounts receivable totaled nineteen claims for over $31,000 due VAMC Kerrville for ineligible hospitalization. Our review of nineteen claims revealed that only three claims had previous collection procedures that were prompt and aggressive. This was a common condition found throughout Disorganized Crime. From a visuals point of view, it made sense. Why go and collect money due? Somebody may get upset; it's only your money anyway.

After Kerrville I joined the audit in progress at the VA Hospital in Tuscaloosa, Alabama. The audit was conducted from February 1979 to April 1979. The report was published on December 15, 1980. The medical center consisted of 45 buildings on 147 acres. The health care facility had 590 hospital beds—442 psychiatric and 148 medical. In addition there was a 120-bed Nursing Home Care Unit. As of December 31, 1978, there were 890 full-time and 62 part-time employees. Cost of nonexpendable equipment on hand exceeded $2.7 million. Fiscal year 1979 operating funds were budgeted at $19.3 million.

As at Kerrville, Tuscaloosa had spent lots of your money on equipment that was not being used, except for visuals. Plans had not been developed that outlined objectives for use of the color closed-circuit television (CCTV) system at this

142

medical center. Medical Media Production Service was responsible for equipment valued over $420,000, of which over $226,000 (54 percent) represented the cost of the CCTV equipment. The color CCTV system was originally purchased to support a statewide network to provide physician education programs. The statewide network was canceled by Central Office because it was too expensive; however, the medical center still had CCTV capability. Our review found limited documented workload to justify a CCTV system at this medical center. We found that during the first quarter of fiscal year 1979 there were only eighty-four programs requested for showing over the CCTV system. We also noted there were no documented plans to show future utilization and needs of the CCTV system; however, there were plans to expand the CCTV system at an estimated cost of about $77,400.

As we found at Oklahoma City, linen controls were inadequate. Linen loss for the consolidated laundry was $71,683, or 23 percent of the total linen stock for the period October 13, 1977 through November 9, 1978. This loss rate represented an upward trend in the amount of linen lost as the two previous inventory periods showed loss rates of 13.7 percent and 18.7 percent.

Station Memorandum Number 137–3, titled "Security of Hospital Linens," had not been revised in five years. At the time of our audit, a draft revision was being circulated, which, if implemented, would have made some improvements, such as assigning specific responsibilities to service chiefs. A log should have been maintained to record the linen issued or replaced daily at each issue point. These logs could have been used to review linen usage and the appropriateness of the linen quota and would have facilitated the study of linen loss at individual issue points.

Equipment planning was not always appropriate. The medical center had a dry-cleaning unit valued at $57,553, which was excessed in October 1978. This equipment had been obtained from VA Medical Center, San Francisco, as excess in June 1977. The equipment had not been installed at San Francisco nor had it been installed at this medical center. The justification by this medical center for excessing the equipment was that it was too large and complex for the space and needs of this facility.

In April 1976, the Chief, Building Management Service, requested a $20,000 dry-cleaning machine. The dry-cleaning equipment was justified to clean draperies on all windows. In June 1976, VA Central Office (VACO) notified the medical center that funds were not available for the purchase of this equipment. VACO later notified the medical center that VAMC San Francisco had excessed a dry-cleaning unit they might be able to use. In March 1977, the request for the smaller unit was canceled by VACO and plans were developed by the medical center to transfer the dry-cleaning equipment from VAMC San Francisco.

The dry-cleaning equipment obtained was twice the capacity of the equipment originally requested by the medical center. We found the medical center did not adequately plan for the installation and use of this larger unit prior to obtaining the equipment. After the equipment was received, it was determined that an additional $12,000 would be needed to provide building support, access for maintenance through an exterior wall, and placement of the unit into the laundry. In addition, $8,500 was spent to purchase anti-vibration mountings necessary for equipment installation. The shipping and handling charges for moving the equipment from San Francisco to Tuscaloosa amounted to $1,900.

Since June 1, 1977, many staff hours had been used at the medical center in an effort to justify, install, and now excess this piece of equipment. The dry-cleaning equipment was placed on excess on October 6, 1978 and still remains stored in the original shipping crates outside the laundry exposed to the elements. This type of storage has resulted in deterioration of many of the rubber hoses and gaskets. More in-depth planning prior to the acceptance of this equipment culd have saved $10,400 for anti-vibration mounts and shipping charges, and untold staff hours expended trying to solve the situation.

Vending machine sales in the canteen reportedly by the vendor were not verified. The VCS contract, dated April 3, 1975, for vending machines, stated:

> The VCS shall have the right to verify quantities of deliveries made to and amounts of collections derived from vending machines. The Canteen Officer or his designee may confirm at random at such times as the operator's representative is engaged in delivery or collection activities on the station.

During November 1978 to February 1979, reported vending sales dropped $1,673 (10.7 percent), from $15,590 for the same period in the prior year to $13,917. Patient and employee population for the comparable periods were approximately the same. The Chief, Canteen Service, on March 9, 1979, drafted a service policy whereby, at random and unannounced times, he would accompany the route man and count and verify each machine. The statement was drafted based on a February 22, 1979, memorandum by Veteran Canteen Service Field Office, Atlanta, requesting vendor data. Controls over vendor sales could have been further strengthened by comparing collections and deliveries shown on count sheets with the sales reported to the Canteen Service and obtaining permission from the vendor to review his records.

The Hospital Director did not concur that the monthly sales reported by the vendor be verified. Fortunately the auditors were able to "dance around" this nonconcurrance by referring to the March 9 service policy and did not drop this condition. It's always fascinated me how someone could disagree on "motherhood and apple pie."

Timeliness of test response to ambulatory care was not satisfactory. Laboratory support to the ambulatory care activity needed to provide improved timeliness for patient services. Requests for chemistry profiles on patients who have had blood drawn at 7:00 A.M. were not received in the ambulatory care activity until 2:30 P.M. This made it necessary for the patient to remain at the medical center all day in order to have the results interpreted by a physician in ambulatory care. These patients were provided a meal ticket for lunch at a cost of approximately two dollars per day. The alternative was to reschedule the patient for another day, but such a procedure would have significantly increased beneficiary travel costs. Patients who lived close to the medical center were sometimes called in one day to get the sample taken and return the next day for an appointment with the doctor. These situations are either an inconvenience to the patient or costly to the government.

With the laboratory equipment, it took five hours to process a chemistry profile. This equipment was past due for replacement, and VA Central Office had authorized the purchase of replacement equipment. The medical district said it would earmark $62,000 toward the purchase of new equipment but not until fiscal year 1980. The proposed replacement equipment was capable of running a chemistry profile in two hours and required only one technicial to operate and accomplish current workload whereas the present equipment required two to three staff to operate. The proposed replacement equipment would have provided more timely and efficient patient service and result in more staff available for expanded service coverage.

Laboratory Service currently had equipment on its consolidated memorandum receipt (CMR) that it did not use. We reviewed use of equipment listed on the service's CMR and found four items that were no longer used. Three of these items were located in the laboratory storage room and had not been used for six months. The items in storage were a blood gas tonometer, valued at $1,525; a pipetting apparatus, valued at $1,230; and a micro gasometer, valued at $643. We also found an explosion-proof refrigerator, valued at $692, which was not being used.

Maintaining unneeded equipment in the laboratory served no useful purpose and took up valuable storage space. These items should have been turned in to Supply Service as excess and a review performed of the equipment listed on the CMR in order to identify other excessible equipment.

Physician coverage for long-term patients was not adequate. We found there was no documented evidence of physician progress notes every thirty days in a majority of the records we reviewed. We sampled 33 medical records for long-term care medical patients and nursing-home residents currently being treated in the intermediate medicine unit and the Nursing Home Care Unit. We noted that 43 of 71 progress notes (61 percent) were in excess of the thirty-day frequency requirement. The average time lapse between physician progress notes in the 43 instances was seventy-five days (i.e., over two months between physician visits).

Physician staff assignments for Medical Service showed there was only one staff physician assigned one-half time to seventy intermediate care beds and sixty Nursing Home Care Unit beds and one staff physician assigned one-fourth time to sixty Nursing Home Care Unit beds. These physicians were assigned to ambulatory care activities for the remainder of their full-time duty schedule.

Utilization reviews were not conducted for outpatient activity. These reviews are conducted periodically to assure that optimum use of facilities and services is made for the best patient care. We reviewed medical records, correspondence files, and committee minutes to determine if the outpatient activity was operated in accordance with VA regulations and if any formal utilization review of this activity was conducted. Our review of medical records showed that outpatients are: (i) treated for and prescribed medicines for conditions other than those for which they were placed in the program; (ii) treated for extensive

145

periods of time (over five years) without documentation of need for further care; (iii) treated for chronic medical problems in the ambulatory care program; and (iv) seen for medication prescriptions while there are existing refills for the same medication.

Our review of committee minutes, correspondence files, and internal review files found no information relating to formal reviews for utilization of outpatient resources. However, we did find a memorandum and notes referring to and supporting the above identified problems in Medical Administration Service files. In addition, we found individual Chief of Staff memorandums setting forth medical center policy in accordance with VA policies relating to outpatient treatment eligibilities. The Chief of Staff told us he intended to develop and publish a comprehensive ambulatory care activity policy in the future.

Bed control is not effective because the bed-control clerk is not maintaining an accurate perpetual bed inventory for each ward. We reviewed the accuracy of the current bed census control sheet by verifying the actual number of vacant beds on ten wards against the number identified on the bed census control sheet. Although the number of vacant beds in three wards agreed with the control sheet, seven wards were not in agreement—four wards had more vacant beds than identified on the control sheet and three wards had fewer.

VA policy provided that persons authorizing admissions were to notify the admissions office to reserve a bed and each ward unit was responsible for notifying the bed-control clerk when a vacant bed was ready for occupancy. This latter function was the responsibility of the ward clerk during regular duty hours and nursing personnel during irregular duty hours.

Inaccurate bed inventories were caused by the failure of persons responsible for reporting admissions and vacancies (including inter-ward transfers) to properly report those changes. In some instances duplicate reporting by both clerical and nursing personnel on the wards caused the error.

One of the Veterans Administration's most fundamental and closely guarded policies is that no patient is to be mistreated or abused in any way, physically or verbally, by any employee. The importance of this policy is shown in the penalties that can be imposed if an employee is found guilty of patient abuse. The administrative penalty action for abuse of a patient is removal. However, a lesser penalty may be imposed when mitigating or extenuating circumstances clearly warrant such lesser penalty or the nature of the abuse is minor.

The reporting of patient incidents to identify patient abuse were weak. Our review showed that procedures for reporting patient incidents are not sufficient enough to ensure that all suspected incidents of patient abuse are reported to the Director. It also provided that steps would be taken to ensure that appropriate officials were kept fully informed of this policy so that not only would all possible measures be taken to avoid abuse and mistreatment of patients, but also to ensure that any responsible and guilty employees would be disciplined in line with VA policy.

Our review showed that sufficient data was not always provided on VA Form 10–2633 (Report of Special Incidents Involving a Beneficiary) so that management could determine if a patient may have been abused. We reviewed fifty VA Forms 10–2633 submitted between February 1 and February 26, 1979, and identified eleven occasions where patients had been injured. According to the information on the VA Forms 10–2633, the injuries were due to patients falling, being struck by another patient, or fighting with other patients. Nursing personnel reported eight of the eleven incidents to head nurses; however, there was no documented evidence the patient was interviewed to determine the validity of the data describing the reported incidents. For example, a nursing assistant reported a patient was found in a hallway bleeding from several small abrasions on the head. The nursing assistant also reported the patient said he had been in a fight with another patient. However, there was no evidence indicating the patient was contacted to determine the accuracy of the data or the identity of the other patient to determine if he required medical treatment.

We also noted that other data required on VA Form 10–2633, such as the unit that the patient was assigned to and the location where incident took place, not always included. Of the fifty forms reviewed, we found that 22 percent did not show where the incident occurred. This type data was required and was necessary for developing trends so that management could determine if a particular unit was having an unusually high number of incidents.

On March 8, 1979, a beneficiary came to the medical center and requested admission. The beneficiary was informed that he would be admitted as soon as his medical records were obtained from the file room. A few minutes later, the admission clerk was informed that the beneficiary had stabbed himself and was outside in a car. At the time of our review, report of contact forms and VA Forms 10–2633a (Summary of Special Incidents) were prepared; however, the above incident had not been reported on a VA Forms 10–2633. We were unable to determine if any other incidents had occurred in the outpatient areas.

Again the director was nor responsive to the problem. He stated

> Policies and procedures are sufficient as evidenced by the fact that all suspected abuse cases and unusual incidents are reported and dealt with in a timely manner. VA Form 10–2633 or a more timely report of contact is prepared to assure appropriate disposition. Existing reporting practices will continue to be reviewed and strengthened, as appropriate, consistent with identified needs.

The Director provided no other response as to why so many of the injuries were not adequately examined. This can only be explained through the "visuals" moral system. Without the necessary data and follow-up, there could not be any embarrassing things reported concerning patient abuse. Things were so bad that VA Form 10–2633a (Summary of Special Incidents) were also not always prepared and placed in the patients' medical records. Also, the incidents are not always recorded in the progress notes. We reviewed ten to fifty VA Forms 10–2633 that were submitted between February 1 and February 26, 1979, to determine if VA Forms 10–2633a were being prepared and placed in the medical records and to determine if the incidents were being recorded in the progress notes. We noted that VA Forms 10–2633a had not been prepared and placed in the medical

147

records for six of the ten incidents. There was also one incident reported on a VA Form 10–2633 concerning a medication error that was not recorded in the progress notes or on a VA Form 10–2633a. This information should have been documented in the patient's medical records to ensure that the doctor was aware of the patient's medical status.

In addition the weak reporting of patient abuse at Tuscaloosa, similar problems were also found at Salisbury, North Carolina; Hampton, Virginia; and, New Orleans, Louisiana. These conditions are discussed later in this chapter and were found by audit teams of which I was a member. Patient abuse was also found by other audit teams. For example, the Patient Anti-Abuse Program at the VA Hospital in Waco, Texas, was audited from July 23 to August 15, 1979. The report was published February 26, 1980. At Waco, employees related fears and frustrations in deciding whether or not to report patient abuse. These fears consisted of fear of reprisal actions from management, the union, and their peers. Their frustrations include hopelessness for change in the patient treatment system and a feeling that management is not responsive to identified reports of patient abuse. In addition, a review of patient medical records showed all incidents involving beneficiaries were not reported. As reported to the audit team by employees, some abuse incidents are reported as accidental injuries, or as resulting from patient altercations with each other.

Appropriate follow-up action was not taken on some identified or suspected patient-abuse problem areas. We found at least two occasions over a two-month period where nursing employees reported alleged patient abuse incidents without appropriate follow-up action being taken by center management. Another reported incident reflected questionable restraint actions by nursing personnel; however, the incident was not questioned.

The following incidents were reported by employees two to three weeks after the fact because of fears of reprisals and for job security. One instance involved a NA trainee reporting patient abuse to a supervising nursing instructor and then to the Associate Chief, Nursing Service for Education (ACNSE), on October 26, 1978. The ACNSE stated she immediately reported this information directly to the Chief, Nursing Service (CNS). The alleged abuse was that of a ward NA beating a wheelchair stroke-victim patient about the ears with cupped hands. The incident was allegedly witnessed by two other NA's (one a trainee) who did not want to get involved. It was unclear what action was taken from this point. The nurse coordinator responsible for the building in which the alleged abuse took place recalls no inquiry or communication from her supervisor concerning this matter. She recalls her knowledge of the incident was obtained through the "grapevine."

The second instance involved an alleged patient-abuse incident that occurred on November 20, 1978. According to several interviewees, and supported by our review of time and attendance records and data from correspondence files, the following sequence of events took place:

Two NA's, one of whom made the above-noted October 26, 1978 report to his supervisor, witnessed what they considered patient abuse on Ward 90A-North by another NA on the 12 midnight to 8:00 A.M. shift. This patient abuse was described as a "swing with his arm and hitting the patient in the stomach area while the patient was in his bed." Other alleged abuses were noted the same shift by one of the NA's.

On December 5 or 6, 1978, the NA involved in the October 26, 1978 report went to the personnel management spacialist for Nursing Service (now transferred from this section) and reported in detail what he had observed while on duty November 20, 1978. He also related other alleged patient-abuse incidents he had observed while in training and since his recent permanent assignment to Ward 90A-North. The personnel management specialist stated the NA related events in detail as to times, places, names of employee witnesses, names of accused employees, and patient names. He further stated the NA expressed what he considered "legitimate fears" concerning job security and possible retaliation for reporting this information. The NA also expressed frustration with what he considered nothing being done about his initial reporting of alleged patient abuse on October 26, 1978, this being the reason he was reporting the information directly to the personnel management specialist.

On the same day, the personnel management specialist accompanied the NA to the office of the CNA where the details of what the NA had reported were related to the chief nurse.

On December 7, 1978, the other NA witnessed one of the November 20, 1978 alleged patient-abuse incidents, corroborated the first NA's report of this incident to the chief nurse.

On December 18, 1978, a memorandum was sent to the CNS to the COS. This memo stated:

> The NA related he had witnessed the following:
>
> a. Patients being hit in the stomach.
> b. Patients being tied in a chair and slapped twelve to fifteen times.
> c. Confused patients being given burning cigarettes and nursing assistants placing bets as to whether the patients would eat them.

The memorandum went on to state the accused NA's name and that both witnessing NA's stated they had witnessed the alleged patient abuse by this employee.

The memorandum further stated,

> I am submitting this report for your information. I do not believe we could ever *prove* anything *at this late date*. The Head Nurse and Supervisor have been informed and urged to be alert to possible abuse and to review the policy regarding abuse of patients with their staff.

The COS endorsed this memorandum as follows: "I do not believe we would gain by investigation of remote and probably unprovable reports. Closer supervision is probable best answer." The director signed a concurrence to the endorsement on December 19, 1978. Investigation should have been conducted, espe-

149

cially regarding the incident where two employees corroborated the account of a highly suspect patient-abuse incident.

Another incident involved the completion of a VA Form 10–2633 (Report of Special Incident Involving a Beneficiary) on October 30, 1978, the date of the incident. This report described an incident and control actions taken by nursing personnel ona psychiatric ward, which suggests the use of inappropriate restraint actions. A registered nurse completed the report and indicated on the form she had not witnessed the incident but it was reported to her by a NA. The report stated, "It took several nursing assistants to control the patient. During the episode the patient received minor abrasions to the face and mouth." The examining physician's remarks stated, "Patient has superficial abrasions on right cheek, upper lip and chin. No healing problems are anticipated from the superficial abrasions." The report was forwarded to the Chief of Staff who indicated no further action was required as did the Medical Center Director. We interviewed a NA who witnessed the incident. As reported to us, this NA did not witness the onset of the incident but walked into the room during the incident. The NA was almost hit by flying fists upon entering the room where three or four other NA's were beating the patient with their fists. The NA stated the patient's face and eyes were red and swollen as a result of the incident. The NA related the head nurse became upset because she thought the incident could have been handled differently. This type of incident, resulting in injuries only to the patient's face from restraining techniques, should have required further inquiry into the actions taken by employees.

Administrative dicssiplinary actions, in cases where medical center investigations have sustained alleged patient-abuse incidents, do not reflect that such actions support the agency's strong patient-abuse policy.

VA Manual DM&S Supplement, MP-5, Part I, Chapter 752, states the administrative disciplinary action for abuse is removal unless extenuating circumstances clearly warrant such lesser penalty or the nature of the abuse is minor.

VA Manual MP-5, Part I, Chapter 752, Appendix C, provides guidelines in administering disciplinary actions to help assure like disciplinary action is taken for like offense. The policy further states that among other factors in determining disciplinary action, the degree of harm or interference the offense has caused with respect to impact on VA operations or public relations should be considered.

We reviewed all ten administrative disciplinary actions taken in sustained patient-abuse investigations over a period of two years. These actions show the minimum disciplinary action or less, as recommended in the above policy guidelines, was administered in 90 percent of these cases. Included in this review were two sustained cases where the action taken was less than that cited in the guide. Our review of disciplinary actions taken for sustained patient-abuse cases showed one employee, for which three allegations were sustained, was administered the minimum recommended action all three times. The auditors did not regard this as supporting agency policy as noted.

We also conducted a random review of actions taken for other recorded offenses to determine the official action taken and their relationship to recommended actions contained in the guide. The results showed only 64 percent resulted in the lowest disciplinary action suggested in the guide.

Disciplinary actions administered for sustained cases of patient abuse should be strengthened. This would, in effect, reinforce to employees the intent of center management to strongly support agency policy on patient abuse and that management will not tolerate abuse of beneficiaries in any form. In addition, this action would help deter any negative impact patient-abuse incidents may have on VA operations.

During the first nine months of fiscal year 1979, there were 113 VA Forms 10–2633 (Report on Special Incident Involving a Beneficiary) completed in just Building 90. One of these reports, dated December 26, 1978, resulted in an investigation of patient abuse. The allegation was not sustained in this case. An oral report of patient abuse in Building 90 was made to the Chief, Nursing Service, December 1978; however, no investigation was initiated.

In May 1978, an investigation was conducted in Building 90 as a result of oral reports by nursing assistant trainees of alleged verbal and physical patient abuse. This investigation sustained the alleged abuse and resulted in the resignation of a licensed vocational nurse after a letter of intent to remove was executed to him. In addition, three nursing assistants were counseled for general vulgar speech while on duty. However, our review of this investigation file found testimony during the investigation implying other employees in Building 90 were involved in verbal and physical abuse of patients. These implications were not thoroughly followed up in the investigation.

An anonymous letter from a concerned nurse dated February 23, 1979, and addressed to the Medical Center Director, described patient mistreatment and abuse conditions in Building 90. A copy of this letter was received by the VA Office of Inspector General. Medical center management stated they have not received or seen this letter. However, a VA Central Office telephone inquiry was received by the Director on April 17, 1979, regarding a congressional inquiry. This inquiry was regarding an anonymous letter from a concerned nurse about conditions in Building 90 and a letter concerning a patient in Building 90. On April 18, 1979, a letter replying to the VA Central Office telephone inquiry was prepared. This letter and enclosures predominately addressed the circumstances of one particular patient. Conditions in Building 90 were described in general regarding physical environment. In addition, the letter referred to the May 1978 investigation and the removal of an employee for alleged patient mistreatment.

Our review of the allegations outlined in the anonymous letter, with respect to conditions in Building 90, particularly Ward 90A-North (a locked ward), found the environment in this building (type patient, employee attitudes, and ward management) would allow the existence of such bad conditions.

Some employees we interviewed who are assigned to Building 90 expressed fear from various reprisal actions, either identified as union reprisals, management reprisals, or peer pressure and are therefore reluctant to report patient abuse. There are also indications that some patient-abuse incidents are reported as accidental injuries. Patients have been verbally and physically abused and other-

151

wise mistreated according to interviews with employees and patients.

We did observe one patient with multiple bruises on his arms and legs. In an interview with his staff physician, the patient was stated to bruise easily due to medical reasons. However, we reviewed this patient's medical record and current nursing treatment plan. We found there was no mention of a skin or bruising problem or condition in the medical record problem list or the nursing treatment plan. We did find one progress note entry by a registered nurse stating, "The skin is like tissue paper and very fragile."

It was related to us by ward employees and supervisors in Building 90 that patients on Ward 90-A North have been restricted from restroom and water fountains. The patients allegedly have been contained in a locked day room, which is separate from water fountains and restroom facilities. These employees explained the reasons for such restrictions were ease of patient supervision, disciplinary measures toward patients, and mistreatment of patients. A former ward supervisor stated these restrictions were not accomplished with her knowledge and when the conditions were reported to her by a NA, she ordered the doors opened. She also stated she had held staff meetings where she advised employees to discontinue the locking of day room doors. Although we did not personally observe such restrictions in practice on Ward 90-A North at the time of our review, it was related to us by the evening nursing personnel that the doors are still being found locked when they arrive for duty. We believe if such restrictions still exist, they are accomplished covertly.

Many patients on Ward 90-A North are not medically oriented or in good contact according to medical records and staff, but some complained to us of their treatment, such as no-smoking restrictions, inability to leave wards or the building, not enough food, and boredom. Ward 90-A North is a locked ward and as such, the patients are not privileged to leave without supervision. It was also the only ward in the hospital that allows no smoking for the patients at any time. A staff physician and the new nurse coordinator stated they have no idea as to why the ward was designated as nonsmoking, considering the fact the mixture of patients on Ward 90A-North is comparable to the mixture on other medically designated wards. It was reported to us in employee interviews, noted in progress notes, and we observed patients taking food from other patients who were less alert or oriented.

Ward employees complained strongly to the auditors that registered nurses were seldom available in the patient care areas, being busy with paperwork and meetings. During our tours of the patient areas, we did not note registered nurses in these areas the first two weeks. However, we did note them present in the patient areas the last week of the audit. (I wonder why?) Some Building 90 licensed vocational nurses, nursing assistants, and a physician also stated staff nurse presence and supervision in the patient care areas had improved somewhat in the last several months. You will read about additional patient-abuse problems later on in this chapter. Back to the specific problems that were found at Tuscaloosa.

Patient medication profiles were not adequately performed. Patient medication profile reviews were conducted only on refill prescriptions. Prescriptions were not dispensed without prior review of the patient medication profile. This review is interpreted by the VA to include both a pharmacist drug interaction review and a review for duplicate prescriptions.

We noted that reviews by pharamacists for drug interaction and by technicians for duplicate prescriptions were generally accomplished on refill prescriptions but not on new prescriptions. The patient profile review is designed to prevent patients from receiving incompatible drugs and duplicate prescriptions. Under the current review practice, the interaction of non-compatible drugs would occur and duplicate drug prescriptions could be filled prior to reviewing the patient medication profiles. Therefore, performing the profile reviews on refill prescriptions did not adequately ensure against drug interactions or duplicate prescriptions.

Investigations of unacceptable length-of-stay study results are not adequately performed and do not always provide sufficient data so meaningful corrective action can be implemented. Based on the instructions received from VA Central Office for performing these tests, the outcome can be either acceptable or unacceptable, depending where the cases are plotted on a sequential chart on the form. Unacceptable tests are required to be investigated to determine the reasons why the length-of-stay exceeded the prescribed standards.

An analysis of the Length-of-Stay Summary Report (VAF 10–5351), for calendar year 1978, showed that seven tests were completed on a total of eighty-two cases for three diagnoses applicable to psychiatric care. A summary of results is below:

Diagnosis	Tests Completed	Cases Tested	Cases over Standard	Days over Standard
Anxiety Neurosis	2	20	11	388
Schizophrenia: Paranoid or Chronic	4	48	24	1,256
Depressive Neurosis	1	14	9	129
Totals	7	82	44	1,773

The results for three of the seven tests, which include forty-one cases, showed the length-of-stay required investigation. The medical center investigated twenty-seven of forty-one cases to determine the reasons why the length-of-stay was unacceptable. The investigation made on the length-of-stay for the anxiety neurosis study identified problems and provided constructive recommendations. However, the results of the investigation of the depressive neurosis test indicated that there was no problem in the length-of-stay because the cases in the test had inaccurate diagnosis and should not have been included in the study. The other investigation mentioned the length-of-stay for the schizophrenia diagnosis were justified; however, the reasons why the study indicated the length-of-stay was unacceptable were not identified. Because adequate investigations were not made on the length-of-stay studies, sufficient data was not available to determine if the length-of-stay is acceptable or within the standards. Also, meaningful recommendations could not be developed and implemented.

Psychosocial assessments were not being prepared by Social Work Service for all psychiatric patients admitted to the hospital. These assessments are required by JCAH and the VA. With regard to written policies and procedures for providing social work services, the NCAH Accreditation Manual for Psychiatric Facilities, 1972, stated in Standard III of its Social Work Service chapter, that:

> Policies and procedures shall include statements relating to at least the following: Patient and family evaluation and assessment including psychosocial history and community relations; . . .

The requirements by JCAH to take into account the implications of the patients physical, social, educational, and psychological condition was restated in its March 20, 1978, letter, awarding a one-year accreditation to this medical center.

As shown in the following table, we reviewed forty-one medical records and found that sixteen did not contain psychosocial assessments.

Category	Reviewed	With No Assessment	Percentage
Intensive Treatment Unit	23	11	47.8%
Extended Care Unit	13	4	30.8%
Alcohol Treatment Unit	5	1	20.0%
Total	41	16	39.0%

A total psychosocial assessment is one of the first inputs into the medical records to document a history of the veteran's illness, factors precipitating admission, family history, and other facts. This data, among others, is used in arriving at a diagnosis and in preparing treatment plans. It's no wonder the veterans were being warehoused longer than they should have been. You, of course, paid for these extra days.

I was the Auditor-In-Charge of the VA Hospital at New Orleans, Louisiana. It was the worst hospital that I would ever audit. My team was there from May to July 1979. The audit report was never published. As a result, there was no follow-up effort required to determine if any of the problems we found were corrected by members of Disorganized Crime. The report would also not be available through the Freedom of Information Act. Another way of looking at it is you paid for an audit; however, you never got a report. After I tell you what we found, you will understand why this report never saw the light of day.

The medical center stands on 5.5 acres and consists of a ten-story main hospital and five other miscellaneous buildings. The health care facility has 569 operating beds: 260 medical, 221 surgical, and 88 psychiatric. As of March 31, 1979, there were 1,203 full-time and 101 part-time employees. Fiscal year 1978 budget expenditures were $34.8 million. New Orleans VAMC operates in a complex environment. The inner city location, the multi-hospital complex, the dual affiliation with Tulane University and Louisiana State University, and the crowded conditions within the hospital contributed to the problems we found.

Followup on correction of previously noted deficiencies was inadequate. Conditions reported in the General Accounting Office (GAO) Report, April 14, 1976 and the Systematic External Review Program (SERP) Report, January 17–21, 1977 continue to exist. Medical center follow-up procedures, Hospital Memorandum 00–2, January 2, 1977, required each service chief to meet annually with the Director and " . . . discuss items that the chief considers of significance." The memorandum further states:

> The current status of implementation of recommendations resulting from external hospital audits of survey and internal surveys and reviews will also be appropriate items for the agenda.

In a new draft of Medical Center Memorandum Number 00–2, June 20, 1979, these requirements have been strengthened. Service chiefs must now include items pertaining to SIR and external reviews on the agenda and were made responsible for the follow-up action and its effectiveness. Prompt implementation of the newly drafted memorandum could have been combined with action by the Director to assure that long-standing deficiencies were corrected. When feasible, those responsible for correction of reported deficiencies should have been required to develop a specific plan on how this would have been accomplished, including an estimated completion date. Specific items previously reported and were still present.

UNSATISFACTORY FOLLOWUP ON PREVIOUSLY NOTED DEFICIENCIES

Deficiency	Audit Report Chapter	When Previously Reported
Ineffective SIR program	Pharmacy Laboratory	SERP, January 1977
Outpatient medication profile review	Pharmacy	SERP, January 1977
Limited ward rounds	Pharmacy	SERP, January 1977
Storage of heat sensitive drugs	Pharmacy	SERP, January 1977
Lack of space	GA&M Pharmacy Fiscal	GAO Report, April 1976

155

Other previously noted reported deficiencies were noted, however, not written as a separate service chapter in the draft audit reports. For example, Radiology Service needed a Medical Center Directive implementing policies concerning the retention and checkout of patients' X-ray films. This deficienty was previously reported in the GAO report, April 1976 and SERP, January 1977. The directive should have specifically addressed who could check out X-ray films from the Radiology Service film library, under what conditions X-rays could be checked out, and how long X-rays may be retained.

Parking for outpatients, the handicapped, and visitors was not sufficiently provided. There are 165 available parking spaces on VAMC property. These spaces are distributed as follows: employees 149, handicapped outpatients and/or employees 7, and special visitors 9. Although, during the time period October 1, 1978 to March 31, 1979 there were over 92,700 outpatient visits to the medical center (an average of 742 daily), there were no parking spaces designated for outpatients or regular visitors other than the seven for use by the handicapped. Members of Disorganized Crime had all the rest of the parking.

DM&S Circular 10–75–212, September 15, 1975, provided guidelines for patients and visitors vehicle parking at DM&S facilities and states:

> All Directors of health care medical facilities on VA property will provide a sufficient number of parking spaces adjacent to the entrances to the principal areas of care and treatment for services for outpatients and visitors arriving on VA grounds. Directors of physically separated outpatients clinics not on VA property will provide parking spaces for patients, especially for the physically handicapped where parking exists. All new locations and/or relocations will include appropriate access and parking. In view of the crowded conditions for some parking areas, it is anticipated that the Hospital Director will take early action to provide those designated facilities of appropriate size and location where they do not now exist.

The concern of the medical center had been employee parking and not patient and visitor parking. In October 1976, an Ad Hoc Subcommittee on parking reported that one of the main problems of parking was that the number of employees authorized to park was three times the number of available spaces.

In the meantime, a new memorandum concerning parking of cars on government property was being written, which management believed would have alleviated these parking conditions. Our review of a draft of the new memorandum found that the new policy would not significantly improve parking conditions. It showed that the medical center's 165 parking spaces were to be allocated to employees in a manner not much different than the current status. There was no change in the number of spaces to be reserved for the handicapped, outpatients, or visitors.

Disorganized Crime's policy of providing for employee parking based on grade or position before providing sufficient parking for outpatients, visitors, or the handicapped was not in compliance with the referenced circular and was not in the spirit of basic VA policy of service to the veteran. Although this area of the city was congested, there were adequate commercial parking facilities within a short distance of the center, and the area had good bus transportation available. Sufficient parking should have been provided on VA property for the handicapped, outpatients, and visitors before employee parking was taken into consideration. Parking provided should have been based upon statistics derived from the number of daily outpatient visits and use of the facility by the handicapped, outpatients, and visitors.

The Hospital Director, of course, did not agree. The Director told us there was no way to provide sufficient parking spaces under existing conditions for outpatient, handicapped, and visitor needs. In addition, this would further complicate recruitment for key employees. This medical center is in a high-crime area with a preponderance of female employees. Evening and night female employees park in parking lots A and C with police in attendance. Despite this special security precaution, we have had an attack on one of our female employees. Recruitment of nurses has been extremely difficult and only through assurance that they can park adjacent to our existing buildings, have we been successful in recruiting adequate nurse staffing. There are short-term daytime commercial parking facilities available in close proximity to this medical center as well as public transportation, which our veterans utilize. We feel the only appropriate solution is to provide adequate parking through the construction of a parking garage directly across the street from the Medical Center on Perdido Street. This plan has been pursued for sometime with the Health Education Authority of Louisiana and appears feasible to them. We are now in the process of submitting a construction project to VA Central Office for land acquisition and funding consideration. Guess who would pay for all that land and construction?

The auditors replied that we shared the Director's concern for the safety of employees and believed that appropriate measures should be implemented to maximize safe working conditions. However, DM&S Circular 10–75–212, September 15, 1975 stipulated that a sufficient number of parking spaces be provided for outpatients and visitors arriving on VA grounds. Therefore, parking spaces should be reserved for outpatients and visitors, especially during the hours of the ambulatory care clinic. These spaces could be used by employees whose work shifts do not conflict with the hours of the ambulatory care clinic. With adequate planning and timely and appropriate notification to employees (e.g., parking lot signs, letters to all employees, or an article in the house newsletter), voluntary compliance by employees with the new parking rules should be obtainable. These methods could be reinforced by methods requiring a minimum of effort by security personnel. Suggested actions to reduce parking violations and to identify and ticket parking violations are:

1. Stationing an officer at the parking lot entrance for an hour, one half hour prior to the main morning shift, to reduce violations.
2. Stationing several officers, once or twice a week, in the parking lot for an hour, half an hour prior to the end of the morning shift, to identify and ticket parking violators.

We believed that employees should have made maximum use of commercial parking facilities and public transportation and that, as necessary, police escorts be provided at night for groups of employees using these facilities. We further believed that our recommendation that VA parking on VA grounds be prioritized for outpatients, visitors, and key medical center personnel reflects the basic VA policy of providing service to veterans. But as I have already told you, it didn't matter, the whole report was never published.

The program for prevention of patient abuse needed improvement. One of the Veterans Administration's most fundamental and closely guarded policies is that a patient may not be mistreated or abused either physically or verbally by any employee. The administrative penalty action for abuse of a patient is removal. A lesser penalty may be imposed when mitigating or extenuating circumstances clearly warrant such lesser penalty or the nature of the abuse is considered to be minor. We identified several areas where management action could improve the implementation of agency policies. There were:

a. Medical center memorandums did not define patient abuse or state the penalty for patient abuse.

b. VA Form 10–2633a (Summary of Special Incidents) were not filed in medical records; and,

d. All medical employees were not given patient-abuse orientation and training.

Plans for utilizing existing closed circuit television (CCTV) equipment have not been developed. This was very similar to what we had found previously at Tuscaloosa. Plans had not been developed that outlined objectives for use of the color CCTV system. Medical Media Production Service resonsible for equipment valued at approximately $271,000 of which over $145,000 (54 percent) represented the cost of the CCTV equipment. The color CCTV system was originally purchased to support an interagency network to provide physician education programs. The interagency network was canceled by Central Office because it was too expensive; however, the medical center still had CCTV capability. Our review found limited documented workload to justify a CCTV system. We found that during the three-week period of May 14 through June 1, 1979, only sixteen films containing less than eight hours of material were shown. We also noted there were no documented plans to show future utilization and needs of the CCTV system; however, there were plans to expand the CCTV system, at an estimated cost to you of about $52,700.

We found the shortage of space to be the number-one problem at the medical center. The lack of space was reported by GAO in 1976. Hospital management completed a study in 1979 and found the VAMC to be deficient by 119,000 net square feet (NSF) overall. Addressing the long-term solution to the problem, the Director had requested acquisition of 1.1 acres of land for $1.8 million adjacent to the facility and funds to construct an eight-floor clinical addition (319,200 NSF), at an estimated cost to you of $57 million. If approved by

Congress in 1979, construction was scheduled to be completed by 1984. In the meantime, interim construction projects and space-use planning had not been directed toward improving chronic space problems in Pharmacy and Ambulatory Care, and more effective use could have been made of existing space in other areas.

The medical center's February 1979 space summary printout showed Ambulatory Care deficient by 5,247 NSF and Pharmacy deficient by 5,998 NSF. The VA and GAO auditors (April 1976 GAO report) found both functions were operating under strained conditions because of their critical space problems.

Pharmacy Service was assigned 4,227 NSF, which was split between the inpatient unit on the second floor and the outpatient unit on the first floor. In 1976, plans were under way to expand and consolidate Pharmacy in the west wing of the first floor (7,627 NSF) by relocating top management, Fiscal, Supply, and Personnel Services. An architect engineer firm had completed 25 percent of the project drawing; however, the project was reduced by management to removal of walls and renovation of Pharmacy's present space from the present project. There were no plans to expand Ambulatory Care prior to the construction of the clinical addition. Effects of the congestion and split operations; unsuitable, hazardous, working conditions; costly staffing patterns; unsatisfactory employee morale; and untimely service to beneficiaries. Although GAO, JCAH, SERP, and veterans' services organizations have addressed the space deficiencies in report from 1975 to the present, no significant improvement has occurred.

In contrast to the Ambulatory Care and Pharmacy Services, Psychiatry Service had 11,486 NSF over criteria. Observations made during the audit found this space to be under-utilized. In addition, Ward 10E, with eight beds, had only a 35 percent occupancy and patients were moved to other floors at night. There had been six alternative plans proposed for the use of the space that would become available when the 8,000 NSF courtyard building was completed. Changes to the proposals were due to the extension of the completion date of the 8,000 NSF courtyard building. The latest proposal had the courtyard building housing Fiscal, Supply, and Personnel Services and would have saved space on the first floor of the main building.

The space described above was either presently available or coming available in the near future. Specific plans should have been developed and implemented in the next year to relieve the chronic space problems in Pharmacy and Ambulatory Care. The need for improved space utilization and planning was also apparent by the manner in which supplies and equipment were stored throughout the building. Many of these areas were observed to have a crowded and cluttered appearance beyond what should be expected even under existing crowded conditions. Hospital management needed to realistically appraise the use of these areas and determine if they could have been more efficiently and effectively utilized. The Director did not agree with us and gave two alternatives that were unacceptable: reduce the number of veterans served or, lease additional space at another location.

Another reason the report was never published was because a time and attendance review was conducted on June 19, 1979 from 7:00 A.M. to 4:00 P.M.

We made random checks of the presence of 135 employees. The review included Medical, Neurology, Nursing, Psychology, Psychiatry, Radiology, and Surgical Services and the Office of the Chief of Staff. We selected 59 residents, 30 Nursing Service personnel, 27 full-time physicians, 16 part-time physicians,and 3 psychologists for our review.

Time and attendance reports often did not accurately reflect duty and leave. A time and attendance review on June 29, 1979 of 135 residents, physicians, psychologists, and nurses showed 22 (16 percent) of the time and attendance reports to be incorrect.

VA Form 4–5631, Time and Attendance Report, is the official record used for time, attendance,and leave for all employees on the rolls. VA Manual MP-6 stated:

> Payment of salaries are based on these records. Initialing of the Time and Attendance Reports indicates that it properly reflects the true status of the employees involved. The timekeeper must have personal knowledge when each employee is on duty and when he/she is on leave or rely upon properly certified subsidiary records.

The Assistant Chief Medical Director for Professional Services in IL 11–78–25, April 25, 1978, concerning timekeeping for part-time physicians, stated: "If hours of duty are not performed as scheduled, appropriate deductions in pay or leave must result." He further states the observations:

> . . . that patient care has not suffered or that much more work is contributed to patient care than is renumerated cannot outweigh the professionals' responsibility to deliver services as contracted.

Timekeepers were ineffective in monitoring actual hours worked by part-time physicians. Appropriate deductions in pay and/or leave were not being made for part-time physicians who fail to perform duty as scheduled. Seven of the sixteen part-time physicians we attempted to locate were not on duty during the hours indicated on Time and Attendance Reports. Three of the physicians were indicated to be performing professional duties outside the VA during VA scheduled hours.

Time and attendance records were found that do not adequately support salary payments to full-time employees. Unit timekeepers relied on the honor system instead of personal observations or subsidiary records. For example, one full-time Medical Service physician was reported to be on leave by his section chief. The physician's Time and Attendance Report did not reflect the leave. One nurse scheduled to be on duty from 7:30 A.M. to 4:00 P.M. was reported to be off duty by ward personnel. The Time and Attendance Report indicated the nurse worked a normal duty tour of eight hours on June 29, 1979.

Non-payable leave is not accounted for by the PAID system. DM&S Circular 10–72–215, September 1, 1972, states:

> Stations will establish their own control system to record and compile the earning and use of non-payable leave for all residents and interns,

160

full-time and intermittents. The control system established locally must provide that a strict daily record be kept, showing accumulated balances, amount used, and for what purposes.

A uniform timekeeping system for noncareer residents receiving non-payable annual leave had not been implemented. Services did not have a consistent, systematic means of recording non-payable leave. Ten residents were indicated to be on leave by service personnel and three other residents could not be located. Leave records maintained by Medical and Surgical Service timekeepers confirmed leave status for only two of the ten residents. This was a system-wide problem.

Residents and staff physicians were late or failed to report for clinics. Management needed to implement controls to improve resident and staff physician's attendance to clinics in both Surgery and Medical Services. In the past, Medical Administration Service (MAS) monitored physician attendance to clinics. The results showed when residents and staff physicians reported or if they failed to report to clinics. MAS discontinued clinic attendance studies shortly after a November, 1978 memorandum was sent to the Director from the Chief, Medical Service. " . . . I find such timekeeping distasteful and would suggest that a more meaningful reporting would be the amount of medical care and quality of medical care delivered in a clinic setting." We summarized the number of time residents and staff physicians were at least forty minutes late or failed to report (FTR) during the period November 6 to December 29, 1978 as shown by the MAS study.

| | STAFF | | RESIDENTS | |
Clinic	FTR	40 Minutes	FTR	40 Minutes
Cardiology	7	1		7
General Medicine		3	1	29
Thoracic	1	4		4
Orthopedic	4	2		2
Pulmonary	8	3		
Plastic Surgery	6			
Urology	5	3		7
Nurse Diabetics	1			
Endocrinology	1			
Neurology	1			
Hypertension	4	10		
Vascular Surgery	1	2		3
Neurosurgery				3
Dermatology	4			
Renal	1			
General Surgery	—	1		6
TOTALS	44	29	1	61

Also, during this period, the report shows the Assistant Chief, Surgical Service, as over forty-five minutes late to Thoracic Clinic on four occasaions and failed to report once. The Chief of Pulmonary Disease Section failed to

161

report to the Pulmonary Clinic seven times and another staff physician was over forty minutes late three times and failed to report once. The staff physician assigned to the Hypertension Clinic failed to report four times and was late an average of four hours on nine occasions.

During the time-and-attendance review, we observed that the attendance problem still existed, residents and staff physicians were late or failed to report for scheduled clinics. Attendance to scheduled clinics is essential to good patient care or why pay the physician to show up at all?

Identified problems with attendance of part-time physicians had not received adequate attention. During 1979, numerous memorandums have been written by the Director and the Chief of Staff concerning VA and Medical Center policy on part-time physician attendance as well as individual attendance problems. The Chief of Staff, in October 1978, wrote in a memorandum to the Chief, Medical Service, that two part-time physicians assigned to his service were scheduled to be at an affiliated medical school during their VA scheduled duty hours. During our time-and attendance review, these two physicians were again scheduled to be at an affiliated medical school during their VA duty hours. Neither physician could be located by the auditor. The director stated in a December 28, 1978 memorandum to all professional service chiefs his objective that "timekeeping procedures at this facility be completely correct and accurate. . . . " Our time-and-attendance review results indicated a lack of support for this objective from the professional staff.

A lot of surgery was being performed by residents without required supervision by staff surgeons. The surgery log book for the period January 17, 1979 through March 16, 1979 showed in 83 out of 462 surgeries performed, the staff surgeon was not in the medical facility. It should be expected that a staff member or a consultant be involved to the necessary degree with major decisions made by the resident staff, and be present in the operating room, if not actually scrubbed, when a resident acts in the capacity of operating surgeon. Whatever the time of day when an operative procedure is performed by a resident in the operating room, a staff surgeon must approve the operation and be immediately available. It was also the responsibility of the resident to insist that the above protocol be followed. This primarily for the safety of the patient but also for the protection of the resident and staff surgeon.

The Chief, Surgical Service, told us when the staff surgeon calls in that he assumes responsibility and it is not necessary for him to show up in the operating room or for the nurse to be in contact with him because often the staff surgeon is on the LSU or Tulane University campus adjacent to the medical center. In an October 16, 1978 memo from District Counsel to the Director, in response to a suggestion by the Chairman of the Urology Service at the Tulane Medical

School, asking that the facility be defined as "the medical complex in this area," that is, Charity Hospital and the twomedical schools, the District Counsel stated:

It is believed that if the current rule requiring a staff physician to be present in the hospital when a resident is operating were changed to comply with the suggestion of the Chief of the Urology Service at Tulane Medical School and as a result of the changes, some injury occurred to a patient which could have been prevented had a staff physician been in the hospital at the time of the operation, the hospital could probably be held liable for damages and the changing of the rule could be used as evidence of negligence on the part of the hospital in approving the change of the rule in the patient's case.

The hospital could be held liable for any injuries sustained by a patient being operated on by a resident unless that resident physician was under sufficient supervision by staff physicians.

The ruling requiring that a staff physician be present in the hospital when his residents are operating should not be changed.

A copy of this memo was mailed to the Chief, Surgical Service, in October 1978. In spite of all this, the policies states above had not been enforced.

Overbooking and delays in starting surgery resulted in a frequent cancellation of scheduled surgery. We found the average surgery started forty-four minutes beyond the scheduled starting time. This prevented the surgery cases scheduled to follow from being completed in time for clinics, which start at 1:30 P.M. As a result, the "to follow" cases were often canceled. Scheduling was done by junior residents who sometimes overbook by either underestimating the length of time it took to conduct a surgery case or scheduling more cases than could be realistically completed in a day. In April 1979 Nursing Service completed a thirty day study that showed that 36 percent of all scheduled surgery was canceled, mainly because of a lack of staff or lack of time. Staff were not well utilized when time was spent preparing the patient for surgery that was canceled. Much staff time was utilized preparing the patient for surgery prior to surgery. For example, prior to surgery, patients were often placed on special diets and medication and given various tests. These duties were in addition to pre-surgery duties performed by resident and staff surgeons that must be done prior to scheduling, such as examination, diagnosis, and monitoring of patients.

We found general medical beds on all wards were under-utilized. The occupancy of all wards were below the national average of 80 percent and the VA planning criteria HO8–9, Paragraph 100A.04, March 1, 1973, for bed use, which was 80 to 95 percent for medical beds. Bed usage by ward was as follows:

BED USAGE

General Medical Beds

Occupancy Rate Percentage

Ward	Number of Beds	Fiscal Year 1978	Fiscal Year 1979 (10/1/78–6/20/79)
10E	8	50	37
10W	12	58	58
5W	28	71	64
5E	28	78	71
7E	34	82	72
7W	34	72	70
3E	40	73	76
3W	40	82	73
Total	224		

Management had monitored bed use; however, necessary reductions to ensure efficient use of beds had not been made. The low utilization of some wards had resulted in Nursing Service moving all patients from the tenth floor, twenty beds, at night to conserve staff. In addition, a sixteen-bed unit on 5 West was closed for a two-month period. Based on the low occupancy rate, the tenth floor and Ward 5 West should have been partially closed and general medical beds should have been reduced by at least thirty-six beds. The benefits from eliminating excess beds were: more intensive nursing coverage, more space; fewer beds for Building Management Service to maintain; and, an increase in the bed-occupancy rate to acceptable levels.

Organization problems existed with the treatment of respiratory diseased patients. Beds were not designated for respiratory disease care. We found patients located on eighteen of the twenty hospital wards receiving respiratory treatments. Patients admitted with a respiratory disease diagnosis were assigned to ten different wards located on four floors in the medical center. The Respiratory Care Center (RCC) should be adjacent to the Pulmonary Function Laboratory and should comprise a specific bed section in a suitable area within the Medical Service of the hospital, should be air-conditioned in such a way that temperature and humidity can be controlled, and arrangements should be made so that once the air-conditioned air is circulated into the Respiratory Care Center (RCC), it should be then immediately exhausted to the outside, and not recirculated into other parts of the hospital. This precaution should be taken to prevent the possibility of cross-infection.

In 1977, Medical Service converted from treating respiratory diseased patients in a subspecialty unit (designated bed section) to dispersing the patients throughout the medical center to receive treatment in general medical beds. This concept of treatment was implemented for teaching purposes. This provided a variety of patients on each ward, as opposed to the subspecialty concept that restricted patients to one area. According to the Chief, Pulmonary Disease Section, many of the patients admitted with a respiratory disease have multiple medical problems and do not require the specialized medical care provided by a subspecialty unit. Patients with extreme respiratory ailments are admitted to intensive-care units and patients with active tubertculosis (TB) were admitted to private rooms on the seventh floor.

Not confining patients with respiratory disease to a specific area increased the possibility of cross-infection. Although patients with active TB were admitted to private rooms, the air in these rooms was not individually controlled and was not immediately exhausted outside the hospital.

Patients were being reported as occupying an RCC and an intensive-care unit bed at the same time. All patients admitted to the Medical Center with a diagnosis of a respiratory disease were reported as occupying an RCC bed, regardless of the ward assignment. The patients were reported as occupying an RCC bed as long as they were in the Medical Center, even if they were transferred to other wards or received treatments for other illnesses. When patients were admitted to intensive-care units, either at the time of the initial admission or inter-ward transfer, they were again reported as occupying that particular intensive-care unit bed.

Clinical chemistry and hematology procedures for nephrology patients were being performed in a satellite laboratory that Medical Service operates. Medical Service had the nephrology laboratory to perform clinical tests on hemodialysis patients despite Laboratory Service's capability to perform the same tests.

Two full-time medical technologists ran the nephrology laboratory, which housed more than $40,000 worth of equipment. Medical Service had requested an upgrading of the laboratory equipment for an estimated $49,400. In response to this request in the Equipment Committee minutes for June 12, 1979, the Director had asked the Chief of Staff to review the need for the satellite laboratory.

The nephrology laboratory performed sixteen types of procedures. These same procedures were being performed by the Laboratory Service for non-nephrology patients at all times and for nephrology patients when Medical Service staff or equipment was unavailable. The supplemental support from Laboratory Service for fiscal year 1978 and through March 31, 1979, was 297 technical staff hours and $1,302 in supplies for nephrology patients.

Since fiscal year 1977, Medical Service's satellite laboratory workload had been decreasing, as follows:

Number	1977	1978	1979 (Projected)
of tests	32,462	22,087	15,336

The supervisory technologist maintained comprehensive workload data, which was reported to the service chiefs annually in an internal review but not reported within VA information systems, as Laboratory Service did for all similar laboratory tests. Also, the Medical Service laboratory was not accredited by the College of American Pathologists. Laboratory Service should have performed the tests performed by Medical Service's laboratory. This would have allowed better staff utilization, assured uniform quality of work, and provided additional space.

Plans to renovate the hemodialysis equipment should have been canceled. The Five-Year Facility Plan for fiscal year 1980–1984 showed for 1981, a $180,000 non-recurring maintenance project to replace the dialysis equipment and compressors on the central Dialysate Delivery System that was being used. DM&S approved on March 26, 1979, the purchase of individual machines and chairs to replace the central Dialysate Delivery System. This equipment had been purchased and the ten chairs have been delivered. The ten individual kidney machines and blood pumps were to be installed by August 7, 1979. Plans to upgrade the old system should have been canceled and removed from the Five-Year Facility Plan. In other words, Disorganized Crime paid for new equipment, while at the same time planned on spending $180,000 to provide maintenance for the old equipment.

Year-end purchases were unplanned and in some instances, did not appear to be bona fide needs and requirements of the fiscal year in which they were made. Over $2 million, 6 percent of the total annual obligation, was obligated between September 27, 1978 and the end of the fiscal year (three days later). VA Manuals required that a bona fide need of the subsequent fiscal year be recorded as an obligation in the fiscal year in which delivery is to be made. This was necessary to ensure purchases were from the appropriate fiscal year funds and not a means of exhausting appropriation balances (your money). On September 15, 1978, Pharmacy Service purchased 264 units of albumisol directly from a supplier. In addition, 252 units were ordered from the supply warehouse, producing a total of 516 units at a cost of nearly $18,000. The usage of this item was only 38 units per month. At this usage rate, supplies purchased in fiscal year 1978 would last until fiscal year 1980. Office furniture for the fourth quarter 1978 would last until fiscal year 1980. Office furniture for the fourth quarter 1978 was originally budgeted at $1,600; however, $74,700 was obligated, $35,000 during the last three days of the fiscal year. Large year-end expenditures were also noted in the replacement equipment and the additional equipment fund control points.

Follow-up on undelivered orders was not timely. As of April 30, 1979, undelivered orders amounted to $2.1 million. This includes items dating back to August 1974 and items valued at nearly $0.5 million from fiscal year 1976 and prior. It should make you wonder why Disorganized Crime ordered these items, if the item had not been received in five years! What was the reason for the initial order? This amount has not changed significantly in the past six months.

The VA required a monthly verification of outstanding orders for supplies and services. Our review of fiscal years 1977 and 1978 undelivered orders revealed that they did not receive timely follow-up. For example, we found two undelivered orders for prosthetic appliances from early 1978. Both orders were for renal dialysis supplies to be delivered directly to the veteran. Both have been open for over one year with no indication of efforts to resolve the orders with the vendor or the veteran. Also, the VA required that permanent duty travel be completed within two years; a permanent duty travel authority from November 18, 1976 showed an undelivered order balance of $7,500. In 1982, a VA-wide audit of undelivered orders showed that over $20 million of these very old outstanding orders should be canceled.

Claims collection was not prompt and aggressive. As of May 7, 1979, employee receivables totaled more than $4,500, and 62 receivables for ineligible hospitalization totaled nearly $140,000. Receivables for ineligible hospitalization prior to fiscal year 1977 totaled $36,000. Progress had been made in reducing the number and amount of receivables outstanding; however, our review of 81 outstanding receivables revealed collection was not prompt and aggressive in approximately one-fourth of the cases. Prompt and aggressive action on a timely basis with effective follow-up should always be taken to effect collection, utilizing every reasonable effort consistent with the nature and the amount of the indebtedness. In the case of $17,822 receivable for ineligible hospitalization, no contact had been attempted in over a year. At the last contact, the patient had been reported as deceased. There was no indication that any attempt had been made by the VA to verify death or pursue collection from the patient's estate. In another claim for ineligible hospitalization of $731, no effort had been made to locate the patient in over six months. Ineligible hospitalization means your money was spent for treatment, and the patient wasn't even a veteran. In these cases the VA found out about the non-veteran status.

Efforts to find alternatives to overtime usage had little result. During fiscal year 1978, nearly 27,000 hours of overtime were used, at a cost of almost $257,000. This amounted to 1.1 percent of the $2.1 million in regular pay. At that usage rate, fiscal year 1979 overtime was projected to cost nearly $280,000. The facility's overtime analysis originally estimated fiscal year 1979 overtime cost would be $328,000. During fiscal year 1978, twenty-one employees used more than 200 hours of overtime. Eleven of these employees were assigned to Radiology Service. Each of thirty-three employees, two from Fiscal Service, used between 100 and 200 hours of overtime during the year. Overtime usage in these services was primarily due to vacant positions, failure to utilize the central transcription unit, records control, special projects and procedures, and required weekend coverage. We noted several VA Forms 1098 (Request for Authorization for Overtime Work) that had been approved after work was completed, in some instances, more than a week later. Supervisory personnel should have obtained proper authorization for overtime before permitting or requiring performance of overtime work by an employee.

A significant number of outpatients were not receiving their medications from prescriptions filled at the medical center pharmacy. During April and May 1979, approximately 14 percent of the patients (an average of twenty-eight patients daily) who brought prescriptions to the facility's pharmacy did not pick

167

up their medications. Lack of timeliness of filling prescriptions contributed to this problem. After one week's time, the pharmacy staff returned the medications to stock for other use. Our review showed that Pharmacy Service staff could have done more to encourage patients to have their prescriptions mailed out. If the patient took the initiative when he left prescription at the pharmacy, arrangements were made to mail the medication. Otherwise, the patient was given a claim check and expected to return later to pick up the medication. Patients who did not receive their medications could not follow recommended treatment. Furthermore, utilization of pharmacy staff time to return medications to stock was costly and created the potential for error, which adversely affected patient care. To increase the number of patients who receive their medication, every effort should have been made to encourage patients, who may not have planned to wait for their medicine, to request mail-out service.

Medical Administration and Pharmacy Services had sought ways to increase the percentage of fee-basis prescriptions filled by the VA rather than participating (hometown) pharmacies. Fee prescriptions filled by the VAMC New Orleans pharmacy had increased from 56 percent in 1977 to a projected 80 percent for 1979. Hometown pharmacy costs for two consecutive years were reduced by 30 percent as shown below.

HOMETOWN PHARMACY COSTS

April 1, 1977 to March 31, 1978	April 1, 1978 to March 31, 1979
$298,980	$210,672

However, as the VA pharmacy's fee-basis workload increased, the adverse cost effect from the use of brand name versus generic drugs had become more significant. We reviewed the procurement requests for the twenty-one drugs with the highest cost difference between brand name and generic products. The cost impact for five brand-name drugs, which required more than $450 each of purchases since January 1, 1978, was analyzed. The results were as follows:

UNIT PURCHASE COSTS

Drug	Brand Name*	Generic*	Difference	Brand Name Expenditures**
Elavil Tablets (50 mg)	$ 91	$ 23	$ 68	$1,932
Elavil Tablets (25 mg)	232	59	173	1,439
Ducolax Suppositories (10mg)	72	20	52	648
Pronestyl Capsules	57	15	42	507
Hiprex Tablets	66	17	49	459
TOTALS	$518	$134	$384	$4,985

* prices effective May 31, 1979
**January 1, 1978 to May 31, 1979

Use of the generic drugs to treat medical center inpatients was well accepted according to the Pharmacy Service's clinical teaching coordinator. There were clinical reasons why changing a patient's medication from the generic drug, which had been administered to him as an inpatient, to the brand-name drug, which the fee-basis physician requested to continue his treatment, were not advisable. Studies had established that a bio-equivalency problem had resulted from switching companies' generic equivalents for Pronestyl and other drugs. Steps should have been taken to minimize the medical center pharmacy's use of brand name instead of generic drugs. Fee-basis physicians should have been asked to authorize the use of generic drugs. In 1982, the Inspector General's

Advisory Council on Fee-Basis Medical Programs stated that no pharmacy within the VA should fill fee-basis prescriptions on a non-generic basis. Or in other words, you paid for the same idea twice.

Improvement was needed in inspection and disposition of controlled substances. Our review of controlled substances on hand on May 22, 1979 in Pharmacy Service showed an unsatisfactory monthly inspection system and maintenance of unused medications. Among 85 controlled substances (58 Schedule II and 27 Schedule III) counted in the pharmacy vault, 14 deviations were found. Seven deviations of Schedule II substances exceed one unit over, or under, the recorded amount, as the table shows.

CONTROLLED SUBSTANCES DEVIATIONS

Substance	Unit	Register	Annual	Difference
Secobarbital Sodium	100mg	327	402	+ 75 capsules
Demeral (Meperidine)	50mg	4,243	4,301	+ 58 capsules
Ritalin	5mg	460	479	+ 19 tablets
*Opium Tincture	cc	238	250	+ 12 cubic
Quaalude	300mg	639	649	+ 10 tablets
Dexedrine Sulfate	5mg	1,217	1,220	+ 3 tablets
*Paregoric	oz	131	128	− 3 ounces

*These deviations were from balances verified during the May 3, 1979 monthly controlled substances inspection, according to the Schedule II, Schedule III Narcotics and Alcohol Register (VA Form 10–2320). No issue or receipts were annotated between the May 3, 1979 inspection and our count.

According to Pharmacy Service monthly inspection records from July 1978 through March 1979, no deviations were reported. Service management stated that because of the staff time required, pharmacy inspections do not include actual counts of all controlled substances (approximately 125 different items). Our review of controlled substances in the Pharmacy also included analysis of utilization of the 85 items counted. Results of the utilization review for 14 controlled substances (7 Schedule II and 7 Schedule III) not issued in at least one year are:

Number of Controlled Substances	Length of Time Not Issued	Range of Quantity on Hand
3	2 years	13 ampules to 114 ampules
11	1 1/2 years	9 capsules to 431 capsules
14	1 year	9 capsules to 999 capsules

Policy and procedural changes were needed in the controlled-substances monthly inspection and the disposition of underutilized items. We identified monthly inspections, which were of limited validity, which did not assure Pharmacy's accountability of controlled substances, and the maintenance of under-utilized drugs, which involved uneconomical usgage of scarce storage space and the responsible pharmacist's time. Missing drugs are an old problem with Disorganized Crime because you are always going to be there to buy some more drugs. In 1975, the General Accounting Office found that 24 to 57 percent of the drugs tested by the auditors could not be accounted for at nine of eleven VA hospitals tested. This amounted to 1.1 million tablets and capsules of the drugs tested. The New Orleans hospital was not one of the eleven audit sites.

Drugs were not being stored in proper climatic conditions in Supply Service. Drugs that were labeled "store in cool, dry place" and "store in 59–86 degree temperature" were found in the warehouse where the temperature was over 90 degrees. Temperatures should have been controlled to avoid loss or deterioration of drugs by the installation of air-conditioning or related equipment to ensure that manufacturers and officials compendia recommendations are met. The Chief, Pharmacy Service, stated some drugs were ruined in the warehouse due to excessively high temperatures. The November 1976 systematic internal review stated the warehouse was extremely warm during the summer months, and many drugs decompose or lose their potency when stocked under these conditions. The problem was reported again in 1977.

Our review of barriers to the handicapped disclosed several areas where improvements could have been made. The front entrance on Perdido Street did not accommodate handicapped persons. Two thirty-by-thirty inch signs raised three feet above the ground directed handicapped persons to the rear entrance. The rear entrance of Gravier Street, with an eighteen-foot wide wheelchair ramp and electronic doors, was the only way for unassisted patients in wheelchairs to enter the main medical building. At the rear entrance, there were seven parking spaces reserved for handicapped drivers; however, any person departing a motor vehicle from the passenger's side had to exit into traffic. This circle was also used as the main ambulance entrance. A speeding vehicle entering the circle could have injured an unassisted handicapped person. A handrail had been installed along a portion of the rampway leading to the entrance. This rail was installed after a patient was injured when his wheelchair rolled from the ramp. The handrail ended about eighteen feet short of the entrance. The eighteen feet of ramp without the handrail was raised as much as one foot above ground; thus, it was still possible for a patient to be injured by his wheelchair rolling from the ramp.

In the medical center main building, the audit team surveyed fifteen rest-rooms. None had satisfied all the VA construction standard requirements. Deficiencies included: doors too small for wheelchairs to enter; commodes installed too low; mirrors, paper towel dispensers, and electric hand dryers installed too high; and insufficient space for access into showers or bathtubs. It was also observed that public telephones and water fountains were installed too high for easy access by wheelchair patients. A construction project adding a two-floor administrative annex to the main building, which is 61 percent complete, did not include any provisions for accessibility of the handicapped.

The Quarters building, approximately a hundred feet from the main building, housed the patient elibibility unit, hospital-based home care, fee-basis, and the office of the Chief of MAS. Handicapped persons could not easily open building doors, and first and second floor restroom doors were too narrow for wheelchairs to enter.

The station did not have a continuous system for ensuring barriers to the handicapped were removed in accordance with agency standards. A summer college hire was conducting a study of barriers to handicapped. This study was to be completed in August 1979.

The Director's solution was to form a committee and immediately ordered installation of eighteen feet of hand rail. In addition he planned to spend $560,000 to renovate patient bathrooms, $300,000 to eliminate architectural barriers for handicapped, and $125,000 to replace drinking fountains and chillers. Not bad visuals on his part; however, the tab to you was a million dollars. Where were the bureaucrats when the hospital was originally built?

Work orders for maintenance and repairs needed priority attention. The records maintained by the Maintenance and Operation Section and the Biomedical Section could not be used to determine the status of accumulated work orders. On 13 of the 22 work orders reviewed for the period October through November 1978, the completion status was not on the report. The requesting units verified these 13 work orders were completed between October 1978 and May 1979. Failure to maintain adequate logs of work orders could result in inefficient use of manpower. Neither section supervisor was able to determine from their work order log book the status of disposition of the work orders reviewed. Maintenance and Operations Section employees were assigned to work on non-recurring maintenance and repair projects, allowing non-emergency maintenance and repair work to go unattended.

As of June 4, 1979, there were 274 incomplete work orders outstanding in the Maintenance and Operations Section. Despite this backlog, the section supervisor acknowledged that higher priority was given to non-recurring projects to prevent return of your unused funds to VA Central Office at the end of the fiscal year. For example, since February 1978, the Maintenance and Operations Section has had a work order from Nuclear Medicine for installation of a power vent. The Nuclear Medicine Service followed up on this work order four times. The work was performed on June 8, 1979; however, the vent was not functioning properly on June 11, 1979. As a result, a radax machine purchased in January 1978 for $7,905 could not be utilized. Unavailability of this machine has resulted in patients being sent to other facilities or tests being postponed.

Adequate competition is not being obtained on some purchases over $500. Our review of sixteen purchase orders, each valued at over $500, showed there were six purchase orders where no competition had been obtained and justification was not documented. Federal Procurement Regulations required obtaining reasonable competition from a sufficient number of sources in order to ensure fair procurement for the government. Certain instances were permitted where sole-source solicitations were appropriate; however, there should have been some compelling reason and written justification was required in these situations. Based on our review, there was no assurance that adequate competition was being obtained.

More economical taxi service should have been obtained by competitive bidding. The medical center paid the same taxi fare as non-VA passengers. The medical center had two open contracts for taxi service with two taxicab companies in New Orleans. The purpose of the contracts was to provide transportation to the medical center for authorized VA beneficiaries. The annual cost to you of these contracts was approximately $66,000. The Chief of P&C Section told us the medical center had used these two companies since 1973. The New Orleans area had twenty-nine companies. The medical center should have obtained taxi service through competitive bidding. This would ensure that the medical center would have been provided taxi service at a fair price.

Procedures for excessing equipment were not being followed. Although all non-expendable property had been inventoried within the last twelve months and spot checks were performed as required, we found excess equipment in Research Service, Nuclear Medicine Service, and Surgical Service. Non-expendable property on hand in using activities should be only the amount necessary to perform the assigned functions. Each station should establish controls to ensure that all using activities continually and objectively evaluate the need for assigned equipment. When excess property is identified, it should be promptly turned in to the Chief, Supply Service, for reassignment or disposed as excess.

In Nuclear Medicine Service, we found an Ohio Nuclear Dual Probe Scanner listed on the CMR at a value of $35,388 that had been unused over two years. This equipment was inventoried in October 1978 but was not identified as excess. The service told us that even though the equipment was obsolete and had been unused over two years, the life expectancy had not yet been reached and therefore could not be excessed. Need and not life expectancy is the criteria for excessing equipment. The function of this scanner was performed by another piece of equipment in an adjacent room. In the Surgical Intensive Care Unit, we found a Cardiopulmonary Resuscitation Unit and a Piling Lite Source that had not been used in over two years. We also found a Centrifuge with no VA identification number that had not been used in over a year. The total value of this equipment was $1,732. This equipment was found in a storage room one month ago by the Head Nurse. The equipment was determined to be obsolete and should have been excessed in order to preclude some other VA hospital from buying identical equipment at your expense.

Research Service was responsible for supporting and encouraging the conduct of high-quality medical research in order to gain insight into the mechanisms underlying the development of various diseases. Staffing consisted of twenty-eight full-time and four part-time employees. There were also research investigators who were involved in over thirty VA-funded research programs. We found that experimental research was being performed on at least six veterans without their knowledge and consent. This had been discovered several years before by the hospital Chief of Staff; however, it had not been stopped in spite

173

of his best efforts. The auditors never did confirm what investigational drugs were given to the veterans. We did determine that investigational drugs were stocked and dispensed by the research physicians without approval by the VA's Research and Development Committee. Nine prescriptions for investigational drugs did not list dosage or frequency. We found at least two instances where adverse drug reactions took place; however, they were not reported to VA Central Office. In fact no adverse drug reactions had been reported for at least three years prior to our arrival in 1979. (I may need to remind you, this audit report never was published.)

My next audit was at the VA Hospital at Salisbury, North Carolina. The audit was conducted from July through August 1979. At the beginning of the audit, the Director of the Hospital demanded that the A-I-C be removed. To calm the Director's nerves, the Audit Manager was flown from Atlanta to Salisbury on a Friday afternoon. You of course paid for his plane ticket and per diem costs; however, the visuals were good (we didn't cave under the Director's wishes and kept an appearance of independence!), at least at first. The audit report was never published.

The medical center had 884 operating beds, consisting of 516 psychiatry, 328 medical, and 40 surgical. In addition, the medical center operated a 93-bed Nursing Home Care Unit. As of July 31, 1979, there were 1,294 employees, including 1,214 full-time and 80 part-time. The budget for fiscal year 1979 was $30.6 million. This includes $19.3 million for personal services and $3.7 million for fee-basis programs.

Action had been taken by nursing service to initiate a service policy regarding patient showers. Patient interviews during the first week of this audit revealed that patients on wards in Buildings 3 and 4 were dissatisfied that showers were only available three days per week. We reviewed the patient-orientation information provided to patients upon admission and noted that instructions pertaining to showers stated that:

> You must let a nursing assistant know when you want to take a shower at times other than shower night. Shower nights are Tuesday, Thursday and Saturday. Clean pajamas, towels and bath clothes are given at that time.

After discussions of this subject with the Chief of Staff and Chief, Nursing Service, action was taken by the Chief, Nursing Service, to allow patients the opportunity to bathe daily if they so desired. Nice of Disorganized Crime to allow the veterans to shower, eh?

Throughout the duration of the audit, we noted patients sleeping on medical center grounds and in hallways. This condition was most prevalent in and around the patient recreation areas of Building 6, but examples were also noted in other patient care buildings. This problem had been longstanding, as evidenced by a discussion by the Joint Conference Council on September 30, 1977. However, corrective policy had not been issued and implemented. Our concern was not only for the constructive activity of the patient, but also that a patient in need of medical help may not be immediately identified by the staff.

During the audit we assessed employee attitudes toward the care of patients at this medical center. Based on interviews and observations, in general, employees were concerned as to their responsibilities toward caring for the patient, but we did not find sufficient effort being taken to motivate patients to participate in scheduled recreational and occupational therapy activities.

Recreation Therapy activities were administered through the Recreation Therapy Section of Voluntary Service. A schedule of recreation activities, including golf, swimming, bowling, and softball, was provided for patient participation. Therapists also helped with social hours, movies, events with local organizations, ward visits, various therapies, and patient government. Although we found many activities planned for patients, actual participation by patients was minimal. As an example, on the evening of August 8, 1979, bowling, golf, and softball were scheduled. Although some patients participated in bowling, we observed that none participated in golf or softball. Also, on the evening of August 9, 1979, a golf tournament, softball, and bowling were scheduled. We observed two patients playing golf and approximately seven patients playing softball. Other patients were also observed bowling.

Increased efforts by medical center staff to encourage patients to involve themselves in planned recreational and occupational therapy activities should have resulted in improved patient participation. The medical safety of patients required the elimination of patients habitually sleeping on the grounds and in hallwys.

The Director did not agree with the auditors. In a three-page rebuttal, the Director basically discussed the audit team's insensitivity, or lack of knowledge, relative to the impact the recommendations would have had on labor-management relationships and the government workers union.

The initial recommendations made by the team and received by the hospital Director on 8/17/79 read as follows:

(1) That policy requiring *all* medical center employees to assist in the elimination of patients sleeping in hallways be established and implemented. (Underlining added.)
(2) That medical center employees encourage and motivate patients to participate in scheduled recreational activities.

We did not concur with these recommendations and on 8/24/79 the team changed its recommendation requiring that management spend considerable time preparing additional comments. Again we found the recommendations unacceptable. It is simply not feasible to publish a policy forbidding patients to sleep on the grounds and in hallways unless staffing ratios are improved enough to permit a roving task force of nursing personnel equipped to deal with these patients.

This team does not appear to recognize and accept the fact that publishing a policy without the means to assure implementation will have definite fall-out when the next IG Audit occurs, i.e., we will be accused of violation of our own policy.

We agree that actions taken to remedy the above cited conditions should have been consistent with the union agreement. However, there was nothing in the recommendation that violated the union agreement. The safety, care, and welfare of the patient was our primary concern. The condition of patients sleeping on grounds and in hallways was due to lack of positive, constructive action on the part of medical center staff. There was a need for such action, and this need was not apparent in the Director's comments. The Director was more concerned with the other members of Disorganized Crime becoming upset with having to provide adequate welfare to veterans.

Nursing coverage was provided at the medical center, including a 93-bed Nursing Home Care Unit, and the Winston-Salem Outpatient Clinic. As of August 20, 1979, this coverage consisted of 122 registered nurses, 52 licensed practical nurses, and 265 nursing assistants. As of this same date, personnel vacancies for the three Nursing categories were one, three, and nine, respectively.

We reviewed the scheduled coverage for each ward for all three shifts. Scheduled coverage for psychiatric areas, especially Buildings 3 and 4, was minimal. This was confirmed through observations of these buildings during the evening shift. Building 3 contained four floors: the first floor housed the Alcohol Treatment Unit; the upper three floors contained two wards each, two of which were locked wards. These six wards contained a total of 159 beds, with a patient occupancy rate of 95 to 100 percent. Scheduled evening-shift nursing coverage for these wards consisted of only one registered nurse, one licensed practical nurse, two nursing assistants for each of the two locked wards, and one nursing assistant for each of the four open wards. On the evening shift of August 8, 1979, during our review, one nursing assistant was on unscheduled sick leave. This left one nursing assistant to cover two open wards, or approximately fifty patients. According to records maintained by Nursing Service, this was a routine occurrence. We did not consider this adequate nursing coverage.

We reviewed documentation of extensive, in-depth analysis of nurse staffing directed by medical center management since May 1978. Management studies had been made of organization, supervision assignments, staffing criteria, scheduling procedures, and leave usage. A study was being performed to assess overtime usage. These studies had identified the need for additional staffing. They had also resulted in recommendations as to ward coverage, staff upgrading, use of additional part-time staff, and improvement in scheduling procedures.

Medical center management had made numerous requests to VA Central Office for additional personnel ceiling to increase its nursing staff. For example, in July 1977, as part of its fiscal year 1978 budget plan, management expressed the need for 35 additional nursing staff; 15 RN's, 15 LPN's, and 5 nursing assistants. In July 1978, for the fiscal year 1979 plan, the need was expressed for 131 nursing staff; 68 RN's, and 63 LPN's and nursing assistants. These additional ceiling requests were not provided.

Internal service ceiling statistics show that staffing increases in nursing had been minimal compared to other services. The following table compares medical center management's established full-time personnel (FTP) ceilings for nursing service with seven other clinical and administrative services (clinical services

176

do not include clerical staff) over a four-year period. This table shows that little change had occurred in FTP ceiling for Nursing.

FTP Ceilings

Service	June 1975	June 1979	1975 to 1979 % increases (decreases)
Medical (Physicians)	8	12	50%
Psychiatry (Physicians)	12	16	33%
Medical Administration Service	63	78	24%
Building Management	77	94	22%
Engineering	68	76	12%
Social Work	18	20	11%
Psychology	10	10	0%
Nursing			
RN	107	111	4%
LPN–NA	304	303	(0.3%)

Our audit of other areas of the medical center did not result in any assessment of overstaffing. Therefore, we were not questioning past position management decisions. As of August 21, 1979, the facility had a total of thirty full-time and twelve part-time personnel vacancies. This included vacancies in Nursing Service. In light of the substantial nurse staffing needs expressed by management, adjustment of current ceilings through the use of existing vacancies would have been an option available.

Hospital Memorandum 137–78–11, dated January 24, 1978, assigned responsibility for terminal cleaning of discharged patients to Nursing Service. Terminal cleaning for discharges or transfers between buildings was also being provided by the Nursing staff. Reassignment of these duties to Building Management personnel would have freed up Nursing time for patient-care functions.

Medical center management had allowed Nursing Service to exceed its locally established personnel ceilings, especially with regard to nursing assistants. This had been done primarily to counteract the effect of periods of employee losses; e.g., employment terminations and leave without pay. However, Nursing Service had not maintained personnel strength above or even at ceiling levels because of the current recruitment practices maintained at the service level. Instead of recruiting for vacant positions on a one-for-one basis, Nursing Service waited for a block of vacant positions. This was done to facilitate formal training classes for new personnel. However, immediate recruitment for a planned termination, or at the time of actual vacancy, would have increased the number of available personnel. Group training classes could have been held subsequently, with controls established to provide for the appropriate use of staff with unmet training needs.

The Director responded that the auditors had merely recommended to borrow from Peter to pay Paul, e.g., arbitrarily take staffing from other services to beef

177

up Nursing Service, which was unacceptable. The auditors responded that the Director's comments did not indicate a propensity to utilize available resources to aid in the remedy of problem areas caused by inadequate nursing coverage. Vacancies at the medical center represented unutilized resources. Considering current Nursing Service deficiencies, terminal cleaning by Nursing Service represented inappropriate utilization of resources. Delayed recruiting to satisfy mode-of-training preferences represented unutilized resources. The combination of such readily available options provided the Director with a means of alleviating identified problem areas, and we believed maximum efforts should be made to use all available resources.

Linen inventory losses, as reported by the medical center, were excessive. The laundry facility at VAMC Salisbury provided consolidated laundry service for VAMC Salisbury and VAMC Durham. Expenditures for linen were $131,906 in fiscal year 1978 and $148,508 in fiscal year 1979 to date, ending June 30, 1979. We reviewed the results of the physical inventories of linens taken by station personnel at Salisbury and Durham in March 1978 and February 1979. Results of the inventories were as follows:

INVENTORY PERIOD LOSSES

Medical Center	March 21, 1977–March 30, 1978	March 20, 1978–February 12, 1979	Total
VAMC Salisbury	$ 9,571	$46,848	$ 56,419
VAMC Durham	25,442	26,313	51,755
	$35,013	$73,161	$108,174

We reviewed the records prepared for the inventory performed on February 12, 1979 and found that they did not account for all items received. The records only accounted for the items placed in service. Inventory items received but not issued were not included. We also noted that some linen items were reported as having more in service than were issued.

In other to evaluate the adequacy of the inventory controls, we attempted to verify inventory counts as reported on February 12, 1979. We could not reconcile the thermal-blanket inventory because of a lack of documentation and confusion over what items were actually counted by hospital personnel during the physical inventory. Interviews with Building Management Service (BMS) personnel showed confusion over whether any white blankets were still on the wards and included in the inventories. Workpapers for the February 1979 inventory were not available to substantiate what was actually counted at that time.

The Winston-Salem Outpatient Clinic was the clinic of jurisdiction for the State of North Carolina and was operated under the direction of the VA Medical Center, Salisbury. The outpatient clinic's total staffing was eighty-five full-time and five part-time employees. The clinic, headed by the Chief Medical Officer

178

who reported to the Medical Center Director, had independent Medical Administration, Radiology, and Prosthetic Services. Dental, pharmacy, social work, nursing, and supply personnel at the clinic were consolidated under their respective services, located at the medical center in Salisbury.

Medical Administration Service had thirty-seven full-time and one part-time staff, primarily associated with the fee-basis programs, and compensation and pension examinations. There were 27,874 staff outpatient visits and 51,327 fee visits reported for fiscal year 1979, as of July 31, 1979. The number of veterans with fee-basis ID cards was 16,171 as of June 30, 1979. During the first three quarters of fiscal year 1979, over 3,000 veterans had more than 29,000 prescriptions filled by 496 fee participating pharmacies. Expenditures for the three major fee-basis programs at the clinic are as follows:

Major Fee Program	Actual Expenditures FY 1978	Projected Expenditures[1] FY 1979
Fee medical	$1,461,355	$1,660,200
Fee dental	1,540,754	1,433,000
Fee pharmacy	622,469	478,894[2]
	$3,624,578	$3,572,094

1. Projected expenditures are based on actual cost for first nine months of Fiscal Year 1979.
2. The cost reduction that took place is due to an extensive letter campaign by the medical center to encourage veterans to use the outpatient clinic mail-out services.

Management of the Winston-Salem Outpatient Clinic required considerable improvement. The outpatient visits to the Winston-Salem clinic were erroneously reported. Systematic Internal Reviews were not being accomplished in Medical Administration Service at the outpatient clinic. Follow-up action on dental spot-check results was inadequate: Eligible veterans were not being referred in many cases to accessible VA facilities for dental care in lieu of authorizing fee dental treatment. There was a serious lack of internal controls over the fee pharmacy program; as a result, there was a high potential for abuse of the fee pharmacy program. Additional cost reductions could have been achieved by reviewing drug costs claimed by fee participating pharmacies. Controls to assure adequate review of fee medical services provided by fee participants had not been implemented. Veterans with fee-basis ID cards were not regularly evaluated. Licensures of physicians were not being verified prior to approval for participation in the fee-basis program. The fee medical participants whose six-month income exceeded $7,500 had not been analyzed.

The conditions at the Winston-Salem Outpatient Clinic were in considerable need of improvement because of:

a. required policies and procedures that had not been implemented;

b. lack of knowledge of the fee program regulations by some of the outpatient clinic staff;
c. inadequate controls over areas that were sensitive to abuse by fee participants;
d. lack of an organized filing system and efficient work flow on the part of fee dental and fee pharmacy staff; and,
e. erroneous reports to medical center management prepared by Medical Administration Service.

Reported outpatient visits to the Winston-Salem clinic for the first ten months of fiscal year 1979 were overstated by an estimated 5,257 visits. The AMIS Report, RCS 10–69 (Outpatient Health Service Workload) showed 27,715 staff visits to the clinic, as of July 31, 1979, although the actual figure was projected at 22,458 staff visits, based on a three-month review.

We reviewed and compared three months of routing sheet (VA Form 10–2875–2) counts (January, April, and July, 1979) with the number of visits submitted for AMIS. (Routing sheets are the source documents for AMIS reporting.) We found that service-connected visits were overstated by 535, non-service-connected visits by 487, and collateral visits by 555, for the three-month period. This totals 1,577 visits overstated for the three months reviewed and projects to a total estimated overstatement of 5,257 visits for fiscal year 1979 from October 1, 1978 to July 31, 1979, if the same condition existed in other months. In addition, we found that there were no routing sheets for "prescription refill only"; however, 230 prescription-refill visits were annotated on the daily worksheet and reported to AMIS for these three months. Each patient coming to the clinic for the sole purpose of having a prescription refilled was directed to a staff nurse and that visit was counted as a service-connected or non-service-connected visit. The overstatement of outpatient visits represented an estimated $184,000 in overestimated budget needs in fiscal year 1979, (This is based on a rate of $35 per outpatient visit.) How's that for creative financing?

Follow-up action on dental spot-check results was inadequate. As a result, the enforcement of necessary controls had been seriously reduced to a level that may have led to abuse. During fiscal year 1979, as of June 30, 1979, 191 fee dental cases were reviewed by VA dentists in order to verify that the services paid for were provided as required by Interim Issue 10–72–5, April 10, 1972. Twenty (10 percent) of the 191 cases resulted in four requests for refunds and sixteen requests that the fee dentist notify the outpatient clinic in writing when treatment was completed so that another spot-check examination could be arranged. Of the 16 requests for response from the fee dentist, 11 had not been received by the clinic as of August 13, 1979. For example, one veteran received $470 of dental treatment performed by his fee dentist in November 1978. The fee dentist billed the clinic and was paid. A spot check, on January 15, 1979, revealed that five items that were certified by the fee dentist as having been performed were not performed (but you had paid for them). Although the outpatient clinic requested on January 15, 1979 written confirmation that the above five items had been corrected, no response had evern been received. The outpatient clinic had no follow-up procedure established to determine whether a fee dentist replies to such a request.

The results of prior deficient spot checks were not provided to the Medical Administration clerk who selects which fee dentist's work was to be spot-checked. This reduced the effectiveness of the spot checks. For example, one dentist was spot-checked on October 3, 1977. This spot check noted three discrepancies. The dentist's work had not been spot-checked again; however, he still had not corrected the previously noted deficiencies and had been paid over $16,000 since October 1977, for additional fee dental services.

The AMIS Fee Dental Report, RCS 10–173, June 30, 1979, reported that 211 spot checks were performed, which resulted in 23 cases of minor discrepancies and zero cases with misrepresentation. We compared the reported AMIS data to the supporting documentation and found that only 191 spot checks had been performed and only 20 cases with discrepancies identified. We analyzed the 20 cases and found that 15 of the cases should have been inputted as misrepresentation. For example, in one case a tooth claimed to have been extracted was found to still be present. No follow-up had been done since December 22, 1978, to determine if the tooth had ever been extracted. The fee dentist had been paid another $98 for other services performed on other veterans. The staff dentist at the outpatient clinic stated that he reports the results of the spot checks as minor discrepancies because he did not know of any written criteria to classify the discrepancies as minor or as (the more serious) misrepresentations. The Chief, Dental Service, stated that misrepresentation should have been coded if work that had been certified as complete had in fact not been performed. Using the definition of the Chief, Dental Service, the majority of the discrepancies found by the spot checks were misrepresentations.

It was possible that the volume of misrepresentations is greater than indicated in the fee dental report. Interim Issue 10–72–5, April 10, 1972, states:

> Cases in which fraud is suspected will be reported in detail to the Chief Attorney for appropriate action.

Without an organized selection, follow-up, and reporting system of spot checks, the potential for inappropriate payment of your money to fee dentists was high.

Eligible veterans were not being referred in many cases to accessible VA facilities for outpatient dental care in lieu of authorizing fee-basis dental care (which was more costly to you). The fee dental program at Winston-Salem Clinic of Jurisdiction, with the third largest number of fee dental cases in the nation, cost $1.5 million in fiscal year 1978 and was expected to cost nearly that amount in fiscal year 1979. The average cost to the medical center of a dental case completed on fee basis was $666, versus a completed outpatient staff case, which costs an average of only $303.

Our review of authorized fee dental treatment cases pending completion, as of August 16, 1979, showed that many of these veterans live close to VA facilities and should have been referred to the facilities in lieu of dental treatment on a fee basis. Of the 535 cases pending, 276 (52 percent) lived within forty miles of a VA facility. We further determined that 84 of the 276 (30 percent) veterans live within the city limits of a VA facility.

The VA required that the clinic of jurisdiction may authorize dental care on a fee basis when VA facilities cannot furnish care because of geographic inaccessibility, or the specific care or service required. The clinic had been sending up to ten cases per month to some of the VA facilities in its jurisdictional area. However, little effort had been made by the clinic to have these facilities accept an increased number of eligible veterans on an outpatient staff basis. Since the audit team's arrival at the clinic, the staff dentist had contacted several of the other VA facilities and had found that most were willing to accept more of these cases. For example, VAMC Durham, would have accepted 15 ormore of these cases per month; VAMC Asheville, would have taken up to 20 per month. The Chief, Dental Service, at VAMC Salisbury, told the audit team that he could take more than ten cases per month. There have been 1,743 completed fee dental cases this fiscal year as of July 31, 1979. This projected to 2,092 cases for the fiscal year. If eligible veterans living near a VA facility were to be treated on a staff basis, approximately $400,000 could have been saved annually. The Director did not concur with the auditor's recommendation to establish needed internal controls. The Director felt enough controls were in place in spite of our findings that $400,000 of your money was wasted. Nationwide to savings in fee dental work in 1982 exceeded $20 million.

There was a high potential for abuse of the fee pharmacy program. We idenfitied two external and three internal factors that cause this condition.

Factors External to the VA

1. Over one-half of the 772 prescription forms (VAF 10–2577b's) that we scanned were not signed by a physician and did not note the method of order. The North Carolina Controlled-Substance Act required that a pharmacist have the physician's signature on Schedule I and II drug prescription requests. For Schedule III, IV, and V drug prescriptions, the method of order must be noted (e.g., "phone"). The clerk involved with processing the prescription forms had no way of knowing whether the pharmacists had satisfied the North Carolina state law.
2. Some fee-prescription forms are sent to the VA for payment as long as two years after the prescription was filled. There was no VA requirement that these bills be submitted timely. For example, a pharmacy that was paid $6,200 (the highest paid fee pharmacy during the first six months of 1979) had been out of business for over nine months when bills were received for a veteran who died in February 1979; however, the pharmacy had not billed the VA until May 1979. The prescription had been filled as far back as September 1977.

Factors Internal to the VA

1. Fee pharmacy prescriptions had not been included in the Pharmacy Patient Profile. It was in the best interest of good patient care that all fee prescriptions

182

be maintained in the patient's medication profile in the VA pharmacy.

After the VA's copy of the prescription (VAF 10–2577b's) had been processed by the Medical Administration clerk, the form went to the Pharmacy. Instead of putting the form in the veteran's Pharmacy Patient Profile, the forms were put in large boxes and stored. This filing procedure also hid the presence of problems from management. For example, during our scan of 287 prescriptions randomly selected, we found 11 prescriptions (4 percent) written by physicians at VA Medical Centers in Durham and Asheville, North Carolina. VA hospital pharmacies should be used to fill all staff prescriptions for drugs and supplies for authorized patients.

In addition, we attempted to reconcile the RCS 10–69 OPF Report 18 to the prescription forms (VAF 10–2577b) for the previously mentioned highest earning pharmacy and could not locate all the VAF 10–2577b's because these forms were stored in boxes, in no systematic order. The following table shows our attempted reconciliation.

Attempted Reconciliation

RCS 10–69 OPF Report 18	$6,195
Prescription Forms	5,111
Difference	$1,084

2. Only one clerk processed the fee pharmacy paperwork in Medical Administration Service. There were no established standards with regard to the processing of prescription forms; however, our observance of the clerk indicated that the volume and magnitude of her required duties were much greater than can be adequately accomplished by one clerk using the current work-flow procedures.
3. The outpatient clinic received the "Fee Basis Pharmacy Payment Analysis" report, generated from the Austin DPC. This report was not used by the outpatient clinic. Management informed us that no instructions had been received from VA Central Office relative to analysis of this report. However, the report listed veterans' names and file numbers, showing year-to-date expenditures by month of payment, and could have been used to analyze payment trends, which would have assisted management in controlling fee pharmacy expenditures.

In reviewing the report, we found that for the period ending June 30, 1979, there were over two hundred "NOT IN FILE" entries, indicating potential veteran ineligibility for benefits. Audit tests of six cases resulted in assurance that entitlement existed in each case, as evidenced by a Rating Decision (VA Form 21–6976). Management should have performed further analysis to insure that payments were not being made to ineligible veterans and to determine the cause of the "NOT IN FILE" entries and report the results to appropriate officials for resolution of deficiencies. The Director concurred with the reservation that additional staff (at your expense) be provided to do the job the existing membership of Disorganized Crime was already supposed to be doing.

There was no review of claimed costs of fee pharmacists. The VA required that Medical Administration personnel, using the VA prescription schedule and instructions, review pharmacy invoices and supporting prescriptions for appropriateness of fees claimed. The lack of review occurred because there was only one clerk to process the fee pharmacy paperwork, and she did not have the time for the review. VA Manual M-1, Part I, Chapter 18, Figure 18.4 provided that the cost of drugs purchased through the fee pharmacies be limited to the wholesale price plus a percentage factor. We selected thirteen prescriptions that had been paid the pharmacist's claimed amount and found the cost of seven prescriptions were excessive. For example, for L-Dopa, one pharmacist billed $69; however, the manufacturer's price plus percentage factor should have limited your purchase price to $38. If this trend existed in all prescriptions paid, significant overpayments had occurred.

The Director only concurred in principle. The Director felt that the schedule in M-1, Part I, had not been updated in eight years and believed pharmacies would not accept payments based on this schedule. Unless additional staffing was made available at your additional expense, the Director saw no way to maintain timely payment and apply those complex time-consuming VA required formulae.

Based on the indicators developed at Salisbury and other VA hospitals, a large VA-wide audit of the Fee-Basis Pharmacy Program was performed. Eleven additional clinics of jurisdiction were audited, with results very similar to what we found at Salisbury. Estimated savings ranging from $2.1 to $2.8 million could have been achieved by having more fee prescriptions filled by VA pharmacies. Ten of the eleven clinics audited were not identifying those fee prescriptions feasible for VA filling and taking action to have the prescriptions filled at the VA pharmacies at a reduced cost. For the eleven clinics audited, an estimated average overpayment rate of 30.8 percent in fiscal year 1980 prescriptions resulted in an estimated financial loss of at least $207,774 and as much as $381,579. The financial loss was the result of failure by the clinics to effectively review and adjust fees claimed by the participating pharmacies.

Revision of the Department of Medicine and Surgery's policy and procedures for pricing fee-filled prescriptions was needed. For a sample of 1,073 prescriptions, we found that one alternative pricing procedure would have reduced fee allowances by 24.4 percent at the eleven facilities audited. Maintenance of fee-basis prescriptions from participating pharmacies was inadequate. We found prescriptions were not maintained alphabetically or in a manner that would allow effective professional reviews at nine of the eleven facilities audited.

A significant number of fee-basis prescriptions were paid without appropriate supporting documentation. Of the 403,958 prescriptions processed by eleven clinics in fiscal year 1980, 20 percent had not contained the fee pharmacist's signature, 15 percent had not contained the veteran's signature, and 6 percent had not contained the fee physician's signature. Performing drug utilization reviews by VA Medical Center personnel would aid in identifying and correcting abuse and waste in the fee-pharmacy program. We requested the performance of professional drug utilization reviews on 149 fee-basis veteran cases, and 34 cases, or 22 percent, were found in need of physician follow-up. However, only one of the eleven clinics audited was accomplishing drug utilization review of fee prescriptions. Drug utilization reviews were conducted at the request of the auditors. In the following examples of discrepancies found, all descriptions of medications and/or effects were provided by the pharmacies conducting the drug utilization reviews. The discrepancies in the files cited as needing physician follow-up were in three basic categories:

Exessive quantities of medications
Inappropriate concurrent combinations of medication
Duplicate medications.

Veteran #1 (VAMC Bay Pines, FL)

The following veteran received excessive quantities of Valium, a Schedule IV substance.*

Date	Medication	Quantity	Prescription (Rx) Life
2–18–80	Valium 10 mg.	50	50 day supply
3–18–80	Valium 10 mg.	50	50 day supply
4–15–80	Valium 10 mg.	50	50 day supply
4–18–80	Valium 10 mg.	50	16 day supply

*The American Druggist Blue Book, 1979 Annual Edition, defines controlled drugs as follows:

Schedule II substances—have a high potential for abuse, which may lead to severe psychological or physical dependence.

Schedule III substances—have an abuse potential that is less than that for drugs in Schedule I and II. Abuse may lead to moderate or low physical dependence or high psychological dependence.

Schedule IV substances—low potential for abuse relative to the drugs or other substances in Schedule III. Abuse may lead to limited physical dependence or psychological dependence relative to drugs in Schedule III.

Veteran #2 (VAMC Bay Pines, FL)

This veteran received Parest (Schedule II) and Tuinal (Schedule II), both of which are sleeping medications. According to the staff pharmacist, even if they were being taken in an alternative fashion, they were being refilled too soon as follows:

Date	Medication	Quantity	Prescription (Rx) Life
11–19–79	Tuinal 100 mg.	30	30 day supply
12–4–79	Tuinal 100 mg.	100	100 day supply
1–8–80	Tunial 100 mg.	30	30 day supply
2–5–80	Parest 400	15	15 day supply
3–5–80	Parest 400	30	30 day supply
3–31–80	Parest 400	30	30 day supply
4–11–80	Parest 400	180 c.c.	--
4–15–80	Parest 400	30	30 day supply
4–29–80	Parest 400	3	3 day supply
5–5–80	Parest 400	3	3 day supply
Not shown	Parest 400	24	24 day supply

Veteran #3 (VAMC Bay Pines, FL)

This veteran obtained prescriptions for Demerol (Schedule II) from three physicians and had these prescriptions filled at four pharmacies during a six-month period. Examples of prescriptions for two months are as follows:

Date	Medication	Quantity	Prescription (Rx) Life
10–5–79	Demerol	50	16 day supply
10–16–79	Demerol	50	15 day supply
10–17–79	Demerol	24	4 day supply
10–23–79	Demerol	100	33 day supply
10–29–79	Demerol	24	4 day supply
11–16–79	Demerol	24	4 day supply
11–26–79	Demerol	24	4 day supply
11–28–79	Demerol	100	33 day supply
12–5–79	Demerol	24	4 day supply
12–12–79	Demerol	50	16 day supply
12–20–79	Demerol	30	10 day supply
12–22–79	Demerol	24	4 day supply

Veteran #4 (VAMC San Diego, CA)

Veteran number four obtained enough 100-milligram Seconal tablets, a Schedule II controlled substance, for 300 days, based on ten prescriptions obtained by the veteran and filled between October 6, 1979 and February 29, 1980. The prescriptions were obtained and filled at intervals ranging from 5 to 22 days. However, each prescription was for a 30-day supply. Veteran number four also received enough 30 milligram Dalmane capsules, a Schedule IV substance, for 262 days based on ten prescriptions obtained and filled between May 6, 1980, and September 19, 1980. Although each Dalmane prescription was for a 30-day supply, the prescriptions were obtained by the patient and filled at intervals ranging from 10 to 20 days.

Veteran #5 (VAMC San Diego, CA)

Veteran number five obtained more Quaalude than needed based on the usage specified on the patient's prescriptions. Quaalude is a Schedule II controlled substance and highly susceptible to abuse. Between October 12, 1979 and September 18, 1980, the veteran obtained seventeen prescriptions for Quaalude, each for an approximate 30-day supply. The time interval between six of the prescriptions was 14 days or less, and only four of the prescriptions were obtained and filled about 30 days after the prior prescription. In addition, veteran number five was prescribed two interactive drugs at the same time, Quaalude and Benadryl.

Veteran #6 (VAMC Decatur, GA)

The veteran received concurrent administration of drugs of the same therapeutic class from two different fee-basis physicians, as follows:

Drug	Controlled Substance-Schedule	Quality	Date
Ativan	IV	50 (25-day supply)	5–12–80
Tranxene	IV	50 (25-day supply)	5–26–80
Dalmane	IV	30 (30-day supply)	5–29–80
Quaalude	II	12 (12-day supply)	6–03–80

This resulted in an 80-day supply of drugs in the same therapeutic class for a 20-day period, or a 281 percent excess supply. In addition, this veteran was prescribed medications from the VA and also from fee-basis physicians. The drugs were filled by the VA pharmacy and six different fee-basis pharmacies. A partial tabulation of drug receipts by this veteran is shown below:

Date Received/Mailed	Drug	Quantity	Days Supply	Source
3–14–80	Digoxin 0.25 mg	100	100	Fee Pharmacy
4–15–80	Digoxin 0.25 mg	30	30	VA Pharmacy
5–20–80	Digoxin 0.25 mg	30	30	VA Pharmacy
6–25–80	Digoxin 0.25 mg	30	30	VA Pharmacy

This resulted in a 160-day supply over a 103-day period, or 55 percent excess supply.

187

In regards to the staff member approving his own sick leave, the Director told us it was not the normal procedure but rather an oversight. Handwritten signatures should have been displayed on all leave requests to assure all leave taken was officially approved. This would also ensure that management was aware of leave taken by the RE staff.

Improper T&A procedures by RE's were not being detected by the Director, Resident Engineer Staff. For example, the RE at VAMC Reno told us that he approved compensatory time and allowed the staff to use earned compensatory time on an informal basis. The RE told us that a record was maintained on his calendar on an accrual basis. We were not able to quantify the extent that compensatory time was earned and used during the project because of incomplete records.

The *Handbook for Resident Engineers* stated:

> When compensatory time is worked, a VA Form 1098, "Request for and Authorization of Overtime Work," must be prepared . . . and forwarded to Central Office . . .

Compensatory time should have been properly requested. This would have allowed a more accurate record of compensatory time earned and used. This would have also provided the Office of Construction with accurate staff utilization statistics for planning purposes.

The RE at the VAMC Reno project also told us he awarded compensatory time for working on federal holidays because the local holidays did not coincide with government holidays. The RE told us the compensatory days earned was taken on the local holidays when the contractor did not work. The compensatory leave is used within thirty days.

The *Handbook for Resident Engineers* provided that compensatory time was not allowed for working on a holiday.

> Compensatory time may only be granted for irregular or occasional overtime duty.
> Holiday pay is double pay in lieu of regular pay. . . . In as much as compensatory time may only be granted for irregular or occasional overtime duty, an employee may not elect compensatory time in lieu of payment at the holiday rate . . .

We reviewed the T&A reports maintained by the RE at Reno and found the staff earned seventy-two hours of overtime for working on three holidays. The overtime was not reported for two holidays, and the other holiday's overtime was reported after the fact. The RE told us that he did not request the overtime in advance because of late notice from the contractor. The RE was not able to furnish any other records of requests for overtime. Overtime should have been requested in advance, whenever possible, and appropriate records maintained.

The VA took custody of a construction project when the project reached substantial completion. When the VA assumed custody of the project, the contractor was relieved of any further assessment of liquidated damages as provided for in the liquidated damages clause in the contractor. The importance of recognizing substantial completion was fundamental in determining when to accept custody of the project from the contractor. A final inspection was scheduled when the contractor reported in writing that the project was ready for inspection. The RE, in forwarding the contractor's request, would submit his comments as to whether or not the project was substantially complete and ready for inspection. The inspection team captain (project supervisor or RE) evaluated whether the project was ready for final inspection and verified the date of substantial completion. After signing a letter of custody accepting the facility from the contractor, the team captain signed another letter of custody transferring the facility to the DM&S official (usually the station Director). Custody had been accepted by the VA from October 1, 1979 to May 1, 1981, for sixty-six projects valued over $225.3 million.

As you by now already suspect, we found that construction projects were accepted without all major systems being fully operational. This occurred because the definition of substantial completion was inadequately defined.

We audited the William Jennings Bryan Dorn Veteran's Hospital, Columbia, South Carolina, and VAMC Augusta, Georgia, and reviewed the project files at the Office of Construction for all sixty-six projects where custody had been transferred to the VA since October 1, 1979, to May 1, 1981. In addition to finding major systems not being operational at Columbia, we also found eleven of the sixty-six projects (including Augusta) were accepted with major systems not having been established as operational when the VA accepted them. The total value of the sixty-six projects exceeded $225.3 million. The value of the eleven projects accepted with major systems not being operational exceeded $95.6 million. The project for the William Jennings Bryan Dorn Veterans' Hospital, Columbia, South Carolina exceeded $22 million.

Veteran #7 (VAMC Decatur, GA)

We found that the veteran was using the fee-basis system to obtain Talwin (Schedule IV substance) and Butisol (Schedule III substance) through four fee-basis physicians, from both fee-basis and VA pharmacies. A partial tabulation of drug receipts by this veteran is shown below:

Date Received/Mailed	Drug	Quantity	Days Supply	Source
5–15–79	Talwin	50	12.5	Fee Pharmacy
6–08–79	Talwin	36	9	Fee Pharmacy
6–17–79	Talwin	50	12.5	VA Pharmacy
7–09–79	Talwin	36	9	VA Pharmacy
7–25–79	Talwin	62	15.5	Fee Pharmacy
7–27–79	Talwin	62	15.5	VA Pharmacy
8–11–79	Talwin	20	5	Fee Pharmacy
8–15–79	Talwin	48	12	Fee Pharmacy
8–21–79	Talwin	48	12	Fee Pharmacy
8–22–79	Talwin	62	15.5	Fee Pharmacy
8–25–79	Talwin	20	5	VA Pharmacy
9–18–79	Talwin	62	15.5	Fee Pharmacy
9–20–79	Talwin	62	15.5	VA Pharmacy
9–28–79	Butisol	100	16	Fee Pharmacy
10–01–79	Butisol	100	16	Fee Pharmacy
10–01–79	Talwin	50	12	Fee Pharmacy
10–07–79	Talwin	12	2	Fee Pharmacy
10–08–79	Talwin	30	6	Fee Pharmacy
10–10–79	Talwin	20	3	Fee Pharmacy
10–13–79	Talwin	30	6	Fee Pharmacy
10–20–79	Talwin	62	10	Fee Pharmacy
10–23–79	Talwin	36	6	Fee Pharmacy
10–26–79	Talwin	50	12	Fee Pharmacy
10–26–79	Talwin	62	31	Fee Pharmacy
11–03–79	Talwin	62	31	Fee Pharmacy

This resulted in a 242-day supply of Talwin for 172 days, or a 41 percent excess supply; and a 16-day supply of Butisol for 3 days.

Veteran #8 (VAMC Decatur, GA)

There were indications of possible abuse of Valium and other medications by the veteran as follows:

Date Received/Mailed	Drug	Quantity	Days Supply	Source
10–28–79	Drixoral	60	30	Fee Pharmacy
11–08–79	Drixoral	60	30	Fee Pharmacy
11–08–79	Valium-Schedule IV	30	105	Fee Pharmacy
11–16–79	Valium	306	10	Fee Pharmacy
11–23–79	Valium	30	10	Fee Pharmacy
02–12–80	Equanil-Schedule IV	50	16.5	Fee Pharmacy
02–19–80	Equanil	90	30	VA Pharmacy
02–19–80	Drixoral	60	30	VA Pharmacy
03–04–80	Drixoral	60	30	Fee Pharmacy
03–04–80	Equanil	50	16.5	Fee Pharmacy
03–15–80	Equanil	90	30	VA Pharmacy
03–15–80	Drixoral	60	30	VA Pharmacy
03–26–80	Equanil	90	30	VA Pharmacy
03–26–80	Drixoral	60	30	VA Pharmacy
04–11–80	Equanil	90	30	VA Pharmacy
04–12–80	Drixoral	60	30	Fee Pharmacy
04–29–80	Equanil	90	30	Fee Pharmacy

This resulted in the veteran receiving a 153-day supply of Equanil over a 77-day period, a 180-day supply of Drixoral over a 152-day period, and a 20-day supply of Valium over a 16-day period.

Veteran #9 (VAMC Decatur, GA)

The veteran received medication prescribed by seven different doctors—only two of whom practice in the same city. The veteran also used six different pharmacies and showed a pattern of use of drugs that could be abused. The veteran's medical records indicate Talwin addiction. Yet the veteran obtained these and other fee-basis prescribed medications at the VA pharmacy and also through local fee-basis pharmacies as follows:

Date Received/Mailed	Drug	Quantity	Days Supply	Source
6–79	Empirin #—Schedule III	135	34	Fee Pharmacy
7–79	Empirin #3	175	44	Fee Pharmacy
	Talwin-Schedule IV	35	6	Fee Pharmacy
8–79	Empirin #	180	45	Fee Pharmacy
	Talwin	105	26	Fee Pharmacy
9–79	Empirin #3	130	33	Fee Pharmacy
	Talwin	30	7.5	Fee Pharmacy
10–79	Empirin #3	80	20	Fee Pharmacy
	Talwin Inj.	120 Ml	-	Fee Pharmacy
11–79	Empirin #3	80	20	Fee Pharmacy
	Talwin Inj.	85	-	Fee Pharmacy
12–79	Empirin #3	160	40	Fee Pharmacy
	Talwin Inj.	10 Ml	-	Fee Pharmacy
1–80	Empirin	36	9	Fee Pharmacy
	Ascriptin #3	48	12	Fee Pharmacy
2–80	Talwin Inj.	10		Fee Pharmacy
	Empirin #4	54	13.5	Fee Pharmacy
3–80	Talwin Inj.	40 Ml	-	VA Pharmacy
	Empirin #3	48	12	VA Pharmacy
	Talwin	198	49.5	Fee Pharmacy
4–80	Empirin #3	78	19.50	Fee Pharmacy
	Talwin Inj.	160 Ml	-	VA Pharmacy
	Empracet #3-Schedule III	48	12	Fee Pharmacy
5–80	Empirin #3	48	12	Fee Pharmacy
	Talwin Inj.	40 Ml	-	VA Pharmacy
6–80	Empirin #3	240	60	Fee Pharmacy
7–80	Empirin #3	144	36	Fee Pharmacy

Due to the veteran's hospitalization, a medical evaluation was conducted by a VA physician at VAMC Decatur, Georgia, on July 1, 1980. The VA physician stated " . . . the veteran is using an undue amount of medication, frequently of an intramuscular route. It is difficult to disagree with the judgment of his personal physician, since he is in charge of his management. I do, however, feel that we should maintain his fee for services within our limitations." Our review of the veteran's prescriptions for the remainder of fiscal year 1980 indicated that medication usage had decreased but a progression to increased strength medication usage was evident.

Veteran #10 (VAMC Chicago, (Westside), IL)

This veteran received a 165-day supply of Noludar, a Schedule III controlled substance, during a 53-day period between October 20, 1980 and December 12, 1980. He also received a 110-day supply of Librium, a Schedule IV controlled substance, during a 27-day period between October 28, 1980 and November 24, 1980. Prescriptions for these drugs were written by two different fee-basis physicians. Three prescriptions for Noludar and two for Librium were filled by the medical center pharmacy. Five prescriptions of Noludar and two for Librium were filled by participating hometown pharmacies.

The auditors also identified duplicate payments at two of three clinics audited for duplicate payments. As with the Salisbury audit, the overall Fee-Basis Pharmacy Program audit was never published; however, rest assured you paid for its being performed. Let's get back to Salisbury. Were you thinking it was over already?

Administrative review by Medical Administration personnel of invoices for fee medical services did not assure that all invoices requiring a medical evaluation and decision were subject to professional review. The VA required Medical Administration personnel to insure that total monthly charges did not exceed forty dollars, or other approved limitations; any fees exceeding the approved limitations were to be evaluated by the Chief Medical Officer or designee. However, Medical Administration personnel were not bringing all monthly bills that exceeded the monthly limit to the attention of the designated staff physician for his review and approval.

Our review of fee medical invoices processed for payment on July 17, 1979 showed that of thirty-five monthly charges over a hundred dollars:

only nine (26 percent) were professionally reviewed and approved prior to certification;

twenty-two bills were not presented by Medical Administration personnel to the designated VA staff physician for his review, although Payment Information Cards had not shown an approved monthly increase;

in three cases, where the Payment Information Card had indicated a monthly limit increase, this increase was not documented nor clinically supported in the medical record. The monthly limit for one of these three payment cards had been waived with the annotation "pay any amount." This bill showed fourteen office visits in one month for injections of aminophyllin, and blood pressure and weight checks; and,

a review of the one remaining case not referred by Medical Administration Service found the monthly limit increase was documented on both the payment card and the medical record, but the higher limit had been exceeded without approval. The monthly limit had been set at a hundred dollars when the ID card was issued in 1977, and this limit had been exceeded for the past thirty months since the card was issued. The charges were for twelve house visits (ten dollars per visit) each month for treatment by an osteopath.

The thirty-five bills, ranging from $108 to $396 per month, may have represented proper medical treatment. However, they should have been subject to professional review and evaluation, as required. Otherwise there was no assurance that the veteran was receiving, and the VA was paying with your money for, appropriate medical care.

Veterans with fee-basis ID cards were not regularly evaluated to determine their continued need to receive medical treatment on a fee basis. Some evaluations by means of a VA staff examination were performed on an irregular basis.

Our random sample of thirty-eight ID card holders showed that twenty-two (58 percent) lived within forty miles of a VA facility. Only one of these had documentation in the medical record showing that the VA facility had been requested to consider furnishing the veteran's outpatient needs. Our sample also showed that twelve (32 percent) of the ID cards have never been used, suggesting questionable medical need at the time of issuance. ID cards should not have been approved unless outpatient services were currently required.

Analysis showed that twenty (53 percent) of the veterans in our sample may not have needed ID cards. Eight of these veterans lived within forty miles of a VA facility and had never used their ID card (six), or had not used it in the past five years (two). Eight other veterans were not accessible to a VA facility but had never used their ID cards (six), or had not used it in the past five years (two). In addition, four other veterans living within forty miles of a VA facility were using the card, but there was no documentation in their medical record as to why they required care on a fee-basis.

The VA required that a specific validity period be given for each veteran-authorized ID card status. Prior to expiration of this established validity period, each clinic of jurisdiction should have evaluated the current medical needs of the veteran. This could have been done by a VA staff examination, review of the veteran's VA medical records, or by requesting special reports from the veteran's fee-basis treatment source. A determination should have been made to transfer the veteran to care by VA staff, terminate ID card authorization, or to continue authorization by establishing a new expiration date.

I was the Auditor-in-Charge for the audit at VA Hospital, Tuskegee, Alabama. The audit was performed from September 1979 through October 1979. The audit report was published one year later on October 30, 1980. Resources available to management included 1,448 employees, nonexpendable equipment costing over $4.8 million, 977 operating beds, and a 112-bed Nursing Home Care Unit. The protection of and control over patient and government property was a prime responsibility of VA managers. By statutory provisions, the Administrator of Veteran Affairs was responsible for the protection of patients, visitors, and employees; the protection of property; and the maintenance of law and order on property under the charge and control of the VA. The basic concept of security at DM&S facilities is to prevent crime. Directors were responsible for providing persons on federal property with the same degree of protection they enjoyed on state property through the maintaining of effective physical security and a visible deterrence to crime.

Control over the agent cashier's cash was unacceptable. Cash variances had been noted by every unannounced cash count conducted since November 1976. In addition, we found that the Federal Bureau of Investigation (FBI) was conducting an investigation of a $957 cash shortage, discovered during an unannounced cash count in July 1979. The agent cashier had been on duty for only six weeks and was untrained for the duties of an agent cashier. The unannounced cash counts did not always audit all the cash on hand. The agent cashier's cash advance was excessive and the alarm system in the agent cashier's office was inadequate.

The Director notified the FBI on July 6, 1979 of a $957 shortage in an alternate agent cashier's cashbox. At the time of our audit, the Director was waiting for the FBI final report. The Alabama Bureau of Investigation conducted a polygraph test on one of the four alternate agent cashiers. The employee who was tested was not the alternate cashier who was missing the $957. The employee has recently been fired for verbally abusing a patient and filed a grievance for reinstatement. The tested employee had also replaced $145 during the August unannounced cash count. During our review of the $957 shortage, we found an alternate's cash box key could open another alternate's cash box. Except for the Director's request to the FBI, top management had not taken corrective action to prevent repeated cash variances. The Director stated there had been many problems in Fiscal Service in the past. Other problems were given priority over the reported cash variances.

We noted that the door to the agent cashier's office was not always locked, money had been left out on desks, cash boxes were left open, and the filing was haphazard. The current agent cashier had been on duty for only six weeks and had not been provided sufficient training and lacked experience.

Unannounced cash counts did not always audit all cash on hand. For example, the audit of May 25, 1979 reported two cash boxes were not audited because the employees were on leave. Our review of the employees' time-and-attendance records revealed only one employee was on leave. The other employees left the cash box key at home. Both cash boxes should have been audited. The Director's safe contained the keys for all the cash boxes. The reported shortages of May 1979 could have been in the unaudited cash boxes. An accurate verification of cash on hand could not be made by a partial cash count.

The agent cashier's advance of $60,000 was $5,000 in excess of station needs. We discussed our review of the cash replenishments for the last year with the Chief, Fiscal Service. The Chief stated the cause for the low cash turnover rate was due to the lack of beneficiary travel claims for this quarter. Total replenishments for the last twelve months was over $656,000, or an average monthly turnover of only $55,000. The advance should have been reduced because one year's replenishment were examined and the amount of cash advance should have been as low as possible.

We tested the alarm system in the agent cashier's office and found it was not connected into the VA Police Station. The Chief of Police said the alarm was not tied into the station; however, they had patroled the area constantly. We reviewed the recommendations made by a VACO internal audit team concerning the security of the agent cashier. The internal audit team recommended a foot-operated buzzer be installed; however, no action has been taken to implement this past recommendation.

Key control procedures had not been implemented at this medical center. Key control is essential to prevent loss of funds. Appropriate records should be maintained that will make possible the location of desired keys and to whom such keys have been issued. Supply Service had prior responsibility for the development and maintenance of lock key production; however, approximately two years ago, Engineering Service assumed the responsibility for key control. The medical center had never established a beginning inventory or a system for controlling keys. As a result, we were unable to determine which employees at the medical center had been issued keys. In addition, failure to maintain key inventory records provided no assurance keys had been properly returned upon an employee's transfer or termination.

Effective controls over patients' personal effects had not been established. Internal controls were weak because the staff were not complying with VA Manual and station policies and were not performing their assigned duties in a timely manner. Our review disclosed that semiannual audits of patient valuables were not being conducted properly, alphabetical index cards (patient locator cards) were not maintained in accordance with station policy, and mailing requirements of the VA had not been implemented.

Our review disclosed semiannual audits of patient effects are not conducted properly.

We reviewed four semiannual audit reports made to the Chief, Building Management Service. The reports were dated and signed; however, the signature of the auditor and date of the audit were not put on the valuables envelope that held the veteran's possessions. Our review of the semiannual audit reports disclosed all inventory envelopes had not been audited as required. Instead, the Building Management auditor had only sampled the envelopes on hand. Audit workpapers were not retained; therefore, there was no assurance that all patient valuables had been audited. In addition, failure to properly conduct the audits had resulted in the failure to identify patient valuables that were not returned upon the patient's discharge and drugs in the patients' effects that were not turned into the pharmacy as required. According to the Assistant Chief of Building Management, who conducted the audits of patient effects, he was unaware of the requirement to audit *all* patient effects semiannually. He stated sampling techniques had always been used to conduct patient effects audits.

Our review also disclosed patient locator cards were not properly completed or maintained by the Patient Effects Section (PES). The patient locator card file was the control used by PES to control the patient effects stored in the Clothing Room. An alphabetical index card file (patient locator card) should have been maintained in the Central Clothing Room to record such information as "no effects stored," "valuables stored in safe," "clothing stored on hanger number—," etc. Our review disclosed PES was not making any of these notations on the patient cards, and therefore, had no way of knowing if a patient had effects stored in the PES without reviewing all items stored in the safe, clothing room, or in the storage area. Patient valuables envelopes for ninety-one veterans had not been returned upon their discharge.

Based on a review of sixteen patients' medical records, nine patients should have gone through clearance procedures, three were discharged based on their unauthorized absence, three patients were currently hospitalized at this medical center based on subsequent admissions, and one had died at this medical center after a subsequent admission. We noted several of these patients had been readmitted and discharged several times after the personal effects were inventoried; however, on none of these subsequent discharges were their valuables returned.

Our review also disclosed as of September 11, 1979, the PES had 1,145 patient locator cards on file; however, there were only 871 patients at the medical center. Therefore, there were 274 patient locator cards on file for discharged patients. The cards should have been removed when the patients were discharged in order to insure the patient locator control file was kept current.

There were ninety-one Valuables Inventory Envelopes on hand from patients who had been discharged in 1977. The staff had not followed the VA mailing requirements to advise the patient or his responsible representative by form letter that personal effects had been left at the medical center. Failure to follow the procedure had resulted in personal effects not being returned to the patient in a timely manner.

During our review of the patient effects of discharged patients, we found drugs brought to the medical center by patients had not been sent to the Pharmacy Service by the PES. Five patient inventory envelopes were noted to contain drugs. All drugs brought into the medical center by patients should have been, upon admission, turned in to Pharmacy Service and not stored in the clothing room. Based on our review, the PES had not taken action to assure drugs were turned in to the Pharmacy when the patient effects were inventoried. According to the Chief, Pharmacy Service, because patients had access to their personal effects, the failure to turn in those drugs could have resulted in an adverse drug reaction if these drugs had been taken with drugs currently prescribed by attending physicians.

Canteen Service had excessive inventory losses. The Chief, Canteen Service, stated the inventory accountability had shortages of 2.88 percent May 8, 1979 and 2.08 percent September 14, 1979. The majority of the shortages was due to thefts of cigarettes. The Chief stated a shortage of over one percent was significant. During our audit, representatives from Veterans Canteen Service Field Office were investigating the losses. According to the Director of Veterans Canteen Service Field Office, recommendations had been made to strengthen controls over inventory. He indicated that the medical center director had concurred with these recommendations and that immediate corrective action would be taken.

Some medical center fire extinguishers are not inspected monthly. Monthly inspection should have been made of all extinguishers to insure that they were not obstructed and for external evidence of deterioration. We reviewed thirty-seven fire extinguishers in patient care and administrative areas to determine compliance with medical center policy. We found eight of the extinguishers reviewed had not been inspected in over one month. As you would expect, the VA Chief, Fire Department, did not know why all the fire extinguishers had not been inspected within the required time period.

I was the Auditor-in-Charge of the audit of the VA Hospital at Hampton, Virginia. The audit was conducted from November 1979 through January 1980. The report was published in March 1980. The medical center stood on eighty-eight acres and consisted of a seven-floor main hospital and fifty-five other miscellaneous buildings. The health care facility had 458 operating beds: 74 psychiatric, 96 surgical, and 288 medical. In addition, there was a 625-bed domiciliary. As of September 30, 1979, there were 1,089 full-time and 106 part-time employees. Fiscal year 1979 expenditures were $29.5 million. There was over $6 million of nonexpendable equipment.

Follow-up on correction of previously noted deficiencies was inadequate. Conditions previously reported in the 1974 Internal Audit Report, 1978 General Accounting Office (GAO) Survey, Veterans Administration Central Office (VACO) Supply Technical Visit, VACO Personnel Management Reviews, Systematic External Review Program (SERP), and internal memorandums are still present. Specific items previously reported and still present at the time of our audit were:

**Unsatisfactory Follow-up on Previously
Noted Deficiencies**

Deficiency Found During This Audit	*When Previously Reported*
Ineffective SIR Program	Internal Audit Service Report—November 1974
Inadequate methods for silver recovery.	Internal Memorandum—May 1979
Employee training and development was unsatisfactory.	Internal Audit Service Report—November 1974; VACO Supply Service Technical Visit—November 1977; and, VACO Personnel Management Review—August 1978
Follow-up on undelivered orders was not timely.	Internal Audit Service Report—November 1974; and VACO Supply Service Technical Visit—November 1977
Shortage of $105 from Supply Service Imprest Fund.	Fiscal Service Unannounced Cash Count—May 1979
Domiciliary Medicine Service	Internal Audit Service Report—November 1974
Limitation on domiciliary staffing was a hazard to patient/members.	SERP 1978
Therapeutic Programming Board policy had not been updated.	VACO Senior Administration Specialist—May 1978

198

Stock control procedures for Schedule II drugs and Schedule III narcotics were unsatisfactory.

GAO Survey—July 1978

Follow-up on Accounts Receivable was inadequate.

Management analyst—May 1978 and June 1979

The Administrative Executive Board (AEB) should have assured that necessary follow-:up actions had been taken. Also, the AEB should have analyzed the Health Service Review Organization-Systematic Internal Review (HSRO-SIR) quality of care administrative program reviews, findings, and recommendations to facilitate implementation of any approved corrective action or improvements.

Though the Director did agree with us, he felt it was inappropriate to refer to previously noted deficiencies reported in November 1974, November 1977 and 1978.

We accepted the Director's concurrence as responsive to the recommendation, since corrective actions on other applicable recommendations in the audit report were indicated by the Director as scheduled for implementation. We noted that ten of the forty-five recommendations that followed in the audit report were previously reported and in some cases more than once. Some were noted as long ago as 1974; however, they had not been corrected in five years. In Disorganized Crime some things take awhile to be corrected. What's the hurry? You will pay for all of it anyway.

There was a shortage of government property; however, a Report of Survey was not made. VA Manuals required a Report of Survey to be made in order to obtain a satisfactory explanation of the circumstances surrounding the loss or damage of government property. The previous VA Medical Center Director retired in April 1978 and moved from station quarters (Building 6). The Chief, Supply Service, upon subsequent inventory of the quarters, discovered $3,200 worth of VA furniture and drapes missing and initiated a Collection Voucher for $2,017. The costs for the furniture were estimates and may not have been accurate. The depreciation charged against the estimated costs were also estimates, both of the age of the items and depreciation rate to be used. The Chief, Fiscal Service, withheld the previous Director's last paycheck pending collection of the receivables. The previous Director sent $1,072 and seven of the twenty items back in May 1978. The Chief, Supply Service, reduced the amount due to zero after receiving the items. The Chief, Engineering Service, stated that during his inspection of Building 6 in June 1978, he noted that the drapes were not put on the windows and were still in boxes. When the Chief of Staff attempted to move into Building 6 in December 1978, the Chief, Building Management Service, found that the sets of drapes sent back from the previous Director either did not fit the windows, were missing, their color did not match the carpet, or they were of very poor quality and condition. As a result, over $2,900 worth of drapes were purchased for Building 6 in January 1979, four years after $2,100 worth of drapes had been purchased. The Chief, Building Management Service, stated he did not know where the returned drapes are now used and they may have been discarded.

Supply Service was not accomplishing its assigned responsibilities in an efficient and economical manner. We found the following: Systematic Internal Reviews performed in Supply Service did not effectively identify problem areas; accuracy rate of warehouse stock inventories was unsatisfactory; uneconomical buying of some stock items had resulted in excessive warehouse inventory; inventory of equipment on Consolidated Memorandum Receipts assigned to Supply Service had not been timely; Accountability for some non-expendable equipment was inadequate; follow-up procedures by Supply Service on unde-livered orders was inefficient; inadequate methods for recovery for silver resulted in the loss of over 330 ounces in the past year; and, a shortage of $105 was found in the Supply Service Imprest Fund, of which only $65 had been returned.

The accuracy rate of warehouse stock inventories was unsatisfactory. The VA required a complete physical inventory of warehouse stock within a 12-month period, either wall-to-wall or by cycle. Annual inventories were being ac-complished, but the accuracy rate had dropped significantly in 1979, as shown by the following:

ACCURACY RATE OF CYCLIC WAREHOUSE INVENTORIES[1]

	FY 1978	FY 1979
Drugs	96.5%	76.1%
Subsistence	97.8%	54.1%[2]
General	91.1%	66.7%[3]
Accuracy rate, all items	94.1%	68.0%
Total number of line items	1,041	1,054
Line items with discrepancies	61	337
Value of shortages	$572	$5,042
Value of overages	$988	$8,142

1. based on number of line items
2. accomplished October 11, 1979
3. first inventory was declared inconclusive and rescheduled

In order to determine potential causes for the decreased accuracy rate, we conducted an inventory of thirty randomly selected items (which included all classes of stock). The final result was 83.3 percent accuracy (with five line items having discrepancies). Our reconciliation of items initially having discrepancies revealed several problem areas. We found:

a. the existence of unmarked "overflow" areas;

b. inventory splitting, where part of stock is in one location and part in another;
c. the wrong item inventoried because it had been placed in the wrong location;
d. inventory lables (containing stock number, nomenclature, and unit of issue) difficult to read because of size and age;
e. some labels have fallen off the shelves, or were placed in wrong location;
f. no labels present for subsistence stock items;
g. the lack of a locator card system; and,
h. an inventory discrepancy identified during a previous cyclic inventory had not been adjusted.

Periodic spot checks of warehouse stock were not being accomplished. The VA required that periodic spot checks be made "for the purpose of good property management and security during the course of the year." These should have been conducted by other than Storage and Distribution personnel who were in charge of the inventory. Prior to fiscal year 1979, spot checks were conducted by the former Chief, Storage and Distribution Section. According to the Chief, Personal Management personnel had never participated in inventory spot checks. The Chief, Supply Service, told us on November 30, 1979 that periodic spot checks would be conducted in the future.

Action taken by Supply Service to correct the identified causes of inventory discrepancies had not been adequate. In January 1979, the causes of a 66.7 percent accuracy rate were cited as errors in receiving, issuing, and storage procedures; improper paperwork processing; and a continuing increased workload. The service identified corrective action to be taken as (a) additional training for Storage and Distribution and Personal Property Management personnel, and (b) more frequent inventories and adjustments. These recommended actions were not implemented. The same causes were identified for discrepancies occurring in the cyclic inventory of drugs in June 1979 (the accuracy rate was 76.1 percent). Additional training to be provided by July 1979 was recommended but not accomplished. A re-inventory by July 1979 of the line items with discrepancies was accomplished (with an accuracy rate of 84.6 percent). Following the inventory of subsistence items in October 1979 (with an accuracy rate of only 54.1 percent), additional training in November 1979 was again recommended. In-service training in Personal Property Management was initiated in November 27, 1979, but no additional training has been provided to the Storage and Distribution staff.

Uneconomical buying of some stock (from sources other than VA Supply Depot) had resulted in excessive warehouse inventory. These overages existed although the stock turnover rate for fiscal year 1979 at 6.4 was within the recommended range of 4.0 to 7.5.

There were 1,015 line items valued over $275,000 in the warehouse on November 30, 1979. We selected a statistical sample of 167 line items to determine if the stockage levels were appropriate. We found that 36 items (22 percent) in our sample were overstocked by $13,610. This projects to 223 line items overstocked in the total inventory, and represents significant funds tied up in excess stock. The following table depicts our findings:

	Sample	Total	Percent
Line items with appropriate stockage or shortages above safety levels[1]	126	762	75%
Line items overstocked	36	223	22%
Line items with shortages below safety levels	5	30	3%
Total	167	1,015	100%

1. Safety level: Stock intended to satisfy any unusual demand or delay in delivery during the lag time period.

Our analysis of those items overstocked showed that most of the overages were for stock procured from sources other than the VA Supply Depot (Source 1) and were not always purchased according to the EOQ principle. The Economic Order Quality (EOQ) is a method that determines the order quantity that produces the lowest cost of acquiring and carrying inventories. Of the thirty-six items with overages, ten were purchased in quantities over the recommended EOQ level or prior to the recommended Reorder Point, and none of these ten items were Source 1 items. For example, we found that a medical item ordered prior to the established Reorder Point and at twice the recommended EOQ level resulted in this item being overstocked by 289 units (with a unit cost of $1.23) valued at $355.47. Another item with a unit cost of $12 was purchased at 3.75 times the EOQ level and resulted in overages of 90 units valued at $1,080.

Inventory of nonexpendable equipment on Consolidated Memorandum of Receipt (CMRs) assigned to Supply Service had not been timely. The VA required an inventory of all nonexpendable property taken at least once within a twelve-month period. The responsible official or designee was expected to complete a physical count within ten days after receipt of notice that an inventory was due. Supply Service had responsibility for equipment on seven CMRs. One supply clerk was responsible for inventorying 1,281 pieces of equipment (with a total value of over $720,000) on five of these CMRs. This represented 27 percent of all the nonexpendable equipment at the medical center. Inventories on two of these CMRs were completed as scheduled. Completion of inventories on the other three CMRs were six, seven, and eleven months past the anniversary dates of the last inventory, respectively. For example, the CMR for Administrative Services was scheduled to be completed by December 1978, but was not actually certified as finished until November 28, 1979 (during the audit, surprise, surprise).

202

Our review of the assigned CMRs showed that not all medical center services and sections had responsibility for equipment accountability in their own area. Supply Service was in the process of creating CMRs for Spinal Cord Injury Unit, and Hematology/Oncology and Endoscopy sections of Medical Service. Personnel Service, Fiscal Service, Psychiatry Service, Medical Intensive Care Unit, Surgical Intensive Care Unit, and Outpatient/Ambulatory Care also did not have CMRs, and equipment in these areas must be inventoried by Supply Service. We counted over a hundred pieces of equipment valued over $189,000, which should have been the responsibility of the respective service or section chief. Because inventories of CMRs for Administrative Services, Hospital Account, and Wards and Clinics took so long to complete, a large amount of equipment came in between the time the CMR listings were started and when they were certified as complete. Our review showed that thirty pieces of nonexpendable equipment valued over $15,000 were received and accepted by the medical center between the time these three CMR inventories were first started and when they were completed in November 1979. Thus, the equipment accounted for on the date these CMRs were certified did not reflect all the equipment present.

Accountability for some nonexpendable equipment was inadequate. Supply Service was required to assign and affix a maintenance tag to personal property to be included in the preventive maintenance program. A completed VA Form 07–6112 (Equipment Record) was required to be forwarded to the Chief, Engineering Service, within seven days of receipt of equipment. Our review of supply records shows that 151 nonexpendable equipment items valued at over $251,000 had been received by the medical center and assigned preventive maintenance (PM) numbers; but, the PM tags had not been affixed to the items. One hundred and forty-five of these items had been delivered to the using service without PM tags. The majority of this equipment was received in fiscal year 1979; however, 12 items dated back two to nine years. None of the VA Forms 07–6112 for this equipment had been forwarded to the Chief, Engineering Service. This backlog of untagged equipment had accumulated because new items had not been tagged before they left the warehouse for the using service. Supply Service was located five hundred yards from the rest of the medical center, and it took considerable staff time to locate and tag the item once it had left the warehouse.

A review of selected CMRs revealed additional equipment not properly identified with a PM number, serial number, and/or an adequate description (such as brand or model number). In addition to the equipment without PM tags described above, we identified 147 pieces of equipment valued over $43,000 on three CMRs assigned to Supply Service without a PM number nor a serial number to properly identify it. Most of the equipment had been VA property for over five years. Without preventive maintenance tags, there is no preventive maintenance program, which means you will buy more equipment sooner.

Inadequate methods for recovery of silver resulted in the loss of over 330 ounces (valued at over $3,000) in 1979. Recovery of silver from used photographic fixer solution was required by the VA. The Chief, Supply Service, was responsible for working with the servicing depot to establish and maintain a program for recovery of the maximum amount of silver from used photographic (hypo) solution. The Director had delegated the operation of the silver recovery units to the chief technician in Radiology Service. Silver was recovered by use of a single Rotex electrolytic machine located in Radiology Service. Used solution containing silver was brought to the Radiology Service in five-gallon jugs and processed in twenty-gallon drums. The chief technician had brought the loss of solution to the attention of the Chiefs of Radiology and Supply Service. The chief technician stated in her May 24, 1979 memorandum:

> The present system is outdated, inefficient, and in some cases nonexistent. . . . In the Cysto Room and the Dental Clinic, the exhausted fixer tubing is permanently fixed to the drain pipe so that all the silver in these units is flowing down the drain, and none is being collected and processed.

The audit team also found the above and that used fixer was being thrown away in Nuclear Medicine Service. The Assistant Chief, Supply Service, in a May 24, 1979 memorandum to the Chief, Supply Service, estimated that approximately 60 gallons (out of a total production of 252.3 gallons) were lost each week (23.7 percent). Despite the fact that this showed a potential loss of as much as $30,000 a year in unrecovered silver, by Supply Service estimates, no action to follow-up, validate, or correct these findings was undertaken by the Supply Service arm of Disorganized Crime.

The Chief, Supply Service, in his briefing to hospital management on July 18, 1979, stated that the silver recovery program was running well. The Chief, Radiology Service, during his briefing to center management on September 11, 1979, stated the silver recovery program was . . . "a disaster."

Our concern about the potential size of the loss was discussed with the Director. As a result, the Chief, Supply Service, requested a survey of the silver recovery program operation by a representative of the Supply Depot, Somerville, New Jersey. The Supply Depot representative arrived December 5, 1979, and confirmed that hypo solution was being poured down the drain in Dental, Surgical, and Nuclear Medicine Services, though not in the volume reported by Supply Service. Hampton was not an isolated occurrence. At fifteen VA hospitals audited, eighteen ounces of silver were lost in the overflow of silver-laden solution from existing silver-recovery equipment. The auditors observed this overflowing down the drain at nine of the fifteen hospitals. This loss, if applied VA wide, represented over $225,000 annually. Maybe the next time someone tells you your stolen money went down the drain you will believe them.

A shortage of $105 was found in the Supply Service Imprest Fund during an unannounced count by Fiscal Service on May 31, 1979. Four Supply Service personnel as imprest fund cashiers were found negligent. The shortages were $10, $20, $30, and $45. A request for a waiver of restitution was made by the Director; however, it was refused by the Director, Finance Service VA Central Office, September 4, 1979. We requested an unannounced cash count on November 14, 1979, and found the $105 shortage still existed. On November 14, 1979, the agent cashier requested that $105 from the four Imprest Fund cashiers. The VA required that when a shortage occurs in the accounts of the

Imprest Fund cashier due to negligence, restitution would be made immediately from personal funds. On December 3, 1979, we requested a repeat unannounced cash count of the Imprest Fund and found a shortage of $40; only two members of Disorganized Crime had reimbursed the Imprest Fund.

The VA's domiciliary program, one of its least known and least publicized programs, provides housing, medical treatment, food, clothing, and related services to needy, disabled veterans. During fiscal year 1976, an average of 9,090 veterans were housed daily in eighteen VA domiciliary facilities, which, combined, spent $62 million. This was an average daily cost of over eighteen dollars per veteran. As of 1976, only 21 percent of the patient/members had service-connected disabilities and 12 percent had six months or less of military service.

The Domiciliary Service at Hampton was divided into two organizational units: Domiciliary Medicine Service and Domiciliary Operations. Domiciliary Medicine Service provided a coordinated professional treatment program organized to attain preventive and restorative goals. The professional care program was administered by the Chief, Domiciliary Medicine Service. Care included providing for the medical needs of the individual patient/member and for the general public health needs of the domiciliary community. Domiciliary Operations was responsible for the administrative aspect of the comprehensive therapeutic programs of care for patient/members.

The workload for the domiciliary included management of 625 beds, 594 of which were occupied. The five-year plan included a construction project that would provide 200 new domiciliary beds. These beds were designed to replace beds to be lost by renovation and construction of privacy partitions.

Staff for Domiciliary Operations consisted of one domiciliary officer, eight domiciliary assistants, and one clerical position. Domiciliary Medicine Service staffing consists of three full-time physicians, one part-time physician, and a secretary. Nursing Service provided seven registered nurses to Domiciliary Medicine Service, two of whom were nurse practitioners. Also, Medical Administration Service (MAS) provided three medical clerks. One additional clerk was assigned from MAS for training, and one work study student provided approximately twenty hours' service per week.

Domiciliary medicine service was not economical and efficient as a separate service. The VA Internal Audit Service in November 1974 recommended that Domiciliary Medicine Service be abolished and its function and staff be absorbed or dispersed into the hospital's Medical Care, Nursing, and Medical Administration elements. The previous Director concurred with the recommendation; however, Domiciliary Medicine Service continued to operate as a separate service. We believe that absorption of the service's functions into other medical center elements was warranted and would have achieved improved economy and efficiency.

The service's workload had declined from 21,335 clinical visits in fiscal year 1974 to 9,253 in fiscal year 1979. Staffing had remained at 4 FTEE since fiscal year 1974 despite a 57 percent decrease in workload. The previous audit report noted that the productivity rate was low. Productivity was lower at the 1979 workload levels.

The integration of Domiciliary Medicine Service with the medical center outpatient/admission functions would have enabled the consolidation of many administrative functions related to the maintenance of medical records, and would have eliminated the interchange of clinical folders between the domiciliary and medical center. With the absorption of Domiciliary Medicine Service's personnel, and more effective use of professional duty time, the ambulatory care activity could have readily anticipated expansion of both its range of services and clinic business hours to include evenings and weekends. In addition, the procedures for members obtaining prescriptions or refills should have become simpler and their appointments with physician consultants would have been expedited.

Management in July 1978 appointed a task force to study Domiciliary Medicine Service, and its plan of action included an effort to abolish Domiciliary Medicine Service. Action coordinated with Engineering, Supply, and Medical Administration Services. In addition, no specific organizational structure for reorganization had been presented to the Director. Also, the Five-Year Facility Plan, fiscal year 1981–1985, states:

> A part of the project to "Renovate Building 66" proposed for FY 1982, cost $1,084,000, is to house the Domiciliary Medicine Service."

The Director agreed with us; however, he said the implementation would not happen for another year. As a result, the absorption of Domiciliary Medicine Service would have taken six years since first recommended in 1974.

The participants in the Incentive Therapy Program were not evaluated timely. Our review of medical records of five participants, who received five hundred dollars or more from Incentive Therapy funds during the period January 1 through November 30, 1979, disclosed that no rehabilitation plans and objectives had been made. Also, time limits were not specified and reviews were not always performed every three months as required. In addition, all five had been participants on the Incentive Therapy Program for over one year. Where monetary incentives are utilized, the rehabilitation plan should be specific as to objectives and time. The time limit shall not extend beyond one year's duration, other than in exceptional cases, which must be approved by the Hospital, Domiciliary, or Center Director. A comparison of Incentive Therapy payrolls with the Compensated Work Therapy Program (CWT) payrolls found twenty-six participants had received both incentive therapy and CWT funds during the period January 1 through November 30, 1979. The chairman of the Therapeutic Programming Board and the Chief, Domiciliary Operations, were unaware that members were on both programs because there was no coordinated rehabilitation plan.

There was no twenty-four-hour civil service employee coverage of Domiciliary Operations. Our review of Domiciliary Operations showed that operating beds had been reduced October 1, 1979 from 700 to 625 because of the installation of privacy partitions and other renovation projects in the five-year plan. Additional renovation projects were expected to reduce the number of beds even further. Reduction of the staff ceiling by one of 1978 and an increase in the size of the incentive therapy program during the past year required that twenty-four-hour civil-service employee coverage be discontinued on January

28, 1979 in the domiciliary. Coverage was provided by member section leaders on the midnight to 8:00 A.M. shift. Medical center security officers reported a need for civil-service support in the domiciliary on the night shift, 12:00 midnight to 8:00 A.M.

We reviewed the VA Hospital Police Daily Operations Journal for January through March 1979 to determine the types of member activity recorded. We found that thirty-seven calls were received. We noted twenty-three (62 percent) of these calls were to report members missing at 12:00 midnight. Our discussions with the police chief disclosed that they were not notified in most cases if the member returned during the night shift. We checked the first eleven calls in our sample and found that no follow-up calls were received by the police. In addition, we reviewed the Uniform Offense Report for 1979. We found one member charged with breaking a window to get back into the Domiciliary after he walked out of the section to get some fresh air at 4:58 A.M. Another member was found lying beside his bed with a bottle of alcoholic beverage, and a third was taken to the Hampton Police Department and charged with assault-and-battery on a police officer after the police were called to the section at 1:05 A.M. to quiet a disturbance in the domiciliary.

We noted also that none of these incidents was witnessed by a civil-service employee other than the medical center police. Periodic section checks and counseling after midnight by a civil service employee familiar with the members would have improved the follow-up and possible prevention of such cases. In addition, having domiciliary members supervise each other during this critical period, with no civil-service employee on duty, was a questionable practice that left the VA vulnerable to possible future litigation.

The Alcohol Treatment activity in the domiciliary was not adequately coordinated with the alcohol rehabilitation unit. The Therapeutic Programming Board was the principal vehicle through which the treatment and rehabilitation efforts of the domiciliary were to be implemented. In addition, the board had the specific function of aligning the therapeutic resources within and outside the domiciliary for the maximum benefit of patient/members. Our review of the treatment plan for members in the domiciliary who were alcohol abusers disclosed that the treatment plan was not reviewed and approved by the Therapeutic Programming Board because center policy requires all alcohol-related patient programs, with the exception of detoxification, to be under the direction of the Chief, Psychiatry Service. In addition, the medical center's Alcohol Rehabilitation Unit staff was not utilized in formation of treatment plans or quality review of the domiciliary alcohol treatment activity.

We reviewed a report of 203 disciplinary cases processed through the domiciliary for the six-month period January 1 through June 30, 1979. This review disclosed that 43 percent of the disciplinary cases during this period involved an intoxicated member. In addition, a center task force appointed by the Director reported September 30, 1979 that alcohol was a wide-spread problem in the domiciliary and recommended special programs of therapy for alcoholism. Failure of the Therapeutic Programming Board to provide leadership in the installation of a program to deal with alcohol problems in the domiciliary had resulted in the attempt of Social Work Service and the Chief, Domiciliary Operations, to provide this service.

Medical examinations for domiciliary members were not timely. Our review of fifteen medical records disclosed that four members had not had a medical examination in over two years. The VA required that each patient/member would have an annual comprehensive medical examination. The staff charged with scheduling of medical examinations had no training in scheduling. Consequently, those members with the most delinquent examinations were not always scheduled first. Also, systematic monitoring was not performed in order to identify and classify the delinquent population. The nurse practitioners stated that sometimes physical examinations were scheduled in the domiciliary, although the patient/member had been hospitalized and received a recent medical examination. The scheduling clerks were unaware of the recent medical examination, and this resulted in duplication of laboratory work and X rays (for which you paid).

Patient/members medically excused from their assigned activities were not reevalutated timely. This occurred because there was no system by which excused patient/members were identified and monitored for reevaluation. The VA requires that any patient/member medically excused from the therapeutic program for more than one month should be reevaluated at that time, to determine the medical need to continue in the domiciliary on the previously prescribed therapeutic program. Our review disclosed that 39 out of 590 patient/members were medically excused from their therapeutic program for more than seven months during fiscal year 1979 and no reevaluations were made. At the request of the Chief, Domiciliary Operations, in August 1979, 14 reevaluations had been accomplished; however, 25 patient/members remained on medical excuse. This delay in reevaluation could have resulted in patient/members remaining in the domiciliary when medically they should not have continued in the domiciliary. In addition, medical excuse affects the patient/members' ability to perform assigned duties in the domiciliary. This resulted in fellow members having to perform details that were the resonsibility of the excused member for extended periods of time. Domiciliary section chiefs stated that this caused problems with patient/member relations in the domiciliary.

Medical center employees did not always comply with reporting requirements involving patient incidents. We reviewed the medical records of ten patients on whom a Report of Incident (VA Form 10–2633) were filed. It was found that VA Forms 10–2633a were not filed in the active medical records in six of the ten cases. In every instance, a progress note had been entered documenting the incident. The VA requires that the VA Form 10–2633a will be filed on the first page of the active medical record.

In our review of the hospital police file of Uniform Offense Reports, we noted a reported occurrence of attempted suicide by a domiciliary member of the Hampton VAMC grounds. The report referred to the Medical Officer for the Day's (MOD) decision to send the patient to a local community hospital for emergency treatment of the stab wound, because the VA's emergency surgical team could not be assembled in time. The community hospital returned the patient to the VAMC without treatment, due to the superficial nature of the wound. Hospital management and the physician's supervisor stated that the physician was counseled regarding this decision. Although there was an entry in the MOD log regarding this incident, there was no VA Form 10–2633 on file at this medical center. The form, not completed by a physician, was found in the medical record at another VA Medical Center.

Staff nurses generally ensured that VA Form 10–2633 were completed and forwarded through appropriate channels in any non-routine occurrence. Three instances were noted by the audit team in which abuse was alleged by a patient or relative; however, VA Form 10–2633 in one case had not been prepared timely and in two cases were not prepared. In the first case, a domiciliary member discussed with the audit team a case of alleged patient abuse. Our review of the patient's medical record showed no VA Form 10–2633a and no notation in progress or nursing notes. The head nurse disclosed that this deficiency had been recognized, and the employees involved in the allegation counseled and instructed to complete a Report of Incident. This was done on the day following the incident and was being properly investigated.

The second case involved an investigation of alleged patient abuse by an employee, which was reported by the wife of a patient. The medical center's investigation uncovered evidence that the employee had abused patients and intimidated employees for as long as five years. The investigation, which was conducted in May 1979, determined that the abuse alleged at the time of the investigation had in fact taken place, and recommended the removal of the employee, a nursing assistant in a medical ward at VAMC Hampton. The report stated:

> Testimony reveals that known incidents of patient abuse occurred from five years ago to early May 1979 . . .

> (The employee) has intimidated staff and co-workers to the point that they have been reluctant to voice or document their observations of patient abuse for fear of reprisal. Some nursing personnel seemed relieved that patient complaints have precipitated this investigation; others seemed afraid to give testimony beyond the question asked. Three types of intimidation were identified in the testimony received by the Board: (1) The inhumane treatment of patients, which, in itself, generated discomfort in the staff; (2) Blatant disregard or defiance of admonitions to modify such treatment of patients, which in effect "dared" and taunted staff to take corrective measures; and (3) his boasting of ways in which he retaliated against staff members who displeased him. . . . There are additional reports that his retaliations against nurses resulted in discomfort to patients, e.g., the removal of IV and NG tubes . . .

> (The employee) has been counseled by supervisory personnel over at least a three year period; however, this counseling was never documented and patient abuse continued wihtout nursing supervisory intervention.

The employee was removed from the VA and the removal was sustained by Office of Personnel Management. No VA Form 10–2633 was made on any of the alleged incidents. In the third case, an employee was accused of verbally and physically abusing a Spinal Cord Injury patient on August 31 and September 1, 1979. An investigation was conducted, which found insufficient evidence to support the patient's charge that he was verbally or physically abused on August 31, 1979. The investigation found that on September 1, 1979 the employee had placed her hand on the patient's face in what was considered an unfriendly manner and an admitted effort to silence the patient. The board of investigation recommended, on October 29, 1979, that appropriate counseling be given to the employee. A VA Form 10–2633 was not made, and the investigation was initiated after the Director received a letter from the patient. Failure to complete the Report of Special Incident involving a beneficiary prevented hospital management from reviewing all suspected incidents of patient abuse or other inappropriate action.

Drug variances were found during our unannounced inventory of Schedule II drugs and Schedule III narcotics. Our inventory of forty items in Pharmacy Service found the following variances:

November 14, 1979

Item Name	Balanced Recorded On Hand	Audit Count	Difference Overage (Shortage)
Dilaudid Tablets 2 mg.	1,100 tablets	1,080 tablets	(20) tablets
Merperidine Injectable 50 mg. Tubex	1,272 Tubex	1,283 Tubex	10 Tubex
Paragoric Camporated	232 oz.	228 oz.	(4 oz.)
Tylenol #3	3,678 tablets	8,910 tablets	5,232 tablets[1]
Whiskey	6,045 ml	6,795 ml	750 ml

1. We later found that 6,000 tablets (valued over $220) had not been recorded on Schedule II Drugs, Schedule III Narcotics and Alcoholics Register, VA Form 10–2320. As a result, an actual shortage of 768 Tylenol tablets existed but was not known by the Pharmacy staff.

These variances were caused by unsatisfactory stock control procedures. Our review of the receiving documents of the four deliveries of Schedule II drugs and Schedule III narcotics, made from November 5 through 7, 1979, disclosed that the signature of a pharmacist was not present. In addition, a transfer of Schedule III through V drugs was delivered to the pharmacy while the audit was in progress; however, the Supply personnel who delivered these drugs returned to Supply Service without any verification or certification by Pharmacy Service personnel that the drugs were delivered. Problems with the transfer of drugs between the supply warehouse and the pharmacy were reported by the General Accounting Office in July 1978.

Ourdated drugs were stocked in the pharmacy and on the wards. Our inventory of forty controlled drugs in the pharmacy disclosed that the pharmacy has quantities of nine outdated Schedule II drugs and Schedule III narcotics on hand. Three of these have been outdated for more than three years. Our review of controlled drug records in the Medical Intensive Care Unit, Ward 2 West and Ward 3 West disclosed that Codeine 60 milligram tablets and Misentil injection had expired by more than two months. The cause for the presence of outdated drugs was due to inadequate inspections. Our review of Schedule II drugs, Schedule III Narcotics and Alcoholic Register, VA Form 10–2320 disclosed that all Schedule II drugs and Schedule III narcotics were not inventoried monthly. Ten different Schedule II drugs and Schedule III narcotics located in the Pharmacy and recorded on VA Form 10–2320 were not inspected each month. In addition, the biennial inventory of controlled substances, required by the Controlled Substances Act (Public Law 51–513), was not performed on controlled substances in Pharmacy Service in fiscal year 1979 because the requirement was not identified during the replacement of the Chief of Pharmacy Service. Inadequate inspection activity prevented the timely identification of and allowed the inappropriate use of outdated drugs. For example, failure to identify and recommend disposition of outdated drugs resulted in twenty capsules of Amobartital 200 mg being dispensed to a veteran on May 22, 1979 although they had expired in March 1977.

Drugs classified by the Food and Drug Administration (FDA) as ineffective, medically worthless, were purchased and used by the medical center. Ineffective drugs were stocked because they were requested by physicians. The VA required that VA funds not be used to order drugs classified as ineffective. VA funds could be expended to order possibly effective drugs when no effective alternative is available. This reference further states that " . . . every effort will be made to treat all VA patients with the most effective therapeutic agents."

Our review showed that five drugs designated as ineffective (Ananase, Biozyme ointment, Dibenzyline, Diutensen, and Vasodilan) and one drug designated as possibly effective (Combid) were purchased in fiscal year 1979. The Chief, Pharmacy Service, stated there was an effective alternative drug for Combid. Ananase, Combid, and Vasodilan were present on the Pharmacy shelf. Vasodilan and Dibenzyline were ruled ineffective on May 25, 1979; however, the Requirements Analysis Report, November 8, 1979, shows an average monthly usage of three bottles of 1,000 Vasodilan tablets since the drug was cited as ineffective. The unit cost per bottle of Vasodilan was over $46. At this level of usage, over $1,600 could have been saved annually by prohibiting further purchase of the ineffective drug (i.e., "snake oil"). We also found five other ineffective drugs on the shelf in Pharmacy Service that had been purchased prior to fiscal year 1979:

Adrenalin in oil; one box of 100 ampules
Arlidin; one bottle of 1,000 tablets

Maraz; one bottle of 500 tablets
Potaba; four and a half bottles of 1,000 tablets each
Salutensin; two-thirds of a 100-tablet bottle

Because of this finding, a VA-wide audit was conducted on the stockage and usage of ineffective drugs. This VA-wide audit never saw the light of day. The auditors found that substantial funds were inappropriately expended on ineffective drugs. During October, November, and December, 1979, ninety different ineffective drugs costing over $100,000 were purchased by 27 VA hospitals. In addition, 137 VA hospitals were stocking and using one or more of twenty-nine of the above ninety ineffective drugs. The on-hand inventory of these twenty-nine drugs, as of February 13, 1980, was 38,303 units, valued over $211,000, and six months usage, August 1979 through January 1980, amounted to 104,195 units, valued at $575,604. The conservative estimate was at least $1.1 million was expended annually for these twenty-nine ineffective drugs.

Control of the bulk-compounding program was inadequate. Bulk-compounding means "home made" drugs. Pharmacy Service was bulk-compounding eighty-nine different substances, although none of these substances had been presented to the Committee on Therapeutic Agents for formula approval. There was no procedure followed for quality control and determination had not been made of the effect of bulk-compounding on the pharmacy budget, even though 67 percent of the drugs compounded were available from commercial sources. In addition, review of the minutes of the Committee on Therapeutic Agents for the past year showed that the committee had not been briefed on any of the drugs compounded, including those compounded with formulas provided by the professional staff. The VA required that formulas should have been presented to the Committee on Therapeutic Agents for consideration and approval prior to beginning bulk-compounding of the preparation. Also, the Committee on Therapeutic Agents should have been informed of the quality controls that would be used and the effect of bulk-compounding on the pharmacy budget. In addition, the committee should have been briefed not only on new products as they were developed but should have been given complete data on the total bulk-compounding operation.

The Recreation Section of Voluntary Service operated a recreational boating and fishing program, providing docking, hauling, and storage facilities, at your expense, to patients and employees of the medical center. The storage facilities consisted of a quonset hut with storage lockers. The purpose of this program was to encourage and support the sport of boating and fishing as a suitable recreation media, to promote the science of seamanship and navigation, to further the center's safety programs as they concerned the use and operation of small craft, and to develop and continually improve the center's small boat facilities. The boat docks were located along the seawall on Jones Creek, which separates the VA Center from Hampton Institute and docks for commercial fishing vessels.

The recreational boating program was operated primarily for the benefit of a few employees, and the boat docks were hazardous due to rotting. The medical center did not own any recreational boats. There were twenty-nine berthing spaces. Patients and domiciliary members were given priority in assignment of berthing spaces for personally owned boats; however, only seven spaces were assigned to patients or members, and there was no formal therapeutic program to support the use of boating facilities. Two spaces were vacant and two were reserved for the applications from patients. The remaining eighteen berthing spaces were assigned to members of Disorganized Crime without charge. We surveyed four commercial marinas in the city of Hampton to determine commercial mooring and docking fees. The fees ranged from $264 to $756 per year for docking privileges. Also two boats moored at the facility exceeded the thirty-foot length limitation specified in the application for mooring privileges.

The action of salt water and weather on the wooden docks had rotted them to a very deteriorated condition. The District Safety Engineer was requested by the audit team for a professional evaluation during his December 3, 1979 visit to the medical center. The District Safety Engineer told us the structural soundness of the docks was in question, and he would recommend the evaluation of the continued need for the boat docks. An additional hazard that existed was the extreme slipperiness of the lower part of the docks, which flood at high tide. There were no handrails and frequent efforts to apply a non-skid surface had only limited success. The medical center had two projects totaling $152,000 to rehabilitate the seawall, boat docks ($72,000) and the boat house ($80,000).

There was a disclaimer of liability for personal injury or damage on the part of the VA, which was part of the application signed by a person requesting boating privileges. However, the VA Disctrict Counsel at Atlanta stated this was not an absolute release of liability for any negligence on the VA's part in failing to maintain the docks in a reasonably safe condition.

The auditors believed that the planned recreational boat docks and boat house projects should have been reduced in size because of: the absence of a formal therapeutic program for patients and members; the fact that the majority of use of the facilities was made by employees, without charge for personal benefit; and the amount of money needed to rebuild the boating facilities, without sufficient justification showing beneficial results to the patient care program. All the above combined to work against the continuation of this program at the planned level of expense. The poor physical condition of the docks, with its associated risk of personal injury or damage for which the VA could be held liable, should have been corrected. The Chief, Engineering Service, told us a locally funded project of less than $10,000 would have solved the current safety deficiencies. This would have saved $142,000 over the current planned expenditure.

Follow-up on accounts receivable was inadequate because the agent cashier only reviewed the accounts receivable when her other duties were accomplished. Measures need to be taken to assure effective and appropriate follow-up on collection of accounts recievable. Accounts receivable totaled over $178,000 on October 31, 1979. We reviewed forty-five receivables with a total value over $79,000 (44 percent). We found that thirty-five of these receivables required

213

additional action and that claims collection procedures had not been prompt and aggressive. The following are results of our review:

Analysis of Accounts Receivable	Number of Receivables	Value
Prompt and aggressive collection action was taken.	11	$12,285
Not prompt and aggressive.	14	12,083
Not submitted to Medicare for possible reimbursement.	18	52,636
Should have been referred to GAO.	1	1,611
Not deleted from accounting records after referral to GAO.	1	1,323
	45	$79,938

The lack of a prompt and aggressive claim collection system had been previously noted. On May 19, 1978, the management analyst conducted a review of accounts receivable. The review disclosed that propeer follow-up on accounts receivable needed to increase. The management analyst reported the same condition on June 25, 1979.

Specialized medical services provided modern care techniques requiring a combination of uniquely trained professionals, special facility capabilities, and sophisticated equipment for implementation. In the VA, national priorities had been established for provision of start up and continuing support, resulting in the centralized control of these programs. VA Central Office policy was to assure acceptable productivity levels of these valuable and expensive resources, since these programs could have provided benefits critical to the quality of patient care only through a high investment of resources.

VAMC Hampton operated twelve designated specialized medical programs funded by VACO and required to need applicable productivity standards. The specialized medical programs were an Alcohol Treatment Unit; Surgical, Medical, and Coronary Intensive Care Units; Nuclear Medicine Service; Orthotics Laboratory; Satellite Dialysis; Pulmonary Functions Laboratory; Respiratory Care Center; Speech Pathology; and inpatient and Home-based Spinal Cord Injury programs. In addition, two programs existed at Hampton that would be categorized as specialized medical programs, except for their dedication to medical research: Electron Microscopy (EM) and Computerized Axial Tomography (CAT) scanning. Specialized medical services available outside the medical center included catheterization, supervoltage (cobalt) therapy, CAT scanning, and additional hemodialysis to meet demand that the medical center's available unit could not furnish.

Supervoltage (cobalt) therapy services are obtained via a contractual arrangement with a community hospital in Newport News, Virginia. The cost per visit has been $23.50 per visit since January 1979, with a patient generally making three to five visits per week. Total expenditures for cobalt therapy were $23,275 in fiscal year 1979; expenditures of $26,400 are planned for fiscal year 1980. No control mechanism had been established for assuring that the medical center was properly billed for contracted cobalt therapy services provided by Riverside Hospital in Newport News. This situation had existed since the function of handling arrangements for transport of patients with their medical records was transferred from Radiology Service to Medical Administration Service (MAS). This was accomplished at the beginning of fiscal year 1980, although the fund control point for cobalt therapy remained in Radiology Service.

Previously, when Radiology Service made arrangements, they maintained records on which patients went to Riverside and the number of visits made. When Radiology Service received bills for therapy provided during the months of October and November 1979, they found that no records existed in MAS of actual services received. The secretary to the Chief, Radiology Service, attempted to reconstruct the number of visits made in October by walking to the various wards for this information. This method was cited as unnacceptable by the Chief, Radiology Service, when the bill was received for services (117 visits totalling $2,749.50) provided in November 1979.

Joint use of the Electron Microscope (EM) had not been planned. The Hampton hospital's Research Service had EM equipment; however, diagnostic electron microscopy was provided to VAMC Hampton with Research Service, because there was no staff to operate the equipment. The Chief, Laboratory Service, at Hampton told us there was very low demand for EM studies (six since his arrival in March 1978), and that he considered the timeliness of service from VAMC Richdmond to be adequate. The electron microscope is a device that produces highly magnified images, sometimes up to 500,000 times the size of a specimen. This equipment is used to see objects too small to be distinguished by a conventional light microscope. The electron microscopy resources were installed in the Research Building in February 1978. The EM resources were included in a package of 247 pieces of equipment valued over $533,000 declared excess by the National Aeronautics and Space Administration (NASA). The entire installation, including staff, were transferred to the VA after interagency negotiations in 1973.

Although there had been very low productivity on the EM equipment since its acquisition, this had been due in large measure to installation and calibration delays, modification of research space housing the equipment, the disability of the unit supervisor, and delays in obtaining approval and funding for personnel to operate the equipment. Recent additional funding included salaries for two technical personnel to operate the equipment, and action had been taken to recruit the two technical personnel. Laboratory Service and Research Service should develop plans for the joint use of the EM, to maximize the usc of the resource available at the medical center. The low demand for diagnostic EM work at VAMC Hampton, and the future availability of technical personnel on station to operate the EM equipment made joint usage feasible.

Underutilized EM's was not a problem just at the Hampton and Oklahoma City hospitals. A year prior to the arrival of our audit team at Hampton, GAO reported that some of the EM's in VA hospitals were under-used. For the period July 1974 to December 1976, fifteen of forty-two units did not examine the required 250 specimens annually. The 250 specimens was a criteria established by the VA. After the Hampton audit, the VA's own auditors performed, in 1980, a VA-wide audit of EM's. The report, issued in June, 1981, stated that of the nineteen VA medical centers reviewed, five had excess capability and another was in the process of applying for an EM that was not needed. Total acquisition cost for the five EM's was over $211,000. Because there was no way Disorganized Crime was going to give up these underutilized expensive microscopes, the 250 specimens annually required was rescinded by VA Circular 10–81–199 in September, 1981. Took care of that little problem, didn't we? You betcha.

The CAT scanner in Research Service was unused. A research project was developed in 1976 to develop a radical new design for Computerized Aerial Tomography (CAT) scanners, to minimize radiation exposure to the patient to less than one second (as compared to the twenty seconds or more of exposure, which was the state of the art at that time). Negotiations were undertaken between the VA, NASA and Pfizer Medical Systems for a research protocol as follows:

a. Pfizer Medical Systems would provide, at no cost to the VA, a current-model CAT scanner, which would be redesigned and rebuilt in accordance with the concept governing the proposal.
b. NASA would make available, at no cost to the VA, the full resources of the fabrication facility (including designing and engineering) at the NASA Research Laboratories at Langley Air Force Base.
c. VA would provide overall guidance of the project, space for the actual work, and patients to be examined.

The research protocol, entitled "Methods for Reduction of Radiation Dose and Scan Speed in CAT Scanner," was submitted to VA Central Office, Medical Research Service, on July 7, 1977. Approval of the project was held up at Central Office, because of a limitation on CAT scanner purchases imposed on the VA. Although detailed responses to specific inquiries from the Associate Deputy Chief Medical Director for Operations were provided by letter in September 1977, and although Research Advisory Group funding and common resources funding were provided to support start up of the project in March 1978, the scanner was not actually certified as installed until May 3, 1979. The newly installed scanner, on loan from Pfizer, broke down on May 24, 1979. The scanner had not been repaired because of disputes between Pfizer and the VA as to who should bear the cost of repair. The issue had not been settled, and there appeared little hope for an early resolution.

In the three-year delay since the concept was first proposed, advances in CAT scan technology had reduced radiation exposure to the patient to three seconds, reducing the impact of the proposal's objectives. In light of the advances that had been made to date by other medical research entities, the lead time that would still be needed to develop and test a new CAT scan design (even if the present difficulties were overcome), and the fact that the present installation remained unusable for any research or patient care applications, the reasonableness of continuing this line of inquiry was questionable.

I was assigned the Centrally Directed Nationwide Audit of the VA's Resident Engineer Audit. As you may have supposed from reading about the Fire Alarm problems at the Kerrville Hospital due to poor construction, we found that construction practices within the VA were full of problems. Though lots of your money was spent on construction and on this audit effort, the overall report was never published. You guessed it, poor visuals for the VA. At one of our audit sites, the problems were so bad that we were able to issue a separate report that was published on August 27, 1981 and also a Flash Report (reserved for only life-threatening situations). The Flash Report stated that during our audit of the 400-bed Veteran's Hospital in Columbia, South carolina, we discovered significant construction deficiencies that affected patient care. The Office of Construction needed to provide immediate assistance to correct these present problems. Also, the Office of Construction needed to review other projects in progress at locations where construction was being performed by the prime contractor to preclude similar unacceptable occurrences. The construction deficiencies, if not corrected, could have led to loss of life. The audit at the Veteran's Hospital, Columbia, South Carolina, began February 23, 1981.

The replacement hospital had been accepted in four phases from February 13 through July 2, 1979. Patients were admitted to the hopsital on July 26, 1979. The original completion date had been November 20, 1978. The contract with the prime contractor was valued over $19 million.

We had identified three long-standing construction deficiencies that may have adversely affected patient care according to the Chief of Staff. These three construction deficiencies were the medical gas alarm system, ductwork system, and portions of the electrical system. A letter from the Office of Construction, dated October 30, 1980, brought to the attention of the contractor these three deficiencies. The contractor, on February 6, 1981, wrote to the Contracting Officer, that the work on these three deficiencies had been completed. We found that the contractor's letter, of February 6, 1981, was incorrect.

	Letter from Office of Construction October 30, 1980		Status as of March 12, 1981
	Subject	Paragraph	
Item 17563—Complete air and water test and balance.		1.e.	Not completed
Item 306—Emergency medical equipment alarms do not operate.		2.(d).	Not completed
Sporadic nuisance trippng of breaker #9.		6.(c).	Not completed

217

The emergency medical gas alarm system had never functioned properly. The testing of this system was Item 17,463 on the List of Items of Correction or Omission (Punch List) prepared in May 1979. Item 17,463 had not been completed, even though it was initialed "AUBY" on October 15, 1979, with the remark, "This was not to be done by Honeywell." The Assistant Chief, Engineering Service, told us the cause of the inoperative alarm system was the incorrect wiring of the alarm system equipment to a Honeywell computer system.

This alarm system was manufactured by the Ohio Medical Company and was installed by the Republic Mechanical Corporation. The system monitored high/low line pressure for the patient's oxygen, nitrous oxide, air and vacuum systems. The alarm system was also connected to the bulk storage for oxygen, nitrous oxide and also monitored vacuum and air pressure in three centrally located areas. The Honeywell computer system, to which the alarm system was connected, was the major portion of the hospital's Engineering Control Center (ECC), which was staffed twenty-four hours a day, seven days a week. When alerted by the computer of various malfunctions throughout the hopsital, the ECC staff was to determine the location, type of problem, and institute corrective action.

The Chief of Staff told us the lack of the emergency medical gas alarm system could put the hospital into an adverse patient-care situation. The most serious problems would have occurred in the Medical Intensive Care Unit (MICU). At the time of our audit, the MICU had eight patients on ventilators and any time delays between ten and thirty minutes in their oxygen supply could cause death. These patients were suffering pulmonary disorders and were on oxygen in order to keep them alive. An operational emergency medical gas alarm system was also a requirement of the Joint Commission of Accreditation of Hospitals and the National Fire Codes of the National Fire Protection Association. The alarm system had been reported to the Office of Construction by the Resident Engineer or the Hospital Director in January, June, and October, 1980.

The ductwork system was not providing sufficient air flow because of sheet metal failures, inadequate sealing of joints with mastic, and large holes left in the ductwork by the contractor. As a result, insufficient air exchange and air pressure was being provided to the hospital.

The contractor was required to provide an air/water balance test (Punch List Item 17,563). The hospital's Director wrote to the Office of Construction that the test had not been received on October 8, 1980. The Assistant Chief, Engineering Service, told us the VA would not receive the test results from the prime contractor because the ductwork system had too many leaks. Contract Section 699, which required the test, stated that a Resident Engineer would be present when the test was conducted. A vibration test was required by Contract Section 699–6. The test was performed on October 5, 1979; however, 78 of the 121 units were found to be unacceptable. Without these two tests, the adequacy of the ductwork system's ability to move air in sufficient quantities had never been established.

On July 1, 1980, the Resident Engineer wrote to the Office of Construction:

This air conditioning unit and several others of the same design are

218

in real trouble. They are literally coming apart. I think the reason is fatigue failure. The fatigue is introduced by excessive flexing of the unit start-up and shut-down. This is clearly a latent defect and should be the responsibility of the contractor.

The Resident Engineer went on to recommend that a qualified Heating, Ventilation, Air Conditioning (HVAC) Engineer be sent from the Office of Construction to observe and recommend corrective action. The Resident Engineer termed this problem as "particularly alarming." However, the HVAC engineer was not sent. This problem was noted again to the Office of Construction by the hospital's Director on October 8, 1980. In January 1981, the contractor sent one worker to attempt to fix the ductwork system.

The Chief of Staff told us that the lack of sufficient air pressure (both positive and negative) and insufficient air exchange was not conducive to adequate patient care. The minutes of the September 19, 1979 meeting of the Infection Control Committee noted the negative pressure rooms were required for limiting the potentially suspended microbes to the patient room. A positive pressure area would mean protection isolation and it would be used for people with depressed host defenses, such as low white blood cell counts and/or extensive burns.

On March 4, 1981, we examined twenty-six rooms to determine if they had the required air pressure. The Foreman, Air Conditioning Section, conducted measurements using an anemometer, which measured the flow of air into/from a room. We found that only thirteen of the twenty-six rooms had the appropriate air pressure. For example, we found one tubercular patient in Room 4C-152 with neutral air pressure when it should have been negative. The criteria for *HVAC Design for VA Facilities* required, in paragraph 3.6, the following air pressures:

a. Maintain positive pressure relative to adjacent areas in Surgery Area, Intensive Care Units, and Reverse Isolation Rooms.
b. Maintain a negative relative pressure in Animal Research Area, Autopsy Suite, Enema Room, Isolation Rooms, Soiled Utility, Soiled Dishwashing, Soiled Sorting Area in Laundries, Soiled and Decontaminating Areas in SPD, and toilets.

HVAC Design for VA Facilities required, in paragraph 3.2, the following minimum total room air exchange rates (changes/hour):

Animal Research Area	15
Autopsy Room	15
Bath or Toilet Rooms (Exhaust)	10
Enema Room	12
Procedure Rooms	12
SPD	10
Surgery Area	
Operating Rooms	15
Recovery Rooms	15

219

The station did not have the equipment to measure the air-exchange rates in the hospital. However, we believed the lack of air exchange was one of the causes for an unsatisfactory smell in some of the patient restrooms.

Portions of the electrical system did not operate properly. Since July 2, 1979, there had been several instances of sporadic nuisance tripping of circuit breakers. These problems had been brought to the contractor's attention several times, the latest being October 30, 1980. The emergency generator had been used six times, for nontesting purposes, since October 30, 1980. The Assistant Chief, Engineering Service, told us this is a very high rate of use.

Electrical Interruptions

Date	Cause
11/09/80	Nuisance tripping
12/19/80	Nuisance tripping
12/25/80	Nuisance tripping
01/22/81	Nuisance tripping
02/19/81	Electrical shock in elevator tripped transfer switch
03/04/81	Nuisance tripping

These interruptions of electrical power were a risk to adequate patient care. For example, the electrical power was out for over two hours in the MICU on December 25, 1980. The memorandum dated December 25, 1980, from the supervisory nurse of the MICU, describes the situation.

When I came on duty, 12/25/80, at 7:30 A.M., the main and auxiliary power to our patients' panels was off. Three MA II ventilators were plugged into the only available power via extension cords. IVACs were also using extension cords and running available power (Room 4A-159) on discontinued and dial-a-flows used. Patients had to be Ambubagged until a power source was found. O_2 was discontinued at one point because smoke was smelled by staff.

We stayed without power at least two hours (6:00 A.M. to 8:00 A.M.). The monitors were inoperative, of course, and we had at least one patient on a Lidocaine drip (for PVCs). CCU had a code at 8:30 A.M., and the monitors were working.

The supervisory nurse told us that the potential effect of a lack of power was gruesome. With only three personnel on duty in the MICU at night and an MICU capability of eight patients, the nurse told us immediate life-or-death decisions would have to be made by the staff. The Chief of Staff agreed that there is a serious life-threatening situation in the MICU during a power shortage.

The contractor had been requested several times to correct these electrical problems. A possible cause for the nuisance tripping may have been due to the deletion of the requirement for switched neutral. We found a letter in the project files dated March 17, 1978, from the Director, Electrical Engineering Service, Office of Construction, to the Project Director recommending the following:

> Issue a change order deleting the specification requirement for switched neutral and request a credit from the contractor.

This letter was forwarded to the Senior Resident Engineer at Columbia, South Carolina, on March 27, 1978. The Architect/Engineer advised the Senior Resident Engineer on April 26, 1978, that elimination of the neutral pole may result in defeating the ground fault protection and may lead to nuisance tripping of the feeder breakers. The Chief and Assistant Chief, Engineering Service, could not tell us what specific equipment is referred to in the letters. The Architect/Engineer could not recall what action took place.

The Resident Engineer Program was audited between November 1980 and August 1981. Except for the previously discussed Flash Report and an overall report on the new Columbia, South Carolina hospital, no interim audit reports were issued at the six audit sites pending the release of the overall audit report. The overall report was never published. The Resident Engineer's (RE) role and responsibilities in administering construction contracts included the following: interrelating with the construction contractor, subcontractors, the Architect/Engineer (A/E), the station engineering staff and VA Central Office officials; documenting actions taken that impact upon the progress of the project; conducting periodic meetings with the contractor; testing materials and equipment to ensure they meet specifications; providing recommendations for approving changes and process orders and progress payments; approving change orders within the Contracting Officer's Authorization (COA's); certifying that work in place was satisfactory and recommending payment of invoices to the contractor; and serving as the VA safety officer at the construction site.

RE's are administratively evaluated, reassigned, hired, and dismissed by the Director, Resident Engineer Staff. The RE's worked for a Project Supervisor. The Project Supervisors worked directly for a Project Director, who was also the Contracting Officer.

The Contracting Officer was responsible for ensuring compliance with the terms of the contract. The RE represented the Contracting Officer and was responsible for protecting the government's interest in the execution of the construction contract work.

As of March 31, 1981, there were 214 employees assigned to the resident engineer staff, of which 139 were resident engineers, 70 were clerical staff assigned to the RE's at construction sites, and 5 were VA Central Office staff. The total estimated cost for fiscal year 1981 for the RE program was over $4.9 million in salary and overtime, and over $130,000 in travel costs. The resident engineers were assigned to 115 projects, valued over $812 million, as of March 31, 1981. The value of construction contracts issued or in progress for fiscal years 1980 and 1981 (estimated) are listed below.

Construction Contracts

Fiscal Year

	1980	1981 (est.)
Construction In Progress:		
Number	119	136
Value	$556.8 million	$788.6 million
Contracts Awarded:		
Number	39	59
Value	$355.5 million	$278.2 million

Our audit of the Resident Engineer Program disclosed several areas in which management attention was needed in order to improve the economy and effectiveness of operations. These areas included: assignment and supervision of resident engineers; compliance with contract requirements; coordination between the Veterans Administration and the Department of Labor concerning labor and job safety requirements; developing and implementing better policies and guidelines for accepting construction projects and assisting VA management in activating the projects; monitoring the contractor's work following final inspection to correct omissions and deviations; and computing and assessing liquidated damages.

The Construction Methods Determination Board (CMDB) determined whether a project would be assigned to an RE or to the hospital's staff for projects valued below $2 million. Projects valued above $2 million were assigned to Resident Engineers. The Resident Engineer Board determined which RE would be assigned to projects valued over $2 million. The Resident Engineer Board was composed of the Project Directors and the Director of the Resident Engineer Staff. Prior to fiscal year 1981, a major construction project was valued over $1 million. Starting in fiscal year 1981, the major construction category was revised to include projects over $2 million. There were a significant number of RE's assigned to minor construction projects as of May 1981.

The assignment of Resident Engineers could have been more economical. Construction projects were being monitored and controlled by either RE's or hospital staff. We found that the CMDB was assigning projects to the RE's when the more economical decision would have been assignment to the hospital staff. As a result, high-dollar-value projects were being provided the same RE coverage as low-dollar-value projects.

We reviewed the minutes of the CMDB meetings for the eighty-eight projects discussed by the Board during the period October 1, 1979, to May 14, 1981. Although most of the projects were assigned to the hospital staffs, RE's were assigned to several low-cost projects that should have been assigned to hospital staffs. Below is a table showing assignment of projects during this time period.

Assignments of Responsibility for Construction Projects

	Hospital Staff	RE Staff
Assignments	69	19
Contract value over $1.5 million	11 (16%)	2 (10%)
Contract value under $1.5 million	58 (84%)	17 (90%)

Range of Project Values

Range for hospital staff	$144,000—$2.5 million
Range value under $1.5 million	$200,000—$1.8 million

In addition, we reviewed all seventy-one stations with RE's assigned as of March 31, 1981. We found that RE's were assigned to a significant number of low-valued projects.

Assignments of RE's on March 31, 1981

	Number of Stations	Number of RE's
Projects valued less than $2 million	24	28
Projects valued less than $1 million	10	10

We believed the assignment of 28 of the 139 RE's (20 percent) to minor construction projects was an uneconomical and inefficient use of the RE staff. The lack of contractor compliance with the contract specifications was partially the result of spreading the limited number of RE's over too many projects. The Director, Resident Engineer Staff, told us that he had to cannibalize ongoing projects in order to staff new projects. For example, RE's were assigned on a temporary duty status at the $8.5 million project at VAMC Charleston until forty-seven days after the VA's Notice to Proceed, at which time RE's were permanently assigned. We also found that after final inspection, RE's were not always left at construction sites long enough to ensure that the contractor has satisfactorily completed all punch list items. The Director, Resident Engineer Staff, told us an RE remains on a project about one month after acceptance. The four Project Directors told us it was a good idea to have the RE's throughout

223

the life cycle of the project in order to ensure continuity from award to completion. The Directors at VAMC Augusta, Georgia, and William Jennings Bryan Dorn Veteran's Hospital, Columbia, South Carolina, told us it would be beneficial to keep an RE onsite until the project is completely finished. Cannibalization has grown to such a large degree that several stations shared the same RE. As a result, the RE staff was not at the project site full time. As of March 31, 1981, seven stations were sharing other stations' assigned RE's.

The uneconomical assignment of RE's and the effects of this practice had been known for several years as evidenced by the following extracts from the minutes of the Resident Engineer Board:

October 30, 1978—Assignments of R/E's to handle station level projects under $1.0M was discussed and it was felt unless a Central Office project was already ongoing and R/E's staffed at the station, we would not commit ourselves to anything under $1.0M.

December 20, 1978—Resident Engineer assignments through May 1979 were discussed. Small projects of less than $1M will be put before the CMD Board for reconsideration of supervision by the engineering officer at the station rather than assigning a Resident Engineer to supervise the project.

Early assignments of Senior Resident Engineers to major replacement hospital sites in order to review the drawings and design of the project and whether or not it is beneficial to the Government was reviewed. The general consensus was that it is beneficial, but the Senior Resident Engineer should not be moved from his present project until after final inspection and it would be better for him to travel from his old project to his new project rather than move him prematurely.

November 14, 1979—Discussions were held on lack of R/E's and staffing of future projects. It was agreed that we should first try to get DM&S to furnish us clerical help and second to see if we have the A/E or testing lab provide us with clerical help the same way we have them provide us engineers. The Director, Resident Engineer Staff, was requested to draft a letter for AA/C signature to CMD asking that Engineering Service supervise construction on all projects $1.5 million and under.

June 23, 1980—The Director, Resident Engineer Staff, advised that we had no more Senior Resident Engineers available and we would have to start transferring R/E's off of active construction projects to supervise new projects.

There was no narrative reason documented why RE assignments were made to minor projects in the CMDB minutes. The Assistant Administrator for Construction told us that, even with the increased dollar value designated for minor

224

construction, minor construction projects had continued to be assigned to RE's instead of station engineering officers because the Department of Medicine and Surgery (DM&S) wanted RE's. We discussed this issue with the Chief, Engineering Service, Department of Medicine and Surgery, VACO, and were told that station engineering officers would have been able to act as the RE for these minor construction projects.

The Resident Engineer was responsible for ensuring contractor compliance with contract requirements, and for ensuring that quality construction was provided within those requirements. In addition, the RE was to give assistance, when possible and feasible, in promoting the work progress without assuming the responsibilities of the contractor.

We reviewed six contract requirements at six construction projects to determine the extent to which the RE's were ensuring contractor compliance. The six contract requirements included: submission of submittals; compliance with wage rates; enforcement of an effective safety program; compliance with equal employment opportunity (EEO); ensuring the appropriateness of materials on site (MOS); and, updating the critical path method (CPM) network.

The RE's were not always ensuring the contractors complied with the contract requirements. We found deficiencies in at least two of the six contract requirements that we reviewed at each site as shown in the following table:

Contract Requirements Enforced[1]

Location	Submittals	Wages Rates	Safety	EEO	MOS	CPM Network Update
Memphis	Yes	No	Yes	Yes	Yes	No
Gainesville	No	No	No	No	Yes	Yes
Bay Pines	Yes	No	No	No	Yes	Yes
Reno	Yes	Yes	No	No	No	Yes
Columbia	No	No	NA	NA	NA	NA
Augusta	No	No	NA	NA	NA	NA

1. Yes means adequately enforced.
No means contractor did not comply with contract requirements.
NA means we did not determine.

There were three causes why the RE's did not ensure that the contractors were in compliance with the contract specifications.

1. The four Project Directors gave different interpretations and importance as to the extent the RE's should monitor the contract requirements.

225

2. The RE's did not know the specific requirements of the Handbook of Resident Engineers.

3. The RE's interpreted the requirements of the contract in order to "keep the job going."

The construction contracts and the *Handbook for Resident Engineers* required the contractor to submit samples, shop drawings, certificates, manufacturers' literature, and test results to the A/E for review. After the A/E's review of the required submittals, they were forwarded to the RE. The submittals provided to the A/E and RE a method in which they could ensure that a proposed construction activity met the specifications of the contract. After the activity was approved, based on the review, construction materials were ordered and delivered.

We found that the required submittals were not always obtained. At the Reno and Gainesville projects, where construction was ongoing at the time of our audit, we found that the RE's annotated the CPM chart to show all the required submittals had been received. However, we reviewed the project files and found that all required submittals had not been received. At the Augusta and Columbia projects, which were completed prior to the audit, we also found that all of the required submittals had not been received. At these completed projects, we found construction problems that were directly related to the required submittals that were not received.

During our audit, we discussed our observations with the Project Directors of the Southern and Western Areas, Office of Construction. They emphasized the importance of submittals as a quality control.

Nursing Home Care Unit, VAMC Gainesville

At the VAMC Gainesville NHCU project, there were twenty-one CPM submittal activities. These represented contract specification items that were important to the timely completion of the project. All twenty-one activities on the CPM chart were shown to be complete. We reviewed six of these activities to determine if all the required submittals had been received. In three of the activities, some of the required submittal items had not been received and approved by the RE. In one activity (resilient tile), the samples had been received but the manufacturer's certificates indicating approved adhesive, primer, crack filler, underlayment, and wax specification had not been received. In another activity (wall covering), the manufacturer's literature regarding adhesive, installation instructions, and cleaning and maintenance instructions for this activity had not been received. The RE told us the reason the CPM chart was updated to reflect the activities as completed was that the samples were received and the samples constituted the most important and time consuming portion of the submittal. The RE also told us that when the major portions of submittals were received, he sometimes updated the CPM chart to reflect the activity as completed. The RE had not sent a follow-up letter on the three activities with incomplete submittals but told us he planned to do this at a later date as a "clean up activity."

226

Boiler Plant, VAMC Reno

At the VAMC Reno Clinical Addition/Boiler Plant project, there were 131 CPM submittal activities. The CPM chart was documented to show the submittals had been received, approved, ordered, and delivered for all 131 submittal activities. The CPM chart was documented to show that the submittals had been received, approved, ordered, and delivered for all 131 activities. We reviewed 13 activities and found incomplete submittals in three activities. The incomplete submittals included incorrect sample sizes, missing samples, missing manufacturer's literature, and missing shop drawings. The RE told us that he had sometimes approved an activity to be ordered without receiving all of the required submittals because he was able to make a judgment that the contract specifications were met, based on past experience with the supplying company. The RE also told us that if the VA determines at a later date the activity does not measure up to the contract specifications, the contractor is still liable.

Replacement Hospital, William Jennings Bryan Dorn Veterans' Hospital Columbia, South Carolina

We reviewed seventeen submittal activities to determine whether the required submittal items were received. We found incomplete or missing submittals in thirteen activities as shown below:

Contract Section	Submittal Activity	Status
4	Concrete	Incomplete
6	Masonry	Missing
12A	Fireproofing	Incomplete
33	Drywalls	Incomplete
45A	Tile	Incomplete
49A	Carpet	Incomplete
300	Plumbing	Incomplete
311	Oxygen	Incomplete
312	Nitrous Oxide	Incomplete
313	Vacuum System	Incomplete
681	Air Ducts, Devices	Incomplete
699	Testing and Balancing	Incomplete
808	Fire Alarm System	Incomplete

When specifications involving tests, qualifications, and inspections were not met, the effects were difficult to quantify. For example, because the submittals describing the results for testing and balancing had never been delivered, the Office of Construction accepted the hospital from the contractor without establishing the adequacy of the ventilation system. Also, the medical gas system alarm had never been tested to document a successful operation. As long as this

227

system's successful operation could not have been demonstrated, the potential for an adverse patient-care situation existed. The Office of Construction accepted two portions of the building without a successful test of the fire-alarm system having been performed.

Replacement Hospital, VAMC Augusta

We reviewed the files for nine activities where submittals were required by the contract and found that seven of the submittals had not been received.

Missing Submittals

Contract Section	Submittal Activity	Status
804	Emergency Generator	Incomplete
699	Testing and Balancing	Incomplete
688	Engineering Control Center	Incomplete
808	Fire Alarm System	Incomplete
69	Landscaping	Incomplete
317	Compressed Air	Incomplete
311	Oxygen System	Incomplete

As in Columbia, South Carolina, we found systems that were not operational when the facility was accepted from the contractor and all the submittals had not been received by the VA. For example, all the submittals for the fire alarm system had not been received and the system was not tested and proven operational. The punch list for the fire alarm system contained 107 items valued over $13,000 (remember Kerrville?). Also, the lack of a complete testing and balancing submittal also contributed to the inoperative heating, ventilation, and air conditioning (HVAC) system at the time the VA accepted the hospital from the contractor in December 1979. The hook-up of the controls in the control panel and the demonstration of the operation of the air-cooled chilled water pump and controls were not performed until February and March 1980. The punch list for the HVAC system contained 473 items valued over $52,000.

Wage Rates

The Department of Labor found labor violations at three active projects and at both completed projects that we audited. The violations included an incorrect ratio of journeymen to apprentices and misclassification of workers. The *Handbook for Resident Engineers* provided that the RE was responsible for ensuring labor standards were enforced by conducting investigations, reviews, and interviews. Paragraph 41.b of the *Handbook* stated:

> Generally, the Resident Engineer, by acquainting himself with local labor customs, by review of the contractor's apprenticeship agreements,

228

by observations on the job, by oral inquiries of workers, and by payrolls and timesheets, should be able to determine whether or not there is compliance.

We discussed this subject with the Project Directors in the Office of Construction and found that some did not expect the RE's to perform the labor compliance responsibility set forth in the *Handbook*. One Project Director told us the *Handbook* should be changed because the responsibility for enforcement of labor requirements is a Department of Labor responsibility. We found that labor violations were present at five of the audit sites. The following schedule lists the value of the reported labor violations found by the Department of Labor but not noted by the RE.

Labor Violations

Location	Amount of DOL Fine
Memphis	$ 2,500
Gainesville	500
Bay Pines	DOL audit ongoing
Columbia	38,000
Augusta	30,000

Safety

We found unaggressive safety programs at the projects in Gainesville and Reno. At the project at VA Medical Center, Bay Pines, Florida, we found an aggressive safety program; but the RE's authority to contact the Occupational Safety and Health Administration in order to obtain a safe worksite was not adequately defined.

The Senior Resident Engineer (SRE) at all VA construction projects was designated as the Safety and Fire Protection Officer. The SRE was responsible for the safety and occupational health of VA employees at the project, the safety of all visitors whose visits were arranged through his office, and the protection of all property under his jurisdiction. This responsibility included, but was not limited to, establishing and conducting an active safety, occupational health, and fire protection program based on the policies, procedures, and standards outlined in the *Handbook for Resident Engineers,* Office of Construction operating instructions, and requirements of the local situation. It required aggressive leadership and continuing efforts to assure program effectiveness. When the contractor was an independent contractor, the VA had no contractual responsibility for safety of the contractor's employees. The SRE was only involved in contractor safety in four situations where contractor activities:

(a) endangered the safety of VA employees or volunteer workers;
(b) endangered VA visitors;

229

(c) endangered VA property or property under VA jurisdiction; and,
(d) were likely to result in conditions for which the VA may be found negligent.

The Project Directors gave us different interpretations of what the SRE's responsibility was as the Safety and Fire Protection Officer. Their interpretations ranged from "the SRE was not responsible for the construction site because he was not a trained OSHA inspector" to "the definition of responsibility was in a period of confusion." Only two of the Project Directors wanted the SRE's to initiate contacts with the Occupational Safety and Health Administration (OSHA) to report safety violations.

Boiler Plant, VAMC Reno, Nevada

The *Handbook for Resident Engineers* required a Safety, Occupational Health, and Fire Protection Program to be established as follows: A Safety, Occupational Health, and Fire Protection Inspection was required each month with a written narrative report sent to the Project Director. Also, each member of the resident engineer's staff should have been consulted each month concerning safety and occupational health matters. Occupational Safety and Health Administration (OSHA) Form 100F (Log of Federal Occupational Injuries and Illnesses, or Fire) was to have been maintained by the SRE to record injuries and sent to the Office of the Director, Resident Engineer Staff, Office of Construction, each quarter. A negative report was required. We reviewed the safety and accident report file and found that it did not contain any correspondence or documentation of safety, occupational health, and fire protection inspections. In addition, we did not find the Log of Federal Occupational Injuries and Illnesses, or Fire was being maintained. The SRE told us he had neither conducted monthly inspections nor forwarded monthly reports to the Office of Construction because he had observed safety practices while on the job site and had brought noted problems to the attention of the contractor. The SRE told us there had been no employee accidents and he had not submitted a negative report.

Replacement Hospital, VAMC Bay Pines, Florida

Several OSHA violations were committed by the prime contractor and subcontractors. OSHA site surveys were performed six times between January 1980 and January 1981. The site surveys resulted in issuance of twelve citations for $4,970 in penalties.

Our review of the SRE's Weekly Safety Reports for the two-year period February 1979 through January 1981, showed that the prime contractor had committed over 280 violations of OSHA regulations. In addition, the SRE had repeatedly discussed the numerous safety hazards with the prime contractor during the weekly progress meetings. In August 18, 1980, letter from the SRE to the contractor states:

A review of this report clearly indicated that action is not being taken as required to correct the safety violations noted in the Weekly Safety Reports. A review of the accident reports show numerous injuries are occurring as a result of safety violations. The numerous nail puncture injuries and others are a direct result of safety violations. If all the items listed in the attached Safety Report are not corrected within one week, I intend to recommend that the Contracting Officer stop work in accordance with Paragraph G-11.D of the Contract Specifications until the unsafe conditions are corrected.

The safety violations were temporarily reduced; however, the violations returned. For example, $3,140 of the $4,970 of OSHA penalties were levied in December 1980 and January 1981. The unsafe construction environment resulted in 191 workers injured between October 1979 and January 14, 1981, to an extent that the injuries resulted in lost time. In addition, during our initial tour of the construction site, one of our auditors almost fell through the interstitial floor. This occurred because the floor had not been "roped off" so that it would not be walked on. Copies of the Weekly Safety Reports had been sent to the OSHA office in Tampa. An OSHA official in Tampa told us, however, that the site surveys were routine and not based on information submitted by the SRE. In addition to sending copies of the Weekly Safety Reports to OSHA, the SRE should also have made a formal complaint to OSHA when the safety environment degraded to an unsafe level as evidenced by his August 18, 1980 letter to the prime contractor.

Equal Employment Opportunity (EEO)

We found that the RE's at three of the active projects reviewed were not monitoring the contractor requirement that the contractors report on minority and female employment. The RE's told us they were unaware of the responsibility to monitor EEO activities. The *Handbook for Resident Engineers* required that the RE receive a copy of the contractor prepared Employment Utilization Report (SF-257) and provide the contractor with assistance. Three of the RE's did not know they were required to do this. Also, one of the Project Directors told us that he did not want the RE's to monitor the contractor's compliance with the EEO terms of the contract because there was insufficient time to watch everything.

With regards to the RE's responsibilities for ensuring the contractor comply with the EEO terms of the contract, the *Handbook for Resident Engineers* stated:

e. The Resident Engineer should keep in mind he is the VA construction "professional" at the site who sees the site situation from the VA viewpoint, and his assistance and opinions may serve as the key to EEO problems which otherwise might not be uncovered or resolved.

g. The Resident Engineer will ensure that all reports required of his office in the administration and enforcement of Equal Employment Opportunity are produced accurately and submitted promptly.

231

Executive Order 11246, establishing affirmative action goals, was incorporated into the construction contracts. Executive Order 11246 required that the Employment Utilization Report (SF 257) be submitted monthly by the contractor. An example of the SF 257 and filing instructions that the RE was to provide the contractor was contained in the *Handbook for Resident Engineers*. The importance of complying with the EEO terms of the contract was noted on SF 257, as follows:

The report is required by Executive Digest Order 11246, Section 203. Failure to report can result in sanctions which include suspension, termination, cancellation, or debarment of contract.

MATERIAL ON SITE (MOS)

VA construction contracts permit payment for materials that were delivered to the construction site even though the material was not required for construction within the next twenty days. This advance buying allowed the contractor to obtain lower prices and ensure that materials were on-site when needed. The total amount of payments for MOS at the time of our audits at the four active projects exceeded $7.4 million.

Payments for MOS

Project	Amount (millions)	Percentage Completed at Time of Audit
VAMC Memphis	$1.2	97
VAMC Gainesville	0.7	63
VAMC Bay Pines	4.0	80
VAMC Reno	1.5	
Total	$7.4	

Boiler Plant, VAMC Reno, Nevada

Controls over payment for materials on site were inadequate. The RE approved fifty-six requests for payments for materials and equipment purchased by the contractor. The cost of the MOS during the project was over $1.5 million. We reviewed twenty-five of the requests for payment and the supporting invoices but did not find any documentation indicating that the materials and equipment had been verified to ensure accuracy of quantities received and compliance with contract specifications. Some of these requests had long itemized listings for which accurate inventory accounting would be difficult without annotating the documents as the items were verified.

232

We also noted that, on three of the requests, the attached invoices did not show the quantities or unit costs. For example, on May 28, 1980, the contractor requested payment, in the amount of $100,753, for aluminum windows and curtain wall materials. The attached invoice showed only a total cost of $97,346 and the sales tax of $3,407, for "Series 2000 Aluminum windows & S-555 Curtain wall medium bronze finish." Quantities and unit costs were not included on the invoice. The RE told us he had not required the RE staff to document that the invoices were accurate on this project. The RE told us that on previous projects, he had written on the invoice and dated it after the materials and equipment had been verified to be the correct quantity and in compliance with the specifications of the contract. When a request for payment is reviewed, there should have been adequate documentation to provide increased assurance that payments for MOS are appropriate.

CPM NETWORK UPDATE

The contractors employed CPM consultants to update the copies of the CPM network for both the contractor and the RE. The scheduling of various tests was noted on the CPM as well as the value of work performed.

Nursing Home Care Unit, Memphis, Tennessee

The CPM had not been updated by the contractor. The contract required:

> After each monthly update the Contractor shall submit to the Contracting Officer three copies (or one (1) set of sepias), of a revised complete arrow diagram showing all completed and new activities, change orders and logic changes made on the subject update.

Without an updated CPM chart, the CPM network lost value as a management tool. This decreased value was due to the lack of current information as to the status of the project. Both the prime contractor and the A/E told us the CPM was not normally used to control construction projects in the Memphis area. They said bar charts were the common management tool. The RE told us that he did not have the CPM charts updated because the project was relatively small and he could manage the project without an updated CPM chart. A change order, lowering the cost of this contract to you, should have been issued if the VA did not receive an updated CPM network as required by the contract.

The resident engineers were evaluated, promoted, reassigned, hired, and dismissed by the Director, Resident Engineer Staff. They were assigned to the Project Director responsible for the project. The Project Director usually had the RE assignment under a Project Supervisor. The Project Supervisor was assigned to a project throughout a project's development and construction life cycle. Project Supervisors monitored and controlled projects through personal visits and reviewing documentation sent from the construction site by the RE. The

Director, Resident Engineer Staff, was responsible for the time-and-attendance records for RE's. During fiscal year 1981, the RE Program costs for overtime and holiday pay were projected to increase by 62 percent as shown below:

Overtime and Holiday Costs

Fiscal Year	Cost
1980	$ 64,230
1981 (est.)	104,028
Total	$168,258

Weekly Meetings

The *Handbook for Resident Engineers* stated that the Resident Engineer in charge of the project should conduct meetings, preferably weekly, to discuss and resolve job problems. Copies of the minutes of the meetings should have been sent to the Office of Construction. We reviewed the project files for the Dayton project and found that meetings were held every two weeks and were well documented. We found, however, that project meetings were not conducted at the Memphis, Hampton, and the Gainesville projects. The Project Supervisor for the Hampton project reported during each of the four site visits that weekly meetings were taking place; however, we reviewed the project file and found only two meetings had occurred.

We found that the project meetings at the VAMC Reno project were generally conducted weekly but did not always include a discussion on construction delays. For example, we found that the contractor had not taken sufficient action to ensure timely completion of the project. According to the Contract Progress Report for the period ending January 28, 1981. The project had been behind schedule since May 1979. We reviewed the twenty-four Contract Progress Reports and found in seventeen that work progress were reported as unsatisfactory.

The specifications of the contract under Section NAS-10, paragraph B, state:

> The contractor shall submit a narrative report as part of his monthly review and update. The . . . report shall include a description of problem areas; current and anticipated delaying factors and their estimated impact on performance of other activities and completion dates, and an explanation of corrective action taken or proposed.

The contractor's responsibility for the timely completion of the project was specified in the contract as follows:

> The contractor agrees that whenever it becomes apparent . . . that phasing or contract completion dates will not be met, he will take some or all of the following actions at no additional cost to the Government.

234

1. Increase construction manpower in such quantities and crafts as will eliminate the backlog of work.

2. Increase the number of work hours per shift, shifts per working day, working days per week, the amount of construction equipment, or any combination of the foregoing to eliminate the backlog of work.

3. Reschedule the work under this contract in conformance with all other NAS and specification requirements.

In order to determine what action the contractor planned to take when work was not progressing satisfactorily, we reviewed the monthly narrative report file. We found that only twelve of the required twenty-four monthly narrative reports were submitted by the contractor. We found only four occasions in which the RE followed up to request the required narrative report. When the monthly narrative reports were submitted, however, they did not always state what action the contractor had taken, or proposed to take, when work was reported as progressing unsatisfactorily. For example, in the monthly narrative report dated February 29, 1980, the contractor acknowledged being ten weeks behind on concrete pouring but did not state what action he planned to take to get on schedule.

The *Handbook for Resident Engineers* provided the following requirements concerning project meetings between the RE and the contractor to deal with problems:

> The Resident Engineer will hold regular, preferably weekly, project meetings in his office at the project site for the purpose of discussing resulting job problems.
>
> The meetings will be conducted by the Resident Engineer in charge. . . . These meetings provide for improved coordination, better understanding, faster handling of changes, discrepancies, submissions, etc. In addition, they provide an invaluable opportunity to recognize and cope with potential problem areas before they materialize.

> Copies of the minutes of this meeting, noting results and discussions . . . should be sent to the Contractor, Architect-Engineer, and Central Office.

We reviewed the minutes of the project meetings in periods when the contract progress reports reported unsatisfactory work progress. We found that the meetings were not always documented to show discussions of the delays noted in the contract progress reports. For example, during the period ending February 27, 1980, the contract progress report reported work progress as unsatisfactory, citing boilers as undelivered and the slowness of concrete form work. The minutes of the project meetings held during February, however, did not show that these delays were discussed. Documentation concerning delays and the actions taken by the contractor was very important when the completion date extended beyond the scheduled contract completion date. Adequate documentation would be important were a claim to be placed against the VA for the delay.

235

We discussed the results of our reviews of individual projects with the Project Directors. Each of the Project Directors told us that no written guidance had been issued to their Project Supervisors regarding follow-up on documentation sent by the RE. Additional direction was needed by the Assistant Administrator for Construction to ensure the Project Supervisors provide closer oversight of RE's activities. This could be accomplished by performing the required supervisory visits and by performing a thorough review of the RE's documentation. Also, follow-ups should have been initiated when problems were identified by the Project Supervisors.

There was insufficient direction and control over time-and-attendance (T&A) procedures. We found that T&A procedures being used by the Director, Resident Engineer Staff, were not in accordance with VA policy. This had resulted in a substantial increase in overtime and holiday pay costs. In addition, leave requests were improperly approved and improper T&A procedures by RE's were not being detected.

Holiday and overtime work costing over $100,000 was inadequately controlled. This had occurred because procedures for requesting and authorizing overtime, holiday work and compensatory work were not in accordance with VA policy. The VA required overtime and holiday work to be approved in advance, except in emergencies and that each request state the nature of the duties to be performed and the justifications. The *Handbook for Resident Engineers* stated: "The request should be in detail, indicating the type of work scheduled, the hours of work contemplated, number of workmen involved, the probable duration of the overtime period, and the number of Resident Engineers required to work overtime." Office of Construction Memorandum Number 08–81–5, February 27, 1981, limited the authority to approve overtime to the Director, Resident Engineer Staff.

We reviewed all 146 requests for overtime/holiday work during the first half of fiscal year 1981. We found that none of the 146 requests for overtime/holiday work had been disapproved, and on 46 of the requests, the Director's signature had been stamped in the approval block of the request. The Director confirmed to us that his staff had stamped his signature in the approval blocks during his absence. We observed that the Assistant Director, Resident Engineer Staff, also signed, for the Director, some of the requests for overtime. Also, we found 64 (44 percent) of the 146 requests were approved after the overtime had been worked.

Sufficient justification stating why the overtime was necessary or what the staff would be doing during overtime hours was not on 49 of the 146 requests. For example, on March 27, 1981, an RE requested overtime work for two staff involving three different days without any justification or explanation of the duties to be performed. RE's often requested authorization to work on a holiday because the contractor would be working; however, the RE's did not justify the number of staff required. Some requests were for the entire staff of as many as eight RE's; some requests included the clerical staff; and, in some instances only one RE planned to work. In one case, the RE requested authorization for a

236

trainee to work on a holiday without supervision. In another case overtime was approved so the RE could oversee removal of a stack of bricks. Another RE requested a total of 416 hours of overtime during nine pay periods, in blocks of time ranging from twenty to sixty hours. The request did not show the dates on which RE's would be working. Also, all nine reports contained the same general reason for the overtime:

> This overtime is needed for amending of Phase II documents, to handle workload, and to keep up with voluminous paperwork.

The Director, Resident Engineer Staff, told us that his policy was to authorize overtime and holiday work when it was requested. The Director told us that the RE's were in the best position to know when holiday and overtime work was necessary.

Based on the policy of approving all requests for overtime and holiday work and the inadequacy of documenting justifications on the requests, there was no assurance that all costs for overtime and holiday pay were necessary. We found that copies of the VA Form 4–1098 (Request For and Authorization of Overtime Work) were maintained in Budget Division of the Program Control and Analysis Staff and the Office of the Director, Resident Engineer Staff. However, no analysis had been performed to determine why overtime costs had increased. The management analyst, in the Management Staff Office, who reviewed overtime for the Office of Construction told us he did not monitor overtime used by the RE staff. The Assistant Administrator for Construction needed to take action to ensure controls over holiday and overtime work were effective and that only holiday and overtime that was necessary and justified by adequate documentation was approved.

Leave requests were not properly approved. We scanned the Time-and-Attendance Repords for the first four pay periods in fiscal year 1981 and found 106 requests for annual or sick leave that had been approved using a signature stamp of the Director, Resident Engineer Staff. We also found an example in which an RE approved forty hours of sick leave for himself.

The Director, Resident Engineer Staff, told us that the signature stamp was used when he was out of the office to provide timely approval of leave requests.

Replacement Hospital, Columbia, South Carolina

The cost of the William Jennings Bryan Dorn Veterans' Hospital, Columbia, South Carolina, exceeded $22 million. It was accepted prior to October 1, 1979; however, several conditions were found to indicate that the hospital should not have been accepted from the contractor. The method of acceptance and turnover of the hospital resulted in several long-standing problems for the government.

Project	Contract Amount	Inoperable System*	Date Accepted By Office of Construction	DM&S
Columbia, S.C. NHCU 544–028	$ 3,575,734	E,F	12/19/79	12/19/79
Columbia, S.C. Med. Lib. 544–030	2,215,509	E,F,A	05/25/79	05/25/79
Montgomery, AL. Stairs 619–018	$ 431,685	S	12/10/80	04/01/81
Hampton, VA. NHCU 590–050	4,745,966	F,A	02/22/80	02/27/80
Salem, Va. Clinical Bldg. 658–041	2,602,729	F	12/06/79	12/06/79
St. Albans, NY. Extended Care Center 527–9AA-001(E)	855,912	F	07/28/80	07/28/80
Augusta, GA. Replacement Hospital (Phase 2) 510–001B	33,743,117	E,F	12/07/79	12/07/79
Batavia, NY. Elect. Mod. 513–029	967,017	E	12/01/80	12/04/80
Bronx, NY. Replc. Hosp. 526–079, J-M, P-S	42,616,000	E,A,F	05/29/80	05/29/80
Omaha, NE. Add. Elevators 636–019	885,723	S	10/25/79	10/25/79
Providence, RI. OP Clinic 650–012	3,043,272	MG,A	10/29/79	10/29/79
Total	$95,682,664			

*A	Air Balance
E	Electrical System/Emergency Generator
F	Fire Alarm
MG	Medical Gas Alarm System
S	Safety Hazard

Examples of three projects accepted too early by the Office of Construction follow.

We found that some systems had either never been tested or the systems had failed their tests; therefore, it had never been established that all the hospital's systems were operational. The punch list was over 800 pages and contained over 22,000 items. We found three significant construction deficiencies that could possibly affect patient care. These were unsatisfactory performance of the medical gas alarm system, the emergency generator, and the ventilation system. In addition, portions of the hospital were accpeted before the fire-and-smoke alarm system was operational.

The Hospital Safety Manager told us that the fire-and-smoke alarm system did not work properly during the final inspection. For example, he told us the annunciator did not properly identify areas being tested. The Safety Manager wrote the Hospital Director a letter dated June 14, 1979 as follows:

> The purpose of this letter is to document this office's views on Bldg. 100 Fire Alarm System. Prior to acceptance of the Fire Alarm System of Bldg. 100, this office was *never contacted or consulted* by management concerning the adequacy of the system.

> I want to go on record stating that the Fire Alarm System was inadequate at the time Hospital management accepted responsibility, nor is it adequate today.

> At this time, it has not been determined as to whether Engineering Service or the contractor has responsibility for the Fire Alarm System. Communication has been poor in dealings with the Fire Alarm Contractor to date. The Resident Engineer invited this office to the final inspection, but we were met with "cool" receptiveness. Since the specifications call for no actual training on the Fire Alarm System, we took the opportunity given at the final inspection to ask questions that would eventually be asked of this office. It was stated by the Central Office Inspector for Fire Alarm Systems, that we should not "bother" the contractor with further questions.

The Safety Manager told us that the day after the test of the fire alarm system, the Office of Construction, Central Office Inspector for Fire Alarm Systems, left. The Safety Manager told us that since that time they have continued to identify and correct problems with the fire-alarm system. The Associate Director of the hospital told us they contacted the manufacturer of the system who visited the hospital to correct the problems.

239

We also found other long-standing construction deficiencies that had not been corrected by the contractor. Some construction deficiencies were corrected by the facility instead of by the contractor. This resulted in an unnecessary additional cost to you of over $15,000. The Hospital Director did not feel the government received a functional product. The Director signed a custody receipt for three of the four portions. The Associate Director signed for the bulk of the hospital on May 18, 1979. Both the Director and the Associate Director told us there were several reasons for accepting the hospital from the Office of Construction.

Reasons for Accepting the Hospital from the Office of Construction

1. The Office of Construction had already accepted the hospital from the contractor for the government. The Associate Director told us the Resident Engineer had said the May 18, 1979, signature of the Associate Director was just a preliminary paperwork transfer in order to give DM&S access to the building areas.
2. The hospital needed storage space for furniture and equipment that was arriving. All the existing storage space was filled.
3. Both cited pressure from the Resident Engineer to accept the hospitals. The Director told us the pressure was greatest in June 1979, when the last portion of the hospital had not been accepted from the Office of Construction by DM&S. The Director would not sign a custody receipt until deficiencies were minimized in the basement.
4. The Dedication Day was established and both told us substantial cleaning was needed after the accepting the hospital from the contractor.
5. Both the Director and the Associate Director told us they depended on the Resident Engineer to deal with the contractor to get the hospital functional. When the Resident Engineer accepted the hospital, they believed that was the best that could be done.
6. The hospital staff was anxious to begin utilizing the new facilities instead of the old facilities.
7. The telephone company needed access to the new hospital in order to install telephone service.

VAMC Augusta, Georgia

Portions of the fire-alarm system and the emergency generator had either never been tested or had failed their tests. As a result, the contractor had never demonstrated that the two major systems were operational. In addition, the punch list contained over 26,000 items of omissions and deficiencies.

Deadend Corridor Stairs, VAMC Montgomery AL

The deadend corridor stair project, VAMC Montgomery, was accepted by the Office of Construction, December 10, 1980, and transferred to the Department of Medicine and Surgery nearly four months later on April 1, 1981. The Final Inspection Report, January 5, 1981, stated: "Custody of this project was assumed for the Office of Construction by the Senior Project Supervisor on December 10, 1980. The Medical Center Director will not accept transfer until the contractor has completed all of the safety items connected with the stairs."

The Acting Director, VAMC Montgomery, stated in a letter dated November 24, 1980, that the project could not, at the time of inspection, be considered ready for beneficial occupancy nor substantially complete. The Acting Director also said that the medical center desired to refrain from taking responsibility for the project until it was substantially complete and ready for beneficial occupancy. The Assistant Director, Resident Engineer Staff, wrote to the Office of Construction on January 7, 1981, and stated the final inspection was premature and poorly organized.

The Assistant Administrator for Construction told us that we would find several definitions of substantial completion. Each of the Project Directors told us different definitions of substantial completion.

The fundamental point concerning custody of a project is the VA determination of substantial completion. A DM&S Manual provided the following guidelines in regard to the acceptance of construction project:

Before a hospital project is ready for acceptance by the Office of Construction and the DM&S, all major elements, including mechanical and electrical systems, must be satisfactorily completed. Only adjustments should be necessary to eliminate minor deficiencies. DM&S staff required to operate the mechanical and electrical systems should be employed sufficiently in advance of the takeover to be fully instructed and qualified to operate all mechanical and electrical systems on acceptance.

The Director, William Jennings Bryan Dorn Veterans' Hospital, Columbia, South Carolina, told us substantial completion was a point in time when the station had to have access to the building. The Director, VAMC Augusta, told us that substantial completion should have included access by the facility for preparation for patient occupancy. A VA manual provided additional guidelines as follows:

Following final inspection, custody of facilities provided by construction contracts will be acceptable by the Office of Construction and will be retained until all major items of contract deviation and omission have been corrected and supervision of correction of the remaining minor items would

241

not impose an undue burden on station management. Custody will then be transferred to the [Health Care Facility Director].

The practice of accepting custody of projects without well-defined and coordinated ground rules has been counter-productive. As illustrated, custody of construction projects had been accepted with major systems having never been established as operational. It could have been concluded from this review of projects that a need existed for ensuring that the contractor was providing specified operational systems to achieve substantial completion. For example, it would seem that an operational fire alarm would be a minimum condition wherever fire alarm systems were being installed, remodeled, or replaced. The VA should have been specific in defining the major systems that must be in service.

The Office of Construction had awarded over $600 million in construction contracts during fiscal year 1980 and 1981. Several of these projects cost over $10 million each. One future individual project was being contemplated that will cost $400 million. With each of these projects costing so much, the transfer and activation from one phase or area of responsibility to the next was critical. Each project, because of its dollar size, must be aggressively and thoroughly understood.

We observed the transfer of the nursing home care unit, VAMC Memphis, Tennessee; the operations of the replacement hospital at VAMC Augusta, Georgia; and the operations of the replacement hospital (the William Jennings Bryan Dorn Veterans' Hospital) at Columbia, South Carolina. In addition, we interviewed Office of Construction and DM&S personnel involved in the constructing projects. The auditors objectives were to determine whether the facility managers experienced problems in activating the projects turned over to them and the adequacy of relevant directives and guidance provided to VA managers in the activation of VA construction projects.

VA managers experience too many problems in activating construction projects. The Directors at Columbia, South Carolina and Augusta, Georgia, had difficulties in activating their new facilities. During our audit we observed that after the transfer of these projects from the Office of Construction to the facility Directors, the Directors were left on their own to activate and make the new facility fully operational. This, in part, is because RE's were transferred from the project soon after acceptance.

Project Supervisors were not adequately controlling the performance of the RE's. The Project Supervisor works for the Contracting Officer (Project Director) and was required to make quarterly visits to assigned construction projects under control of the Contracting Officer. The purpose of these visits was to enable the Project Supervisor to become familiar with the project and to conduct intermediate inspections. Project visits also provided an opportunity for the Project Supervisors to monitor the RE's performance.

We found that project visits were not made quarterly as shown in the following examples:

Location	Area	Number of Quarterly Visits	Duration of Construction
Gainesville	Southern	1	14 months
Reno	Western	1	13 months
Bay Pines	Southern	4	25 months
Memphis	Southern	2	13 months
Dayton	Central	2	23 months
Hampton	North East	4	23 months

The Project Directors told us that, next to the RE's presence at the projects, Project Supervisor inspections were the most important item for ensuring the successful completion of a construction project. These inspections enabled the Project Supervisors to develop a working relationship with the RE, contractor, and facility Director, and also allowed the Project Supervisor to determine whether the RE's were protecting the government's interest during contract execution.

In addition to the lack of quarterly visits, we found that the documentation of work activities submitted by the RE's was not thoroughly reviewed by the Project Supervisors. Our audit disclosed several findings that indicated a lack of control or follow-up by the Office of Construction staff. These areas are discussed below.

Area of Findings[1]

Project Location	Safety	Change Orders	Weekly Project Meetings
Memphis		x	x
Gainesville	x		x
Bay Pines			
Reno	x	x	x
Dayton		x	
Hampton	x	x	x

1. x denotes finding at a particular location.

SAFETY

We found that monthly safety inspections were not conducted by some Resident Engineers. The VA's *Construction Project Handbook* required the RE to submit a safety and accident report to the Director, Resident Engineer Staff, and the Project Director. The *Handbook for Resident Engineers* stated that the Assistant Administrator for Construction was required to assure that effective safety programs were conducted at VA construction projects. This same manual required the RE to conduct a monthly safety inspection and submit a report to the Project Director no later than the fifth of the following month. We also found that OSHA Form 100F (Log of Federal Occupational Injuries and Illnesses or Fire) was not being submitted to the Management Staff, Office of Construction, at the end of each quarter. The submission was required by the *Handbook for Resident Engineers*. Neither of the above was being reviewed nor was follow-up being performed to ensure accomplishment of the requirement for an aggressive safety program.

The Project Director for the Southern Area told us that he did not feel the RE's should conduct safety inspections. He told us that the *Handbook for Resident Engineers* should be changed to delete this requirement. The Project Director for the Western Area told us that the RE's should conduct safety, fire, and health inspections and report the results of each week on the daily logs. This Project Director told us the Project Supervisors should monitor this. The Project Director for the Northeast Area told us that the safety inspections should be made and that the Project Supervisors should monitor this during their site visits. The Project Director for the Central Area told us that he had instructed his Project supervisors to contact the RE's when the RE's did not indicate that safety inspections were being performed weekly. We reviewed the project files for a construction project in Dayton, Ohio, for which this Project Director was responsible and found that weekly and monthly inspections were reported as being performed.

CHANGE ORDERS

We found that methods used by the RE's to establish and issue change orders did not ensure changes to contracts were accomplished at fair prices to the government. For example, independent estimates were not always obtained to compare against the contractor's price proposals when they exceeded a thousand dollars. The A/E did not always review the contractor's price proposal when they exceeded a thousand dollars. The contractor's price proposal would be accepted when the independent cost estimates did not support the contractor's proposals. The RE did not document how he arrived at his cost estimates. None of the contractors submitted price proposals timely when proceed orders were issued. The *Handbook for Resident Engineers* required that copies of these documents (contractor's price proposal, A/E's review, independent cost estimates, and the RE's memorandum of justification and explanation for accepting the price and change) required the Project Supervisor to analyze and code each proceed and change order and stated that the Project Supervisor would conduct a review to assure that change and proceed orders were correct. Effective reviews had not been done to ensure the issuance of changes to the contract are at a fair price to the VA.

Examples of the problems follow:

Southern Area

Memphis
1. Contractor did not provide price proposals within 30 days of proceed order date.
2. A/E did not provide independent estimates in all cases.
3. The change order would be issued at the contractor's proposal when the A/E estimate did not support it and there was no documentation to support why the contractor's proposal was accepted.

Western Area

Reno
1. The RE did not always submit the contractor's price proposals to the A/E for review when the change orders exceeded $1,000. In the memorandum for the record justifying the change orders, the RE did not always cite the reason why an A/E estimate was not required.
2. Sometimes the A/E would review the contractor's proposal and recommend that it be accepted but not support the recommendation with an independent estimate.
3. We found examples where the A/E would recommend that the contractor's price proposal be rejected and the RE would increase the scope of the work and go with the contractor's proposal but without having the A/E review the changed scope.
4. Change orders were issued at the contractor's proposal when the A/E's estimate was not within 10 percent.
5. Change orders were issued where estimates contained incorrect arithmetical calculations.
6. Contractor price proposals were not received within 30 days of a proceed order.

Northeast Area

Hampton
1. Contractor's proposals were not detailed or broken down.
2. No copy of the A/E's estimates were in the project files or contract administration files.
3. Contractor's proposal was not within 10 percent of A/E estimate and not referred to Director, Estimating Service, Office of Construction, for review.

Central Area

1. A/E's estimates and reviews were not in the project files in all cases.
2. A/E estimates were not within 10 percent of the contractor's proposal.
3. A/E estimates were not detailed.

The majority of the information given to the hospital staff was provided during the pre-construction conference, conversations with the RE, and during the acceptance of the facility. There were few directions or guides to VA managers in activating the construction projects. In addition to a lack of clear guidelines as to when to accept a construction project, the facility Director was also presented with several obstacles before a construction project was made operational. For example, at Columbia, South Carolina, we found that there were numerous difficulties in activating the new hospital. There were four major systems that were not operating correctly: the emergency medical gas alarm system, the ventilation system, the electrical system, and the fire-and-smoke alarm system. The hospital staff had to move in all of the government-furnished equipment and furniture and had to clean the new hospital. The Hospital Director told us the hospital staff had to correct some of 22,000-item punch list before patient occupancy on July 26, 1979, because they could not wait for the contractor to complete the items.

At VAMC Augusta, Georgia, we found that the Director had experienced similar problems as had the Director in Columbia, South Carolina. Two major systems were not operating correctly: the fire-and-smoke alarm system and the energy-management system. The hospital staff also had to move in all the government-furnished equipment and furniture. The date of patient occupancy was delayed eight months because of the 26,000-item punch list.

Several other similar problems were experienced by both Hospital Directors. For example, control of work orders was inadequate for the replacement hospital; and there was no preventive maintenance program for the replacement hospitals. There had not been any testing of the emergency gas-alarm systems and neither hospital's staffs had been given adequate training on the medical gas alarms. Also, neither hospital's Supply Service had inventoried contractor-furnished material. Failure to inventory contractor-furnished equipment resulted in both hospital's CMR's being inaccurate, guarantee and maintenance tags not being attached to the equipment, and updated maintenance cards not being furnished to the Engineering Service. Without guarantee tags it was possible that defective equipment was repaired at government expense. Without maintenance cards, neither Engineering Service could update their respective Engineering Management Information Systems for use in their preventive-maintenance programs. The stations had not confirmed if they had received all equipment required by the contract and did not know whether any equipment had been lost or stolen. As a result of the lack of a preventive maintenance program at VAMC Augusta, Georgia, the dryers for the compressed-air system were not removing water from the compressed air. We were told that water was choking patients because water

246

was in their air/oxygen lines, which were inserted in the patients' noses. The Acting Chief of Staff and Chief, Surgical Service, told us this was adverse patient care. In addition, the water was damaging the ventilators. We discussed these problems with the Director and were told that corrective action would be taken immediately.

At the final inspection, a List of Omissions and Deviations, commonly referred to as the punch list, was prepared by the final inspection team for listing work to be accomplished before final contract settlement. One of the responsibilities of the RE was to monitor and inspect the omissions and deviations to ensure that appropriate corrective actions were taken by the contractors. When the work was acceptable, the Resident Engineers were to document their acceptance on the omissions and deviations reports. In order to accomplish this, the Resident Engineer should have established communications with DM&S engineering counterparts who were to operate the project upon completion. This would facilitate an orderly transition to the station engineering staff. In cases where the Resident Engineer was transferred from the project before the punch list was completed, the Station Engineering Officer was designated to function as the Resident Engineer and assumes responsibility for ensuring completion of the punch list items.

Relevant statistical data concerning the two completed projects audited is shown in the following schedule:

Statistical Data

Item	Columbia, S.C.	Augusta, GA.
Project Value (Phase 1 and 2)	$11,000,000	$43,000 000
Date of Substantial Completion	May 31, 1979	December 3, 1979
Date of Patient Occupancy	July 26, 1979	August 13, 1980

The VA was not adequately monitoring the contractor's work after final inspection. This was caused by the early transfer for the RE from the construction project and the lack of adequate performance of the RE activities that were delegated to the hospital staff. We found problems with methods used to ensure omissions and deviations were corrected at the replacement hospitals at Columbia, South Carolina and Augusta, Georgia.

William Jennings Bryan Dorn Veterans' Hospital, Columbia, South Carolina

At the time of our audit, the VA had not been adequately monitoring the contractor's performance following final inspection. This resulted in long-standing construction problems with the new hospital, unnecessary cost to the government, and the contractor being paid for work the government performed and for work that was not performed.

We reviewed the final and partial final punch lists and determined the following punch-list items had not been corrected.

Schedule of Punch List Items Not Corrected

Number of Punch List Items Remaining	As of Date
	August 1979
846	January 1980
63	June 1980
12	March 1981
6	

Since July 2, 1979, the hospital's resources had been used in some instances to correct punch list and other deficiencies were the responsibility of the contractor. The engineering staff did not document which of the over 22,000 punch-list deficiencies the engineering staff corrected. In addition, we found 342 punch-list items that were never initialed as being completed. We found two items for relocation of commodes were never completed. We did not review the other 340 items to verify whether they were completed.

Additional contract deficiencies were identified by the station. We were not able to verify their costs because the station did not document the costs involved in their correction. According to the Assistant Engineering Officer, some of these deficiencies were corrected by the station in order to provide proper patient care. This resulted in unnecessary additional cost to you of $15,720.

Additional Government Costs to Correct Contractor Deficiencies

Remove sand and mud from water lines	$ 7,000
Repair sheet metal failures	4,700
Tighten loose commodes	3,000
Investigation of air/water balance	700
Investigation of emergency medical gas alarms	320
	$15,720

VA Medical Center Augusta, Georgia

Completion of punch-list items at the VAMC Augusta, Georgia, replacement hospital had not been accomplished effectively. This resulted in an eight-month delay in activating the hospital and inefficient operation of the air-conditioning system following activation. In addition, the hospital used its resources to correct punch-list items.

Delay in Activation

The Office of Construction accepted custody of the hospital on December 3, 1979. The punch list for the final inspection, dated December 3, 1979, and the partial final inspection, dated November 5, 1979, listed over 26,000 items of omission or deviation. These items were not sufficiently completed to allow patient occupancy until August 13, 1980,and as a result the VA was delayed in using its $43 million investment.

Air Conditioning System

The Engineering Control Center (ECC) had not operated properly from the acceptance of the hospital to the time of our audit. A principal function of the ECC included efficient operation of the air-conditioning system. As of July 2, 1981, the punch list showed three computer software packages for the ECC that had not been installed. These software packages control and optimize the temperature of the hospital. The station's computer system analyst told us that, because the ECC had not operated properly, the loss in excess electrical consumption had been $134,000 during the period since patient occupancy (August 1980 through May 1981). The consultant hired to oversee completion of the punch list told us the programming required to operate the ECC would not be available until 1982. We estimated that even if the ECC became fully operational in January 1982, the hospital would have incurred an additional cost of $94,000 for unnecessary electrical consumption, due to the lack of the computer software packages.

Punch List Items Corrected by
Station Resources

The Chief, Maintenance and Repair Section, Engineering Service, told us that the Engineering Service staff was sometimes used to correct punch-list items and other contract deficiencies in order to provide for adequate patient care. The Chief also told us the extent of this work had not been documented nor was the station reimbursed for the work by the contractor.

Consultant Used As RE

A purchase order was issued for a consultant to provide administrative services for the Engineering Officer while acting as the RE. We found several problems with this purchase order. The purchase order was issued on a sole-source basis; however, a Memorandum of Determination and Findings stating why a sole-source procurement was justified was not prepared by Supply Service. The purchase order stated that the limitation was $5,000; however, neither the number of hours nor the hourly cost for the consultant was documented. There was no time period nor specific accomplishments listed. The total amount of invoices paid by the VA under this purchase order exceeded $9,900 at the time of our audit. The Chief, Engineering Service, did not keep any documentation to support the hours claimed by the consultant.

We also could not locate any documentation to support the hourly cost of twenty-two dollars being billed by the consultant. The Chief, Engineering Service, and the consultant were personal friends. We found that only 106 of the 336 punch-list deficiencies had been corrected during the period of the purchase order, October 3, 1980, to June 26, 1981. We discussed this purchase with the Director, VAMC Augusta, and he told us the consultant's services would be terminated July 7, 1981. Also, the Chief, Engineering Service, told us that the consultant would not charge the VA for any services incurred since his last invoice dated April 30, 1981. Just as a coincidence, this was the consultant's last invoice prior to the arrival of the audit team.

Liquidated damages represent the final amount, agreed to in advance between the contractor and the government, to be paid by the contractor for each day work exceeds the extended completion date. Liquidated damages protect your interest in the event the contractor does not complete the contract in the allotted number of days.

Liquidated damages were assessed only by the VA Contracting Officer and were based on the Contracting Officer's finding of fact concerning the delay in project completion. The Federal Procurement Regulations provided for inclusion of a liquidated damages clause in government contracts as follows:

> A liquidated damages clause may, in the discretion of the contracting officer, be included in construction contracts. Where such a provision is used, the invitation for bids or request for proposals shall include a clause reading substantially as follows:

> **Liquidated Damages**

> In case of failure on the part of the Contractor to complete the work within the time fixed in the contract or any extension thereof, the Contractor shall pay to the Government as fixed, agreed and liquidated damages, pursuant to the clause of this contract entitled "Termination of Default-Damages for Delay-Time Extensions," the sum of $— for each calendar day of delay.

After the delay was over, the government may have expected the contractor to submit to the Resident Engineer a claim for the time the contract as a whole was delayed due to the government. This claim should give the dates the delay began and ended, the cause of the delay, the particular part or parts of work affected, and the number of calendar days the delay affected the completion date of the contract as a whole. In forwarding the contractor's claim, the Resident Engineer would include comments and definite recommendations, referring to previous correspondence and including any additional information available. The use of liquidated damages served a two-fold purpose. A financial deterrent was effected against the contractor to maximize prospects for on-time delivery of the project to the government. Also, a reduction in final financial obligation of the government to the contractor was made possible.

The amount of liquidated damages included in the construction contracts for the projects included in our audit were:

Schedule of Liquidated Damages

Site	Project	Liquidated Damages/Calendar Day
Memphis	NHCU[1]	$ 445
Gainesvilled	NHCU	348
Bay Pines	Repl. Hosp.	9,000
Reno	Boiler Plant	940
Columbia	Repl. Hosp.	1,890
Augusta	Repl. Hosp.	2,400

1. Nursing Home Care Unit.

The Schedule of Minimum Liquidated Damages had not been updated since 1968. The practice of the Office of Construction was to establish a liquidated damage amount in the contract specifications clause covering liquidated damages. This amount was based on the Schedule of Minimum Liquidated Damages, dated October 9, 1968. The daily rate to be assessed as liquidated damages was computed using this schedule, which assigned rates according to the estimated amount of contract as minimum guidelines.

The amount assigned (based upon these minimum guidelines) was not representative of the construction business because of higher costs associated with every aspect of the industry. For example, the schedule peaked with an assigned bracket of estimated costs of $26–30 million. The schedule recommended a minimum for contracts over $30 million. The cost of building a hospital had increased along with all cost in the construction industry and, together with inflation, the cost of a project in 1981 bore little resemblance to 1968 costs.

The effect of not using an updated schedule meant that the amount to be withheld would not have been sufficient economic incentive for the contractor to complete his work on time. Also, the amount withheld would not have been enough to cover anticipated costs by the VA in providing an alternative method of finishing the uncompleted work. These rates should have been for and representative of what Disorganized Crime expected to suffer if the contract was not completed in the time allowed in the contract. The Schedule of Minimum Liquidated Damages was an agency responsibility. Officials within the Office of Supply Service were responsible for updating the appropriate VA Procurement Regulations (VAPR) as needed. For matters requiring their action, appropriate VA officials prepared requests for changes to appropriate VAPR sections. This had not been done for over thirteen years. What's the hurry?

251

The method used to compute liquidated damages was inadequate. The present method for assessing liquidated damages was an application of a percentage to the daily rate specified in the contract. This percentage was derived based on the value of the unaccapeted work to the total contract amount. A liquidated damages clause was included in all construction contracts and was worded as follows:

If any unit of work contracted for is accepted in advance of the whole, the rate of liquidated damages assessed will be in the ratio that the value of the unaccepted work bears to the total amount of the contract. If a separate price for unacceptable work has not been stated in the Contractor's bid, determination of the value thereof will be made from a schedule of cost furnished by the Contractor and approved by the Contracting Officer, or as otherwise stated in the contract.

We reviewed the project files at the Office of Construction for thirty-one projects reaching final settlement between October 1, 1979 and May 1, 1981. We found that six of the projects reaching final completion were finished late.

Late Projects Reaching Final Settlement

Project Name	Value	Daily Liquidated Damages	Days Late
Chicago, Illinois Remedial Surgical Area	$1,563,000	$185	224
Chillicothe, Ohio Emergency Power Distribution	488,288	90	55
Chillicothe, Ohio Modernization of Buildings	6,328,338	530	30
Columbia, South Carolina 120-Bed NHCU	3,630,193	340	114
Marion, Indiana Correct Electrical Deficiencies	1,367,504	150	34
Omaha, Nebraska Additional Elevators	885,767	150	121

The contracted amount of daily liquidated damages in the Chillicothe, Ohio, modernization of Buildings 7, 26, and 27 project per day. The Project Director,

252

in accordance with the liquidated damages specification, computed a daily liquidated damages rate as follows, based on the value of the unacceptable work:

Percentage Complete	99%
Liquidated Damages Prorated	$5.25 (1% of $530)
Days Late	30
Total Assessment	$157.50 x $5.25)
Nonprorated Assessment	%15,900 (30 x $530)

This practice of prorating liquidated damages does not reflect the true cost (actual damages) to the VA of the contractor being late in completing the project. The Project Supervisor submitted a Memorandum of Justification that showed damages amounting to $302 per day.

Employee Salaries		Daily Rate
Senior Resident Engineer	GS 13–4	$157
Resident Engineer	GS 7–4	82
Clerk	GS 4–4	54
Duplicating Equipment		6
Telephone		3
		$302

Liquidated damages were to be prorated in all Office of Construction contracts according to the general policy of the Office of Construction. The Office of Construction had opted to collect damages in this manner rather than try to validate actual damages. The Director of Contract Administration told us the validating procedure for liquidating damages was simply including a Memorandum of Justification stating anticipated damages at the time the Invitation For Bid was issued. The Director also told us validating and collecting actual damages was a long, tedious affair for Disorganized Crime that would not result in an actual collection until all legal matters concerning the project were settled, taking months or years.

The Contract Attorney for General Counsel, VACO, said the present clause for liquidated damages used in all Office of Construction contracts did not provide for collection costs incurred by the VA as described in the project's Memorandum of Justification. The Contract Attorney told us that eliminating the prorating clause would be beneficial to the VA in administering late contracts and collecting costs incurred by the Office of Construction when projects run past the contractual completion date.

Now after all these years of audit reports being dropped, you can imagine that I couldn't be naive about the importance of visuals. But I still, deep down, believed that if the auditors found something *really* crooked or *really* gross, then those items, in spite of the bad visuals they would create, would be reported. My last two audits at the VA hospitals in Augusta, Georgia, and Miami, Florida, proved me wrong.

The VA Medical Center (VAMC), Augusta, Georgia, was audited by the Office of Inspector General from January 4, 1982, through March 2, 1982. The audit report was published April 15, 1982. VAMC Augusta was composed of two divisions. Lenwood (uptown) was located approximately four miles from the new facility (downtown). Lenwood was the psychiatric division, which had been constructed in 1912, with operating beds as of February 28, 1982, consisting of 396 psychiatric and 208 intermediate medicine, for a total of 604. The new 390-bed facility (downtown) was activated for patients in August 1980. The downtown facility replaced the Forest Hills Division, which was vacant and pending disposal by GSA. The planned fiscal year 1982 budget was over $62 million.

The medical center had twenty-two projects that were either ongoing (two) or planned (twenty) that would have resulted in over $3 million of unneeded construction. A technical evaluation of the Lenwood Division was completed by an Architect/Engineer firm that contained recommendations that would be used to revise the Lenwood Division's Master Plan. The recommendation in the technical evaluation changed the need for some of the projects in the medical center's Five-Year Facility Plans for fiscal years 1982 and 1983. However, these projects had not been reevaluated nor had the facility plans been updated to ensure that unnecessary construction projects were not being initiated. In addition, the Lenwood Division complex had been determined eligible as a historical site. Installation of elevators in Buildings 2 and 6, an ongoing construction project, was an apparent violation of the National Historic Preservation Act of 1966.

There were twenty-two projects approved by Central Office, as of January 4, 1982. The total estimated cost of the twenty-two projects was $3,620,000. Two of the twenty-two projects, with estimated cost of $1,681,000, were included in the medical center's Five-Year Facility Plan for fiscal years 1982–1986. Contracts had been awarded and work had started on the two projects. The remaining twenty projects, with an estimated construction cost of $1,939,000, had been approved for fiscal year 1983. The projects were included in the budget that had been submitted for fiscal year 1983.

The Master Plan—which is a twenty-five-year plan—identified the medical center's facilities, the lifespan of the facilities, the future workload of the medical center, concepts on usage of current facilities, and future construction requirements to satisfy the medical center's workload. The Five-Year Facility Plan was the management tool used by medical center personnel to establish priorities of construction projects to achieve the overall requirements that had been identified in the Master Plan.

On August 10, 1981, the Architect/Engineer (A/E) firm of Jova, Daniels, Busby, Incorporated submitted a technical evaluation of existing facilities at VAMC Augusta Lenwood Division to the Office of Construction, VA Central

Office. The technical evaluation report was the basis for which a revised Master Plan would be developed for the Lenwood Division. In the technical evaluation report, the A/E firm stated in part:

> Aside from age, the greatest impact on the usefulness of the present buildings has been changes in the minimum standards for health care, patient privacy, operational efficiency, life safety, fire prevention, energy conservation, earthquake resistence, etc. Although many of the deficiencies resulting from these modern standards can be corrected, too many compromises and too much expense would result from trying to correct them all. The money would be better spent on new facilities tailored to current standards and treatment techniques.

Discussion with the VAMC Augusta's Project Supervisor at VA Central Office on February 17, 1982 disclosed that an A/E firm had developed ten design concepts that would be discussed with medical center management, Department of Medicine and Surgery (DM&S) and Office of Construction personnel to determine which concept would best meet the needs of the medical center. The A/E firm presented the ten design concepts to medical center management on March 3, 1982. DM&S and Office of Construction personnel were to be briefed in April 1982. After the design concept was selected, a master plan would be developed for the Lenwood Division.

The Director received a Determination of Eligibility Notification, dated May 7, 1981, from the Keeper of the National Register of Historical Places, which stated that the entire 105.7 acres of the Lenwood Division had been determined eligible as a historical site. Section 110 of the National Historic Preservation Act of 1966 gave the VA resonsibility for the preservation of historic properties. Section 110 provided that prior to acquiring, constructing, or leasing buildings to carry out agency responsibilities, the agency would, to the maximum extent feasible, use available historic properties.

Our review of the twenty-two projects in the fiscal year 1982 and 1983 Five-Year Facility Plans disclosed that:

a. The facility plan included ten projects, with estimated construction cost of $514,000, for buildings that were recommended for demolition in the technical evaluation report. These projects included construction of a porch, construction of an addition to the recreation building, renovation of toilets and adding enclosed fire escapes to seven buildings.

b. There were six projects, with an estimated construction cost of $1,152,000, that the Program Analyst said were to be reevaluated. These projects included installation of storm and sanitation sewers, paving of service areas, construction of a cycle-run and exercise track, weatherproofing quarters, increasing the capacity of the chiller plant, and renovating the second floor of Building 20.

c. There were four projects, with estimated construction cost of $1,172,000, for buildings that the Program Analyst stated the functional use would be changed from patient-care buildings to administrative buildings. The four projects included installing of linen and trash chutes in Buildings 12 and 76, installing medical gas and nurse call systems and providing new fire-alarm devices to both buildings. The contract for the medical gas and nurse call systems and the fire alarm project had been awarded and work had started.

d. One project, with construction cost of $297,802, had been awarded to install elevators to the front of Buildings 2 and 6. Buildings 2 and 6 were included in the list of buildings that were recommended for demolition in the technical evaluation report.

e. The Program Analyst stated that the project to renovate classrooms 211 through 213, 301 and 310 in Building 19 was going to be reevaluated. However, follow-up on this project showed that the project had already been completed and should not have been in the plan. The construction cost of this project, per the Five-Year Facility Plan, was $46,000.

The twenty-two projects in the Five-year Facility Plans have not been re-evaluated because the facility plans are not reviewed and updated when other actions impact on the projects in the plans. Medical Center Memorandum Number 001–1–80 provided for the Management Analyst to update the Five-Year Facility Plan continuously. The Five-Year Facility Plan for fiscal year 1983 was submitted to Medical District Number 9 on February 25, 1981. The technical evaluation was provided to the medical center in August 1981. Even though the recommendations in the technical evaluation significantly impacted on the fiscal year 1983 Five-Year Facility Plan, there was no evidence that the plan was reevaluated to determine if the projects were still needed or if the postponement or cancellation of the projects would affect the operations of the medical center.

The Management Analyst, who was responsible for coordinating and updating the facility plan, terminated his employment with the medical center on September 26, 1981. Another coordinator was not assigned until December 1981 after the audit team requested information concerning the facility plan. As a result, nine projects, with estimated construction cost of $1,893,000, were not reevaluated to determine if the projects were still needed since a new master plan was being developed for the Lenwood Division. For example, Project Number 80–127 was planned to construct an addition to the recreation building at an estimated cost of $219,000. The technical evaluation report recommended that the building be demolished. This project was still included in the facility plan and funding had been requested for fiscal year 1983.

Two construction contracts, valued at about $1,243,800 were awarded after the medical center had received the technical evaluation from the A/E firm. Both contracts were funded by Central Office. Contract Number V101C-966, valued at $945,000, was awarded on September 8, 1981, and Contract Number V509C-135, valued at $197,802, was awarded on September 30, 1981. Contract Number V101C-966 provided for new fire-alarm devices in Buildings 12, 34, 76, and 94, medical gas systems for selected rooms in Buildings 12 and 24, and an emergency nurse-call system in bathrooms in Building 12. Contract Number V509C-135 provided for the installation of elevators for Buildings 2 and 6.

The Program Analyst, who was responsible for coordinating the Five-Year Facility Plan, stated that the functional use of Buildings 12 and 76 may be changed from patient care to administrative. The change in the functional use of the buildings would have negated the need for the medical gas system and the nurse call system that was to be installed in Buildings 12 and 76. Therefore, Contract Number V101C-966 should have been postponed and the contract requirements reevalutated to ensure that unnecessary renovations were not made to the buildings. The contract cost that was attributed the medical gas and nurse call systems were not available, therefore, the cost for these contract requirements could not be determined.

Per the technical evaluation report, Buildings 2 and 6 were recommended for demolition. Therefore, the need to install elevators in the buildings may have resulted in unnecessary expenditure of construction funds. In addition, on May 7, 1981, the entire 105.7 acres of the Lenwood Division was designated eligible as an historical site. Section 106 of the National Historic Preservation Act of 1966, as amended, states:

> The head of any Federal agency having direct or indirect jurisdiction over a proposed Federal or federally assisted undertaking in any State and the head of any Federal department or independent agency having authority to license any undertaking shall prior to the approval of the expenditure of any Federal funds on the undertaking or prior to the issuance of any license, as the case may be, *take into account the effect of the undertaking on any district, site, building, structure, or object that is included in or eligible for inclusion in the National Register*. The head of any such Federal agency shall afford the Advisory Council on Historic Preservation established under Title II of this Act a reasonable opportunity to comment with regard to such undertaking (Author's italics).

Contract Number V509C-135 provided for the installation of elevators to the exterior of Buildings 2 and 6, which would alter the exterior structure of the buildings. The proposed design for the installation of the elevators in Buildings 2 and 6 was approved by Central Office on June 10, 1981, with the proviso that the drawings be submitted to the Georgia State Historic Preservation Officer for their concurrence. On August 6, 1981, the Medical Center Director forwarded a letter to the Georgia State Historic Preservation Officer requesting approval to construct elevators to the front east side of Buildings 2 and 6. The Georgia State Historic Preservation Officer's reply to the Director, dated October 2, 1981, stated:

> Within the Medical Center complex, Buildings 2 and 6 are contributing structures to the historical significance of the district. The proposed alteration to these buildings consists of a large addition to the front of each building to accommodate stairs and an elevator. The location of this addition is inappropriate as it is, the addition substantially alters the original entry "courtyard" character of each building and destroys the original open porch.

The addition also connects to the original building in a way that would destroy the original exterior fabric where they meet. Therefore, this addition would have an adverse effect on both Building 2 and 6, as well as on the district as a whole.

In accordance with 36 CFR 800.4(c), the Veterans Administration should now forward the appropriate documentation for this project to the Advisory Council on Historic Preservation. . . .

On November 2, 1981, the Director requested approval from the Office of Construction to proceed with the renovation project even though the Georgia State Preservation Officer had ruled that the construction would have an impact on the historical significance of the district. The Office of Construction's reply to the Director's letter, dated December 21, 1981, advised him that since he disagreed with the Georgia State Historic Preservation Officer's decision, that a letter to the Advisory Council on Historic Preservation was the next step to take to obtain approval to renovate Buildings 2 and 6.

Even though the Director had not received approval from the State Preservation Officer or a reply from the Office of Construction, a notice to proceed was sent to the contractor on October 23, 1981, and the contractor started work on November 2, 1981. The Director had not submitted a request to the Advisory Council on Historic Preservation. As a result, the renovation to Buildings 2 and 6 was being performed without obtaining approval from the Advisory Council. The altering of Building 6 was an apparent violation of Section 106 of the National Historic Preservation Act of 1966. Work being performed under Contract Number V509C-135 should have been canceled and approval should have been obtained from the Advisory Council on Historic Preservation prior to completing the contract.

Because the Lenwood Division had been designated eligible as an historical site and a revised master plan was being developed, there was need for the medical center to reassess the projects to determine the impact that the historical designation and the revised Master Plan would have on the planned projects. The twenty-two projects (ongoing and planned) in the Five-Year Facility Plans (FY 82 and FY 83) should have been canceled. The medical center should have reevaluated all of the proposed projects to determine which projects or portions of projects had been affected by the development of the revised master plan and the Lenwood Division's eligibility as an historical site. The reevaluation of these projects would have reduced the possibility of unnecessary construction work being performed and could have resulted in cost avoidance of as much as $3.1 million.

Veterans were enrolled in the Ambulatory Care Program prior to the physician documenting their medical determination and justification. Veterans enrolled in the Outpatient Treatment/Non-Service Connected Program were receiving treatment for conditions not related to the condition for which they were hospitalized. Veterans in both programs were not discharged from the programs after a professional determination had been made by the physician that the patients' condition had stabilized. There were two VA employees enrolled in the Ambulatory Care Program. These conditions were caused by: (1) medical determinations justifying the enrollment of veterans into the Ambulatory Care Program were not always being required during the admissions process; (2) veterans are cross-consulted to other clinics for treatment of conditions not related to the conditions for which they were enrolled in the program; (3) the lack of an effective control system to account for veterans in the outpatient treatment programs; and, (4) Ambulatory Care Committee not ensuring that the veterans enrolled and maintained in the Ambulatory Care Program comply with VA criteria. This had resulted in about 3,437 unauthorized treatments costing an estimated $331,842 during fiscal year 1981, and approximately 1,088 unauthorized treatments during the first quarter of fiscal year 1982, costing an estimated $116,253. During the remainder of fiscal year 1982, it was estimated that a potential $299,308 could be saved by complying with VA criteria.

During fiscal year 1981 and the first quarter, fiscal year 1982, the medical center's total outpatient workload was 90,790 and 22,417 visits, respectively. These figures represent service connected and non-service connected visits. The cost for the outpatient treatment programs was $8,766,452 for fiscal year 1981 and $2,395,263 for the first quarter, fiscal year 1982. As of December 31, 1981, there were 2,723 veterans on the Ambulatory Care (A/C) roll and 4,639 veterans on the outpatient treatment non-service connected (OPT/NSC) roll. MAS personnel estimated that the A/C and OPT/NSC programs' workload during fiscal year 1981 was about 12,436 and 21,175 visits respectively. The estimated workload during the first quarter, fiscal year 1982, for A/C program was 3,010 visits and 5,124 visits for the OPT/NSC program.

Using statistical sampling techniques, we selected 142 of the 7,362 veterans enrolled in the outpatient programs (67 A/C and 75 OPT/NSC), to determine if the veterans met the criteria to be enrolled in the outpatient treatment programs and if the documentation justified the number of visits. We used a 95 percent confidence level. We received comments from the Associate Chief of Staff for Ambulatory Care (ACOS/AC) and the Chief, Medical Administration Service (MAS) on the veterans whom: (1) we believed to have been enrolled in the A/C Program prior to the physician documenting his medical determination and justification and, (2) veterans enrolled in the OPT/NSC Program who were receiving treatment for conditions not related to the condition for which they were hospitalized. The purpose of obtaining these comments was to determine why these veterans were on the A/C and OPT/NSC rolls. We compared procedures used by the medical center for treating non-service connected veterans on the outpatient program rolls to the criteria set forth in VA and DM&S policies and procedures.

Title 38, United States Code, Section 612, stated in part:

(f) The Administrator, within the limits of Veterans Administration facilities, may furnish medical services for any disability on an outpatient or ambulatory basis—(1) to any veteran eligible for hospital care under section 610 of this title (A) where such services are reasonably necessary for preparation for, or (to the extent that the facilities are available) to obviate the need of, hospital admission, or (B) where such a veteran has been furnished hospital care and such medical services are reasonably necessary to complete treatment incident to such hospital care (for a period not in excess of twelve months after discharge from in-hospital treatment, except where the Administrator finds that a longer period is required by virtue of the disability being treated) . . .

Interim Issue 10–73–42 provided the following instructions for enrolling and maintaining veterans in the A/C program:

Ambulatory care may be provided to veterans . . . when:

. . . a medical determination indicates that such care is . . . necessary. . . . This determination should be made by the examining or treating physicians, and should be based on his professional judgment that the medical services to be provided are necessary to treat a condition which would normally require bed care, or which, if untreated, could reasonably be expected to require such care in the immediate future. This would not, however, cover routine maintenance treatment of chronic conditions which do not normally require hospital care, such as daily insulin injections for diabetes, administration of anti-hypertensive drugs, etc. Such determination will be recorded on VA Form 10–10m, Medical Certificate, by the examining physician.

. . . Ambulatory Care will be terminated when the patient's condition has improved or stabilized to the extent that further care is no longer required to satisfy the purpose for which it was initiated.

Department of Medicine and Surgery Manual M-1, Part I, Chapter 17, dated November 17, 1981, provided the following instructions for enrolling and maintaining veterans in the OPT/NSC program:

. . . Certain NSC veterans may be furnished outpatient care that is reasonably necessary to complete an episode of VA authorized inpatient care.

. . . Not all patients released from inpatient care will require outpatient care.

. . . This program will provide medical benefits for the NSC veteran requiring outpatient care as a part of a period of hospitalization will be administered in such a way as to encourage patients to return to their family physicians for continuation of treatment at no expense to VA.

. . . entitlement will cease and treatment will be terminated when (1) it is professionally determined that the condition for which hospital care was provided has become stable or (2) there is no longer a close relationship to the preceding episode of hospitalization.

. . . Outpatient treatment of patients placed in the program will be limited to the conditions for which hospitalization was furnished.

Ambulatory Care Program: Using statistical sampling techniques, we determined that about 1,625 (60 percent) of the 2,723 veterans on the A/C roll were enrolled in the program without the physician documenting his medical determination and justification for placing the veterans in the program. We statistically determined that approximately 284 (10 percent) of the 2,723 veterans were not discharged from the program after a professional determination established that the patient's condition had stabilized. The following schedule shows veterans on the A/C program where the physician did not document his medical determination and justification.

Schedule of Four Veterans in A/C Program

Veteran	Date Enrolled	#Visits FY 81	FY 82	Remarks
A	04/23/81	10	6	Veteran admitted to the program for arthritis and poor circulation. Veteran received A/C treatment at seven clinics for the following conditions: shortness of breath, rash, obesity, lump on face, impacted wisdom tooth, and microscopic hematuric urology. The veteran made 7 visits after 8/10/81 when the Chief, Ambulatory Care, said veteran was ineligible and veteran was picked up on the rolls of a non-VA hospital.

Veteran	Date Enrolled	#Visits FY 81	FY 82	Remarks
B	04/20/76	11	4	Veteran admitted to the program for ulcerated area on left arm, diagnosed as basal cell carcinoma. Resolved 8/17/77. Veteran received A/C treatment at 5 other clinics for for the following conditions: high blood pressure, gout, renal stone, leg pains, and arthritis. The veteran made 11 visits after he told Social Work Service on 12/12/80 he could maintain his medical condition with a private physician.
C	11/14/74	19	4	Veteran admitted to the program for advanced periodontal disease. Veteran received A/C treatment at 3 other clinics for the following conditions: hypertension, warts, and allergy.
D	06/01/81	3	1	Veteran admitted to the program because he wanted to get his medicine from the VA. All conditions were diagnosed as stable on the date enrolled due to treatment by veteran's private physician.

We identified two veterans employed at VAMC Augusta who were enrolled in the A/C program. These cases are discussed below.

Veteran Number One is a social worker for the medical center and is a GS-11, step 6, who earns $27,496 per year. The Chief, MAS, told us this employee was seen as a veteran and the veteran certified on the Application for Medical Benefits that he was unable to defray the necessary expenses of medical care when he applied for treatment on September 30, 1981. We found that this veteran was not on sick or annual leave during the periods he attended clinic (9/30/81, 10/23/81, and 10/30/81). The cost of this care was $176. Veteran Number 1 also had Blue Cross/Blue Shield high option health insurance.

Veteran Number Two was treated in the A/C program four times (12/18/79, 1/8/80, 9/28/81, and 10/6/81). His medical record was documented to show he retired from military service at the grade of E-7. He is currently a GS-4, step 1, and receives a salary of $11,490 per year. He was also covered by CHAMPUS. The cost of his outpatient care was $201.

We believed these conditions represented prima facie evidence that these veterans had the ability to defray the necessary expenses of the medical care provided and we believed the Medical Center Director should have taken action to ascertain if the veteran/employees had the ability to pay. The medical center had the latitude to pursue this based on the instructions contained on the VA Form 10–10 (Application for Medical Benefits), which states:

> . . . The VA will make the final determinations of whether to provide the needed care based on the following factors:
>
> 1. The applicant's monthly income from all sources. (Including that of the spouse.)
> 2. The cash value of the applicant's ready assets other than home of residence (cash, savings deposits, stocks, bonds, property, etc.).
> 3. The applicant's entitlement to medical care under an insurance liability of third parties in accident cases and CHAMPUS or Medicare coverage.

Outpatient Treatment/Non-Service Connected Program: Using statistical sampling techniques, we determined that about 1,113 (24 percent) of the 4,639 veterans were receiving treatment for conditions not related to the condition for which they were hospitalized. We also statistically determined that about 989 (21 percent) of the 4,639 veterans were still enrolled in the program after the attending physician had assessed their medical condition as stabilized. The following schedule shows four veterans on the OPT/NSC program receiving treatment for conditions not related to the condition for which they were hospitalized.

Schedule of Four Veterans in OPT/NSC Program

Veteran	Date Enrolled	Number of Visits FY 81	FY 82	Remarks
A	11/07/78	13	0	Veteran was an inpatient for degenerative arthritis of the right knee. Veteran's condition was stabilized on 1/4/79. OPT/NSC treatment has ben received at 7 other clinics for the following conditions: weight reduction, acne, blackout spells, and angina evaluation. The veteran made 10 visits after Social Work Service determined the veteran's income exceeded $13,800 annually.
B	10/24/79	17	5	Veteran was an inpatient for orthostatic hypertension. Veteran's condition was stabilized on 7/9/81. OPT/NSC treatment has been received at 7 other clinics for following conditions: basal cell carcinoma, skin specimens lab work, hernia, adhesive capsulitis, shoulder pain, and osteoarthritis.

Veteran	Date Enrolled	Number of Visits FY 81	FY 82	Remarks
C	05/04/79	13	1	Veteran was an inpatient for back muscle strain and eye muscle disease. Problem noted as clinically stable on 7/9/81. OPT/NSC treatment has been received at 3 other clinics for the following conditions: swollen ankle and fractured arm.
D	03/10/81	3	3	Veteran was an inpatient for bursitis and coronary bypass. Veteran's conditions were stabilized on 6/24/81. OPT/NSC treatment has been received at 3 other clinics for the following conditions: hearing loss and back pain.

During the audit, we requested comments from the ACOS/AC and the Chief, MAS, on 65 of the 142 cases we reviewed. These included cases where the physician did not document his medical determination justifying enrolling veterans in the A/C program, veterans who were not discharged after they were assessed by the attending physician as stabilized, and veterans who were treated for conditions unrelated to their episode of hospitalization. We received written comments and discussed our findings with the responsible officials to give them an opportunity to explain any mitigating circumstances. Generally, the comments we received did not adequately address the issues we raised. These members of Disorganized Crime denied responsibility for monitoring the problems we identified, refused to comment, or provided extraneous comments.

The reason the medical certificates (VA Form 10–10m) have lacked the required documentation of the medical determination justifying placing the veterans in the A/C program was due to the ACOS/AC not enforcing this requirement during the admissions process. The ACOS/AC told us that MAS routinely picks up a 10–10m on ambulatory care if they were referred to a clinic or if they returned on a second visit, they were placed on ambulatory care status. The Assistant Chief, MAS, told us if the 10–10m was not "explicitly" documented, that the veteran was placed in the A/C program to obviate the need for bed care, that it was implied as such when the veteran was referred to clinic. Interim issue 10–73–74 required the medical determination to be documented on the VA Form 10–10m to place the veteran in the A/C program. Also, we found that in processing the veteran into the A/C program, a Health Benefits Advisor (HBA) received the medical certificate, established a medical record, and enrolled the veteran into the A/C program. However, the HBA had not always obtained the required medical determination from the physician before placing the veteran into the program.

On January 5, 1980, the Clinical Executive Board assigned the ACOS/AC the authority and responsibility for carrying out established policies and procedures and providing direction for the outpatient programs. Medical Center Policy

Memorandum Number 11C-1–80, dated August 13, 1980, established the Ambulatory Care Committee to monitor the A/C program. The ACOS/AC was the chairman of that committee. The ACOS/AC had not provided the required direction to ensure that veterans whose conditions had stabilized were discharged from the clinic rolls. The A/C Committee had not monitored the programs to ensure veterans enrolled and maintained in the A/C program comply with VA criteria.

The Chief, MAS, was responsible for establishing controls over patients in the outpatient programs. The Chief, MAS, had not maintained an effective control system to account for veterans in the outpatient treatment programs. MAS was responsible for screening and referring for discharge veterans who had remained in the A/C program and OPT/NSC program in excess of one visit and in excess of twelve months, respectively. Using statistical sampling techniques, we found that an estimated 568 (21 percent) of the 2,723 veterans in the A/C program had been scheduled beyond the second clinic visit without having their record screened for possible discharge. We also found that an estimated 990 (21 percent) of the 4,639 veterans in the OPT/NSC program had been enrolled in excess of twelve months without being screened and referred for evaluation for discharge.

The veterans were also receiving unauthorized treatments because the ACOS/AC had established procedures that allowed veterans to be treated for conditions not related to the reason they were enrolled in the A/C or OPT/NSC program. For example, veterans were cross-consulted to other clinics for treatment of conditions not related to the condition for which they were enrolled in the program and these veterans were followed for long periods of time. The ACOS/AC established the procedure of not completing a new VA Form 10–10m, Medical Certificate, during the A/C Committee meeting of May 27, 1980. According to the minutes of the meeting, the ACOS/AC stated:

> . . . On checking into the procedures for making out a new 10–10m for each complaint of the patient, this seems to be double work. We will continue to use consult forms as we are now doing.

The minutes of the A/C Committee meeting, dated December 23, 1980, were documented to show that a doctor from Neurology Service had stated he was told he could no longer refer patients that he was following for a neurological condition to the admission area for hypertension or other minor illnesses. The ACOS/AC replied that the admissions area was strictly for admissions and the doctor should fill out a consult form and refer the patient to MAS who would contact the appropriate physician. Because of these procedures, the veterans were not required to complete a VA Form 10–10r, Reapplication for Medical Benefits, and the physicians were not completing a VA Form 10–10m, Medical Certificate. Consequently, the authority and justification for treating the veterans for other conditions had not been established (at a high cost to you).

Using statistical sampling techniques, we determined that approximately 3,437 (4 percent) of the 90,790 outpatient visits during fiscal year 1981 and

1,088 (5 percent) of the 22,417 outpatient visits during the first quarter, fiscal year 1982, were for treatment of medical conditions other than the condition for which the veterans were put on the rolls, for conditions that had stabilized, or treatments were provided without appropriate processing. The cost associated with these visits visits was $331,842 for fiscal year 1981 and $116,253 for the first quarter, fiscal year 1982. We also determined that if the A/C and the OPT/NSC programs had been properly controlled, the total outpatient program could have been reduced by an estimated 3,226 visits. The reduction in the program would have resulted in cost savings of about $299,308 during the remaining quarters in fiscal year 1982.

Selection of Architect/Engineer firms and award of Architect/Engineer contracts were not supported. Architect/Engineer (A/E) firms had not been properly evaluated by the Architectural Engineering Evaluation Board (AEEB). This was caused by Engineering Service personnel circumventing the requirements established in October 1981 for A/E firms to be evaluated by the AEEB. Also, procedures had not been implemented that would allow the AEEB to objectively rank A/E firms. As a result, there were no assurances that the most qualified firms were being selected to provide the medical center with A/E services.

During fiscal year 1981, there were five A/E contracts, valued at $69,158.30, awarded to A/E firms. As of February 1, 1982, there were four A/E contracts, valued at $72,600, in the process of being awarded. Also, Central Office was developing a new master plan for the Lenwood Division. Once the plan was completed, the need for numerous construction projects would have developed and the cost of A/E services that would have been needed could exceed $1.7 million.

During the audit survey, we noted that a contracting specialist had filed a memorandum in the A/E contract files which stated that:

> The terms, conditions and price on the contract were negotiated by Engineering Service without knowledge or presence of any Supply or contracting people. The procedure for negotiating A/E contracts has been told to Engineering as well as being sent in writing, and they refuse to do the A/E contracts in accordance with FPR or VAPR regulations.

We reviewed procedures used to award all five A/E contracts that had the memorandum filed in the contract folders. We reviewed one A/E contract, valued at $24,800, that was awarded on September 28, 1979 (fiscal year 1979). We reviewed the procedures that were being used to award four A/E contracts, valued at $72,600, for construction projects that were scheduled to start during fiscal year 1982. We contacted two of the three A/E firms that were evaluated by the AEEB for one of the A/E contracts that was to be awarded. In addition, we interviewed the Chief, Engineering Service, the Chief, Supply Service, and the contracting officer.

Our review of the six A/E contracts issued during fiscal years 1979 and 1981 showed that: (1) the A/E firms had not been properly evaluated by the

AEEB; (2) that the Director had not authorized negotiations with the top-rated firms; and, (3) the Chief, Engineering Service, had negotiated the contracts without the knowledge of the contracting officers.

The VA Procurement Regulations (VAPR) provided that an Architectural Engineering Evaluation Board (AEEB) be established to evaluate the professional and technical qualifications of A/E firms interested in providing VA A/E services. The composition of the board would include the Senior Contracting Officer, Engineering Officer, and the responsible contracting officer. The evaluation criteria required that values be assigned to factors in determining the relative qualifications of the firms. VA Form 08–3375 (Architect/Engineering Evaluation Board Evaluation Criteria and Scoring) had the factors that should have been used to evaluate the A/E firms. The AEEB may have adjusted the values after interviewing the A/E firms. After firms had been evaluated, the three most qualified firms, in order of rankings, were to be submitted to the Director for approval before the contracting officer entered into negotiation with the top-rated A/E firm.

The Chief, Engineering Service, selected all six of the A/E firms that were awarded the A/E contracts valued at $93,958. Our review of the six A/E contracts showed that there was no documentation that indicated the firms had been evaluated by the AEEB. The AEEB recommendation was submitted to the Director on two of six contracts. However, the selection of the firms was based on the Chief, Engineering Service, recommendations because there was not an established AEEB at the medical center prior to October 1981.

The Chief, Engineering Service, negotiated the cost of the contracts without the knowledge of the contracting officer who finalized the contract. VA form 7–2237 (Request, Turn-in, and Receipt for Property or Services) was used by using services to request that a procurement action be initiated by appropriate Supply Service personnel. However, the VA Forms 7–2237 for five of the six A/E contracts awarded were prepared from one to seven days after the dates of the A/E firms' proposals and the amount on the VA Forms 7–2237, with the exception of one, agreed with the amounts proposed by the A/E firms. Details are:

Contract Number (V509P-)	VA Form 7–2237 Date Prepared	VA Form 7–2237 Estimated Amount	A/E Firm's Proposal Date	A/E Firm's Proposal Amount	Number of Days
3680	01/27/81	$26,850.00	01/21/81	$26,850.00	6
3450	09/25/79	24,800.00	09/18/79	24,800.00	7
3681	02/03/81	20,599.80	02/02/81	20,599.80	1
3682	02/06/81	11,050.00	02/02/81	13,350.00	4
3679	01/27/81	9,107.50	01/26/81	9,107.50	1
3566	03/24/80	1,551.00	NOT IN CONTRACT FILE		-

Even though the former Supply Officer was told of these procurement deficiencies, no action was taken to correct the contracting procedures. The Director stated that he was told by the Central Office Supply Technical Review Team that one A/E contract had some problems, but he believed that his new Supply Officer had probably corrected the problems.

The medical center had established an AEEB in October 1981. However, as of February 1, 1982, there were only four A/E contracts in the process of being awarded to A/E firms. Three of the contracts were being negotiated with minority small businesses under the 8a Program. We also noted that the Chief, Engineering Service, had submitted a memorandum, dated December 28, 1981, with the names of the three top-rated firms to the Director for approval on the fourth A/E contract valued at $24,400. The Engineering Officer told us that the AEEB had met and that the Supply Officer and contracting officer attended the meetings; however, there were no minutes of the meeting. The Supply Officer and the contracting officer told us that they were not at the AEEB meeting. The contracting officer also stated that he did not know that he was on the AEEB. In addition, on February 8, 1982, we contacted two of the three firms that were listed in the memorandum and found that they had discussions concerning the A/E contract with the Chief, Engineering Service, and project engineer.

Even though the medical center had established an AEEB, the board had not implemented the use of VA Form 08–3375 for the purpose of evaluating A/E firms that were interested in providing the medical center A/E services. Consequently, there were no assurances that the same factors were being considered when the A/E firms were being evaluated.

Based on the method used to select the A/E firms in December 1981, we concluded that adequate controls had not been established to ensure that the AEEB was properly evaluating the A/E firms and that the three most qualified firms were being selected to negotiate for the required A/E services. We also concluded that there were no assurances that the Engineering Officer was not negotiating with A/E firms since he had circumvented the AEEB requirements that were established in October 1981. The need to establish good A/E contracting procedures would be more imperative since a new master plan was being developed by Central Office. This established the need for numerous construction projects that could result in A/E services that could cost more than $1.7 million.

Though the final audit report did discuss questionable negotiations and awards for A/E contracts, a more serious finding was dropped from the final report. Due to its sensitivity this finding was referred to the IG's Office of Investigation. No action had been taken on it prior to December 1983 when I left Disorganized Crime.

The dropped finding dealt with negligence in the administration of contracts, which may have cost the VA significant amounts. This situation was caused by: (1) the Engineering Officer establishing a "sweetheart" contract with a personal friend and, as a result, not performing his duties as a Resident Engineer in an acceptable manner, (2) several individuals negotiated contracts without authority, (3) acceptable controls over contracting officers had not been established to insure that goods and services contracted for were necessary and received by the VA, and (4) several employees falsified procurement documents in order to circumvent VA and Federal Procurement Regulations (FPR). As a result, these contracts were inappropriately negotiated and administered.

We reviewed 37 of 48 contracts valued over $10,000 awarded during the fifteen-month period October 1, 1980, through November 30, 1981. On 23 of the 37 contracts, there were problems. In addition, we reviewed 67 other contracts that came to our attention through employee interviews, referrals from the Office of Investigations, IG, and survey work performed on work orders and preventive maintenance. The 67 contracts were either below $10,000 or awarded prior to October 1, 1980. The total value of the 104 contracts we reviewed was over $8.2 million. The total value of the universe of 115 contracts was over $9.1 million.

In conjunction with the Office of Investigation, IG, we determined that the Engineering Officer had established at least one "sweetheart" contract with a personal friend. This contract was for consulting services to act as Resident Engineer in lieu of the Engineering Officer after the construction of the new Downtown Division. We found the description of services to be performed inadequate, documentation was not maintained to support what was billed to the VA, and little actual services were rendered by the consultant. Total payments made to the consultant exceeded $9,900. After we brought this to the Director's attention, he discontinued further consulting services on this contract.

The Engineering Officer was negotiating contracts outside his responsibility. We have discussed this in the previous finding. In addition, we also found employees in Social Work Service negotiated contracts for Community Nursing Home Care and a key-and-lock survey was negotiated by a staff liaison in the Director's office. The above individuals were not contracting officers. Only contracting officers were authorized to enter into and administer contracts for personal property and nonpersonal services. Generally, these contracts were inappropriate because the terms and specifications of the contracts were ambiguous or very general.

Acceptable controls had not been established over the contracting officers to insure that goods and services contracted for were necessary and received by the VA. We discussed earlier the six architect-engineer contracts. The Engineering Specialist responsible for monitoring these A/E contracts did not document when the A/E firm made site visits. We were told that the drawings and specifications given Engineering Service by the A/E firm were proof that site visits had been made because the service could not have been performed without a site visit. The Engineering Specialist did check and recommend for approval invoices for payments of $65,677.60 submitted by the A/E firm for the contracted work, which included six site visits. In addition to lack of documentation for site visits, progress reports did not contain percentages of completion.

We also found a lack of documentation in the receipt of goods and services for five preventive-maintenance contracts, V509P-3626, V509P-3648, V509P-3658, V509P-3645, and V509P-3574, to support payments of invoices totaling $46,024. We found that 100 inspections were required of the five contracts, but only thirty-three were documented in the Engineering Service files as service performed. There were no logs maintained to show time and dates of visits from companies providing required service. Twelve of the thirty-three service tickets were inadequate because of service documented as received were signed by unauthorized VA staff to certify services had been received. Voucher Audit did not detect unauthorized signatures certifying services had been received nor did Voucher Audit determine if the contract amounts ahd been exceeded in the payments that had been made previously by the VA.

Several employees falsified procurement documents to circumvent VA and Federal Procurement Regulations. Fifty-five contracts, with a total value exceeding $3.5 million, were awarded with falsified documents in the contract files. Generally, these contracts dealt with Invitation for Bid (IFB) procurements. Though the IFB's were listed on the Abstract for Bids or Informal Proposals (VA Form 07–2232) as having been sent to several vendors, the IFB's in fact were never sent. As a result, the one bid received and awarded was to the only vendor who had actually received an IFB. Also, the Synopsis of contract awards was falsified to show it had been mailed; however, in reality it was never mailed. Though VA Procurement Regulations allowed an award when only one bid was received, this was allowed only if adequate competition had been solicited. Because of the grossly negligent manner in which these contracts were awarded, we believe they were inappropriate.

So in spite of the fact that procurement documents had been falsified for $3.5 million of contracts, it was never published. For at least the next year, no further investigation was performed. Maybe some action was taken after I left, but I'll leave that for you to decide.

My last audit was at the VA hospital in Miami. It finally hit me after all those years that I was not only wasting my time, but that by drawing a salary, I was contributing to the visuals that are the lifeblood of Disorganized Crime. Miami was no worse than the other organizations of Disorganized Crime, but it had its own style. The VA Medical Center (VAMC), Miami, Florida, was audited from April 19, 1982 through June 8, 1982. The report was published in July 1982. VAMC Miami was constructed in 1968, with operating beds as of May 2, 1982, consisting of 157 psychiatric, 66 intermedidate medicine, 275 medical, and 206 surgical, for a total of 704. There also was a 120-bed Nursing Home Care Unit. The planned Fiscal Year 1982 Budget was over $76 million.

Improvement in the management of Prosthetic Service could have saved $128,000 and eliminated abuse of the Prosthetic Program. Inadequate supervision of Prosthetic Service by the service chief had resulted in a large amount of waste and abuse. This inadequate supervision was caused by a lack of planning, direction, internal controls, and failure to follow established regulations. As a result, we found: (1) excessive stockage of prosthetic items ahd accumulated because of unnecessary purchases, no physical inventory, and lack of coordinated buying by the two outpatient clinics and the main facility; (2) the automotive and adaptive equipment program lacked internal controls to prevent abuse from occurring; and, (3) the loaning of prosthetic items had not been effectively controlled. As a result, we found $128,000 of excessive inventory and abuse of the automotive and adaptive equipment program.

During our survey of the Prosthetic Service, we observed a lack of internal controls. In addition, little direction had been given by the service chief. For example, only two Medical Center Policy Memorandums had been issued, one in 1971 and the other in 1979. The purpose of both was to establish a committee. No internal service policies had been made by the chief. We also found no planning for the service, such as size of the inventory, identification of deceased veterans who had received loaned prosthetic items,and the amount of verification needed for payment of high dollar repairs and purchase of automotive adaptive equipment. We found no evidence of any follow-up by the service chief to determine if: (1) the inventory was overstocked; (2) the automotive and adaptive equipment program was subject to abuse; and, (3) the loaning of prosthetic items was conducted in an economical and businesslike manner.

We discussed our concerns with the Chief, Prosthetic Service. The Chief appreciated our suggestions to improve the service's operation; however, he felt that only an increase in staff (sounds familiar?) would permit the implementation of the recommendation without affecting patient care. We believed that implementing required internal controls and performing basic supervisory functions would have resulted in more economical and efficient patient care with no reduction in quality.

We found excessive stockage of prosthetic items had accumulated because of unnecessary purchases, no physical inventory, and lack of coordinated buying by the two outpatient clinics and the main facility. The following schedule shows the purchases for prosthetic items for the eighteen-month period from October 1, 1980, through March 31, 1982:

Schedule of Purchases for Prosthetic Items

Location	Fiscal Year	
	1981	1982 (3/31/82)
Main Facility	$1,122,940	$480,651
Riviera Beach	130,948	74,243
Oakland Park	4,080	33,942
Total	$1,257,968	$588,836

No physical inventory as required by the VA had been taken prior to the arrival of the audit team. The Chief, Prosthetic Service, estimated that the inventory was composed of 125 line items valued at $60,000. At our request, the Director had an inventory conducted during the four-day period from April 3–6, 1982. The actual inventory was found to be composed of 1,023 line items valued at $279,434. We accepted for audit purposes, one-year stockage onhand. Using statistical sampling techniques, we project that the overstockages were in 637 line items and were valued at $128,718.

Schedule of Overstocked Prosthetic Items

Item	Onhand	Amount Due In	One-Year Usage	Units	Overstockage Amount	Years
Abdominal Binders	43	40	20	63	$ 778	3
Acromioclavicular Splint	39	0	0	39	792	39
Dextrometer	16	0	2	14	3,337	7
Hinged Knee Cage	24	12	0	36	293	36
Jobst Waist High Stocking	30	0	0	30	599	30

We were not able to determine if there was an overage or shortage of the inventory because the perpetual-inventory system had never been established, as required by the VA. There was no locator system established for the inventory. The Chief, Prosthetic Service, had no established safety levels, reorder points, or economic order quantities, as required by the VA. Each of the three locations was independently purchasing prosthetic items without knowledge of what was onhand at the other locations. As a result, overstockages in one location were not being reduced by transfers to the other locations.

We found the automotive and adaptive equipment program lacked internal controls. We reviewed records of 16 of the 110 veterans who had received new automotive adaptive equipment or repairs to previously acquired adaptive equipment during fiscal year 1982 as of March 31, 1982. In addition, we reviewed the records of the chief and assistant chief of Prosthetic Service. The cost of the repairs was $59,000, and the new automotive adaptive equipment cost was $55,000. We found that 12 of the 15 veterans did not have prescriptions in their medical records for adaptive equipment costing $9,292 (CB radios, air conditioning, etc.). Prescriptions were required by the VA.

It was to the veterans' economic advantage to have repairs made and new adaptive equipment installed in their old automobile before they trade in on a new automobile. Each eligible veteran or serviceman was permitted payment of, or reimbursement for, automotive adaptive equipment for three voluntary automobile replacement transactions within a two-year cycle. Only one automobile may be owned at any one time if the veteran wishes replacement, reinstallation, or repair of adaptive equipment. We contacted the Department of Motor Vehicles, State of Florida, and found that 3 of the 16 veterans we reviewed had not transferred title of their previous automobile when they purchased a new automobile.

We found there were 218 VA Forms 10–1439, Prosthetics Inventory Card-Loaner Items—Medical, with a total value of $284,369. Loaned items included televisions, electric wheelchairs, scooters, etc. All these items had been loaned on an indefinite basis. No equipment had been loaned on a temporary basis. We found that no follow-up was performed, as required by the VA. Also, there was no action noted on any of the VA Forms 10–1439 to show any repairs, complaints, reissues, condemnation, or recovery of any of the items. We requested Target

M-11 printouts from the VA Regional Office at St. Petersburg, Florida, and obtained 151 of the 197 (76 percent) requested. In 46 cases ($73,362) where M-11 printouts were not obtained, we performed no further audit tests to determine if the information provided to target was incorrect or if the equipment was loaned to a nonveteran. We found that the control over and accountability of the loaned items was inadequate. For example, over $67,000 of items loaned do not have the current address of the location of the item on the VA Form 10–1439.

Schedule of Target M-11 Printouts

	Veterans	Loaned Item Value	Value Percent
Received M-11 Printouts			
Address of M-11 Matches VA Form 10–1439	92	$137,538	48
Address Does Not Match VA Form 10–1439	53	67,838	24
Deceased Veteran	6	5,631	2
Subtotal	151	$211,007	74
Did Not Receive M-11 Printouts	46	73,362	26
Total of VA Forms 10–1439	197	$284,369	100

In our audit of the sixteen veterans sampled in our audit of automotive and adaptive equipment, we found three had received loaned prosthetic items per their VA Forms 10–2319. VA Forms 10–1439 had not been prepared for the loaned items received by two of these three veterans. This further weakens the control over and accountability of the loaning of prosthetic items.

Problems with prosthetics items, of course, were just not limited to the VA hospital in Miami. Another audit team audited the VA Rehabilitation Engineering Center (VAREC) in New York during 1982. Part of VAREC's mission was to manufacture and distribute orthopedic footwear and prosthetic/orthotic devices. The review disclosed substantive management and operating problems in most functional areas. The auditors attributed these conditions to management's failure, both at VAREC and at higher levels in VA, to establish well-defined program goals and to monitor operations so as to assure that the goals were accomplished.

The review raised serious concerns about the effectiveness of spending nearly $10 million annually in VAREC operating costs. For example, the auditors found that inventory and stock controls were inadequate. Of the $6.5 million inventory of prosthetic/orthotic components, over $1.3 million were not usable. A test of the inventory records of one component, electric hands, found that 725 were purchased between 1972 and 1977 at a cost to you of over $622,000. At the time of the audit, physical count showed there were 398 in stock at VAREC, 55 percent, and at least 332 had never been issued. Based upon average cost, this stock was valued at $340,000. Inventory records showed, however, that 501 components should have been in stock. Significant discrepancies between inventory records and physical count existed for most line items in VAREC's inventory. There were 680 components in stock at the time of audit, which were powered by nikel cadmium battery packs, which had to be periodically recharged to remain serviceable. These battery packs cost approximately $90 each. During the audit, samples were tested and would not hold a charge (surprise, surprise). Let's go back to the Miami audit.

Internal controls were so weak as to invite fraud, waste, and abuse in the million dollar non-VA hospitalization program. Weak internal controls in the non-VA hospitalization program had resulted in payment for inappropriate treatments, duplicate payments, and overpayments for treatments provided. As a result, we questioned $102,057 of the $122,002 (83 percent) of invoices paid by the VA.

The VA authorizes (38 U.S.C. 17), in certain circumstances, to contract with public or private hospitals for the care of veterans. The VA authorizes the admission of a patient to a public or private hospital at VA expense only when: (1) the medical condition necessitates emergency care; (2) a long distance of travel was involved; and, (3) the nature of the treatment required made using public or private facilities instead of VA facilities necessary or economically advisable. Authorizations for care by non-VA hospitals at VA expense must be authorized in advance. In emergencies, this authorization could have been obtained if the veteran, or someone on his behalf, notified the VA within three days after admission to a non-VA hospital. A veteran would be treated in non-VA hospitals only until the patient's condition stabilized or improved enough to permit transfer to a VA medical facility. The only exception was when the veteran was scheduled for discharge from a public or private hospital and movement to a VA facility was impractical.

The eligibility criteria was divided into two different classes. The treatment was considered "prior authorization" if the VA was notified within three days of admission to a non-VA hospital. The treatment was considered "not previously authorized" (unauthorized) when the claim for payment was received by the VA within two years of when the services were provided.

The following schedule provides background information concerning this program:

**Background Information Showing Size of Non-VA
Hospitalization Program at VAMC, Miami**

Item	1980	1981	1982 (3/31/82)
Total Authorized Claims	471	512	257
Total Unauthorized Claims	24	76	30
Cost Authorized Claims	$973,565	$1,133,808	$795,248
Cost Unauthorized Claims	22,844	162,440	42,433
Amount of Original Budget	536,514	1,109,895	764,706
Amount Spent	996,409	1,296,248	837,681

274

Internal controls had been seriously weakened by the following three causes: (1) there was no verification of the fees charged to the VA, and there was inadequate documentation to support appropriateness of treatments performed and the fees charged; (2) little daily physician follow-up was performed to encourage patient transfer; and, (3) financial and budgetary controls were weak.

There was no verification of the fees charged. We sampled twenty-three claims made during fiscal year 1982 ending March 31, 1982. The sixteen authorized claims were all over $6,000, and the seven unauthorized claims were all over $1,500. The value of the twenty-three claims was $194,006. We obtained invoices for the twenty-three claims we sampled from the Data Processing Center, Austin, Texas. We audited $122,002 (63 percent) of the $194,006 sampled and discussed our results with the Director. The Director acknowledged that the condition was improper and was widespread, and that future gathering of evidence could be avoided by the audit team. As a result, we limited our review to the $122,002 worth of claims. We found improprieties in payments with the claims audited as shown in the following schedule:

Schedule of Improprieties Found by Audit Team
In Audit of Non-VA Hospitalization Program

Claims with Duplicate Payments	$ 4,587
Claims with Payment Exceeded VA Established Limits	4,110
Claims with Lack of Documentation to Support Payment	93,360
Claims with Appropriate Payment	19,945
Total	$122,002

Example 1.—A duplicate payment was made to the Miami Heart Institute of $4,587, which was certified for payment by Medical Administration Service (MAS) on January 11, 1982. A portion of the same service was certified on February 1, 1982, and the Miami Heart Institute was paid $3,377. Example 2.—A veteran was treated for a ruptured aneurysm from December 2–10, 1981. A surgeon billed the VA and was paid $2,900. The authorized maximum allowed per VA Manual M-1, part 1, appendix A, was only $2,400. Example 3.—The Martin Memorial Hospital billed the VA and was paid $10,927.11 for the same period of treatment and the same veteran, as in Example 2 above. The only documentation sent to MAS was the Authorization and Invoice for Medical and Hospital Services, VA Form 10–7078. As a result, there was no assurance that the surgeon fees (in Example 2) were not included in this invoice. Also, there was no way to determine if the services the VA was billed for were those which were authorized.

Inadequate documentation was also found in our review of the discharge summaries, which were required by the VA from the private hospital. Without discharge summaries, it was impossible to determine if the treatments provided were appropriate and should have been paid by the VA. For the claims we

275

sampled, only fifteen of the twenty-three discharge summaries were in the patients' medical records when the invoices were paid.

Little Daily Physician Follow-up. We found little physician follow-up as required by the VA. This follow-up would include:

a. continuous physician-to-physician contact in an effort to get veterans admitted to the non-VA hospitals to transfer to the VA facility;
b. timely transfer after the veteran's condition had stabilized; and,
c. the requirement in the authorization for timely transfer when the patient's condition had stabilized.

The following schedule shows the results of our review in the sixteen authorized claims where transfers may have been possible:

Schedule of Follow-up

No Action by Anyone to Transfer Patient	4
No Action by Physician to Transfer Patient	6
Action by Physician to Transfer Patient	6
Total	16

In none of the sixteen cases were letters sent with the timeliness of transfer requirement documented, notifying attending physicians. The VA's contract with the private hospital, the VA Form 10–7078, also did not limit the authorization to when the veteran's condition stabilized and he could be transferred to the VA facility. Also, during the initial contact, the timeliness requirement was not conveyed.

Lack of physician follow-up may also cause inappropriate treatments to be provided at VA expense. We identified one veteran who refused to be transferred to the VA facility, even though his condition had stabilized and he could have been safely transferred. Medical Administration Service certified for payment the entire stay by this veteran, including the period after he had stabilized. Included in this payment was $460 for psychological tests, consultations, and nine psychotherapy sessions. The veteran, however, had been admitted for chest pains.

276

Financial and budgetary controls were weak. We found that the Status of Funds Report (CALM 826 Report) and the Fund Control Point Log 138 were not in balance, as shown in the following schedule:

Reconciliation of Status of Funds Report to the
Fund Control Point Log Performed at Request of Audit Team

Status of Funds Report

Fiscal Year 1982	Before	Adjustment	After
First Quarter	$360,813.33	$ 6,375.84	$367,189.17
Second Quarter	389,604.67	1,582.30	391,186.97
Total	$750,418.00	$ 7,958.14	$758,376.14

Fund Control Point Log

	Before	Adjustment	After
First Quarter	$366,382.34	$ 806.83	$367,189.17
Second Quarter	256,962.97	134,224.00	391,186.97
Total	$623,345.31	$135,030.83	$758,376.14

This was caused by improper posting of transactions to the wrong fund control point, addition errors, and failure to post transactions. The patients' subsidiary cards maintained by MAS were not posted timely, and the posted invoice amounts were not always supported. The cost ceiling for the program had been consistently overobligated. The amounts budgeted were not consistently applied nor realistic. As a result, there was little ability to plan for the controlled growth of this program. Also, accrued services for this program had been inflated.

The workload and costs of the non-VA hospitalization program had consis-

277

tently grown prior to the arrival of the audit team. The following schedule shows this growth and decline:

Schedule of Growth and Decline of the
Non-VA Hospitalization Program

Time Period	Average Daily Census	Number of Claims
Fiscal Year 1980	8.1	479
Fiscal Year 1981	9.0	537
Fiscal Year 1982		
1st Quarter	9.4	167
2nd Quarter (notified of audit—3/17/82)	7.1	120
3rd Quarter—5/31/82 (during audit)	2.6	49

We believed this decline in program costs was due to our presence and interest in the program.

Follow-up on accrued services valued over $2.7 million could have reduced these obligations. There had been insufficient review of accrued services payable by the appropriate services when requested by Fiscal Service. Our review of the April 5, 1982, CALM 852 Report, Accrued Services Payable, showed $2,788,132, of which $601,807 was for outstanding obligations for the non-VA hospitalization program. At our request, an analysis of these non-VA hospitalization obligations was performed by MAS and Fiscal Service. This review resulted in deobligation of $217,881 of the $301,729 (72 percent) of pre-January 1, 1982, obligated balances. Medical Administration Service was not conducting required analyses of outstanding obligations, and obligating procedures did not provide for consistent estimates. This had resulted in excess funds being committed to the program.

Accrued services had grown to over $2.7 million, as shown in the following schedule:

Schedule of Accrued Services
as of March 31, 1982

Fiscal Year of Obligation	Accrued Services Obligated
Pre-1980	$ 4,099.32
1980	53,189.71
1981	440,332.79
1982	2,290,511.04
Total	$2,788,132.86

possible payment by non-VA sources nor incorporate consistent estimating procedures. Medical Administriation Service personnel told us the initial obligation

A review of the April 5, 1982, CALM Report, Accrued Services Payable, pre-January 1, 1982, showed $301,729 in outstanding obligations for the non-VA hospitalization program. We reviewed all of these outstanding obligations and coordinated deobligation efforts between MAS and Fiscal Service. As a result of this review, $217,881 was deobligated. This included $100,461 of pre-fiscal year 1982 funds and $117,420 of obligated first quarter fiscal year 1982 funds.

Obligations procedures did not include required analyses of outstanding obligations. The original obligations had remained committed as long as twenty-one months after the patient was discharged from the hospital. Medical Administration Service personnel had not performed routine analyses of these outstanding obligations to rejustify the obligations. The VA required that MAS perform an analysis of obligations outstanding for more than forty-five days and promptly notify Fiscal Service of appropriate adjustments. This review would have ensured that obligated balances were relevant to anticipated expenses.

Procedures used by MAS to obligate funds had not provided realistic estimates for the initial obligations. The current procedure did not provide for was computed from a base figure of $400 per patient day. We found no consistent formula applied, and some estimates used to comprise the initial obligations were based only on the hospital per-diem charge. This did not represent expected future expenses. For example, only two of the seven patients shown in the following schedule used $400 per patient day as the base figure:

Schedule of Obligated Amounts and Actual Expenditures

Patient Days	Base	Obligations Original	Obligations 5/24/82
5	$500	$2,500	0
5	600	3,000	0
12	400	4,800	$2,757.15
2	400	800	190.10
3	468	1,405	76.50
3	620	1,860	1,080.25
4	528	2,113	0

In addition to these inconsistencies, $132,500 was obligated the last two calendar days of 1981. The unit supervisor told us the authorization clerk's position had been empty for some time. He attempted to obligate all funds remaining in the account for the year. After our review, funds totaling $70,890 were deobligated from these two days' obligations.

In addition to increasing the outstanding balances for accrued services, these inappropriate obligating procedures had resulted in the excessive use of scarce/earmarked funds. We found that VAMC Miami, had consistently requested additional funds for non-VA hospitalization prior to the arrival of the audit team. During the period the audit team was at the facility, $200,000 was anticipated to be turned back to the Florida Medical District.

Schedule of Funds Requested or Turned Back
for Non-VA Hospitalization

Time Period— Quarter and Fiscal Year	Amount Original	Change	Total	From/To
1st 1981	$ 262,145	$ 50,000	$ 312,145	District
2nd 1981	281,750	0	281,750	
3rd 1981	285,250	100,000	385,250	District
4th 1981	$ 280,750	75,000	355,750	District
Total	$1,109,895	$255,000	$1,334,895	
1st 1982	$ 257,353	$100,000	$ 357,343	District
2nd 1982	257,353	150,000	407,353	VACO
3rd 1982	$ 257,353	($200,000)[1]	$ 57,353[2]	To District

1. This includes $117,000 of first quarter funds deobligated in the third quarter FY 1982.
2. This is not indicative of the $280,686 average maintained for the fiscal year (this data does not include any deobligations from second quarter obligations).

According to the Chief, Ambulatory Care and Processing Section, an unusually high turnover rate in the key clerical position for the non-VA hospitalization program had hindered their efforts to properly train and expose personnel to the complexities of this position. The chief also cited poor unit supervision of personnel assigned to this position inasmuch as the present incumbent was not sufficiently apprised of the position's responsibilities.

Inconsistent obligation procedures, coupled with lack of follow-up by MAS with Fiscal Service for rejustification of outstanding obligations, had resulted in excess funds being committed to the program. During our review of the accrued services payable for this program, $217,881 was deobligated.

Compliance with VA policy on medical treatment to non-service-connected veteran/employees could have saved approximately $106,655. Non-service-connected veteran/employees were receiving treatment in the ambulatory care and outpatient treatment programs despite VA policies that prohibited such treatment. Also, a non-veteran service organization employee received extensive continuing medical treatment. These conditions were caused by physicians and other medical personnel providing treatment despite policies prohibiting such and veteran/employees and non-employees (Disorganized Crime) ignoring and circumventing established procedures. This had resulted in approximately 1,014 ineligible visits at a cost of $47,335 and 332 ineligible patient days at a cost of $59,320, for a total projected cost of $106,655.

280

Medical records for non-service-connected veterans treated on an outpatient basis or on the ambulatory care roll were reviewed. The medical records of veteran/employees maintained in the locked files had the following problems: (1) There was a disparity in treatment for veteran/employees versus veterans who were not employees. Veteran/employees were being provided ambulatory care even though their 10–10m forms indicated neither hospitalization nor outpatient treatment were required. The 10–10m was marked AC/DC (indicates Ambulatory Care Program/Discharge), yet further review of the medical record indicated the veteran/employee was given a clinic appointment or advised to return for additional treatment if the condition did not improve instead of being referred to their private physician. (2) The ambulatory care area had become the "family physician" for employee/veterans as they come through this area for everything from common colds and sore throats to requesting birth control devices/medications. (3) All veteran/employee medical records had not been identified, stamped to indicate "employee," and placed in locked files. (4) The service-connected emblem had not been placed on all files for service-connected veterans, even though some have had recent episodes of hospitalization or outpatient treatment. (5) Material filed in the veteran/employee medical record was filed haphazardly and was not in chronological or any other logical order. (6) Material was filed in the veteran/employee medical record when the person went to the Personnel Health Physician as an employee.

We determined from review of the P-31A that the universe of NSC veteran/employees was 590. Utilizing variable sampling with a 20 percent ratio of sampling error to standard deviation with a 95 percent confidence level, we selected ninety-six medical records for review. Thirty-five medical records were located, of which only four were in locked files. The other thirty-one had never been identified as employee medical records and/or placed in locked files. We compared treatments received by the employee from October 1, 1977, through the date of audit (April 26, 1982) to the VA, DM&S, and local policies and procedures.

There are several criteria controlling what treatments can be received by a veteran/employee. These criteria are: (1) Chief Medical Director Information Letter 10–80–54, dated October 7, 1980, entitled "Ability to Defray Medical Care Costs and Recovery of Costs"; (2) VA Circular 00–81–56, dated October 21, 1981, entitled "Recovery of Costs of Care Provided to Ineligible Federal Employees"; (3) DM&S Circular 10–81–234, effective date: October 29, 1981; (4) DM&S Circular 10–82–41, effective date: March 19, 1982; (5) Medical Center Policy Memorandum Number 05–33–77, effective date: August 10, 1977, entitled "Employee Health Services"; and, (6) two medical center employee news bulletins, dated January 1981 and May 1982. These criteria only allow NSC veteran/employees to receive emergency treatment at a VA medical center. All chronic and acute illnesses treated by the VA will be billed to the NSC veteran/employee. This was to allow the VA to be in compliance with the Federal Medical Care Cost Recovery Act.

Using statistical sampling techniques, we determined that twenty (20.8 percent) of the ninety-six non-service-connected veteran/employees received outpatient and/or ambulatory care treatment at an approximate cost of $7,702, for which they were not billed. Two of these employees did not have hospital insurance. We also determined that nine of these veteran/employees also had a total of seventy-eight inpatient days of hospitalization at an approximate cost of $13,298. Examples of treatment provided are as follows:

Examples of Treatment Provided to
NSC Veteran/Employee

Vet/ Employee	Date of Treatment	Type of Treatment	Disposition Remarks
A	2–14–80	Wants birth control pills	Progress notes show refer to GYN clinic ASAP.
B	5–24–78 through 1–30–80	Allergy treatments	This vet/employee had a total of 64 allergy treatments ranging from 2–4 treatments per month.
C	5–23–78	High blood pressure	Vet/employee had a 1973 hospital admission for high blood pressure and has been in OPT/NSC status since that time. Vet/employee had a 1-day hospital admission on 8–17–81 and another 1-day hospital admission on 12–15–81. Progress notes stated "Being admitted for administrative purposes and continue his clinic privileges." In addition, patient treated arthritis and a skin condition at two other clinics without completion of a 10–10m to justify need.
D	7–03–81	Burning type mid- epigastic pain	Referred to A&D by Personnel Physician who requested an Upper GI series. Told her to return PRN.
	6–11–81	Feels funny, nervous like	Return PRN (as needed).
	6–03–81	Laryngitis	Told to return to clinic PRN.
	8–07–80	Routine—Re-exam and pap smear	GYN clinic.
	8–06–80	Routine—Pap smear	GYN clinic.
	6–07–79	GYN	GYN clinic.
	7–20–78	GYN	GYN clinic.
	3–25–78	Pap smear–viral syndrome	Hospitalization not required.

Vet/ Employee	Date of Treatment	Type of Treatment	Disposition Remarks
D	1–12–78	GYN	GYN clinic.
	1–04–78	Barium enema	Not shown.
	12–21–77	GI	Not shown.
	11–03–77	Routine—Pap smear	GYN clinic.
	10–28–77	Pelvic pain & vag.	A/C GYN clinic. GYN clinic gave pelvic exam, preg. test, antibiotic and told vet/emp to return to clinic 11/3.
E	2–26–82	Human bite—Tetanus shot	Bitten 2 days ago by son. Waited until Monday to be treated. Treated as an employee but progress note filed in his veteran medical records.
	10–03–81	Migraine headache	Duty hrs. 12 noon to 8:00 P.M. Treated at 3:00 A.M.
	7–25–81	Migraine headache	Duty hrs. 4:00 P.M. — 12 A.M. Treated at 12:15 A.M.
	7–10–81	Migraine headache	8 hrs. SL—Treated at 12:35 A.M.
	6–27–81	Migraine headache	Non-work day. Treated at 12:50 A.M.

While reviewing the veteran/employees' medical records, we noted several progress notes that indicated "EMPLOYEE," indicating the person was treated as an employee. Reviewing of those progress notes further indicated that employees were receiving extended, continuing, and definitive care.

In addition, we found the following treatment was provided to a non-veteran employee of the State Service Organization as follows:

Nonveteran/Nonemployee

Dates of Treatment	Type of Treatment Provided	Cost If Billed
1–02–80	EKG & CBC (complete blood count)	$ 51.00
1–03–80	SMA-12	51.00
No Date	Lightheadedness—6 days Duration	51.00
1–13–80	Thyroid Scan	51.00
1–23–80	Not Shown	51.00
1–29–80	L Muscular Swelling	51.00
2–01–80	CBC	51.00
2–15–80	T3 & T4	51.00
3–17–80	Diarrhea & Nausea	51.00
3–19–80	Auto Accident	51.00
6–02–80	Tooth Pulled–Area Aching/Sinus Series	51.00
6–16–80	Chills, Vomiting–Overexposure to Sun	51.00
12–02–80	Sore Throat & CBC	51.00
12–08–80	Abnormal Loss of Hair & T4-RIA	51.00
12–09–80	Cough	51.00
12–11–80	Cough & Chest Pain	51.00
12–15–80	Inj. to L Elbow	51.00
2–17–81	Headaches & Vertigo	51.00
3–11–81	Diarrhea	51.00
6–04–81	Diarrhea & Nausea	54.00
6–15–81	Earache—3 Days Ago for 24 Hours	54.00
10–20–81	Coughing for 2 Weeks	54.00
10–26–81	Cough Continuous & Left Ear Drainage	54.00
2–10–82	Throat BC&S	61.00
3–08–82	Auto Accident	61.00
4–23–82	EKS	61.00
Total		$1,371.00

Timecards for the twenty veteran/employees were reviewed for the period January 1979 through May 1982. We were unable to review timecards prior to January 1979 as they are not maintained prior to that date. While we determined that some employees were not charged leave when they attended clinics, we were unable to determine if employees working from 3:30 P.M. to 12 midnight attended clinics before their duty hours began.

And that was the last hospital audit that I finished. The next chapter deals with VA Regional Offices. The story, of course, is the same but the details are slightly different.

Chapter 7

Veterans Administration
Regional Offices

It's a fallacy to think of tax reduction measures as "costing" the government anything. A "cost" is something that is owed to someone in exchange for something. But the taxpayers don't "owe" the government anything, other than the money they choose to give them in exchange for services.

—Michael Burch
(Executive Director of the National Taxpayers Legal Fund)

The fifty-nine Regional Offices of the VA are responsible for spending the majority of the money stolen from you and given to the VA arm of Disorganized Crime. I did audits of regional offices during the same four-year period that I audited VA hospitals. Though the type of problems found were different than at hospitals, there are only two things you should recall before proceeding. You paid for all these activities and these activities were all screwed up.

My first Regional Office was at Columbia, South Carolina. The audit was conducted from July 10 through August 4, 1978. On June 30, 1978, the Regional Office employed 241 full-time employees and 11 temporary employees. Total administrative budget for fiscal year 1978 was $5.1 million. In fiscal year 1977, compensation and pension award payments exceeded $166 million and education award payments approached $76 million.

In Columbia there were 605 education account receivables (overpayments) valued over $245,000, which were over thirty days old as of June 30, 1978. All receivables were due from veterans claiming some form of benefit, such as education, compensation, or pension checks. A major computer problem prevented prompt and aggressive action that would have identified $68,000 (28 percent) of the receivables as being overstated or where other manual action was needed to terminate the receivables. Receivables were listed where the veteran did not owe any money. This occurred because education awards had been submitted without the VA receiving from the veteran's school/college his certification of attendance information. This certification was to be input to clear the overpayment; or the certification had been submitted, but the computer had rejected it and the computer's advisory message had been filed in the claims folder by some member of Disorganized Crime without any action. Also, we found many receivables that were over one year old, but still reported the veteran drawing checks.

This problem was found at ten VA Regional Offices over the next three years. These results were summarized into an overall report in February 1981. This computer problem and lack of corrective action by Disorganized Crime had resulted in $2.8 million of account receivables not being collected. This overall report was never published.

The Regional Office's Systematic Analysis of Operation, dated April 26, 1978, noted problems with the maintenance of ninety-seven veterans' liability accounts, valued over $157,000, and made recommendations to solve these problems. It was noted that follow-up and reminder notices were not being sent timely. Recommendations were made to review the cards and send collections letters. This condition was still present on July 21, 1978 when the auditors arrived. A sample of twenty-four home-loan defaults, valued over $45,000 and under station responsibility, revealed that action in six cases had been neither prompt nor in accordance with the procedures for collection letters. For example, one home-loan default of over $2,600 was established October 1, 1964. The third collection letter, FL 4–409, was to be sent December 31, 1964; however, it was sent May 20, 1976. There had been no action since May 31, 1977, when a credit report was obtained, although the debtor was drawing $59 per month in compensation and both he and his wife were federal government retirees.

This was not an isolated problem at the Columbia Regional Office. Another audit team reviewed 152 loan liability debt cases at four regional offices for which they had collection and basic maintenance responsibility. Those auditors found that Liability Account Cards for 23 debts, totaling $81,655, could not be located and that 73 of the cards available had not been properly maintained as shown below:

Regional Office	Number of Cases Reviewed	Number of Missing Cards	Number of Cards Not Properly Maintained
Atlanta	50	6	40
Chicago	25	-	6
Huntington	35	7	-
Philadelphia	42	10	27
Total	135	23	73

As you may already suspect, this audit report also was never published

Collection Contracts. Address Locator Cards, FL-20, were used to verify addresses. In some instances, the FL-20 was sent to the Postmaster more than once. Certified mail, wire, or skip-locators were not used for large claims, although the VA provided for their use. Credit reports were not obtained simultaneously with the second demand letter for debts over two hundred dollars. The use of the telephone to make collections was not made as required. Finance Division personnel did not participate in a "Phone Power" seminar conducted in the Loan Guaranty Division by a phone company representative. The seminar emphasized increased use of the telephone in collection activities.

Repayment Agreements. Of the twenty-four audited home loan defaults, seven had repayment agreements. All seven had repayment schedules in excess of three years as follows:

EXAMPLE	MONTHLY REPAYMENT	PRINCIPAL	YEARS TO REPAY PRINCIPAL
1	$15	$2,572	14
2	$15	$2,153	12
3	$15	$2,062	12
4	$25	$2,853	10
5	$30	$2,245	6
6	$41	$2,640	5
7	$38	$2,034	4

Arrangements to pay by installments should provide for complete liquidation within a reasonable time, considering the size of the debt and the debtor's ability to pay and should not normally extend more than three years or be less than ten dollars per month.

No attempts were made to obtain either the executed confess-judgment notes or the acceptable financial information before accepting an offer to pay by installments exceeding one year as required.

Non-Veteran Claims. The lack of a proper and aggressive collection program was also present in non-veteran home-loan defaults. A review of all seven of the non-veteran home-loan defaults with a total value over $15,000 revealed that two accounts, totaling $3,000, should have been written off and no collection actions had been taken on the other five.

Estates. The Finance Division had written off six defaulted home-loans during fiscal year 1978 because of the death of the debtor. A review of the six write-offs revealed that there were no attempts to determine if there was an estate. When there is evidence of an estate or assets, prompt action will be taken to protect the interests of the government. The division had been automatically writing off these debts based on an opinion from a now-retired loan guaranty attorney.

GAO Referral. The Finance Division was not prompt in referring claims to the GAO. Five of seventeen claims were properly referred to GAO in fiscal year 1978 within thirty days of the last administrative action as required. Some claims that should have been referred to GAO had not been. For example, one claim for a home-loan default of $9,699 had only eighteen payments totaling $361 since August 30, 1974. The debtor had been located, but had been un-cooperative (at his present repayment rate it would have taken 545 years to pay off the principal and interest). Financial data indicated the debtor had the ability to pay. No response was received when an offer of compromise was solicited. There is not sufficient positive evidence to adequately support suspension or termination of collection, and the debt is not exempted from referral to the GAO.

Terminations. The division did not use all sources of information to insure that terminations are made in accordance with VA policy. There were nineteen terminations of home-loan defaults, valued over $35,000, during the first nine months of fiscal year 1978. The VA required that reasonable locator actions be taken. These should be prompt and aggressive and normally include a review of loan dockets and claims files. A review of fourteen home-loan defaults found:

a. prompt and aggressive action was taken in only two cases;
b. the loan docket was reviewed in only three cases; and,
c. the claims files supported the termination in all fourteen cases.

Disorganized Crime has so many receivables outstanding that it is trying to hire collection agencies to get the money.

I was a member of the audit of VA Regional Office (VARO), Houston, Texas. The audit was conducted during the period November through December 1978. At the end of fiscal year 1978, authorized employment was 629 full-time and 17 part-time positions. The VARO is organized into Administrative, Adjudi-cation, Finance, Loan Guaranty, Personnel, and Veterans Services Divisions. Approximately 50 employees from Loan Guaranty (VAO) in San Antonio. Also, 29 veterans representatives are based at 49 colleges in south Texas. For fiscal year 1978, VARO had a total operating budget of $10,582,000. The station's region, which includes South Texas (ninety counties) and Mexico, has a popu-lation of 731,000 veterans. Available VARO Houston work load data from the last two fiscal years is summarized as follows:

Compensation and Pension (C&P)	Fiscal Year 1977	Fiscal Year 1978
Number of awards (effective 9–30)	117,785	118,341
Value of payments	$275,339,573	*
Education		
Active payments (average number per month)	*	25,672
Value of benefits	$124,336,376	*

288

Number of Loans

Home (guaranteed)	18,405	19,262
Mobile home (guaranteed)	59	189
Vendee (portfolio)	1,737	880

*Data not available at the time of audit.

Appraisals were found to affect some loan defaults. To determine if a correlation existed between differences in initial Certificates of Reasonable Value (CRV) and foreclosure CRVs, which exceeded $3,000, we reviewed a sample of fifteen foreclosed home loans. We found wide variances between the initial CRV (appraisal) and foreclosure appraisal in four cases (26 percent). The results are summarized below:

Case	Initial CRV	Foreclosure CRV	Difference
1	$38,500	$24,000	$14,500
2	48,500	42,500	6,000
3	20,000	14,500	5,500
4	14,625	10,625	4,000

The time span between the pairs of appraisals cited was nine to eleven months. CRV differences of $4,000 to $14,500 are unsatisfactory and significant. The auditors could not determine why the two appraisals in each of these four houses were so different.

COUNSELING RESOURCES (STAFFING AND CONTRACTS)

Our review of the counseling work load showed that VARO staff counseling psychologists were significantly under-utilized and three counseling contracts (estimated cost $162,475 in fiscal year 1979) should have been canceled immediately.

In addition to the Chief, Counseling and Rehabilitation (C and R) Section, the VARO had six full-time staff counseling psychologist positions. Since May 1978 one position had been vacant, but recruitment was underway. Another position, which had been part-time, became full-time on December 17, 1978. Also, for Fiscal Year 1979, five counseling contracts were budgeted at an estimated cost of $188,660. Houston Community College, Pan American University, St. Mary's University, Texas Southwest College, and Trinity University all had counseling contracts with the VARO.

Counseling Work Load Summary For Fiscal Year 1977–1979

The number of counseling cases (VARO and contract) during fiscal year 1977–1979 is shown below:

Fiscal Year	Total Cases	Contract Cases	Contract Counseling Cost
1977	3,594	1,463	$138,784
1978	3,370	1,512	152,813
1979	*	1,1920 est.	188,660 est.

*Because total counseling work load is significantly affected by external developments, such as a Department of Veterans Benefits (DVB) blanket mailout to veterans/dependents, an overall counseling work load projection for fiscal year 1979 would not be reliable.

Although counseling work load decreased six percent, contract counseling increased three percent from fiscal year 1977 to fiscal year 1978. The contract counseling work load, as budgeted for fiscal year 1979, is estimated as increasing 27 percent in number of cases from fiscal year 1978.

DVB Counseling Psychologist Work Load Standard

According to the VA, each counseling psychologist (other than the Chief or Technical Supervisor) generally will see at least four counselees per day, of whom two will be initial counseling cases. Using the fiscal year 1978 VARO staff psychologists' work load of 1,858 counseling cases, staff psychologists saw an average of 1.58 counselees per day. The Chief, C and R, did not counsel. The computation was based upon 251 work-days for 4.68 staff counseling psychologists—5.35 available psychologists less 0.67 psychologist (leave used).

The VA revised its Counseling and Rehabilitation (C and R) work-rate standards effective October 1, 1977. These new standards were developed from time actually expended. The VA noted that the revision of the standards should result in reducing the national C and R effectiveness ratio average to about 100. In fiscal year 1978, VARO Houston staff counseling psychologists averaged 134 percent effectiveness, computed by dividing the standard manhours by available General Operating Expense (GOE) manhours minus leave. Standard manhours consist of the number of work units multiplied by the applicable work-rate standards. The VARO staff psychologists' average effectiveness does not include clerical overhead. Agency policy noted that work-rate standards represent typical averages of the time (including allowance time) required to complete the work in the established work units, and not the precise processing times for each station. The rate at which work is performed at a particular facility is affected by varying levels of employee competence, population density and distribution, geographic and climatic conditions, work load mix, personnel turnover, and other local factors. The VA manual continues, high effectiveness is not of itself proof of a highly efficient and effective use of manpower.

Analysis of Staff Counseling Psychologist Utilization

Although their individual effectiveness averaged 134 percent in fiscal year 1978, VARO staff counseling psychologists were underutilized. We reviewed the VARO staff counseling psychologists' work load for six months, from May 22, 1978 through November 20, 1978. The work load review showed 45 workdays when at least one of the four full-time staff counseling psychologists saw no scheduled counselees. On another 118 workdays, at least one psychologist saw only one counselee. Also, the part-time psychologist's work load could have been increased. There were seven workdays when this staff member saw no counselees and 37 workdays when he saw only one counselee.

Each station will analyze its "no show" rates for various types of cases and will take these rates into consideration in scheduling such cases. The risk of having a larger than expected number of counselees appear on a given day is one that must be lived with. What is not tolerable is to schedule on a basis which may result in one or more counseling psychologists not seeing an appropriate number of counselees on a given day. Various techniques for handling overflow may be used including group procedures; initiating individual counseling with a brief interview and having any necessary tests administered and then rescheduling for another day; and having the Chief, C and R (Counseling and Rehabilitation), available to take overflow cases.

The division did not comply with these provisions. Effective overscheduling to take into account the "no show" rates were 58 percent for Houston and 48 percent for San Antonio. Group procedures and counseling by the Chief, C and R, were not used to handle incidents of overflow.

Counseling psychologists' noncounseling responsibilities do not consume significant amounts of time; however, clerks should perform some of these duties. According to the VA, the review and distribution of all cases referred to C and R (approximately 20 per day) is a clerical responsibility. However, counseling psychologists were performing the review. Also, two counseling psychologists' typing summaries was inappropriate use of their (high dollar) time. Improved staff utilization would allow the psychologists additional time for counseling.

Other noncounseling activities do not require significant amounts of time or are not accomplished by the counseling psychologists. The review of all Chapter 34 change of program or objective for possible memo action takes one counseling psychologist approximately five hours per week. The Chief, C and R, stated that personal-adjustment counseling is rarely done. One counseling psychologist stated that he has done two of these in three years. The Vocational Rehabilitation Board meets for approximately one hour per week; however, only one counseling psychologist serves on the board. The Chief, C and R, said that hospital liaison is very seldom done in Houston. He also reported that one San Antonio counseling psychologist spends one afternoon a week on liaison. The unit's vocational rehabilitation specialists (not the counseling psychologists) do the motivational visits.

For fiscal year 1978, C and R unit's unmeasured work was 97 hours; at most, the impact of unmeasured work to the counseling psychologists would have been 20.7 hours per psychologist in fiscal year 1978 (97 hours divided by 4.68 available staff psychologists). Group counseling should be used. The majority of the contracted cases were Chapter 34 and 35 type counselees, who are most appropriate for group counseling and who require less documentation than Chapter 31 cases.

Use of Contract Counseling Is Excessive

In fiscal year 1978, VARO Houston's use of contract counseling (1,512 cases) was double the national average (757 cases). If VARO staff counseling psychologists had counseled the Houston Community College, St. Mary's University, and Trinity University contract cases, they would have seen an average of 2.8 counselees per day. Among the five counseling contracts, only two—Pan American University in Edinburg and Texas Southwest College in Brownsville— are needed. These contracts are justified because the two schools are approximately three hundred miles from San Antonio where the closest VARO psychologists are based. In fiscal year 1979, these two contracts were projected to cover 300 counseling cases (estimated cost $26,185). Improved use of VARO staff counseling psychologists would allow an 84 percent reduction in the use of contract counseling.

Based upon current fiscal year cost estimates ($188,660), the VA would save $162,475 in fiscal year 1979 by cancelling the Houston Community College, St. Mary's University, and Trinity University counseling contracts. According to our review, by complying with VA requirements, VARO counseling psychologists would be able to effectively handle the workload which elimination of the three contracts would add.

As you may already suspect, the Houston RO Director did not concur with the auditors to reduce the number of contracts and save over $160,000 of your money. The Director's comments to the auditors did not address the finding that the VA's own staff counseling psychologists were significantly underutilized. And that's where the matter stopped!

I was a member of the audit team at VA Regional Office, Waco, Texas. The team was at Waco from November through December 1978. The audit report was published in September 1979.

Staffing at the end of fiscal year 1978 consisted of 546 employees. This includes persons assigned to Veterans Assistance Offices at Dallas, where there is a 25-person Loan Guaranty Division, Lubbock, El Paso, and Fort Worth. The general operating expense budget for fiscal year 1979 was $10,581,524.

292

Housing Loans Processed or Granted, FY 1978

	Loans	Amount
Guaranteed	18,401	$611,180,360
Direct	68	1,132,565
TOTAL		$612,312,925

Education Loans Processed, FY 1978

	Loans	Amount
Applications processed	4,058	
Adjudication approved	1,685	
Active in Finance	1,650	
Disbursements		$1,490,555
Oustanding, including		
defaults		1,513,740

Veterans Going to School as of September 30, 1978

	Number
Chapter 31 (Vocational)	1,036
Chapter 34 (GI Bill)	26,495
Chapter 35 (Dependents)	3,128
TOTAL	30,659
Estimated Total Payment in	
Fiscal Year 1978	$113,408,000

Estimate of Monthly Compensation Payments for Fiscal Year 1978

	Participants	Payout Year-to-Date
Compensation	101,811	$283,208,974
Pension	85,120	125,231,049
TOTAL	186,931	$408,340,023

The Director was generally not receptive to the recommendation that the audit team made in the audit report. As with the previously discussed Houston audit report, the auditors found that your money was spent both for VA staff and contractual services to perform the same function.

Counseling psychologist workload in Waco, Dallas, and Lubbock did not justify staffing and/or contractual services. The number of cases counseled in-house and the number counseled by guidance centers were inconsistent with staffing and workload. DVB Circular 20–75–118 stated that each counseling psychologist generally will see at least four counselees per day. The present counseling workload at Waco, Dallas, and Lubbock is such that current staffing and contractual services cannot be justified.

Waco Regional Office

The average number of cases seen by the four counseling psychologists at the regional office, for the period October 7, 1977, through October 5, 1978, was 2.3 cases per day per counselor. Texas State Technical Institute (counseling contract) for the same period averaged 2.8 cases seen per day. The workload of the regional office counseling psychologists does not justify having a guidance center contract with the Texas State Technical Institute, which is also located in Waco, Texas, when that workload could be handled in-house.

Dallas Office

The counseling psychologist's workload at the field location in Dallas does not justify two counseling psychologists. The combined workload of the two counseling psychologists at Dallas, Texas, for the period October 7, 1977, through October 5, 1978, was an average of 1.8 cases actually seen and counseled per day.

Between October 7, 1977 and October 5, 1978, the counseling psychologists stationed at Fort Worth, Texas, averaged 2.4 cases actually being seen and counseled. The counselor at Fort Worth could be utilized to alleviate peak workloads that may be realized by the counseling psychologist in Dallas, Texas. This would bring the Fort Worth counseling psychologist's average caseload closer to the standards of four per day.

Lubbock Office

For the period October 7, 1977, through October 5, 1978, the Lubbock counseling psychologist workload averaged 2.2 cases seen per day; the guidance center workload was 2.0 cases seen per day. The workload could be handled by two counseling psychologists at Lubbock.

Because of the low workload in Dallas, relocation of a counseling psychologist from Dallas to Lubbock would alleviate the need for a guidance center contract in Lubbock.

Summary

The following chart shows that projected workload per counselor is well within the standards established in DVB Circular 20–75–118, if the two counseling contracts are canceled and the Dallas and Lubbock staffing is adjusted. Projected annual savings of $76,484 will result.

	Present Workload	Projected Workload	Projected Annual Savings
VARO, Waco	2.3	3.0	-0-
Texas State Technical Institute (Contract	2.8	-0-	$41,200
Dallas Office	1.8	3.3	-0-
Lubbock Office	2.2	2.7	-0-
Texas Tech (Contract)	2.0	-0-	35,284
			Total $76,484

As expected, the Director disagreed with the audit team, but the Director's comments were unresponsive to the recommendation. In addition, after this and the Houston audit reports reached VA Central Office in Washington, D.C., the requirement for a standard number of counselors to be scheduled per day was deleted. Took care of that problem, didn't we!

I was a member of the audit effort at the VA Regional Office at Nashville, Tennessee. The audit team was there from November through December 1978. The audit report was published November 7, 1979. Staffing consisted of 276 full-time and 12 part-time employees as of December 1978. Total station operating cost was $5,930,000 for fiscal year 1978 and $5,799,776 planned for fiscal year 1979. In fiscal year 1978, compensation and pension payments exceeded $17.7 million each month.

Leased GSA vehicles were used for home-to-work transportation. Our review of VROC schedules and interviews with the VROC Coordinator disclosed that GSA vehicles are used for transportation from home to place of employment on days when official travel is not scheduled. Under no circumstances should an employee be authorized to operate an assigned vehicle from his place of residence to his place of employment for the purpose of performing an assignment or duty at his place of employment that will comprise the normal hours of duty.

Although we did not attempt to quantify the number of times this situation occurred, we did note that one VROC traveled 1,394 miles for home-to-work transportation not associated with official travel during August, September, and October 1978.

Also, dispatched GSA vehicles had been obtained unnecessarily. We reviewed the mileage records and logs for GSA-dispatched cars used by the regional office during fiscal year 1978 and found that on forty-six occasions the cars had been obtained on Friday for use the following Monday. This resulted in weekend charges totaling $628 during fiscal year 1978. In twenty-four of the cases (52 percent), official business travel did not begin until normal business hours Monday. These problems with vehicles are also discussed later on at St. Petersburg, Florida.

Besides GSA vehicles, Disorganized Crime also spends lots of your money on chauffeurs, limousines, and air travel.

Twenty-three Defense and State department officials are using unauthorized chauffeur-driven limousine service between their homes and offices. The GAO estimated the yearly cost of providing chauffeur service for each official at $35,000, for a total exceeding $800,000.

If that isn't expensive enough for your blood, the Defense Audit Service reviewed 777 military flights and found that 180 (23 percent) were termed uneconomical misuse. An example of this would be the Air Force general ordered a C-140 aircraft for a trip between Washington, D.C., and Offutt Air Force Base, Neb., because it is fastesr than a T-39, which normally would have been used. The general and his party saved a total of 15 minutes on the round trip. The additional cost was $12,400.

But let's get back to the Nashville Regional Office.

Our review disclosed that due, in part, to inadequate communication between Loan Guaranty and Finance, debts owed by the veteran to the VA were not being considered when processing a veteran's application for a home-loan guaranty. We selected a hundred loan guaranty cases approved in 1978 and compared them to the Finance Division accounts receivable listings. We found that none of the individuals had an educational loan default but, of the hundred cases reviewed, six individuals owed the VA money because of educational overpayments. Five of the educational overpayments existed at the time Loan Guaranty approved the guaranty and issued a Certificate of Commitment.

Date Educational Overpayment Occurred	Amount of Debt	Date of Certificate of Commitmennt Issued
April 1974	$ 476.80	January 10, 1978
August 1975	2,796.75	December 29, 1977
December 1975	218.67	December 27, 1977
April 1976	200.00	January 11, 1978
July 1976	395.90	January 10, 1978

In all five cases, the educational overpayment was outstanding more than one year at the time the home-loan guaranty was approved. Our review of the loan files for these five cases also showed that the veterans failed to disclose their education overpayments on their home-loan application.

We also selected fifty loan guaranty cases defaulted in 1978 and compared them against Finance Division's local accounts-receivable listing for educational loan defaults and against the quarterly listing of educational overpayments. One of these individuals had an educational loan default, but four had education overpayments. One of these had an education overpayment of $3,983 at the time the Certificate of Commitment was issued. The amount owed to the VA was not listed on veteran's application. The veteran subsequently defaulted on his home loan, which resulted in an additional $1,466 debt to the VA.

We discussed this case with the Loan Processing Section and were told that had Loan Processing known about the education overpayment at the time the loan was processed, the loan would not have been approved.

The Regional Office Director has the obligation to take whatever steps necessary to reduce the number of home-loan defauts and to operate the Home Loan Guaranty program in an efficient and economical manner. Since the VA does not report veterans' debts to credit bureaus, the lenders have no way of knowing if the veteran is indebted to the VA unless the veteran volunteers this information on his application. Our review disclosed that in all cases (six) where the veteran had an overpayment at the time the Certificate of Commitment was issued, this information was not stated on the veteran's application, and therefore not considered in determining the veteran's ability to repay the home loan. In order to ensure that the veteran is capable of repaying the loan, Loan Processing must determine that all debts owed the VA are considered when analyzing the loan application. Failure to consider these debts has and may continue to result in home-loan defaults. The approval of a loan to an unqualified veteran is a dis-service since it will result in the veteran losing his home, a debt being owed the government, and an adverse effect on the veteran's credit standing.

The auditors later found this same situation in most other regional offices. As a result, the VA changed its procedures in April 1979 and has since collected millions of dollars in repayments before veterans are granted a home loan.

Telephone service is underutilized. During the audit we found telephone lines and equipment in three units within VSD that were either not being used or were not used enough to justify the service.

Excess telephone service is in the Telephone Unit. There are nineteen incoming telephone lines in the Telephone Unit used to conduct telephone interviews with VA beneficiaries in Tennessee—two state-wide WATS lines, seven intra-city lines, and ten local lines. Five of the local lines are excess, and should be discontinued.

The VA required that each October telephone traffic studies be conducted. The purpose of these studies is to analyze telephone utilization to determine that number of telephone lines needed to provide sufficient service.

Regional office management told us that numerous contacts were made with the telephone company during 1978, to arrange for a telephone study to be conducted in October. Our review of records for 1977 and 1978 disclosed reports of a partial study conducted in the spring of 1978 and a report of a September 1978 study. We found that these studies were not in the required manual format because division management had not analyzed the data to determine the need for existing telephone service. In addition, the telephone company told us that the September study was not conducted, but rather a report was developed based on the spring study. We compared regional office telephone usage data and the September 1978 report, and found the September report to be inflated.

During the audit, we analyzed the volume of telephone calls received and the number of missed calls for October 1978. Based on our review and standards contained in M27–1, Part I, only five local lines were justified.

In addition, the Telephone Unit is equipped with fourteen telephone answering devices. The Chief of the Telephone Unit told us that fifteen answering devices were initially installed because they were all going to be staffed. One

297

of these answering positions was subsequently removed. During the audit, the Veterans Services Officer identified two of these devices as excess. Our review of staffing schedules for fiscal year 1978 and 1979 disclosed that when all staff assigned to the Telephone Unit are present, only eleven of the fourteen answering devices are utilized. Currently, there are no plans to staff all of the answering devices. Also a December 1977 Central Office staff visit reported that during November, the peak month of the year, staffing of the Telephone Unit averaged only eight staff. By eliminating two of the telephone answering devices, the VA will save $602 annually. Telephone costs were also a problem at the St. Petersburg, Florida, Regional Office, which will be discussed later on.

My next three audits of Regional Offices were conducted at Little Rock, Arkansas (February-March 1980); Pittsburgh, Pennsylvania (May-June 1980); and, St. Petersburg, Florida (July-September 1980). Only the Little Rock audit report was not thrown away, and was published in July 1981. The auditors began to realize in the beginning of 1980 that the VA's $100 + billion Home Guaranty Program was all screwed up. Fortunately, the Little Rock report was published before Disorganized Crime realized the magnitude of the problem being found. The other two audit reports, as well as the overall audit report (in which hundred of thousands of your dollars was invested), were all thrown away. As a result, I'll talk about the overall report on the Home Loan Program and some other interesting examples of Disorganized Crime at work at St. Petersburg. By the way, my audit team (all of us based out of Atlanta) had been assigned Pittsburgh because the previous audit team (based out of Maryland) had refused to complete the audit guide for the Home Loan Guaranty Program. The previous auditors thought the audit guide was too difficult to perform. As a result, you paid for three more round-trip airline tickets from Atlanta to Pittsburgh (don't forget, the Pittsburgh report was never published).

The VA Mortgage Credit Assistance Program, often called the VA Home Loan or Loan Guaranty Program, provides assistance to eligible veterans acquiring homes of their choice. The program also provides the veteran assistance in retaining the home once it has been purchased. The program is also designed to minimize the loss to the government when a VA loan is liquidated through voluntary deed or foreclosure.

VA loan guaranty activity is the responsibility of the Loan Guaranty Division of each regional office. Loan Guaranty Divison operations include appraising properties to establish their value, supervising the construction of new residential properties, determining veterans' ability to repay loans and evaluating credit risks, servicing and liquidating defaulted/foreclosed loans. To accomplish these functions, Loan Guaranty Divisions are generally organized into Loan Processing, Construction and Valuation, Loan Servicing and Claims, and the Property Management Sections. The Division is under the overall supervision of the Loan Guaranty Officer.

I know this is going to be hard to believe, but hundreds of thousands of veterans have defaulted on their home loans. As a result, the VA uses your stolen money to pay the bank that loaned the veteran the money to buy the house in the first place (no money down, naturally). The VA gets the house, which it needs to sell back to the public. The houses are usually in need of repairs in order to get the house sold. The Property Management (PM) section of the Loan Guaranty Division is responsible for overseeing the protection, maintenance, repair, and disposition of acquired property. The goals of PM are to realize the maximum market value of acquired property and minimize loss to the VA (you).

Overall lack of control in Property Management operations has resulted in payments for repairs and services not rendered as well as delays in analysis, repair, and listing of properties for sale. As a result, the holding period has increased, which increases the loss to the VA. For example, in Fiscal Year 1979, each day properties managed by the St. Petersburg office were held, cost the VA approximately $5,612, and that's just one of fifty-nine Regional Offices.

Our review of quality controls over management brokers found that the VA has paid for repairs not made or repairs of poor quality. We also found that management brokers services are not properly documented. Repair programs are not always completed promptly. Acquired houses are not always secured or maintained in a marketable condition, and vandalism and theft is not always reported to law-enforcement authorities. In addition, unsatisfactory property management brokers are not properly removed or suspended. Prompt and effective action is not always acquired in a timely and economical manner.

We found that internal controls are not established to ensure that properties are prepared for prompt resale. The initial analysis and reanalysis are not always prepared timely. Controls in Property Management had not identified untimely analyses. Undocumented and unnecessary staff inspections were partial causes for these untimely inspections.

Our reviews over the repair program in Property Management showed the need for repairs over $1,500 is not always established, controls over approval of subsequent additions to repair contracts costing over $500 are inadequate, bulk bidding and contracting is not used, and competitive bidding is not always solicited. We also found repairs are not always properly authorized and repair programs costing over $4,000 and repairs after sale costing over $500 do not always have Central Office approval.

After the properties have been prepared for sale, we also found properties are not posted for sale, consolidated sales listings are not published for all areas of the state, and controls over sales listings are ineffective. Our review also found that attorneys are used routinely and unnecessarily for closing loans. We also found losses exceeding the guaranty are not systemically reviewed, and the results are not used to limit future losses wherever possible.

The VA paid for repairs that were either not made or were of poor quality. For example, at St. Petersburg, we inspected fifty-one houses identified by the Property Management (PM) Section as having been in the custody of the Veterans Administration for over two years as of August 1, 1980.

All repair work noted below was authorized on VA Form 26–6724, Invitation, Bid, and/or Acceptance or Authorization. The VA Form 26–6724 should be completed in the appropriate space to certify that the services have been satisfactorily completed where that form is used to authorize the services. We

299

found that in ten (19 percent) of the fifty-one houses, the repairs were certified as completed by the property management broker; however, our review disclosed the repairs were not made or are of poor quality. Examples of this situation are shown below:

Property One

The VA authorized general repairs, including replacing missing framing and rescreening the porch, on December 12, 1978. The repairs were completed on May 2, 1979, and inspected by the PM broker on May 20, 1979. The VA paid for the repairs, including $120 for rescreening the porch, on June 4, 1979. An unsigned and undated note in the file states, "Suggest that we don't screen the porch until the house is sold." On July 10, 1979, the file is annotated, "Repair side patio screen on porch when house is sold as noted in file." On September 30, 1979, a VA Form 26–6705a, Agreement to Repair and/or Acceptance by Purchaser, which lists repairs to be made after acceptance of an offer to buy, was prepared stating, "Screened porch will be repaired and rescreened."

During our inspection on July 22, 1980, we found that the porch was not rescreened. The neighbors told us that the porch had never been rescreened. It is apparent from an inspection of the house that the porch was never rescreened, although the VA has paid for this repair.

Property Two

On October 12, 1979, the VA authorized general repairs, including replacing Formica counter tops in the kitchen and completely repainting the exterior. The repairs were completed on February 4, 1980, and certified as complete and meeting specifications by the PM broker on February 5, 1980. The VA paid the contractor $1,771 on February 25, 1980. On May 7, 1980, a VA staff inspection report, which lists numerous problems, states, "O/S (outside) paint job is very poor." This report was sent to the PM broker who wrote the contractor on May 19, 1980, advising him to correct all deficiencies in the repairs.

On the date of our inspection, July 25, 1980, the exterior paint was still in poor condition. In addition, we found only one of the kitchen counters had been replaced.

There is no documentation that any further action has been taken to correct the deficient repairs or to admonish the PM broker for not doing a satisfactory inspection of the repairs prior to certifying that all specifications had been met.

Property Three

The VA authorized general repairs on June 5, 1979, including painting exterior stucco and replacing any rotten wood. Repairs were inspected and certified as meeting specifications by the PM broker on September 11, 1979. On September 14, 1979, the VA authorized payments of $3,224 for the repairs. On September 18, 1979, a staff inspection reports states, "Clean-up in general leaves a lot to be desired. My notes show repairs are not complete." The report does not indicate which repairs are incomplete. The PM broker's response addresses the clean-up problem, but not the incomplete repairs. There is no follow-up action documented on the incomplete repairs.

We inspected the house on July 31, 1980 and found the paint had washed off large portions of the stucco. A portion of the eaves in the rear of the property was completely rotted through.

Property Four

On May 29, 1979, the VA authorized general repairs costing $2,264, including $95 to replace two screen doors on the front porch. The repairs were certified as meeting specifications by the PM broker on September 10, 1979. Payment was approved by the VA on September 22, 1979. On October 16, 1979, the VA authorized roof repairs costing $1,050. The repairs were certified by the PM broker as meeting specifications on October 26, 1979. The VA approved payment on November 6, 1979. The report of a staff visit, on December 12, 1979, notes no problems with the general repairs, but states, "Roof not repaired yet." No follow-up action is documented in the file.

Although our inspection on July 30, 1980 revealed no obvious problems with the roof, we found that only one of the screen doors on the front porch was new.

Property Five

On October 4, 1979, the VA authorized general repairs costing $2,126, including $50 to remove the dishwasher and cover the opening with a panel to match the cabinets. Work was certified by the PM broker as being complete and meeting all specifications on January 5, 1980. The report of a staff visit on March 27, 1980, which lists numerous problems with the repairs, states, "While we have paid (the contractor) on this, I expect him to go back and repair the house according to the specs." However, the deficient repairs noted during the staff visit were corrected by another contractor in May 1980 at additional cost to the VA of $607.

A staff visit on June 10, 1980, states, "Repairs look good now. Floors need a good waxing and cleaning." There is no record of any action being taken to clean the floors. During our inspection on July 25, 1980, we found the floors were still dirty and that the dishwasher space was covered with ordinary plywood. It did not match the kitchen cabinets.

There is no record of the PM broker being admonished for not making an adequate inspection prior to certifying that all work met specifications.

As the above examples indicate, property-management brokers have certified repairs as completed when they had not been completed. Our review disclosed that this condition resulted, in part, because no effective system of follow-up was established to ensure PM brokers take corrective action on problems noted during staff field inspections. Additionally, our review found no documentation in the files to show that PM brokers are routinely counseled or admonished when they do not make thorough inspections before certifying the repairs complete and meeting all specifications.

Failure of PM brokers to thoroughly inspect repairs prior to certifying that the required repairs have been completed satisfactorily and the lack of VA follow-up on problems noted during staff field inspections has resulted in increased repair costs and delays in completing the repair program and listing the property for sale.

Management broker (usually a Real Estate agent) services are not properly documented. We reviewed the VA Form 26–6722, U.S. Government Property Inspection Report, in forty-eight houses identified by the Property Management (PM) Section as having been in VA custody for over two years as of August 1, 1980. This form is maintained in each vacant property and must be signed by VA employees, management brokers, sales brokers, and contractors when they enter the property. We found that seven (14 percent) of the forty-eight had not been inspected each calendar month according to the VA Form 26–6722. There are five management brokers involved who, according to the VA Form 26–6722, did not make a total of twelve required monthly inspection visits. A review of the brokers' consolidated invoices showed that the VA paid the $15 monthly management fee in all twelve cases. One broker made only five documented inspections of the eleven required for one property from September 1979 through July 1980.

DVB Manual M26–5, paragraph 5.10, provides that management brokers will be paid a monthly fee for supervising of property. DVB Circular 26–80–18, dated May 7, 1980, states in paragraph 4(a) that in some cases, it may be necessary for a management broker to visit the property more than once a month.

This situation was caused by inadequate monitoring of the VA Form 26–6722 during VA staff visits. In one case, the PM broker failed to document any visit to the property in March 1980. VA staff inspections were made in May and June 1980, but there is no documentation indicating that action was taken regarding the lack of a PM broker inspection in March. In another case, a VA staff inspection was made on June 10, 1980. The VA Form 26–6722 shows the last inspection by the management broker prior to that was April 5, 1980, over two months earlier. No action was taken regarding the failure to inspect the property in May, 1980.

Failure of the brokers to complete the VA Form 26–6722 and the VA staff to follow up when the condition is identified provides no assurance the required service was received and the VA payment was appropriate.

Repair programs are not always completed promptly. We reviewed twenty-one properties that had been repaired and in VA custody since July 1, 1978, but had not been resold as of July 1, 1980. This review showed that it took an average of over seven months to complete initial repairs, excluding emergency repairs or initial cleanups, from the date the VA had both the title and the VA Form 26–8463, Property Inspection Report, which lists the necessary repairs, to the date the repairs were completed and inspected by the management broker. It took an average of 3.6 months to authorize repairs and an average of an additional 4 months to complete and inspect the repairs. The initial repair program is normally to be initiated as soon as possible after completion of the property analysis and as soon as absolute title is acquired. The VA Form 26–6724, Invitation, Bid and/or Acceptance or Authorization, stipulates the number of days required to complete repairs. In no case reviewed was more than thirty days allotted for completion of repairs.

Examples of the cases reviewed are shown below:

Property One

The VA received the property inspection report documenting necessary repair on July 17, 1978. Absolute title to the property was received August 10, 1978. The bids for general repair work were not prepared until November 10, 1978. Repairs were authorized on January 16, 1979, with thirty days allowed to complete the work. The VA was informed of the need for additional general repairs on February 22, 1979, and of the need for electrical repairs on February 26, 1979. The bids for the additional general repairs were prepared on February 22, 1979; a bid was not accepted until September 18, 1979, but these repairs were never made. Bids for the electrical repairs were not prepared until January 15, 1980. Repairs were authorized the same day and completed February 21, 1980. Additionally, a new roof was authorized on July 19, 1979, and completed August 20, 1979.

On April 1, 1980, the VA changed management brokers. On June 3, 1980, the VA wrote to the contractor who had been authorized in January 1979 to make the general repairs, stating that he would be held liable for four months of the delay (February to May 1980). Computing lost interest at $300 a month, the contractor was found liable for $1,500. However, the contractor eventually completed repairs on June 20, 1980 and was paid the full amount for the work.

Invitations to bid for additional repairs were prepared on June 23, 1980. As of August 1, 1980, these repairs had not been authorized because repairs beyond those in the bids prepared June 23, 1980, were required. The house was listed for sale "strictly as is" on August 1, 1980.

As of the date of our audit (August 11, 1980), over $4,400 had been expended for repairs to the property, two years had elapsed, and the property still had not been repaired to meet minimum property standards.

Property Two

The VA received the property inspection report documenting needed repairs on May 1, 1978. Absolute title to the property was obtained on September 1, 1978. Bids for general repairs were prepared on November 10, 1978. Repairs were not authorized since only one bid was returned. On January 23, 1979, the VA requested that the management broker obtain bids from additional contractors. On July 12, 1979, bids were prepared for a new roof, repairs not included in the general bids. A new roof was authorized July 24, 1979, and work was completed August 8, 1979.

303

On August 28, 1979, new bids were prepared for general repairs replacing the one dated November 10, 1978. Repairs were authorized October 4, 1979, allowing thirty days for the work. Repairs were not completed until January 5, 1980. The property was listed for sale February 13, 1980. It took the VA seventeen months to repair and list this property.

Property Three

The VA received the property inspection report listing all necessary repairs on September 29, 1977. Bids were prepared on September 29, 1977. A bid was accepted on November 15, 1977, but work was delayed pending acquisition of title. Absolute title was received on January 23, 1978. No action was taken until May 19, 1978, when the VA told the management broker to have the contractor begin work. On May 23, 1978, the management broker reported severe vandalism. New bids were prepared on the same day, but work was not authorized until November 3, 1978, allowing thirty days for completion. Work was completed January 29, 1979. It took the VA twelve months to repair this property.

Property Four

The VA received absolute title to this property on October 16, 1978. Due to adverse occupancy, the property inspection report was delayed until March 13, 1979. Bids were prepared on April 25, 1979 and repairs were authorized on May 21, 1979, allowing thirty days for completion. On July 11, 1979, the VA realty specialist contacted the management broker concerning the overdue contract. On August 22, 1979, the specialist made an onsite visit and noted delays due to roof repairs. Roof repairs were authorized on October 16, 1979, and completed October 20, 1979. However, the general repair work, supposedly delayed by the roof repairs, was certified completed on September 10, 1979, by the management broker. The property was not listed for sale until January 23, 1980. It took the VA ten months to repair and list this property.

This condition was caused by a lack of effective controls over timeliness of authorization of repairs. Management had not established a procedure to determine that authorized repairs were completed in a timely manner after the VA had absolute title and all other necesary documentation. Additionally, there were no controls over how much work was assigned contractors or how long it was taking them to complete the work. Consequently, management could not readily identify contractors who were assigned too much work or who were consistently late in completing repairs.

Failure to ensure that repair programs are promptly completed delays placing houses on the market. Each day a house remains unsold costs the VA lost interest, taxes, management fees, and increases the risk of vandalism.

Acquired houses are not always secure. We inspected fifty-one houses identified by the PM Section as having been in the custody of the Veterans Administration for over two years as of August 1, 1980, and found ten (19 percent) of the fifty-one houses were not secure. The Loan Guaranty Officer was immediately notified of these cases so that these houses could be secured. The types of problems found are shown in the chart below:

Number of Houses	Problem
2	Door could not be locked
2	Door could be locked, but was not
4	Windows broken out
1	House boarded up, but boards removed
1	Door removed

The VA requires that appropriate steps will be taken to minimize the risk of loss by fire and other hazards, to prevent damage by the elements and protect abandoned properties against theft and vandalism.

Houses that are not secure have a greater risk of loss due to theft or vandalism and of damages by the elements. Currently, the Property Management Section requires that houses be inspected by the PM brokers only once a month. Most of the houses inspected are in areas in which VA-owned houses have been vandalized. The risk of the house standing unsecured in such areas can be decreased by more frequent inspections. Regional Offices should make clear to VA management brokers that the monthly fee for management of a VA-owned property is not payable simply for one inspection per calendar month. In some instances, it may be necessary for a broker to visit a property more frequently in order to provide satisfactory management of that property.

Houses are not always maintained in a marketable condition. We inspected fifty-one houses identified by the Property Management (PM) Section as having been in the custody of the VA for over two years, as of August 1, 1980.

Twenty-five (49 percent) of the fifty-one houses had dirty interiors. Sixteen of these twenty-five needed only minor cleaning, such as sweeping or mopping the floors, but nine were littered with trash, broken glass, and filth, including excrement, throughout the house.

Thirty-one (60.8 percent) of the fifty-one houses had unkempt yards. The condition of these thirty-one yards ranged from twenty-three that needed cutting or raking to eight that had large amounts of rubbish. Six (11.8 percent) of the fifty-one houses had neighbors' cars or abandoned cars in the yard or driveway. Seven (13.7 percent) of the fifty-one houses had swimming pools that were very unattractive, being partially filled with slimy green water and trash. It is VA's policy generally to place acquired properties in such a condition that they will compare favorably with competitive properties in the neighborhood and present an appearance that is reasonably conducive to pride of ownership.

Sound business practices dictate that houses offered for sale be kept clean and attractive, especially when the VA has spent considerable amounts of money on cosmetic improvements, such as interior painting. In our opinion, fresh paint on the interior walls adds little to the attractiveness of the house in the mind of the buyer if the floors are covered with filth.

305

Management has not emphasized to PM brokers the need to maintain the property in a salable condition. The last memorandum to the management brokers from the VA, addressing this condition is dated August 4, 1978. It states, "On your monthly inspections, evidently your eyes are closed to the debris, grass, etc., which is overgrown and corrective action is not taken." In many houses we inspected, such conditions still exist.

This condition results in loss of appeal to the buyer, which can lead to delays in selling the property. Delays in selling a house cost the VA additional lost interest, management fees, and property taxes.

Vandalism and theft of fixtures in VA-owned houses is not reported to law enforcement authorities. We inspected fifty-one houses identified by the PM Section as having been in VA custody for over two years as of August 1, 1980. Twenty-six (51 percent) of the houses had evidence of vandalism or theft at the time of our inspections July 21, 1980 to August 6, 1980. The most common form of vandalism was broken windows. The most often stolen items were window screens and electrical fixtures. However, much more valuable items were also taken. Examples of these problems are shown below:

Property One

The VA acquired title to this property on June 19, 1978. In August 1978, a VA staff visit showed that both air-conditioning condensors were stolen. On January 29, 1979, general repairs costing $2,730 were inspected by the management broker and certified as complete. These repairs included replacing twenty-two window panes and extensive repairs in the bathrooms. A report of a staff inspection on December 11, 1979 notes numerous broken windows. The house had to be boarded up. A report of a staff inspection on February 12, 1980 states all plumbing fixtures in one bathroom are missing. During our inspection on July 31, 1980, we additionally found that the kitchen sink was missing. There is no documentation to show that the local police or other law enforcement agencies were contacted.

Property Two

The VA acquired the title to this property on March 22, 1978. General repairs were inspected and certified as meeting specifications on August 3, 1978. Vandalism and theft of fixtures to the house were reported to the VA by the PM broker in February 1979 and May 1979. At the time of our inspection (July 27, 1980), we found the air-conditioning condensor and thermostat missing and there was damage to the exterior walls. However, no report of theft or vandalism was made to the police or other law-enforcement agencies.

Prompt and effective action is not always taken to terminate adverse occupancies. Adverse occupancy is the continued occupancy of a house by the borrower or his successors after foreclosure.

A review of thirty guaranteed loans in which custody of the property was conveyed to the VA prior to July 1, 1978, and which had not been resold as of

July 1, 1980, showed that in sixteen cases (53 percent), the property was still adversely occupied at the time of our review. These properties remained adversely occupied an average of ten months after the VA was notified of the condition. Examples of the properties reviewed are shown below:

Property One

The VA was notified of the adverse occupancy in June 1978 and acquired absolute title to the property August 1978. No action was taken to remove the occupants until January 1979, when the VA wrote the lender and requested assistance, even though the lender no longer held any interest in the property. No action was taken by the lender. The next action took place in May 1979, when a VA employee talked to the occupants, who promised to vacate the property by July 1979. A staff visit in August 1979 showed the property was still adversely occupied. No further action was taken until February 1980, when the case was referred to the District Counsel who contacted a fee attorney in March 1980. The occupants vacated the house in April 1980, after contact by the fee attorney.

The VA paid the lender's claim in July 1978. During the nineteen months of adverse occupancy, the VA lost over $6,000 in potential interest (computed at nine percent) and management broker fees (computed at $15 per month).

Property Two

The VA was notified of adverse occupancy in June 1978. The lender's claim was paid in July 1978. There is no record of any action taken to remove the occupants until July 1979, when a fee attorney took legal action on behalf of the VA to have the occupants evicted. The property was vacated July 1979. During the twelve months from the date of the lender's claim to the date the property was vacated, the VA lost over $2,600 in potential interest (computed at nine percent) and management broker fees (computed at $15 per month).

The Property Management Section also identified nine additional properties that are currently adversely occupied. The average length of occupancy was 7.3 months from the date of notice to the VA to the date of our audit (August 11, 1980). Four of the cases are foreclosures on vendee loans in which the VA holds the mortgage. These vendee loans are discussed in a separate finding.

Delays in ending adverse occupancies in the cases of guaranteed loans were caused in part by a local policy of requesting that the lender's attorney, who handled the foreclosure, also handle the eviction since the foreclosing attorney had "standing" in the court. However, because the lender no longer held any interest in the property, help was often not given to the VA. In addition, there was no policy for follow-up action if the lender did not respond. Additionally, there were no controls to identify properties adversely occupied or to ensure action was taken to end the occupancy. In those cases reviewed in which a fee attorney was eventually engaged, the adverse occupancy was promptly terminated. By directly contacting fee attorneys, the PM Section could more effectively and efficiently end adverse occupancies.

307

Sound business practice dictates the adverse occupancies be brought to an end as swiftly as possible. If a house is adversely occupied, it cannot be inspected, repaired, or placed on the market. Each day a house remains unsold means increased loss to the VA. In fiscal year 1979, it cost the VA $5,612 for each day properties were on hand.

Titles to portfolio loans are not acquired in a timely and economical manner. We reviewed a sample of thirty portfolio loan properties sold between December 1978 and February 1980 and found the average time from the date of the foreclosure sale to the date clear title was received was 6.8 months. The time required to receive clear title ranged from five days to three years. The lengthy time to gain clear title to a property is not an unrecognized problem by the Loan Guaranty Division or VA Central Office. After a reasonable length of time, cases in foreclosure on which there are no satisfactory explanations for the continued delay are reported to Central Office. A number of field stations have commented on the untimely processing of judicial foreclosures of portfolio loans by the U.S. Attorneys. VA has been in communication with the Department of Justice for a long time concerning this matter.

Loan Guaranty management has also written several letters to the District Counsel (another member of Disorganized Crime) in St. Petersburg concerning these delays. As pointed out in a letter from the Acting Chief, Loan Service and Claims Section, to the Loan Guaranty Officer, dated August 19, 1980, (and substantiated by appropriate workpapers), over $131,000 was lost on accrued interest on ninety cases referred to the U.S. Attorneys for over seven months. These ninety cases were referred from August 1977 to January 1980. In addition to interest, Property Management incurs management expenses on these properties.

According to the Loan Guaranty management and the District Counsel, the delays in receiving clear title have been caused by the untimely processing of judicial foreclosures by the U.S. Attorneys. As a result, repair programs are delayed until clear title is obtained, accrued interest is lost, and Property Management expenses are incurred. The additional time required to acquire title to the property increases the likelihood of additional repairs and vandalism to the property.

The need for repairs over $1,500 is not always established by a VA staff or a fee compliance inspection. We reviewed thirty repairs costing in excess of $1,500 each, authorized in June 1980, and found ten (33 percent) which did not have an inspection by either VA staff or fee compliance inspectors before being authorized. These ten repairs are categorized below:

No documentation of an inspection—5
File annotated as not inspected because of lack of travel funds—4
File annotated as not inspected because of riots in the Miami area—1

In contrast with these ten repairs, one repair program, in Jacksonville, costing $1,500 had *six* staff inspections. A new roof was put on one house, even though there was no established need for this repair by either the liquidation

308

appraisal or the property management broker's inspection. We did not find a documented staff field on this property. Repair jobs in excess of $1,500 should generally not be undertaken unless the need for the repairs has been established by a physical inspection of the property made by staff personnel or VA compliance inspector.

The former Chief, Property Management, told us repairs authorized during June would probably not have had a staff inspection prior to authorizing the repair, because of limited travel funds during April, May, and June 1980. He also told us that fee-compliance inspectors had never been used by the Property Management Section. Instead, a staff inspection is attempted before repairs are authorized and again after repairs are completed. Without proper inspections, management cannot be ensured that repairs in excess of $1,500 are needed. Failure to employ fee-compliance inspectors in appropriate situations results in inefficient use of both staff time and travel funds.

Controls over approval of subsequent additions to repair contracts costing over $500 are inadequate. We reviewed seventy-four repairs costing less than $1,500 and found nineteen (26 percent) were additions (extras) to a larger repair contract. Our review of repairs costing over $1,500 found eight that had additions to the repair contract. These twenty-seven extras ranged in cost from $123 to $2,199, and totaled over $16,000. In two instances, the additional request was for more than the originally approved repair.

Particular care will be exercised in the preparation of specifications for technical or structural work, such as repairs to plumbing, heating, and electrical systems, reroofing, termite treatment, waterproofing and foundation repairs, drainage and sewage disposal. . . . Individual specifications under the major heading will clearly and adequately indicate the extent and nature of the work and material. Provisions will generally be made for a sum of 10 to 20 percent for contingencies (as the type or conditions or work dictate) in all estimates and requests for authorization for repair expenditures. When substantial repairs are to be made, even though such repairs be decorative only, reasonable efforts will be made to ascertain that the plumbing, heating, and electrical systems are in proper order, and that there are no serious construction defects, such as termite condition. In some cases, it will be necessary for a test to be made by a qualified plumber, electrician, or exterminator. Such report will enable inclusion in the entire scope of the repair program, thus obtaining the benefits of competitive bidding, instead of compelling the VA to deal exclusively with the contractor who was the successful bidder on other parts of the repair program.

We found that the Invitation, Bid, and/or Acceptance or Authorization, VA Form 26–6724, was not always clearly written or was not specific. Eleven of the seventy-four repairs costing under $1,500 were inadequate in instruction of specifications. For example, one VA Form 26–6724 was annotated with the instruction "replace light carpet to match existing carpet." No other details were furnished as to the room(s), number of square feet, or grade of carpeting involved. Another VA Form 26–6724 was annotated, "all work completed, Payee: Chastain Fence." There is no mention of how much fencing or where it was installed. A VA Form 26–6724 for a roofing repair was annotated, "Call management broker to inspect when ready to replace rotten wood." If rotten wood was suspected, it should have been included in the original estimate. The management brokers currently prepare the VA Form 26–6724's; however, realty specialists have not always insured that VA Form 26–6724's were always detailed and contained specific instructions. Inspections are not always made by a qualified specialist, especially on roofing repairs, to ensure that all construction defects are identified before bids are requested.

Additions to a repair or a repair contract can cause delays in completing the repair(s) when work must be stopped for inspection and authorization. Unclear instruction and specifications for needed repairs invites requests for additional work. Each delay in completing a repair program increases the time the VA must hold the property before listing the property for sale. Each day the property is on hand, additional cost is incurred to the VA. Repairs not originally identified, because an in-depth inspection by a qualified specialist was not conducted, could lead to more expense than if the additional repair had been identified and considered in the original bids or put out for separate bidding.

Authorization of repairs and fee expenses in Property Management is inadequate. We reviewed the authorization control records for fiscal year 1980 and found various errors. The authorization control records are listing of control numbers assigned to all repairs and fees in excess of fifty dollars. Authorization numbers are assigned to show the need for a repair or service has been established and that appropriate approval has been obtained. Pages were not always dated, individual entries were never dated, and payment processing dates were missing on authorization that should have been cleared (paid). Amounts authorized were also missing. For example, one page of the authorization control record (twenty-three authorizations), dated December 26, 1979, has five missing processing dates, two missing amounts, and one missing coding classification.

We also found VA Form 26–6724, Invitation, Bid, and/or Acceptance or Authorization, which showed authorization dates after work had actually been started and completed. Authorization should have been given when the need for the work was established. These post-authorizations were usually extras (items or work not identified in the original contract) to a repair contract. From our review of thirty repairs over $1,500, we found eight that had requests for extras to the contract. These extras totaled over $6,400 and were not properly authorized prior to the starting of the work. An example of post-authorization is shown below:

Original authorization on June 30, 1980, to install a new roof for $1,798.
Extras were completed on July 14, 1980.
Extras to the contract were authorized and paid on July 28, 1980.
These extras were for replacing rotten wood.
Extras cost $2,199.

The VA established the format of a control register for authorization, but does not specify how the control register is to be maintained. Sound business practice requires that management authorize and record all obligations prior to

310

completion of work or submission of vouchers for payment.

There were no controls established over the control register. Each realty specialist maintained a separate page of the authorization register and gave it back to a clerk who maintained the register when the page was full. The importance of the register has never been stressed to the realty specialists nor have periodic reviews been made to ensure that all repairs and fees have been properly authorized, paid, or canceled. Realty specialists have not always documented the files or the control register to show that the VA had knowledge of all repairs prior to completion and submission for payment.

As shown in our example above, lack of proper control over authorizing repairs and fees can result in the VA having to pay for repairs after the fact, without prior knowledge of the need for the repair or its cost. Management cannot be aware of outstanding obligations if extras and emergency repairs are not properly documented or authorized until the invoice is received for payment.

Repair programs costing over $4,000 and post-sale repairs and expenditures over $500 do not alwys have VA Central Office (VACO) approval. We reviewed thirty repairs authorized in June 1980 costing over $1,500 each and found seventeen repairs that involved additional contracts of $4,000 and should have had VACO approval; however, eight did not have VACO approval prior to authorization of the repair program. One of the nine programs that did have VACO approval has an additional authorized repair that will exceed the total amount of repairs authorized by VACO. A follow-up request has not been made for this additional expenditure.

We also examined the authorization control records for the period June 7, 1980, to August 7, 1980, and found seventeen post-sale repairs, each in excess of $500. From our review of these seventeen repairs, we found five (29 percent) did not have prior VACO approval.

DVB Manual M26–5, paragraph 4.06c(2) and DVB Circular 26–80–18, dated May 7, 1980, states that Central Office approval must be obtained for repair programs over $4,000, even if the program is to be accomplished through separate repair contracts. Even the absence of any showing of legal liability, a settlement may be effected, provided that in such cases the total amount paid by VA for the cost of any repairs or other expenditures to be made by VA shall not exceed $500 in connection with anyone sale. Cases not conforming to the foregoing limitations shall be submitted to Central Office. Commitments to make adjustments will be avoided until a final decision has been reached in the case.

The above situations occurred because not all realty specialists were aware that all identified repairs must be considered as one repair program regardless of the number of different contracts involved; however, the former Chief, Property Management, and the realty specialist told us they were aware all repairs after sale (in excess of $500) require VACO approval, and that the five repairs rated in our review were authorized without proper approval.

The Chief, Property Management, issued a memorandum on November 6, 1979, which attempted to clarify the need for VACO approval; however, the example used in the memorandum has been interpreted, by some of the realty specialists, as a method to circumvent the need for VACO approval on repair programs over $4,000. If proper controls had been maintained over the authorization process, these repairs would not have been authorized without VACO approval.

As a result, not only are manual requirements not followed, but VACO has not had the opportunity to review the need for repair programs in excess of $4,000 or expenditures, after sale, in excess of $500, to determine if the extent of repairs is justified. Management should follow all manual requirements that establish controls to avoid expenditures of funds not in the best interest of the VA.

Properties are not posted for sale in Broward, Dade, and Palm Beach counties. We inspected forty-four houses and four lots in south Florida identified by the Property Management (PM) Section as having been in the VA's custody since July 1, 1978, and not resold as of July 1, 1980. We found that thirty-seven (84 percent) of the houses and three (75 percent) of the lots were not posted for sale by any type of a For Sale sign. (Makes you wonder why the houses were not sold, eh!)

Sound business practices dictate that properties currently for sale be clearly posted to inform the public of their availability. DVB Manual M26–5, paragraph 5.14, encourages maximum use of VA Form 26–6389a, VA—FOR SALE—Sign, Acquired Property (Aluminum). Never thought that Disorganized Crime would give a form letter to a For Sale sign, had you?

These properties were not posted for sale in south Florida because management felt that posting properties with VA for sale signs was an invitation to vandalism. No documentation was maintained to determine if removal of the VA for sale signs had an effect on vandalism. While we recognized that in some rare instances, it might be in the government's interest not to use the VA's for-sale sign, the property should still be posted for sale with enough information to be useful to the prospective buyer. Additionally, vacant lots stand little chance of being vandalized.

By not posting properties for sale, the VA is decreasing properties' sales opportunities. Each day a property remains unsold means lost interest to the VA and increases the risk of vandalism.

Property Management (PM) Section does not publish consolidated sales listings for all areas of the state. In areas of the state that have a large number of properties for sale, such as Broward, Dade, and Duval counties, newspaper advertisements are used to list property for sale. Properties *are advertised for one day* as they become available. If no offers are received within thirty days, the case is referred to the appropriate realty specialist for consideration of changing the listing status. VA Sales Listing (Multiple), or any adaptation thereof should be issued on a recurring basis, not less than once a month, to reflect an appropriate consolidated listing.

Consolidated listings were published for all areas of the state until June 25, 1980. At the time, management decided that in those areas of the state covered by the newspaper advertisement, consolidated listings were no longer useful because the properties had been listed previously *for one day in the newspaper*. Due to the time lag in publishing the consolidated listing, some properties were no longer for sale by the time the listing was distributed.

By not publishing a consolidated listing, the PM Section is not giving maximum market exposure to these properties, making sales more difficult. Since an advertisement appears only one day, it is possible that prospective buyers or sales brokers will not be aware of a property's availability.

Controls over sales listings are ineffective. We reviewed the system used to list properties for sale and found there is a lack of control over when properties are removed from the market for contemplated repairs or if the property has been listed for sale over thirty days and when they are returned to the market. Control cards, which reflect the sales status of the property (e.g., currently listed, offer being processed, offer accepted) are routinely removed from the sales unit and given to the realty specialist responsible for the property. This occurs when the property has received no offers for thirty days after it is listed for sale or when the realty specialist needs to evaluate the repair program. When the control card is removed from the sales unit, the property is removed from the sales listing and not relisted. There are no controls to ensure that the cards are promptly returned to the sales unit so that the property can be returned to the market for sale.

A review of thirty properties acquired by the VA prior to July 1, 1978, still on hand as of July 1, 1980, revealed that eight (26 percent) were not currently listed for sale and no offers were being considered. The control cards were not in the sales unit. Examples of these properties are shown below:

Property One

This house was last listed for sale on January 9, 1980. The control card was on a realty specialist's desk. A review of the PM file shows that extensive additional repairs are being considered, but invitations to bid were not mailed out until July 14, 1980. In the six-month interim, the property remained off the market.

Property Two

The property was last listed for sale on February 13, 1980, at which time the VA received four bids on the property. The control card was on a realty specialist's desk. A review of the PM folder showed that on April 16, 1980, the realty specialist documented that house was being held off the market until it could be repaired again. On May 16, 1980, he documented additional vandalism. On July 14, 1980, invitations to bid were mailed out, but the file is documented, "Don't award, list SAI (sell as is)." However, house had not been relisted as of August 15, 1980.

We also found that there are no adequate controls to ensure that properties are initially listed for sales promptly. Examples of properties not listed for sale promptly are shown below:

Property Three

Repairs were completed and inspected on October 16, 1979. The house was listed for sale on January 23, 1980. A note in the file states, "Delay in listing due to removal of file from technician's desk."

Property Four

This house was demolished and debris removed on May 23, 1978. The lot was not listed until July 12, 1978.

Property Five

Property was secured on December 13, 1979. No further work was done on the property. The property was listed for sale "as is" on February 13, 1980.

Sound business practice dictates that properties for sale receive maximum exposure to the market. Effective controls over sales listings are needed to ensure all property ready for sale is in fact listed for sale.

The above situations are caused by a control system that does not effectively monitor the sales status of properties. When sales control cards are distributed to the individual realty specialists, the system no longer has the required controls. Additionally, there are no effective procedures to determine when a property is to be removed from the market. Properties are routinely removed from the market while additional repairs are being considered. Properties one and two, discussed previously, are examples of this condition. Such properties could remain on the market "as is" until repairs are actually authorized. Additionally, by proper use of VAF 26–6705a, "Agreement to Repair and/or Acceptance by Purchaser," the VA can, when appropriate, agree to make repairs after acceptance of an offer to buy, rather than take the house off the market.

Without proper controls of sales listings, including when and why properties are removed from and returned to the market, management cannot be assured that all property receives maximum sales exposure. Each day a property remains unsold increases the loss to the VA in interest and increases the risk of vandalism.

Attorneys are paid routinely and unnecessarily on loan closings. During our review, we found that attorneys are used for all loan closings on term sales and also on most cash sales. A $100 fee is paid to attorneys for closing a term sale and a $75 fee is paid for closing a cash sale. In fiscal year 1979, the St. Petersburg regional office paid over $150,000 to attorneys for their services. In fiscal year 1980 (October 1979 through June 1980), there has been over $86,000 spent for attorney services, of which $12,000 was for the closings of sales in the Jacksonville area. These loans could have been closed in the Property Management Section (PM), by VA personnel. For the $100 or $75 fee, the attorney checks the accuracy of closing statements, fills out the standard VA mortage and note, ensures the deed is recorded, and mails the document to the VA. All information necessary to complete the mortgage and note is provided to the attorney in a closing package prepared by the VA. The loan closing package also contains the deed, which has been prepared in the PM Section. The attorneys then return the prepared mortgage, note and deed, after closing of the sale, to the Jacksonville office. PM Section copies the documents and sends them to District Counsel in

St. Petersburg. If errors are found, District Counsel notifies the PM Section. PM Section then informs the fee-attorney of necessary corrective action needed.

There have been no documented studies to show fees normally charged by attorneys for similar services in Florida. Although there are no specific manual requirements stating that Central Office approval must be obtained to routinely pay attorneys more than the $50, Central Office should be advised that all fee-attorneys are paid $75 to $100 in Florida for closing loans. Sales may be closed in the most expeditious manner by a qualified attorney, salaried employees of the VA, sales brokers, or management brokers. Such attorney, unless he or she is a salaried employee of VA, shall be retained on a fee basis, and will be paid by VA a fee for the preparation of the closing instruments and for the closing of the sale. The amount of such fee shall be based on the fees normally charged in the locality for such services, but should generally not exceed fifty dollars. A fee larger than fifty dollars may be warranted in certain situations, such as in any case in which considerable travel was necessary, or the attorney was called upon to perform unusual or extended services not anticipated in the usual case. In cases in which the closing instruments have been prepared and appropriate instructions have been issued by the office of the District Counsel, it will generally be found expeditious and economical to have the sale closed by a VA salaried employee or by the VA sales or management broker who negotiated the transaction. Sales and management brokers are not paid an additional fee for closing a sale. Sales brokers currently receive a 5 percent fee for doing little more than showing the home to the prospective buyer.

Both management and staff told us that they could not rely on the sales broker or management broker to properly close a sale, even after all necessary legal instruments (deed, mortgage, and note) have been prepared. However, we contacted the Jacksonville Board of Realtors and found that a licensed sales broker is qualified to completely close a sale. We were also told that the loan closing is an intricate part of the real estate examination. Florida laws do not allow a sales broker to prepare legal instruments; however, if the mortgage and note are prepared by the VA (the owner) prior to closing, there is no need, in most instances, to have a fee attorney present at the closing. Prior to 1978, there were three attorneys from District Counsel stationed in Jacksonville. These attorneys did close cash sales in Jacksonville. At the present time, all District Counsel attorneys are located in St. Petersburg. Fee attorneys have always been used to close VA loans in Florida. District Counsel told us that the Florida Bar had confirmed the use of the sales broker in closing sales if the legal instruments (deed, mortgage, and note) were prepared under the supervision of our attorneys. This confirmation was in 1968.

By routinely using attorneys for loan closings, the VA incurs unnecessary costs and makes inefficient and uneconomical use of both sales and management brokers, as well as salaried employees. Training brokers, as well as development of alternative methods for handling loan closings are worthy of consideration.

Some resold properties have losses greater than the guaranty. We reviewed the VA Forms 4–5308, Property Management Record Printout—Fiscal, furnished by the Finance Division for properties sold in fiscal year 1979 and fiscal year 1980 through June 30, 1980, to determine how many VA acquired properties had losses exceeding the guaranty. We found sixty-seven properties resold by the VA had losses greater than the guaranty. We found 2,480 VA acquired properties were resold during the same period for a total loss of $10,203,929. The sixty-seven properties represent three percent of the properties sold in fiscal year 1979 and 1980 to June 30, 1980, and 12 percent of the total loss. For fiscal year 1980 to June 30, 1980, the thirty properties sold represent three percent of the total sold, but 21 percent of the total loss. The following chart shows the total and average losses for the sixty-seven properties:

	Fiscal Year 1979	Fiscal Year 1980 (To June 30, 1980)	Fiscal Year 1979 & 1980 (To June 30, 1980)
Properties Sold	37	30	67
Total Loss	$612,673	$614,981	$1,227,654
Average Loss Per Property	16,559	20,499	18,323
Total Loss Above Guaranty	106,514	228,958	335,472
Average Loss Above Guaranty Per Property	2,879	7,632	5,007

We did not identify a trend of specific causes for losses for these properties. However, since these few properties do represent a considerable percentage of the total losses, we feel a significant savings could be effected by instituting a systematic review. Good management practice should ensure all contributing factors to this situation are analyzed and the results used to limit future losses whenever possible.

The Chief, Construction and Valuation Section, told us his section receives no feedback from Property Management concerning the accuracy of liquidation appraisals other than those designated as, "cash only—strictly as is," sales. The Chief, Property Management Section, told us the final sales price is not communicated to Construction and Valuation Section for their information. Both chiefs told us that several different circumstances might cause a property to lose its value beyond the VA guaranty. For example, properties might become vacant in high-risk areas where vandalism and shifting market values could create a decrease in the value of the property. Delay in repairs, untimely listing for sale, lengthy foreclosure proceedings, and untimely or inaccurate liquidation appraisals could contribute to significant changes in property value. One example of a circumstance that could affect the loss on acquired property is the accuracy of liquidation appraisals.

The following are ten examples of properties that have liquidation appraisals that differ significantly from the sales price. We are not stating that the liquidation appraisals were inaccurate, as the final sale occurred an *average* of thirty-two months after the liquidation appraisal and the condition of the property could have changed significantly during the inerim period.

Property	Liquidation Appraisal	Final Sales Price
1	$27,750	$ 5,000
2	38,000	19,525
3	30,500	12,000
4	30,000	12,001
5	77,500	46,350
6	22,800	7,300
7	33,000	12,600
8	27,500	13,100
9	26,500	14,500
10	10,600	6,300

Because a systematic review of VA acquired property having losses exceeding the guaranty has not been conducted, specific causes for these high losses have not been identified and corrective action ahs not been taken. In our opinion, these cases warrant a systematic review to ensure appropriate personnel are aware of all factors that led to the high losses.

A systematic review of these properties should have included the following steps:

A review by Loan Service and Claims Section,
A review by Construction and Valuation of appraisals and inspections made to verify that factors affecting the value of the house were consistent with the appraisal value,
A review by Property Management accounting for value of repairs accomplished, explanation of excess elapsed time between actions taken to correct deficiencies, summary of deficiencies, and possible reasons for deficiencies, and,
A review by the Loan Guaranty Officer of his assistant of the section reviews to take necessary action to correct identified problems when warranted.

Another section within the Loan Guaranty Division is the Construction and Valuation Section. The Construction and Valuation (C&V) Section is responsible

317

for determining the reasonable value of properties to be purchased, constructed, or repaired for which Veterans Administration guaranty, insurance, or direct loan is sought. Appraisals are also made on foreclosed property. The appraisal function is intended to provide the veteran with a degree of protection within the Loan Guaranty program as well as ensure that the Veterans Administration has sound security for its guaranty or direct loans. Compliance inspections are made to ensure that dwellings under construction are in accordance with Veterans Administration approved plans and specifications and meet minimum property requirements. Appraisals and compliance inspections are generally conducted by non-VA employees, called fee appraisers and fee compliance inspectors. Tens of millions of your dollars are spent annually by the VA on fee appraisers and compliance inspectors. The fee appraisers and inspectors are supposed to be reviewed by VA employees called staff appraisers or staff inspectors. Generally the VA's review of these "for hire" appraisers and compliance inspectors was dismal.

For example, at Little Rock, field reviews of fee appraisal reports needed considerable improvement. The majority of the field reviews performed were desk reviews of documentation at the office of the fee appraiser. As a result, these properties were not physically inspected by the VA staff appraiser. Also, the number of field reviews of fee appraisals performed is overstated. We reviewed the documentation of the 589 field reviews performed during the six-month period August 1979 through January 1980. During the six-month period, the VA staff appraisers conducted field reviews on seventeen days.

The VA allows 0.628 standard man-hours (SMH) for performing a field review of a field appraisal report. This does not include additional time required for travel. We found that when the standard man-hours are applied to the reported workload, staff appraisers reported performing more field reviews than could be completed on thirteen of the seventeen days. This is shown in the following field reviews reported by one staff appraiser:

Dates Field Reviews Accomplished	Number of Field Reviews Reported Accomplished By One Staff Member	Standard Man-Hours To Accomplish Reported Workload
August 16, 1979	60	37
September 17 & 18*	72	45
September 24	35	22
September 25	97	60
September 26	93	58
December 11, 12, & 13**	52	32
December 18	67	42
December 19	24	15
December 20	22	13
January 25, 1980	41	25

*Averages to over 22 SMH of work for each of the two staff days.
**Averages to over 10 SMH of work each of the three staff days.

318

We interviewed the staff appraisers and found different procedures used to conduct field reviews. One staff appraiser told us that since 1976, he has gone to the fee appraisers' offices and performed desk reviews of the documentation concerning the subject property without physically inspecting the property. Another employee told us that he physically visits the subject properties but remains inside his car, does not visit all the comparables, and spends only a few minutes at the property.

We accompanied a staff appraiser in the field to observe the staff appraiser's performance of the field reviews. The staff appraiser's methodology needs improvement. The staff was unable to locate two of the seven appraised properties that were selected for field review because one was a vacant lot and the other property (that had a house constructed) had no house number, lot number, or any other identification. Loan Guaranty personnel contacted the fee appraiser to verify the existence of the property and this was physically verified by Loan Guaranty personnel.

The staff appraiser visited one comparable sale property for one appraisal report and then visited another comparable sale property for a different appraisal report. This method of switching reviews before completing field review of one appraisal report resulted in the staff appraiser missing one comparable sale. The Chief, Construction and Valuation Section, told us the proper way to conduct a field review was to visit the subject property (appraised property) followed by visits to the three comparable sales to determine if they support the appraised value of the property.

None of the five properties located were complete. Two of the properties were about 40 percent complete, one property had a foundation poured, the footing had just been dug on another property, and one property was being cleared. It is preferable that field reviews of appraisals of proposed construction be made after construction has been completed. At that time, the value of the completed structure can be compared with the original value, taking into account the quality of workmanship and materials.

The staff appraiser did not get out of the car to inspect the two properties that were only 40 percent complete. He paused in front of one property less than one minute and the other property two minutes. This field trip, including forty minutes for lunch and two hours for travel, required four and a half hours. This results in almost two hours to conduct field reviews of the five appraised properties located.

Staff appraisers should be directed to physically inspect the appraised property in order to compare the original appraised value to the value determined at the time of the field review. Proposed construction cases should be visited after construction has been completed. This should strengthen quality control over fee appraisals.

A lack of quality controls over fee appraisers can result in unwarranted losses to the VA in the sale of acquired properties. It can also result in the veteran paying an excessive amount for a property. In our review of defaulted loans, we found inconsistencies in appraisal reports for a property originally appraised for $51,500 on July 17, 1976. The property's value of $51,500 included $33,000 for sixty acres of land ($550 per acre). The staff appraiser who reviewed the appraisal report established the reasonable value at $47,000 so as not to exceed the sales price of $47,000. The loan went into default and received a default appraisal on November 21, 1977. The default appraisal showed a value of $36,000 "as is" and $40,000 "as repaired." These values include $18,000 from the original appraisal made sixteen months before. The staff appraiser who reviewed the appraisal report increased the value of the property to $43,000 "as is" and $45,800 "as repaired." The increase was due to the staff appraiser valuing the sixty acres of land at $25,800 ($430 per acre). In the loan docket file, there is a notation on Form Letter 25–565 that noted the difference between the original value and current value was caused by "depreciation and poor care." However, the property alone was devalued by $15,000 (45 percent) by the default appraisal and $7,200 (21 percent) by the staff appraiser who reviewed the default appraisal. We cannot make a professional judgment on the previous value of the land; however, we do not believe that land would decrease in value 21 to 45 percent over sixteen months in an inflationary economy.

Other inconsistencies that we noted in the appraisal reports on the above property not resolved by any documentation, were:

ITEM	ORIGINAL APPRAISAL JULY 17, 1976	DEFAULT APPRAISAL NOVEMBER 21, 1977
1. Number of Rooms	5	5-1/2
2. Number of Bedrooms	2	3
3. Main Square Footage	996	1,025
4. Carport Square Footage	180	264
5. Cost Approach Appraisal	$51,460	$40,000

We visited the property on March 12, 1980, and found five and a half rooms. There were two bedrooms. No additions or deletions had been made to the house from July 1976 to March 1980. We did not measure the main square footage and the carport. The Little Rock regional office sold this property on October 20, 1978, for $42,500, with a loss of $11,053.

The exact same problem was found at other regional offices. At St. Petersburg, the second largest regional office in the VA, our review of staff appraisers and staff compliance inspectors showed that the quality of field reviews conducted is questionable due to the documented number conducted in a single day.

Interim Issue 26–79–13, dated September 26, 1979, provides that 0.628 and 0.305 standard manhours (SMH) for field review of an appraisal report and compliance inspection report respectively. The allowance given for miles traveled is 0.028 SMH's. Standard man-hours include all actions in connection with a field review, including the case selection and processing of reports.

We reviewed records of field reviews reported as accomplished from January through June 1980 and found for five days, the amount of SMH's earned by one staff appraiser significantly exceeded the number of hours in one day. The number of SMH's earned by one of three construction analysts, who documented the date field reviews, performed in March and May 1980, for field review of compliance inspections, significantly exceeded eight hours for six separate days.

Appraisal Field Reviews

Date	Number of Completed Field Reviews	DVB Work-Rate Stand-ard (Hours)	Number Of Miles Traveled	DVB Work-Rate Stand-ard (Hours)	Total Standard Hours Earned
4–07–80	54	0.628	208	0.028	39.73
4–22–80	54	0.628	251	0.028	40.94
5–13–80	81	0.628	155	0.028	55.21
6–17–80	58	0.628	mileage not known	0.028	36.42
7–30–80	53	0.628	127	0.028	36.84

The total standard hours earned for compliance inspection field reviews are shown below:

Compliance Inspection Field Reviews

Date	Number of Completed Field Reviews	DVB Work-Rate Standard (Hours)	Total Standard Hours Earned
3–11–80	118	0.305	35.99
3–12–80	67	0.305	20.44
3–13–80	101	0.305	30.81
5–13–80	84	0.305	25.62
5–14–80	96	0.305	29.28
5–16–80	87	0.305	26.54

These figures do not reflect the additional time required and earned for

321

travel, because we could not determine the number of miles traveled each day for the compliance inspection reviews.

We accompanied the staff appraiser who reported completing a large number of field reviews in one day, to observe the performance of field reviews. On the day of our review, the time expended per field review ranged from three minutes on occupied property located in a subdivision to forty-four minutes for a vacant property not located in a subdivision. (I don't have the foggiest idea how he spent forty-four minutes looking at an empty lot, but you paid for it.) The average time per field review of an appraisal for the one day was fifteen minutes, which is below the SMH allowed by DVB. The total standard man-hours earned during the eight hours we accompanied the staff appraiser was 12.6.

We also accompanied a construction analyst on August 14, 1980, who reported accomplishing a large number of field reviews of compliance inspection reports in one day. For the day we accompanied the construction analyst, no itinerary was prepared in advance. Subdivisions were selected for review where construction, meeting VA specifications, was in process. Each review lasted from 1 to 10 minutes, with an average time of 3.6 minutes. A total of sixty-five field reviews (19.5 SMH) were accomplished this day. Five of these properties were locked and the construction analyst did not gain entry to the house; however, these inspections were still counted as reviews. The number of field reviews conducted in a single day at this office causes us to question the quality of field reviews since considerably less than the SMH allotment was used for the days identified above. Management should adopt local guidelines for conducting field reviews to ensure acceptable quality of work is performed by fee personnel.

These inspections and appraisals are the basis for the values given in the VA Loan Guaranty Program.

The Loan Service and Claim Section of the Loan Guaranty Division is responsible for servicing home loans that have gone into a default status. This responsibility consists of portfolio loans (direct loans and vendee accounts for which the VA is the mortgage holder) and guaranteed or insured loans. The mortgage holder also has a responsibility for adequate and proper servicing of guaranteed and insured loans. Loan Service and Claim Section prepares vouchers for the payment of claims, reviews record printouts, perform coding, and analyzes output pertaining to portfolio loans. The purposes of servicing defaulted loans are:

(a) to cure minor delinquencies before they become serious defaults;
(b) restore seriously defaulted loans to a current basis before the defaults become insoluble, and,
(c) to terminate loans expeditiously by the method most advantageous to the government when, in the best judgment of station management, the defaults are insoluble.

Servicing of defaulted guaranteed home loans is the responsibility of lenders whose loans have been guaranteed by the Veterans Administration. Lenders are required to provide adequate and timely servicing to ensure that all reasonable efforts are made to bring the loan to a current status. Supplemental servicing is initiated by the Veterans Administration after the lender has reported that attempts to bring the loan into a current status have been unsuccessful. No guaranteed loan should be foreclosed unless justified by adequate servicing by the mortgage holder and the Veterans Administration.

The servicing of home loans is a three-step life cycle:

1. The lender attempts to work out a payment plan with the veteran to correct (cure the default);
2. the lender (bank, savings & loan, etc.) notifies the VA the veteran is in default, and,
3. the VA provides supplemental servicing to the veteran to cure the default by working out an alternative payment plan, financial counseling, etc.

What we found, as you already suspect, none of the above three items were performed in any organized and consistent manner.

The Little Rock audit team reported that lender notification of default was not timely. We reviewed a sample of a hundred loan dockets in default and found twenty-two instances in which the lender did not notify the regional office within the 105-day time requirement. The notification ranged from 106 to 293 days. The date of the notice of default and date of intent to foreclose was the same in eighteen of the hundred loans reviewed. As a result, the VA does not have sufficient time in order to provide timely supplemental servicing.

Supplemental servicing of defaulted home loans is not always performed. We reviewed a sample of a hundred loan dockets in default and found twenty loans had no VA supplemental service. No guaranteed or insured loan should be foreclosed or otherwise terminated unless such action is justified following the performance of adequate and proper loan servicing as reflected in the loan docket.

Our review of the hundred loans showed that additional low-cost efforts can be made by the Service and Claims Section through the increased use of letters and the telephone. The preferred method of performing supplemental servicing is personal servicing; i.e., personal contact either by a face-to-face interview or, if feasible, by telephone. Our review disclosed that eighty-three of the hundred loans had no telephone contact. Only five of the loans had received a letter from the Loan Guaranty Division. Insufficient efforts to provide supplemental service will not give the veteran every reasonable opportunity to continue homeownership.

Lender servicing of defaulted home loans is not always performed. Our review of the previously mentioned twenty defaulted home loans that had no VA supplemental service disclosed that seven had no lender servicing. A local policy has been established as to how management wants the loan specialists to enforce VA Regulations on lender servicing. This policy was not always enforced by the Chief, Property Management, and Loan Service and Claims Section. Our review disclosed that organized action is not performed to make certain that lender servicing is adequate. If not personal contact has been accomplished when the notice of default is received, the Loan Service and Claim Section returns the notice to the holder for further servicing. We contacted the Loan Guaranty Officer concerning the seven loans to determine why there was no lender servicing. The Loan Guaranty Officer informed us that he did not know; however, he stated that the property is usually unoccupied. We reviewed the seven loan dockets and found that only one house was not occupied.

The exact same conditions were found in Pittsburgh, St. Petersburg, Atlanta, Baltimore, San Francisco, Philadelphia, and Roanoke Regional Offices.

Regional Offices did not contact the borrower in all cases where a Notice of Default was received and supplemental servicing was not always timely. VA supplemental servicing by the regional offices was conducted in only 58 percent of the cases reviewed where a Notice of Default was received. The percentage of cases reviewed where contact was made with the borrower ranged from 27 to 96 percent. In those cases where contact was made, an average of thirty-five days elapsed from the date the Notice of Default was received to the date of first contact with the borrower. The timeliness of supplemental VA servicing ranged from seventeen to fifty-two days. Of those cases where a Notice of Intent to Forclose was received, 45 percent received no supplemental servicing. Additionally, 28 percent of those cases that resulted in foreclosure received no VA supplemental servicing.

Notice of Default is not received from mortgage holders within 105 days of default in all cases. In our sample an average of 15.4 percent of the Notices of Default were not received within 105 days. The percentage received within 105 days ranged from 72 percent (Baltimore) to 100 percent (Atlanta). VA regulations require that the holder of any guaranteed or insured loan shall give notice to the VA within 105 days after any debtor has been in default. Failure to report default status to the VA within the 105-day period increases the potential for foreclosure on the property because VA monitoring of lender servicing and supplemental VA servicing is delayed. Prudent servicing standards require that contact be made as soon as possible after a delinquency occurs for maximum effect.

To make matters worse, at Roanoke and San Francisco, the VA employees did not review the Notice of Default when received from the lender. As a result, no supplemental servicing was provided. Though the lack of supplemental servicing was found by the auditors in 1980 and the subsequent decision not to publish the reports was made soon thereafter, the problem just didn't go away.

Because of this, the Veterans' Affairs subcommittee is considering a bill to provide money to assist unemployed veterans who are facing foreclosure. This measure would allow the VA to make payments totaling no more than $8,400 on behalf of an unemployed veteran homeowner who has a reasonable prospect of being able to repay both his mortgage lender and the VA.

As a result, instead of cleaning up its act, Disorganized Crime is going to spend lots more of your money in behalf of the largest lobbying group in the country. Now that's what I call solving a problem. Just think of the visuals.

Just one more "little" item for your bemusement before we leave the VA's Loan Guaranty Program. A veteran receives a green sheet of paper, called a Certificate of Eligibility (COE), from the VA, either by mail or if he shows up at a Regional Office and asks for one. The COE is what the veteran presents to the lender (usually by way of a real estate agent). The COE is then processed (credit checks, employment verification, etc.), the VA-insured mortgage issued, and the veteran gets title to his house with no down payment. Or in other words, the COE is a house waiting to be processed! You would think the COE's would be kept under lock and key—do you actually believe that after coming this far with me?

Another audit team found that hundreds of veterans had tens of millions of dollars of housing in excess of their legal ceiling. Though this audit report also was not published, one of the reasons was found at the Pittsburgh Regional Office. The accountability of COE's was weak.

We conducted an inventory of COE's on May 29, 1980 and could not locate 22 of the 5,417 COE's that were to be on hand. There are six causes for the weak accountability of COE's.

1. Security of the COE's is inadequate.
2. Accountability for the COE's has never been formally established at the Loan Guaranty and Veterans Service Divisions.
3. Receipt of COE's from Administrative Division is informal.
4. Destruction of COE's is inadequately documented.
5. The register of COE's in Loan Guaranty Division is inadequate. The register in Veterans Services Division has good accountability since August 1979.
6. There has been no inventory of the COE's.

There were 3,000 of the 5,417 COE's on hand at the Corps of Engineers. These were sent to the Corps six weeks prior to our inventory in order to have the regional office's address printed on the COE's. These 3,000 COE's were on a shelf in the printing office. The printing staff told us there were no secured files or safes in their office. When we brought this to the attention of the Chief, Administrative Division, he immediately secured the 3,000 COE's. The Director also instituted a change in the manner of the printing of the address on the COE's. In the future, a rubber stamp will be used to put the address on the forms.

Accountability for the COE's had never been formally established at the Veterans Services and Loan Guaranty Division. The secretary of the Assistant Chief, VSD, had signed for the COE's received from the Administrative Division. The Chief, Interviewing Unit, had established a register for the COE's and had physical possession of the COE's in his office. When the Chief, Interviewing Unit, took possession of the COE's on hand, there was no inventory of the COE's on hand. His predecessor retired in May 1979 and there was no inventory when he retired. In the Loan Guaranty Division, accountability was never established.

Receipt of the COE's from the Administrative Division is informal. As previously noted, the secretaries of the division would sign as to the receipt of the COE's. The secretaries told us they would not inspect the COE's to insure that all the COE's were present when they received them. We noted in one instance that 1,000 COE's were issued to VSD; however, the Administrative Division had no signed receipt from VSD. The Corps of Engineers had not signed for the receipt of 3,000 COE's that they had received from the Administrative Division.

The destruction of COE's is inadequately documented. On July 10, 1979, a work-study student disposed of 4,775 COE's with control numbers less than 6340001. The disposal of these COEs was noted on a Forms or Publications Requisition and Shipping Document VA Form 3–3242. The VA Form 3–3242 noted that the COE's were from VSD; however, 2,000 of the destroyed COE's had been issued to Loan Guaranty Division. Another 1,000 COE's had never been receipted by VSD from Administrative Division; however, they were also included in the 4,775 COE's received from VSD. There were no entries in either of the Division's registers showing the receipt or release of any of the 4,775 COE's. During our review of the Loan Guaranty Division log, dated July 1979, we found 77 COE's that were listed on the log as being issued but were reported destroyed on the VA Form 3–3242. The disposal of the 4,775 COE's was not certified by a disinterested full-time VA employee. During our inventory, we found 3,013 COE's with control numbers less than 6340001. The Chief, VSD, had 13 COE's voided when brought to his attention. The Chief, Administrative Division, destroyed the other 3,000 COE's.

My last Regional Office audit was at St. Petersburg, Florida. I've already discussed the Loan Guaranty Program in Florida, but most of the other programs were also screwed up. Office supplies cost over $300,000 from 1978–1980; however, we found that inventory procedures did not provide an accurate accounting of office supplies and forms on hand. We reviewed fifteen of three hundred line items for office supplies and forms and found eight had significantly more stock on hand than indicated on inventory records. According to inventory records, the cost of the eight items was $918. Our review, however, showed the cost was actually $1,779, $861 more than inventory records indicated. For example, the Procurement Request Card for compress paper fasteners indicated 150 boxes were on hand as of August 22, 1979. No further purchases were indicated, but on August 12, 1980, our inventory disclosed 306 boxes.

An example of inadequate follow-up on inventory discrepancies is VA Form 22–6553c. The Automatic Requisition Card, VA Form 23–6582, for this form indicated an inventory of 300 on August 1, 1979. On August 3, 1979, 12,000 additional forms were ordered. An inventory in October 1979, revealed 50,000 forms were on hand. Inventories were conducted quarterly from October 1979 through July 1980, yet no follow-up was taken on this item until the Chief of the Publications Unit was questioned by the Audit Team. The Chief of the Publications Unit told us that forms in bulk storage were overlooked during the August 1, 1979 inventory. During the audit, more than one year after the inventory error, the Chief of Publications Unit took action to dispose of the excess forms. The Chief called other regional offices to determine if they needed these excess forms.

We reviewed thirty-six high-use VA Forms stocked by the Publications Unit and found that thirty-one (86 percent) had stock on hand that will last for more than one year. VA Forms are ordered by the Publications Unit from the VA Forms and Publications Department, Alexandria, Virginia. These forms were all depot-stocked items ordered on a quarterly basis. Inventory levels should be established to permit replenishment in accordance with the schedule established by the Director, Publications Service. Local controls should be established to prevent accumulation of excesses within the station.

The accumulation of excess forms is due to the outdated reorder points and usage levels. The Publications Unit is currently updating the reorder system using the low watermark (safety level) technique. However, based on current usage figures, we found that twenty-five (69 percent) of the thirty-six forms reviewed had reorder levels that were incorrect because they were outdated. Sixteen reorder points were too high and nine too low.

Estimated usage levels on Automatic Requisition Cards were found to be outdated. We found twenty-six (72 percent) of the thirty-six forms reviewed had either incorrect usage data or no usage data indicated. For example, VA Form 10–1394, Application for Adaptive Equipment—Motor Vehicle, has an estimated annual usage of 3,000 units and a reorder point of 2,000 units. The actual usage of this form has been 1,000 per year. With a reorder point at 2,000 units, the minimum inventory level for this form would equal a two-year supply. The 7,500 units currently on hand, at the present usage rate, would last for seven years.

Duplicating activities are not economical. We reviewed 108 requests for reproduction made during June and July 1980 and found that the copies produced exceeded the number requested by 15 percent (28,699). A total of 217,592 copies were produced, although only 188,893 copies were requested.

One of the VA's objectives of paperwork management is to reduce paperwork to the absolute minimum consistent with responsibilities. It lists the elimination of unnecessary copies as one of the controls to accomplish this objective. The Chief Benefits Director in December 1979 established goals to reduce printing and reproduction costs.

The Chief of the Publications Unit was unable to explain all the excess copies produced. Some reasons given were spoilage and counting errors; however, all Reproduction Requests, VA Form 07–3011, were not on file in the Publications Unit for review and those on file did not explain the variances. For example, on July 17, 1980, Personnel Division requested 760 copies of a fifteen-page employee newsletter (15 × 760 = 11,400 pages). The Publications Unit produced 14,899 pages, 3,499 pages or 30 percent more than requested. No explanation was given for the overage. Direction and control should be provided to eliminate unnecessary copies and ensure adequate documentation regarding significant variances is maintained.

As in Nashville, St. Petersburg also had cost control of its telecommunications. Telecommunications costs exceed $280,000 annually ($268,000 for fiscal year 1979 and $288,000 estimated for fiscal year 1980) for telephone, teletype,

327

telegram/mailgram, and telecopier operations. The largest single cost, approximately $132,000 (47 percent) for fiscal year 1980, is incurred through operation of the Telephone Unit of the Veterans Services Division. The Chief, Administrative Division, is responsible for the efficient and economical usage of telecommunications. The Chief is also responsible for obligation of funds for telecommunication costs.

The Telephone Unit is equipped with forty incoming telephone lines used to conduct telephone interviews with VA beneficiaries. The telephone lines include thirty intra-city (FX) lines, five state-wide WATS lines, and five local lines. The Telephone Unit is assigned twenty-eight staff and there are thirty answering stations as of August 31, 1980.

The telecommunication system is not operated in an efficient and economical manner. We found unused telephone service and equipment at the main regional office building, the Tyrone Towers location, and the Loan Guaranty Office in Jacksonville. The Telephone Unit is not efficiently utulizing the forty incoming telephone lines used to conduct telephone interviews. We determined that over $60,000 (20 percent) of the $280,000 annual telecommunication costs were not efficiently and economically used. Management has been aware of these excessive costs for over two years; however, it took no action. The Chief, Administrative Division, relies on the other regional office divisions to reduce unnecessary telephone service.

We identified the major cause as the Chief, Administrative Division, not adequately monitoring telephone use to determine what telephone service is needed. Regional Office Circular 23–76–8, dated October 14, 1976, gives the Chief, Administrative Division, the overall responsibility for telecommunication costs. The Chief, Administrative Division, should provide direction and control to assure efficient and economical operation of the telecommunication system. This would include assuring that the annual telephone utilization survey, for which the Chief, Administrative Division, is responsible, is conducted as required. Also, additional coordination is needed between the Chief, Administrative Division, and other division chiefs to assure that excess telephone service is identified and promptly removed.

Current telephone service is excessive. We determined that staffing in the Telephone Unit is insufficient to justify seventeen of the forty incoming telephone lines used to conduct telephone interviews.

The VA provides the requirements regarding staffing in the Telephone Unit. Proper staffing of Telephone Units and full utilization of telephone equipment available are essential to good service. The ratio of staffing for local lines will be three VBC's for each four incoming lines, with an increase in assigned personnel as necessitated by peak workload periods. Preferred staffing for FX/WATS lines should be a VBC for each incoming line.

Although there were twenty-eight staff assigned to the Telephone Unit as of August 31, 1980, actual available staffing has averaged fifteen employees from April through June 1980. This is because staff assigned to the Telephone Unit are sometimes on leave, on compressed work schedules, or utilized in other units of the Veterans Assistance Section. During the audit we surveyed staffing of the Telephone Unit and determined staffing ranged from fifteen to twenty-two employees. This staffing includes VBC's assigned to the Telephone Unit on a temporary basis during peak workload periods. Veterans Services Division has no plans to increase staffing in the Telephone Unit. The Personnel Director told us there are no short- or long-range plans for additional positions for Veterans Services Division, except in the Counseling and Rehabilitation Section. We computed the incoming lines should be reduced by seventeen to a level of twenty-three, because there are only twenty-two staff utilized in the Telephone Unit.

The regional office is currently experiencing a missed call rate of over 29 percent (callers put on "hold," for a VBC to answer, who eventually hang up). We consulted with the Federal Accounts Manager at General Telephone Company who is responsible for the forty incoming lines. He told us the regional office is paying for telephone service they cannot use, because of an insufficient amount of staff to answer the telephone calls. Adding incoming lines to meet the demands for service without the personnel to staff the lines serves no purpose. The result is more callers placed on "hold," awaiting availability of a VBC.

A reduction of seventeen incoming lines would reduce communication costs by over $55,000 per year. As additional staffing becomes available, more telephone lines can be installed. The cost of installing an FX or WATS line is about $125, according to the account manager; this cost is less than the monthly cost of any of the FX or WATS lines.

Telephone traffic studies were conducted in October 1978 and October 1979, by VSD personnel. Their review determined that only thirty incoming lines were needed in 1978, and only twenty-seven incoming lines were needed in 1979. However, no action to reduce the number of incoming lines was recommended. Based on the average cost of forty incoming lines, we estimate that over $68,000 of the telephone service should have been eliminated for the last two years.

The Assistant Veterans Services Officer was reluctant to recommend eliminating telephone lines for fear of hindering chances of obtaining additional staffing. The Chief, Administrative Division, told us he depended on division chiefs to ensure all telephone service is needed. A desire for additional staffing is not valid criteria for unneeded telephone service. Staffing in the telephone unit has not increased since October 1978, when it was thirty employees. Management should monitor telephone service and ensure that only telephone service that is utilized be maintained.

Telephone traffic studies are inadequate. The October 1978 and October 1979 studies were not performed to assess the telephone needs to an individual service area, and the annual October 1979 telephone traffic study did not include blocked calls. Blocked calls are identified as a caller getting a busy signal while trying to call the regional office. Effective management of telephone operations requires periodic traffic busy studies that identify the number of missed/blocked calls. Studies of this type will be conducted on five randomly selected work days during the month of October, in accordance with the agreement reached with the local telephone company. Those stations possessing capability will conduct their own studies without assistance from the telephone personnel.

The VA requires that data on missed and blocked calls will be used for each specific type of line; for example, the local lines, FX lines and WATS lines. We discussed these guidelines with a representative of the Telecommunications Service in VA Central Office, who told us a study should be conducted on each service area. This would include each city with FX line service, the local area lines, and statewide WATS lines. For VARO, St. Petersburg, a study should have been performed on the five incoming WATS lines, a separate study should have been performed on each of the fifteen cities served by an FX line(s) and on the five incoming lines serving St. Petersburg. The study that was performed measured all the forty lines as one unit.

The regional office cannot compute the number of blocked calls. In October 1979, the regional office received a report concerning the blocked calls from the telephone company. The report from the telephone company was not in the proper format, because the Chief, Administrative Division, did not request that the report specifically show the number of blocked calls. The Federal Account Manager, General Telephone Company, told us that the number of blocked calls can be obtained if this information is requested in advance.

Telephone studies were not performed on each FX location, local lines and WATS lines, because the previous Veterans Services Officer did not interpret the manual instructions to require an individual study on each service area. As a result, it is not possible to accurately determine the extent of blocked and missed calls by location, the appropriate mix of WATS and FX lines, and grade of service affecting the individual service areas.

The 1980 telephone utilization survey had not been conducted. The Director notified the Office of Data Management and Telecommunications in VA Central Office on June 11, 1980, that the annual telephone utilization survey of telephone equipment, features, and services, was conducted. He certified that the annual survey of installation and use of telephone equipment was accomplished and corrective action had been initiated to correct the deficiencies noted. The clerk in Administrative Division responsible for conducting the survey told us that the survey was for inventory of equipment to verify billing charges and did not include verification of use. The clerk told us that the Regional Office Circular Number 23–76–8, dated October 14, 1976, requires a semi-annual inventory of telephones and associated equipment and reporting thereon. The station policy on telephone use should be updated to require an annual survey, which would also include a review of utilization.

The annual telephone survey was limited to verification on inventory and billing charges and did not include utilization. As a result, under-utilized telephone equipment and lines were not identified and removed. We surveyed the use of telephone service at the main regional office building, the Tyrone Towers location, and the Loan Guaranty Division Office at Jacksonville, and found excess telephone service at all locations. The cost of maintaining the excess telephone service identified by the audit team exceeds $5,600 annually.

In the Administrative Division's data terminal room, we found two telephones, on adjacent desks, for answering one incoming line. There are two employees who use these telephones, but since only one person can use the telephone at a time, one instrument should be removed. VA Manual MP-6, Part VIII, paragraph 204.04e, provides that one telephone will serve the needs of two or more persons at adjacent desks.

We found a telephone in the Office of the Chief, Administrative Division, with three incoming lines that was not utilized. The division chief told us that the desk and telephone were sometimes used by the Chief, Central Transcription Section (CTS), who had assigned work space elsewhere in the building. The Chief, CTS, told us she used the second desk when performing quality reviews. Since this telephone is not essential to carry out her assigned duties, it should be removed.

In the operation activity of the Veterans Assistance Section (VAS) of Veterans Services Division, we found seven incoming telephone lines that are excessive. The Acting Chief, VAS, developed a plan in May 1980 to reorganize the physical layout of this activity and remove the excess telephone lines. The proposed action of VSD to streamline the required telephone service indicates an improvement in organization; however, the seven lines had been under-utilized for two years when VSD converted to the modular office concept in 1977. During our audit, the Chief, Administrative Division, requested the elimination of the seven lines on July 28, 1980, two months after the reorganization plan was developed.

There are thirty answering positions and related equipment in the Telephone Unit. As of August 31, 1980, there are twenty-eight Veterans Benefits Counselors (VBC's) assigned to utilize the thirty answering positions. However, due to the compressed work schedule of the VBC, a maximum of twenty-two positions are occupied at any one time. The unit chief also told us, and we confirmed, the space is congested in the telephone unit area. The unit chief stated he did not feel it was necessary to occupy space with answering positions that were not being manned. By removing seven of the answering positions, the congestion in the telephone unit could be reduced while eliminating unnecessary costs.

In the Counseling and Rehabilitation (C&R) Section, located at Tyrone Towers, we found three telephones that were not being utilized. One telephone had not been used since February 1980. The section chief told us that they had been actively recruiting for a counseling psychologist who would use this instrument. We identified another telephone that had not been used since February 1979, and a third telephone not used since June 1980, because assigned staff had left. The Chief, Personnel Division, told us there are no plans to staff the latter two positions and therefore the telephone should be removed.

In the Operations Section of Finance Division, located at Tyrone Towers, we found three telephone lines and three telephones that were not being utilized. These telephones and lines have not been used since February 4, 1980. According to the Chief of Operations, they were temporarily not being used to determine if the current clerical staff can provide adequate dictation support. These telephone lines have not been used for six months and should be eliminated. We found two telephones to answer the telephone number 3398 in Finance Division. This line is used by two voucher auditors whose desks are adjacent. One of these instruments should be eliminated because one telephone would be sufficient.

In the Loan Guaranty Division, we found an unused telephone outside the photocopy room. In the specially adaptive housing work area, we found a telephone on a desk that was occupied by a work-study employee.

Costly WATS lines are used by callers in areas served by FX lines. At our request, a telephone survey was conducted during the period July 23–29, 1980. VBC's answering the telephone documented incoming calls on the five WATS lines and the origination of the calls. We found that 40 percent (350) of the 872 WATS line calls documented in the survey, originated from areas with FX(s) line service, and that 52 percent (183) of these calls were from locations served by three or more FX lines.

The annual cost of a WATS line is $11,748, compared to the annual cost of an FX line, which ranges from $1,484 (Tampa) to $3,480 (Pensacola). Uneconomical usage of the WATS lines occurs when 40 percent of the calls (approximately two lines) are made by callers located in areas served by a less expensive FX line.

We determined some of the callers calling from locations served by FX lines could have learned of the WATS line telephone number from local directory assistance. We called directory assistance and found that Jacksonville, Tallahassee, and Sarasota had the WATS line telephone number listed as a number to call for benefits, information, and assistance. Also, we found that the Sarasota FX line was not listed in directory assistance. The Assistant Veterans Services Officer told us that attempts had been made to delete the WATS telephone number from the local telephone book at Jacksonville. We reviewed the telephone directories maintained at the regional office and found that the Jacksonville telephone book listed the WATS telephone number and the Tallahassee and Sarasota telephone books listed only the FX numbers. The Jacksonville, Tallahassee, and Sarasota locations account for over 10 percent of the WATS calls recorded during the survey. In addition, we found that the regional office sent mail-outs informing veterans throughout the state of toll-free telephone numbers. Consequently, veterans living in areas served by an FX line were made aware of the expensive WATS line telephone number.

The annual cost for use of GSA vehicles is about $81,000 ($70,000 for Fiscal Year 1979 and $81,000 estimated for Fiscal Year 1980). This amount includes dispatched and leased GSA vehicles. The Chief, Administrative Division, is responsible for control of GSA vehicles and obligation of funds for GSA vehicles costs.

We found that the regional office has not been performing travel in the most efficient and economical manner. We reviewed the GSA billing printouts for the period January through May 1980 and found nine of the 29 GSA-leased vehicles are driven an average of 865 miles per month or less.

Administrative Division should maintain controls and statistics on GSA vehicles. The purpose of maintaining controls and statistics on leased GSA vehicles is to ensure travel is economically and efficiently performed. The regional office required a minimum of 800 miles per month to justify assigning a GSA-leased vehicles. The manager at the Tampa GSA motor pool told us that assigned GSA vehicles should be utilized at least 1,000 miles each month to justify leasing.

One of the six automobiles assigned to the Loan Guaranty Division in Jacksonville averaged 542 miles of monthly use during January through May 1980. Travel could be performed more efficiently by use of POV or increased use of the other five vehicles assigned to the Jacksonville Loan Guaranty Division. This would save $960 per year. In addition, GSA dispatched vehicles are available for daily rental at the same location that the leased cars are garaged.

During January through May 1980, two of the four cars assigned to Administrative Division averaged 355 and 485 miles of use per month. The other two cars averaged 804 and 865 miles of use. By returning the two GSA-leased cars used the least, the 840 miles (355 plus 485) could be absorbed by increased use of the two remaining GSA-leased vehicles. This would save $2,160 per year in leasing fees and increase the use of the other vehicles to a point where it would be economical to continue leasing them.

The car assigned to Finance Division averaged only 164 miles permonth of use during January through May 1980. This car was used to travel between the main regional office location and Tyrone Towers, and occasional trips to the bank. This travel could be performed by use of the shuttle van that travels between the regional office and Tyrone Towers three times each day, and by pooled use of one of the cars assigned to Administrative Division. Additionally, POV could be used as necessary. This would save over $1,000 per year.

As at Nashville, the use of leased GSA vehicles is not monitored for outbased employees. We reviewed the use of GSA-leased vehicles and found that travel performed by outbased employees is not reviewed by first-line supervisors or Administrative Division, which is responsible for control of GSA cars. In addition, we found that assignment sheets provided to outbased employees assigned leased GSA cars do not define the conditions under which the vehicle may be operated between the employee's place of residence and place of employment.

We reviewed the Field Activity Reports from January through June 1980, which showed that employees in the Fiduciary and Field Examination Unit, stationed in Miami and Pensacola, were using GSA-leased vehicles to travel to and from work when no away-from-office travel was reported.

We were not able to verify that mileage reported by the Vocational Rehabilitation Specialist (VRS) in Pensacola was for official purposes because travel logs are not maintained. Also, the supervisory VRS discarded records of the itinerary of the VRS in Pensacola prior to the audit (What a coincidence!). These records would have allowed reconstruction to determine the estimated miles required to travel to visit the Chapter 31 trainees. The Supervisory VRS told us after contacting the VRS assigned to Pensacola that the GSA-leased vehicle was parked at home when no official travel was performed. This contact was made during the audit in July 1980. We reviewed the report of travel for the month of August and found that the VRS in Pensacola officially traveled on five days and reported driving 189 miles. However, between September 1979 and June 1980, prior to our inquiry concerning travel, the VRS's reported travel ranged between 330 and 1,058 miles of travel each month. Reported mileage for this period averaged 631 per month.

Effectiveness and productivity are low at some VSD satellite locations.

Satellite locations are established at Fort Myers, Miami, Orlando, Riviera Beach, Jacksonville, and Pensacola, Florida. They were staffed with seventeen employees as of June 30, 1980. The primary mission of the satellite locations is providing assistance and information concerning VA benefits to VA claimants in the local areas. We reviewed the station's effectiveness and productivity data for the six satellite locations for fiscal year 1980 through June 30, which were computed in accordance with work measure standards defined in DVB Manual M27–1, Part I, Chapter 7. Effectiveness is a measure of the units of work produced in relation to available staff-hours. Productivity is a measure of units of work produced in relationship to gross available staff-hours.

Cumulative Effectiveness and Productivity
Data for FY 1980 Through June 30

Location	Effectiveness (Percent)	Productivity (Percent)
Fort Myers	48	45
Miami	81	51
Orlando	80	66
Riviera Beach	95	88
Jacksonville	95	61
Pensacola	90	84

There are no published standards for effectiveness and productivity at the satellite locations; however, the Assistant Veterans Services Officer told us that effectiveness of 90 percent and productivity of 70 percent were standards he wished to meet within the division. The Assistant Veterans Services Officer also told us that no study of the satellite locations based on effectiveness and productivity has been conducted to evaluate staff utilization.

The Finance Officer furnished the following costs of the VSD satellite locations for fiscal year 1980:

Location	Number of Staff as of June 30	Salaries	Space Rental	Communications Costs	Total
Fort Myers	2	$ 29,657	0	DM&S	$ 29,657
Miami	4	109,944	$ 7,272	$ 4,299	121,515
Orlando	3	82,245	0	DM&S	82,245
Riviera Beach	2	35,276	0	DM&S	35,276
Jacksonville	4	85.096	0	DM&S	86,382
Pensacola	2	46,210	4,075	1,082	51,367
TOTAL	17	$338,428	$11,347	$ 6,667	$406,442

334

Work measurement has value to top management for budgeting, long-range planning, and policy formulation. The effectiveness and productivity data for the satellite locations indicate the need for a management study to determine if the staff resources could be used more effectively.

As with the satellite locations, we also found that the Career Development Center (CDC) was underutilized. The VA provided instructions for the installation of a CDC in the Counseling and Rehabilitation Section of Veterans Services Division. The objectives are to provide veterans with current career and job information, using printed and audiovisual materials. In addition, it will provide training in job-finding skills, career development, and direct placement contacts, or appropriate referral for job placement assistance. Sounds like motherhood and apple pie, doesn't it, but Disorganized Crime always tries for good visuals.

We determined the CDC was established and functioning in accordance with the VA's requirements. Efforts to publicize the CDC include radio and television commercials and printed literature. Also, various organizations, such as VA Medical Centers, service organizations, and state employment services have been informed of the availability and function of the CDC Unit. We reviewed the first three months of operations June through August 1980. The CDC has a proposed budget of $85,855 for the first year and $58,928 annually after the initial year. The first year budget consists of funds for rental space, audiovisual equipment, furniture and software (film strips, publications) totaling $28,590. Staffing for the CDC consists of three full-time positions and partial use of a Counseling Psychologist at an annual cost of $57,265.

During the first three months of operation, sixty-three workdays, 109 veterans visited the CDC for an average of less than 2 veterans per day. The VA provides no criteria for utilization of the CDC and no local criteria has been established. In our opinion, the CDC unit is being underutilized and does not justify the current expenditures for staffing. We feel that staff could be reduced during this period of low utilization and the workload of the unit should be closely monitored to determine the potential for effectively implementing a CDC at this regional office.

Chapter 8

The National Debt

The authorities increase the size of their texts of laws. They pile up back-break-ing burdens and laythem on other men's shoulders.

—Jesus (Matthew 23)

Now for the punch line of the joke. I lied to you, you didn't directly pay for anything I've described to you. But wait a second, you're thinking, where did my tax money go? The answer is your money went just to pay off the interest. It's incredible but it's true. It takes all the stolen money collected from the bottom 80 percent of taxpayers just to pay the interest on the huge federal debt (the counterfeited money I told you about way back in Chapter 1). Stated another way, it takes all the taxes paid by 61 million taxpayers just to pay the *interest* on Disorganized Crime's debt. And the debt isn't just growing, it's exploding. And that explosion is right now blowing away everything you and I ever knew, all because of Disorganized Crime. Only five years ago, the total federal govern-ment debt was little more than half its estimated level by the end of 1983. That's right, by the end of 1983, the debt would be $1.383 trillion compared to $780.4 billion at the end of 1978 ($1,383,000,000,000 versus $780,400,000,000). It took our forefathers 153 years to accumulate a $100 billion federal government debt (1809–1962). Then it was 23 years, 1975, when the federal debt reached $500 billion (1962–1975). But, over the last 8 years (1975–1983), the debt has soared by over 130 percent to $1.38 trillion. Isn't that the sound of a bubble popping? Don't shrink away from the void in your heart. Think about what it was squandered on—nothing, absolutely, nothing.

What's really a laugh, is when I think about the guys who started the revolution back in the 1770s. They would not only talk about the government being a bunch of lying crooks, but would actually dress up as Indians and throw tea off boats rather than pay higher taxes. Our forefathers would actually get so worked up that they lived in snow and killed tax collectors and other uniformed riff-raff sent by the government. Today, I've seen people actually get so scared that they couldn't sleep, when they would get a *machine-generated form letter* from the IRS demanding more money, and (here's the amazing part) actually

337

send more money to be frittered away by Disorganized Crime!

I have only two more facts to present to you. The debt grew over $1.2 trillion in our lifetime and there's no end in sight. Have you ever heard of any rumor of a plan to pay off the debt? Think now, don't get confused with the propaganda you've been fed your whole life. I'm not asking about "reduction in federal spending" or "slowing the rate of federal spending," I'm talking pay off the debt. I've never even heard of any rumor, and I believe you haven't either. That means the debt can only get bigger. Let's play a game and say the debt will only grow another $1.2 trillion in the next thirty years, just like the last thirty years. At what point will the remaining 20 percent of taxpayers' money also join their fellow victims in just paying off the interest?

The last fact describing the impossibility of this continuing. Disorganized Crime will spend about $848 billion from October 1, 1983 to September 30, 1984. That's just the take of one year's theft of your money. A trail over one mile wide could be paved with dollar bills from San Francisco to New York. Isn't that simply amazing?